POETICALITY

Poeticality

IN REFUSAL OF SETTLER LIFE

Jeffrey Sacks

FORDHAM UNIVERSITY PRESS NEW YORK 2026

Fordham University Press gratefully acknowledges financial assistance and support provided for the publication of this book by the University of California, Riverside.

Fordham University Press also publishes its books in a variety of electronic formats. Some content that appears in print may not be available in electronic books.

Visit us online at www.fordhampress.com.

For EU safety/GPSR concerns: Mare Nostrum Group B.V., Mauritskade 21D, 1091 GC Amsterdam, The Netherlands, gpsr@mare-nostrum.co.uk

Library of Congress Cataloging-in-Publication Data available online at https://catalog.loc.gov.

Printed in the United States of America

28 27 26   5 4 3 2 1

First edition

For Leah, Leila, Bella

Contents

ACKNOWLEDGMENTS xi

PREFACE xv

Introduction: Poeticality 1

1 Settler Life 19
Reading Life, 21 • Property, 27 • Pacification, 38 • Translation, 48 • Politick Societies, 53

2 Anontological Form 66
Patience, 68 • Mere Being, 73 • Demonstration, 83 • Insubstantiality, 92 • Common Things, 97 • Necessity, 101 • Generosity, 112

3 Insurgence: A Poetics of Things 118
Reverberation, 121 • Inessential Gathering, 130 • Language, 140 • Poetic Being, 148 • Insurgent Life, 165

NOTES 175

WORKS CITED 247

INDEX 273

Plates follow page 92

Will you not memorize a little poetry to halt the slaughter?

—MAHMOUD DARWISH

ألا تحفظون قليلا من الشعر كي توقفوا المذبحة؟

ـ محمود درويش

Acknowledgments

This book was revised and completed during the ongoing genocide of the Palestinian people, within and outside of Gaza, a collective decimation carried out by the Zionist settler state, and which has come to include genocide through starvation. Perhaps this book contributes, in a certain way, to a collective thinking of such violences, where if "defeat drowns with the defeated, like fish," as the poet and painter Etel Adnan wrote, struggle in common, a certain being or doing together and with others, creates occasions for "the formulation of new propositions," a practice in sociality among beings and things.[1] I remain grateful for the kindness and generosity of friends and colleagues who, over the years, have read, listened to, commented on, or spoken with me about parts of this work, and who have provided sustenance and conviviality in destitute times. I wish to thank, in particular, Hosam Aboulela, Soraya Abuelhiga, George Abraham, María del Rosario Acosta López, Refqa Abu-Remaileh, Siraj Ahmed, Tony Alessandrini, Samer Ali, Dina Al-Kassim, Michael Allan, Shir Alon, Sinan Antoon, Sophia Azeb, Rana Barakat, Amanda Batarseh, Sara R. bin Tyeer, Heidi Brevik-Zender, João Costa Vargas, Emily Drumsta, Ayman El-Desouky, Huda El Shakry, Marwa Elshakry, Sarah Doebbert Epstein, Nergis Ertürk, Samera Esmeir, Huda Fakhreddine, Joseph Farag, Keith Feldman, René Gabri, Nouri Gana, Jared Gee, Erin Graff Zivin, Hala Halim, Jens Hanssen, Lara Harb, Olivia Harrison, Heeba Hartit, Nizar Hermes, Beth Holt, Rana Issa, Amira Jarmakani, Rebecca Johnson, Fady Joudah, R.A. Judy, Christian Junge, Dina Al-Kassim, Christophe Katrib, Leen Kawas, Maya Kesrouany, Alexander Key, Samiha Khalil, Sami Khatib, Kyle Khellaf, Jodi Kim, John Kim, Mariam Lam, Latipa, Jacques Lezra, Annette Damayanti Lienau, David Lloyd, Alex Lubin, Saree Makdisi, Ussama Makdisi,

Peter Makhlouf, Sean Matharoo, Karim Mattar, Anne McKnight, Sonja Mejcher-Atassi, Natalie Melas, Lucie Kim-Chi Mercier, Jeannie Miller, Mark Minch-de Leon, Ayman Mleitat, Liron Mor, Fred Moten, Anahid Nersessian, Sonali Pahwa, Fatima Quraishi, Najat Rahman, Hany Rashwan, Kamran Rastegar, Marc Redfield, Trisha Remetir, Maisam Rizvi, Dylan Rodríguez, Na'ama Rokem, Lubna Safi, Steven Salaita, Sara Salih, Sarita See, Rana Sharif, Stephen Sheehi, Setsu Shigematsu, Amira Silmi, Nadine Sinno, Anna Ziajka Stanton, Shaden Tageldin, Pauline Homsi Vinson, and Veli Yashin. Tom Lay, at Fordham University Press, supported this project from the beginning and shepherded it through the review and production process, and I thank him for his generosity and care. Kem Crimmins, at Fordham, provided support and guidance as the book went into production, and Teresa Jesionowski copyedited the manuscript, closely reading each of its sentences with a sensitivity and attention to detail for which I remain grateful. I am grateful as well for the thoughtfulness of the anonymous reviewers who read the manuscript. I've learned immensely from their comments, engagement, and recommendations. I wish to thank Simone Fattal, and the Estate of Etel Adnan, for granting permission to publish the images of Adnan's poetry, painting, and drawing that appear in this book, as well as Patrice Cotensin, Laurine Royer, Eleanor Hooker, Suheyla Takesh, Rémi Homs, Sophie Jones, and Kaelen Wilson-Goldie, for helping to navigate copyrights, permissions, and captions. Part of chapter 3 has been published in *PMLA*, under the title "Lafẓ: Language Praxis," and I thank the journal for allowing the article, in a slightly edited form, to be reprinted with permission. A number of friends and colleagues thought of me on several of occasions over the years. I want to thank Christian Junge and Kirill Dmitriev for Arabic philology in Bamff; Nouri Gana and Gil Hochberg for Fanon in Tunis; Sarah Doebbert Epstein and Sami Khatib for "Simplicity at War" at Sanayeh House in Beirut; Sami Khatib and Vanessa Ohlraun for "The Promise and Compromise of Translation" at the Office of Contemporary Art Norway, in Oslo; Suzanne Stetkevych for the Arabic Poetry Colloquium, at Georgetown University; Mushin al-Musawi and the organizing collective for "Thresholds to Arabic Literary Criticism"; Anna Ziajka Stanton, Jeannie Miller, and Lara Harb, for the "Arabic Theoretical Lexicon"; Peter Makhlouf and René Gabri for the "Conference of Butterflies"; Veli Yashin for "Critiques of Violence/Languages of Critique"; Tony Alessandrini, Sophia Azeb, and Nouri Gana for "Fanon and West Asia"; Samera Esmeir and the editorial collective of *Critical Times* for "Critique and Translation"; David Lloyd for "Poetics of Law/Poetics of Decolonization," and for everything; Saree Makdisi, for inviting me to give a talk about this book in the Department of English at UCLA, where I realized, finally, what its title needed to be; and Sami Khatib and Paula Schwebel for "Benjamin in Palestine," the beginning, if one that had already started, of this book. Sophia Azeb shared with me an Arabic translation of Cedric Robinson's *Black Marxism*, and I remain grateful for this gift. Sara Salih was a partner in wandering, in Ramallah and elsewhere, and I hold those walks and our conversations in memory closely. David Lloyd and Sarita See invited me to dinner and read an early draft of the manuscript, and I am grateful for their generosity and insight, and for their noting a moment that called for a more sustained reading. I thank Leah, for all she gave during the time of this book's writing, and for her unending support and love. And I thank Leila and Bella, for so many hugs, and more, without which I wouldn't have made it. Much of this book was written during the pandemic years, in the garage beneath our kitchen and, later, at a table to the side of it. As I noted at the beginning of these acknowledgments, this book was revised and completed during the ongoing genocide of the Palestinian people. If something, the Gaza genocide demonstrates that it—like the settler forms I study in this book—ought not be exceptionalized. It belongs, instead, to the normative terms for collective existence in Western-hemispheric life and its racializing formations in capitalist and state legality, terms in which a particular form of life, and what the poet Aimé Césaire noticed we may understand to be a "habit," are coagulated.[2] It is in a shared effort toward the dissolution or de-posing, the abolition of such existence, and the juridical, linguistic, and social forms that sustain it, that I offer *Poeticality*, in solidarity with the Palestinian struggle for liberation, survival, life, and love.[3]

Preface

The time of writing may not be reduced to a point of origin, and yet a site from which this book emerged was a gathering in collective study around the work of Walter Benjamin, a workshop and conference organized by Sami Khatib and Paula Schwebel titled "Benjamin in Palestine." The event took place over five days in Ramallah, Palestine, December 5–11, 2015, at the International Art Academy Palestine, the Khalil Sakakini Center, and Birzeit University. Artists, filmmakers, students, activists, and scholars gathered to read Benjamin, and the intensity of conversation, the being together in study, reverberate today as the carceral-settler state reinvents itself anew and as the wars against Indigenous and Black peoples, and against non-white, non-Christian, and non-hetero-normative beings, modes of thought and relation, senses of language, and forms of collective life continue unabated, mutating in still recognizable ways. The task of critique—the task of reading—remains, now more than ever, a "task," *Aufgabe*, in the sense in which Benjamin gives us to think this term. As Lucie Kim-Chi Mercier writes in her report on the conference, the interventions that constituted the event strove to locate "points of passage" between the writings of Benjamin and the present-day context in Palestine, as much as its participants, and "the dense nexus of relations formed throughout the conference, between people, between people and places, strived to create its own unconventional mode of readability."[1] It is a mode we may consider in relation to what Benjamin called "the tradition of the oppressed": "The tradition of the oppressed teaches us [*belehrt uns*] that the 'state of exception' in which we live is the rule. We must attain to a conception of history that is in keeping with this insight. Then the bringing about of a real state of exception will stand before our eyes as our task [*Dann wird uns als unsere Aufgabe die Herbeiführung des wirklichen Ausnahmezustands vor Augen stehen*]; and this will improve our position in the struggle against Fascism."[2] This passage in Benjamin points to the German jurist Carl Schmitt, who had written that "Sovereign is whoever decides on the state of exception [*Souverän ist, wer über den Ausnahmezustand entscheidet*]."[3] If, in Schmitt, the sovereign is a single being, where *wer* is the one who decides, in Benjamin, in place of a single being, the "sovereign," *Souverän*, there is a "tradition," *Tradition*, and this tradition is sent to "us," *uns*, in "teaching," *Belehrung*; in place of "decision," *Entscheidung*, there is a teaching and a passing on, in relation to the first person plural pronoun, "us," a lingual form through which a collective is called into being in that teaching, which the tradition of the oppressed carries; and in place of a reading of the relative pronoun *wer* in the singular, there is a collective, appealed to through the "task," *Aufgabe*, Benjamin also names: the bringing about of a real "state of exception." And so Benjamin's task does not call into being a world of substances but only relations, not recognizable forms but instead doings in the social, and not solely a receptivity in teaching but what he also terms "struggle," a manner of being together where the sort of doing, which "we" do, is not, and never will have been, our own.

What does it mean, then, to read "Benjamin in Palestine" today, here and now, from the spaces where I live and write, read and listen, and teach and gather with others? If somewhere, the spaces in which I teach and learn, study and live, are the occupied lands of the Cahuilla, Tongva, Luiseño, and Serrano peoples, in what is now called "Southern California"; and these are, simultaneously, spaces of the American settler state and its histories of transatlantic chattel slavery, colonial genocide, the theft of Indigenous lands, and their ongoing transmutations in the regimes of carcerality, property, legality, and whiteness. It is the argument of this book that each of these transmutes practices of reading, being, and language, in the advance of a sense of relation and the social where these are to be grounded in a being that is itself, a subject in property-centric form.[4] Edward W. Said, in *Orientalism*, taught us that philology invests—and invents—categories, that it makes "religion," "race," "language," and, one might also underline, "politics"; Werner Hamacher noticed that there is more than one philology, and that the linguistic life of philology subtends, on the one hand, the disciplines for hermeneutic reading and historical understanding—what he terms "logology"—and, on the other hand, a manner of doing language in excess of these terms, where philology is a kind of indefinition: "The nearer philology comes to its object of concern, the farther it withdraws," Hamacher wrote; and Talal Asad observed the manner in which a particular sense of language privileges the ideational over the sensory, where "a message can always be separated from its medium," and where the sociality or materiality of language is subordinated to the meaning to which it is coerced to refer.[5] Sense—a temporal abstraction—is privileged over sound in its subordinating capture: "All Names, that are more than empty sounds, must signify some *Idea*," John Locke wrote. But how may we think the understanding of the social, which this sense of language advances? What is the social form that is pressed forward—and exteriorized—through the philological disciplines and the modern, European practices of language and sense? What sense of being is privileged in these? How does this sense of being relate to language, capital, race, and form? What is the relation between reading and settler colonization, transatlantic chattel slavery, and the ongoing practices of anti-Black and anti-Indigenous life? How does a reflection on reading compel attention to that sense of life, which has been generalized since at least Europe's twelfth, Christian century—a century during which, as Cedric J. Robinson underlined in *Black Marxism*, racial capitalism, transatlantic chattel slavery, colonial-settler and racial genocide, and settler colonization find a point of origination?[6] How may we think this sense of life, and of being and language, in its extensions and transmutations of itself outside of European and Western hemispheric frames? And how may we think the reproduction of statal existence, and its subordination of language and the social to the self-determined subject of experience, in post-Ottoman social formations, and in the white, settler, Zionist decimations—the ongoing *Nakba*, before and after 1948—directed against the Palestinian people, and in the genocidal obliterations of the wars against Iraq?[7]

In the fourteenth-century historian and philosopher Ibn Khaldūn an understanding of language as a "lingual act," فعل لساني, *fiʿl lisānī*, is passed on: "Know that language," he writes, "as it is commonly understood, is the speaker's expression of their intention. And that expression is a lingual act, given through that intention, in the medium of speech. So language must be a learned practice that has been established in the organ that enacts it, which is the tongue."[8] In the introduction to this book and the chapters that follow I study Arab and Arabic art, translation, philosophy, and poetry, which reformulate, which receive and transmute, the terms shared out through Ibn Khaldūn's tongue, where there is not a subject of language but a practice of doing in insubstantial form. To study the reformulations of this sense of language I begin, in chapter 1, with the modern, normative terms for language, the social, and being—what I refer to as "settler life." Settler life is a manner of reading, a sense of language, and a pose in philosophical explication, which extends and reproduces itself, from the Crusades, initiated in 1095, to the Lockean thinking of property and legality, the Kantian explication of the subject—of "I," in the taut section on "transcendental apperception" in the first

Critique—and the Tocquevillian formulation of the social; it is also, in terms Martin Heidegger underlines in a 1955–1956 lecture course I study in the introduction to this book, a mutation in the history of metaphysics and ontology.[9] In studying settler life in this manner I decline the exceptionalization of settler forms: Settler life does not refer solely to the settler colony—it is not the settler's form of life—because it is what divides the settler from the native—as in Frantz Fanon—as it links and separates the self-reflective, self-determined being to and from the slave, the animal, and the savage, and as it divides a sort of being that is capable of language—as well as the social and the political—from another sort of being, incapable of these, and mired in its never-ending incapacity, what Denise Ferreira da Silva has termed "subjects of affectability."[10] Settler life is a transmuting reformulation of whiteness in the fields of language, being, and the social; it is, at the same time, a counterinsurgent attack.[11] Chapter 2 studies several Arabic-language treatises, letters, and commentaries of the ninth- through eleventh-century philosophers al-Kindī, al-Fārābī, and Ibn Sīnā, to observe a tradition of what I term "anontological form," where what a being is does not temporally coincide with itself, where being is formally excessive. It is a tradition wholly other than what is privileged in post-Latinate frames for the reading of Aristotle in Europe and its global self-extensions in the mutation of Christian theological terms into philological, colonial, racial, and historical ones.[12] Chapter 3 studies the Lebanese and American, French- and English-language painter and poet Etel Adnan and the Iraqi poet Khālid al-Maʿālī and his Arabic-language translations of the German-language, Romanian Jewish poet Paul Celan. I observe reiterations of the tradition of anontological form, its being passed on, in Adnan, al-Maʿālī, and, as al-Maʿālī gives us to read him, Celan. And I notice that in Adnan, al-Maʿālī, and Celan—in poetry, translation, and painting—language is not recalled to a properly composed subject, but instead occasions a non-selfsame doing, an insurgence in refusal of settler life's accumulative, self-oriented, statal social logic and sense.[13]

I wish to underline this refusal: It is an adverbial form, not an act of a subject but instead a material doing, already a kind of repetition, a *re*fusal in which we may also hear a sharing or a leaning, a non-self-sufficiency, which gives a form of life and a manner of being wholly unlike that one which is pressed out at the world in settler life. In the "re" of this "refusal" there is not a self-formed being but instead a sonority in temporal acts, where there is no "I" that sustains or lies beneath such acts as a subject but instead a collectivity, which does not precede but is only given through such acts, where "I"—or "we"—temporally exceeds itself. And refusal is, at the same time, a refutation of and a withdrawal from a field of terms, a form a life, and a sense of language and world.[14] In this frame, I observe the "use" in the word "ref*us*al," as well as the "refuse" it carries, the leftover or left-behind materials, the detritus and rubble, where refusal is a certain re-use, which destabilizes a distinction between subject and object, form and formulation, and beings and things, given in the verb *refundere*, from which the Latin word *refusum* derives, as in the *Oxford Latin Dictionary*, which offers: "1. To cause to flow back, pour back, (in pass.) to flow back. B (pass., of rivers) to flow back (over their banks), i.e. flood. C (pass., of an action) to recoil, redound (on)." *Refundere* is also, this lexicon explains, "To restore to a fluid state, thaw" and "To give back, restore, refund."[15] Refusal, as *refundere*, is a flowing back, a flooding again; it is a surge, which, in a Lucretian manner—and I underline, in chapter 3, several of Etel Adnan's references to Lucretius—overflows the temporal determination of beings or forms.[16] I observe that refusal, further, as one is given to read it in the materials I study in this book, and as I translate these in the chapters that follow, is several: It is a refusal of a sense of world and being; a refusal, in post-Ottoman, Arabic-language frames, of the ongoing orientalist-philological violences, and their reordering of language, a reformulation, in Arabic, of what "language" is; a refusal of juridical-linguistic life and subjective comportment in self-reflexive interiority; a refusal of the terms of life and death, of unsurvival and collective obliteration, in the settler colony; and it is, finally, an indetermined practice with matter, an anaccumulative doing in refusal of settler life. Refusal is not a critique of settler life but a withdrawal from it, a "disengagement" with it, as Audra Simpson has written, and its cadastral, plantational, and state-determined juridical terms.[17]

Theodor Adorno wrote in *Minima Moralia* of "the good life" and its loss: "The melancholy science from which I make this offering to my friend relates to a region that from time immemorial was regarded as the true field of philosophy [*als der eigentliche der Philosophie galt*], but which, since the latter's conversion into method, has lapsed into intellectual neglect, sententious whimsy and finally oblivion: the teaching of the good life [*die Lehre vom richtigen Leben*]. What the philosophers once knew as life has become the sphere of private existence and now of mere consumption, dragged along as an appendage of the process of material production, without autonomy or substance of its own [*ohne Autonomie und ohne eigene Substanz*]."[18] And yet "life," in the harsh division of "life" from "the good life," is sent out, distributed, and reformulated; it is the division that divides, on a global scale, within polities and across social formations, in the repeatedly formulated and collapsed division of a sort of being capable of language from another incapable of it, one sort of being that owns and possesses language, that retains a capacity or faculty for it, and another—differentiated, and ever-differentiating—that does not. "Life," in this sense, becomes a coercive locus for the generalization of a sort of being that is properly itself, separate from and linked to the animal—"Speech differentiates man from the other animals," Rousseau wrote—and which is said to come to be itself in its properly cultivated relation to language and form.[19] If in Adorno life has been lost—"Our perspective of life [*Leben*] has passed into an ideology which conceals the fact that there is life no longer [*daß es keines mehr gibt*]," he offered—it becomes the task of reading to think life differently, in terms not reducible to these.[20] This, not in order to recuperate a vitalism, biologism, or organicism, and even less to affirm a biopoliticality of forms, but instead to observe that the life of living beings, if it is something, it is in excess of the terms to which it is subordinated in the normative practices of philosophical self-reflection, and the demand that living beings lift themselves from their materiality or corporeality to abstraction and universality, and, through this, from death to life. And it is to observe that if there is life, it may only be what is given in relation to, and yet not identically with, the individual and collective losses—including those which, as the poet, translator, and critic Sinan Antoon has written, "are never mentioned or seen"—which settler life has not ceased to impart, asymmetrically, to the world.[21] "For the value of a thought is measured by its distance from the continuity of the familiar," a distance, one might also say, refiguring Adorno's prose, from what is already known, *des Bekannten*.[22] If the thinking of life is not to return life to itself, I approach life, and if also what I call "settler life," neither to affirm an "autonomy" or "substantiality," as Adorno promises—"without autonomy or substance of its own"—nor to affirm a sense of being that would be its own—the word *eigen* appears twice in the sentences I've cited here, as Adorno laments its loss in relation to "philosophy" and "life"—but only to listen, in a kind of slow, distracted reading, to the manner of doing, which language occasions. In this, the labor of reading becomes a kind of yielding, which does not affirm a proper listening or reading subject—a proper subject for language or life—but a practice in sociality, a collective mode without return to a self-possessed being as its ordering principle or ground.[23]

This book was in revision as the Israeli occupying forces began their bombardment of Gaza on October 7, 2023. The bombardment reiterates the terms of settler life and form, an acute penetration and what Nadera Shalhoub-Kevorkian has called a "dismemberment" of Palestinian being and life, commensurate with the forms of genocidal deworlding pursued by the Zionist state since 1948.[24] If the work I offer can make this deworlding, and its collective and social obliterations, intelligible, if these may be situated within a history of the Zionist colonization of Palestine as well as the regional, global, and Western hemispheric institution of settler form and sense, of white settler existence and propertied life, I offer the pages that follow to bring out a wholly other sense of being, language, and life, in which the poetry of Mahmoud Darwish, and others, shares. A principal argument of this book is that poetic and artistic practice shares in an insubstantial, anaccumulative, non-self-determined sense of being, language, and life, inidentical in relation to that one that is generated through the terms I study in chapter 1. In 2002, at the time of still yet another Israeli siege, this time of the West Bank, Palestinian city of Jenin, Darwish wrote: "To poetry: place your siege under siege [إلى الشعر: حاصر حصارك; *ilā al-shiʿr: ḥāṣir ḥiṣāraka*]."[25] If Darwish appeals to poetry as a locus for collective insurgence, and if he suggests a manner in which poetry may place the siege under siege, to disinstall it and render it inoperative, this is also to point to a particular manner of being or doing, a practice in the social, and to an indistinction among these, carried in the word "poetry," الشعر, *al-shiʿr*, and Darwish's address to it. What is held and sustained in Darwish's language, I wish to observe, is a refusal of the modern terms for legality and property, and the subordination of collective form to state-juridical existence—terms reformulated in the thanatocentric acts and cartographic destructions of the Zionist settler state. "They did not mean to kill the children./They meant to," the poet and translator Fady Joudah has written of the ongoing genocide in Gaza. "Too many kids got in the way/of precisely imprecise/one-ton bombs/dropped a thousand and one times/over the children's nights," he notes, as he points to love and life: "Life says: I will make you to make love./Love says: I make life so that I am."[26] There is an intersection of love with life, life with being, and being with the poetic, which Joudah teaches us to read and with which I linger in address and devastation and rage. Poetry's placing of the siege under siege resounds, therefore, in a wholly non-Lockean manner, distinct from the sense of language privileged in normative, self-exteriorizing European formulations, their white social being, and their unending reduction of sonority to sense, matter to abstraction, and the social to the juridical—a practice of domesticating capture in the formation and persistence of a quite particular sense of life. In this book I remain with Darwish's imperative, his injunction to the poem, to notice a particular sort of doing in the poetic, which his language continues to give. I do so to advance what Benjamin, to draw upon a term I noted in this book's acknowledgments, and to which I return in the introduction and chapter 3, called the "de-posing," *Entsetzung*, what we might think of as the dissolution or abolition of the state form and the manner of life it fosters and through which it is sustained. And I do so to affirm the demand for Indigenous sovereignty, in Palestine, in Turtle Island, and elsewhere, in refusal of law, the state, and self-determined form, a demand which, therefore, through the collective acts occasioned in it, decomposes and disinstalls, deregulates and disallocates, that de-poses all sovereign forms and all state legalities, in refusal of that form of life, which coerces such forms to be understood as sovereign, or as temporally selfsame, at all—in refusal of settler life.

Claremont, California
November 2, 2023/July 28, 2025

Introduction

Poeticality

> Everything is in the language we use.
>
> —LAYLI LONG SOLDIER

"Will you not memorize a little poetry to halt the slaughter?" the Palestinian poet Mahmoud Darwish wrote in a poem that appeared in a volume titled *Eleven Planets* (أحد عشر كوكباً/*Aḥad ʿashar kawkaban*), published in 1992.[1] The poem in which this passage appears is titled "The 'Red Indian's' Penultimate Speech to the White Man" and in it the poetic subject speaks in the voice of the "'red Indian'" to the "white man," addressing the colonizer, in Western hemispheric life, in a language that exceeds the terms of that life and is wholly other than it. I notice that if the language of this poem addresses itself to that life—what I term, in this book, "settler life," a mode of being and doing that reiterates an ongoing genocidal and social obliteration—as it does so it speaks to the colonizer and asks them to memorize poetry. The "speech," which this poem is, is an instance of language, in Arabic, and in this the linguistic subject, the one who speaks and offers a poetic word, stands "before" the colonizer and addresses them, as if the subject of poetic speech, through this address, had called into being a world, at once a practice of sociality and linguistic life, at odds with that of the colonizer, even as the poet explains that "the white master will not understand the old words/here, among our free souls, between the sky and the trees [لن يفهم السيّد الأبيض الكلمات العتيقة/ هنا/في النفوس الطليقة بين السماء وبين الشجر; *lan yafham al-sayyid al-abyaḍ al-kalimāt al-ʿatīqa/hunā fī al-nufūs al-ṭalīqa bayna al-samāʾ wa bayna al-shajar*]" (38). The "white man" directs their acts into the earth and water, and at living beings—"The stranger utters strange words, and digs, in the land, a well/in order to bury in it the sky. The stranger utters strange words / and hunts our children and the butterflies" (43)—and as they "utter," يقول, *yaqūl*, in this manner they proliferate a sense of language, being, and life. It is perhaps for this reason that Darwish, addressing the colonizer—at once "the stranger," and "the white man"—asks them to "memorize," to do a particular sort of act occasioned, in Arabic, in the word "poetry," الشعر, *al-shiʿr*. To read Darwish's poetic utterance is not to subject it to linguistic understanding—historical, hermeneutic, or philological—but it is instead to yield to or share in the manner of address formulated in the poem. One might further say, reframing "understanding" and displacing it through the poem, that to understand poetic statement in Darwish is to do the sort of act the poem recalls: It is to memorize "a little poetry."

There is an address to the colonizer: "Will you not memorize a little poetry to halt the slaughter?", ألا تحفظون قليلا من الشعر كي توقفوا المذبحة, *alā taḥfaẓūna qalīlan min al-shiʿr kay tūqifū al-madhbḥa*, and in this there is not an appeal to the poetic in order to move thought away from the social, or from the matter of genocidal obliteration, but instead we are directed to the poetic as site of linguistic practice and being. The poetic subject asks: "Will you not memorize?" and because the verb "memorize" is in the second person plural, I notice that Darwish addresses a collective, not any single colonizer or settler, but a plurality of beings in settler life. Poetic utterance calls into being and transmutes—in the material form of three letters in the conjugated verb, the *tāʾ*, the *waw*, and the *nūn*, indicating the second person plural—a sense of language, the social, and world through the particular sort of doing, which language, in the poem, is. In reading this poem Steven Salaita has observed that Darwish invokes a "cosmos" and a "landscape," and this invocation gives an indistinction of the cosmological and the poetic, and the material and the formal.[2] "Here," Darwish writes, "our bodies evaporate, in one cloud and another, in the sky / here, our spirits glimmer, one star and another, in the sky's song."[3] Language intersects "our" evaporating bodies as the poetic mirrors mutating droplets of water, and yet this is not because "sky" or "star" presumes a self-possessed form for contemplation or an observing subject in interiorizing self-reflection, because what is given in the poetic is a certain doing, a mode of being that is also a being together, where the motions of water droplets are indistinct from "song," نشيد, *nashīd*, in a poetic and lingual formulation with matter—what Darwish, in the passage with which this introduction begins, and which I also place as an epigraph to this book, recalls with the word "memorize." In Darwish language does not return to a self-owning subject, it is in excess of the social logic of property advanced in the settler, plantational, capitalist terms of cadastral life and its privileged philosophical form—the form and manner of the Western hemispheric and global life of the "white man" to whom the "penultimate speech" is addressed.[4]

Darwish observes, in the language practice of the settler, a sort of translation: "For it is the right of Columbus the free," he writes, "to find India in any sea,/and it is his right to name our ghosts pepper and Indians," and Darwish relates this "right," حق, *ḥaqq*, to the settler's self-allocated sense of world, where language is reduced to the activity of a being in its interiorizing self-understanding; where the social institution of such a being is reiterated, globally and hemispherically, in what Marx, in the first volume of *Capital*, termed "primitive accumulation"; and where primitive accumulation is ongoing and foundational for capital.[5] "Columbus the free," Darwish also wrote, "was searching for a language, which he didn't find here,/and for gold in the skulls of our kind ancestors, even as he took/what he wanted of the living and the dead in us [وكولومبوس الحرّ يبحث عن لغةٍ لم يجدها هنا، / وعن ذهبٍ في جماجم أجدادنا الطيّبين، وكان له / ما يريد من الحيّ والميت فينا; *wa Kulūmbūs al-ḥurr yabḥath ʿan lughatin lam yajidhā hunā,/wa ʿan dhahabin fī jamājim ajdādinā al-ṭayyibīn wa kāna lahu/mā yurīd min al-ḥayy wa al-mayyit fīnā*] (39). Glen Sean Coulthard has observed that "rather than positing primitive accumulation as some historically situated, inaugural set of events that set the stage for the development of the capitalist mode of production through colonial expansion, we should see it as an ongoing practice of dispossession that never ceases to structure capitalist and colonial social relations in the present," and I notice, thinking with Coulthard, that this temporal excess of primitive accumulation mutates and crosses fields, to materially afford practices of the social and modes of knowing lodged in an accumulative practice for property-centric form.[6] In this sense, settler life may be understood as a practice of language, where primitive accumulation is an interiorizing action for the formation of a subject, an internalization and linguification of what Sarita Echavez See has termed "knowledge *nullius*," an "epistemic accumulation" which, rather than exteriorized in the form of an institution is interiorized as the literary and linguistic life of a subject.[7] In such interiorization, a pedagogical practice of self-cultivation in *Bildung*, the destruction occasioned in primitive accumulation is reformulated in properly cultivated literary and linguistic subjectivity and philosophical self-representation, as it advances a redefinition of what language is, in the subordination of the sonority of utterance to subjective linguistic existence.[8] Darwish points to the excessive form of settler life—he continues the passage I've cited, addressing "Columbus," a name that stands in for "the white man" as well as, more generally, the settler subject, to ask, "So/why does he continue his war of extermination, from his grave, until the end? [إذاً/لماذا يواصل حرب الإبادة ، من قبره، للنهاية; *idhan/limādha yuwāṣil ḥarb al-ibāda, min qabrihi, lil-nihāya*]"—as he notes its relation to language and the poetic, and its exteriorization of itself, in its "continuing" wars of "extermination," الإبادة, *al-ibāda*, in relation to capital, race, and the global forms of juridical life.[9] This, even as the "end" is not something Darwish affirms—the speech Darwish relates is the "penultimate speech," the speech "before the last," ما قبل الأخيرة, *mā qabla al-akhīra*—but is the temporal mode of linguistic understanding privileged by the settler and its hermeneutics of domesticating sociality, where settler practice extends itself endlessly, and where this extension exceeds the life of any single colonizing being: "Columbus," for example.[10]

The reflection on Indigenous extermination is offered, in the volume of Darwish's I'm reading, "after Iraq," a reference to the 1991 American-led invasion of Iraq, which Darwish thinks in its triangulated relation to the Zionist colonization of Palestine and settler colonization in its Western hemispheric frames: "No space remained, upon the earth, for the poem, Oh my friend," Darwish wrote, addressing an unnamed Iraqi poet, to which the final poem in the collection is dedicated, "So is there, in the poem, a space, still, for the earth, after Iraq? [فهل في القصيدة متسع، بعد، للأرض، بعد العراق; *fa hal fī al-qaṣīda muttasiʿ, baʿd, lil-arḍ, baʿd al-ʿIrāq*]."[11] Darwish gives us to think the poetic as a space for earth, as the decimating aggressions, which target Iraq and Palestine, are thought in relation to the ever-proliferating wars against Black and Indigenous existence and life. They are wars which mutate and advance what Nick Estes, Melanie K. Yazzie, Jennifer Nez Denetdale, and David Correia have termed "settler ontology," where "everything in a settler world is a border," and in this we may think of settler life as a property-centric management of language and the social—settler life is also a logistics, as Stefano Harney and Fred Moten have given us to think this term—which constrains a particular sense of being.[12] I wish to underline that settler life, if it is something, *is* ontology. By this I mean two things: If ontology is a discourse on being, where beings are to be grounded in an atemporal being, settler life is the affirmation of an understanding of being in property-centric form; and if ontology is a particular manner of dividing beings—if it is the division of the temporal from the eternal, and of what perishes from what does not—settler life exacts an asymmetric imparting of death and a withholding and allocation of life as it sets itself against what it understands to be the unruly, riotous form of non-white, non-European collectives—against beings incapable of abstraction and the proper setting of limits. In this book—learning from the traditions of Black Study, Indigenous Studies, and Arab and Arabic Studies—I offer a contribution to the collective study of this form of life. I do so to address the senses of language, being, and life it exteriorizes, in its eviscerating violences, as it generalizes itself in the social.[13] And I do so to precipitate or accelerate, in a shared thinking or doing, the disinstallation, and what Walter Benjamin termed the "de-posing," *Entsetzung*, of settler life.[14] And yet this book, instead of privilege settler life, is offered only in part as a reading of it, as I underline—in Arab and Arabic poetics, art, philosophy, and translation, as I study these in chapters 2 and 3—a wholly other manner of being, an anaccumulative doing or making, where language is indistinct from the social, the social from the ontological, and the ontological from the poetic—what I call "poeticality."

In Darwish poetic practice is in excess of the grammar of linguistic utterance. "Columbus the free," he wrote in a passage I cited above, "was searching for a language, which he didn't find here, / and for gold in the skulls of our kind ancestors, even as he had / what he wanted of the living and the dead in us." There is a relation to "ancestors" أجداد, *ajdād*, through which "we," نحن, *naḥnu*, is called into being, a social or lingual form in collectivity given in the poetic. Because it acts in this manner, we may read Darwish's language in relation to the tradition of "resistance," مقاومة, *muqāwama*, theorized—and anthologized—by the Palestinian literary critic, novelist, playwright, and militant Ghassan Kanafani, who was assassinated by the Israeli state on July 8, 1972. And yet resistance, in this frame, and in excess of it, is not an act grounded in a subject, individual or collective, but instead an insurgence—a social and ontological refusal, a practice in non-self-determined form, and a manner of doing in excess of temporal stabilization. Here, collectivity is called into being through material or lingual acts, inidentical practices of form in the social.[15] Thinking these two texts together—Darwish's "Penultimate Speech" (and the sense of form given in Darwish's poetic corpus, from the "earliest" to the "latest" writings) and Kanafani's *The Literature of Resistance in Occupied Palestine* (أدب المقاومة في فلسطين المحتلّة / *Adab al-muqāwama fī Filasṭīn al-muḥtalla*), published in 1966—we may consider the manner in which settler life is an exertion of a particular sense of form, exteriorized in settler colonization, transatlantic chattel slavery, colonial-settler and state genocide, racial capitalism, and modern law.[16] Kanafani's anthologization, like Darwish's poetry, refuses the thanatocentric, obliterating practice of the Zionist state—in its acute particularity and in the manner in which it reiterates modern juridical-centric collective existence—as it gives a sort of act where, in its material formulation, there is no "subject" that "does" language, but instead a sharing in and passing on of a tradition, what Nouri Gana has formulated as "an opaque undercurrent of resistance," a "loyalty to the remainder" in "militant *ṣumūd*," in excess of the time of the modern state and its linguistic sense.[17] I offer this book, then, as a sort of translation, and I offer this particular translation—in declining to think about language as an occasion for autonomous acts in the social—to think a sense of the social in affirmation of manners of being and doing in anaccumulative form—what I call, in chapter 3, "a poetics of things." Because the readings I offer study language in this manner, and because language is what this book does and is, as well as the "object" "about" which it writes, it is translationally in default, in excess of temporal or epistemic closure. And this work—each of its sentences—is therefore amethodological, formally improper, and constitutively wanting; it is, one might say, a translational catachresis. Rather than presume a stability of objects I offer readings which, like the poetic and artistic work I study, only give themselves away, in what the poet Layli Long Soldier has termed, in a passage I'll cite below, a kind of love.

Settler life is the exteriorization and mutation, the transformation and rephrasing, of a particular sense of form, and, in particular, of the terms privileged in ontology, the discourse on being in the European philosophical tradition. To think the relation between settler life and ontology I turn to a lecture course presented by Martin Heidegger at the University of Freiburg in Winter 1955–1956, and published under the title *The Principle of Reason* (*Der Satz vom Grund*). There, Heidegger notes that the European philosophical tradition, and what he also terms "metaphysics," is installed through the setting up of a "partition," which it does not cease to reiterate: "The setting up of this partition between the sensible and the nonsensible, between the physical and the nonphysical," he writes, "is a basic trait of what is called metaphysics and which normatively determines Western thinking."[18] It is a normative determination, Heidegger explains, that does not cease to desire to ground beings in an atemporal being, and to think beings on the basis of such a being, and this is because "human understanding, whenever and wherever it is active, always and everywhere keeps on the lookout for the reason why whatever it encounters is and is the way it is" (13/3). Heidegger's lectures take as a starting point the Latin statement of Leibniz, "*Nihil ist sine ratione*," which Heidegger translates and comments on: "Nothing is without reason [*Nichts ist ohne grund*]. There is nothing—and here that means any something [*ein Etwas*] that in some manner is—that is without reason" (16/5). There is, then, to have been a principle of reason, and if this principle is "general"—"But the principle of reason intends to say more, namely, that generally, and that means as a rule, every being has some sort of reason for being, and for being the way it is" (18/6)—it posits objects or beings or things in the field it generates without exception: "What the principle of reason posits, it posits as being without exception [*Was der Satz setzt, setzt er als ausnahmlos*]" (18/6). The principle of reason posits as it extends itself in a manner that is both general and exceptionless, because whatever being or thing or object, anything that is "something," *Etwas*, is to be recognized in relation to the principle of reason. The principle of reason, one might therefore say, advances a language practice, which designates things or beings as objects, and which subordinates language to being, where, as Heidegger wrote, "The word 'is,' in one way or another, invariantly names being [*nennt stets auf irgendeine Weise das Sein*]" (92/50), as it sends itself everywhere, where anywhere and wherever is there where it gives to itself the authority to speak and extend its sense of language and world.

In elaborating the positing form of the principle of reason, a "principle," *Satz*, which is, itself a kind of "positing," *setzen*, Heidegger calls upon a being that listens well, and which "we," the addressees of this lecture, are to be. "Everywhere we move in the aura of the demand to render reasons and at the same time we have an uncommonly difficult time simply paying attention to this demand so as to hear *that* language in which it genuinely speaks" (57/28–29). "We" are to have paid attention properly, and if this passage commands "us" in a pedagogical mode, this is because it cyphers a history of pedagogical formation—of *Bildung*—in the European tradition; and, further, this demand, which compels an attention to reasons, and which requires that reasons be "rendered," is to have spoken to us in a language that "genuinely speaks": "so as to hear *that* language in which it genuinely speaks," *um darin* die *Sprache zu vernehmen, die er eigentlich spricht*. There is a sort of "hearing," where one hears in a "genuine," *eigentlich*, manner, and this term relates to what is "proper" and to "property," *Eigentum*, to what is one's "own," *eigen*.[19] This passage reiterates a sense of being formulated through a social logic of property, and, more particularly, the capitalist form of property characterized, since at least the sixteenth century—as Marx outlines in *Grundrisse* and the first volume of *Capital*—by the expropriation of surplus value and set in motion through and ongoingly repeated in primitive accumulation.[20] What is congealed in Heidegger's explication is a social relation and manner of being, where the "proper" and "property," and the value associated with these—including the value placed on the subject of self-understanding and interiorizing self-reflection—are shown to be derivative of, and founded through, the global practice of primitive accumulation in its relation to settler colonization, transatlantic chattel slavery, and capitalist relations, terms which are formatively and ongoingly interrelated, as Eric Williams has shown in his 1944 study *Capitalism and Slavery*, and as Cedric J. Robinson has elaborated.[21]

Jacques Derrida has underlined the privilege of the "proper" in Heidegger, in "*Ousia* and *Grammē*," an essay published in 1968, and one may trace his discussion of this term as well through his 1964–1965 lecture course, *Heidegger: The Question of Being and History*.[22] In this book I learn from the reading practice of Derrida, a thinker and writer of inidentical form, of non-selfsame, self-differentiated being, and I learn from his intervention, in particular, in thinking about the animal (in chapter 1, in relation to Aristotle, Fanon, Marx, and Locke), and in thinking about Emmanuel Lévinas in relation to language, being, ontology, and form (in chapter 3). I draw attention to the terms "proper" and "property" to introduce the question of being and its relation to settler life, and to address the normative forms of modern philosophical self-understanding in relation to the history of metaphysics and ontology, which Heidegger traces in *The Principle of Reason*. If Heidegger places an emphasis on Leibniz—"This means," he writes in a comment on Leibniz's "principium reddendae rationis," "that reason is what must be rendered to the representing thinking person [*Der Grund ist solches, was dem vorstellenden, denkenden Menschen zugestellt werden muß*]"—this is to underline that in Leibniz, "What is encountered is presented to a cognizing I, presented back to and over against it, made present."[23] And if, to study this rendering, one is to neither "stumble"—"The question of the supreme fundamental principles and their hierarchy certainly stumbles around in the fog [*irrt freilich im Nebel herum*] as long as we are unclear about what a fundamental principle is" (22/9)—nor "blur" one's sense of what a principle is—"The principle of reason does not help us much when we try to clarify what the essence of reason is. Yet it is necessary to know this if, when discussing fundamental principles, we do not want to have a blurred notion [*einer verschwommenen Vorstellung*] of what a fundamental principle is" (23/9)—I notice that the reflection on the principle of reason becomes an occasion to think the form of a subject that hears properly, and that neither "stumbles" nor "blurs," in a manner wherein it owns itself and is a kind of property. It is not only that Heidegger's address presumes that it is surrounded by beings that "stumble" and "blur," but that his language reiterates a tradition, for and through which the social is instituted in relation to a particular sort of being, in propertied self-understanding, and in a generalization of "whiteness as property," as Cheryl I. Harris has explicated this term, and as J. Kēhaulani Kauanui has given us to read Harris.[24] Darwish's poetic statement is instructive: It is the "white man," الرجل الأبيض, *al-rajul al-abyaḍ*, the subject of settler enunciation, which gives to itself a right to name—"It is the right of Columbus the free to find India in any sea,/and it is his right to name our ghosts 'pepper' or 'Indians,'" Darwish wrote in a passage I cited above—and we may think of this self-giving as the exertion of a right to translate, which subordinates language, and sonority, to a propertied sense of being and life, in a racializing formulation of the social.[25]

It was Heidegger who underlined Kant as a figure in "modern metaphysics," and in the lectures I'm discussing here Kant is a thinker of "foundations": "According to Kant, reason is the faculty of principles, that is, of fundamental principles, of the giving of foundations" (125/71–72), and, Heidegger notes, Kant responds to the demand for grounds: "Insofar as thinking becomes a critique of pure reason through Kant, it responds to the demand of the *principium rationis sufficientis*" (127–128/73). And yet in Kant—as in Leibniz—the demand for reasons is proffered by and returns to a cognizing subject, what Heidegger termed "the representing, thinking person," for whom all beings and things appear as objects: "It is in relation to the I as subject that beings, placed before the I in representation, have the character of an object for a subject. Beings are beings as objects for consciousness. Since consciousness allows an object to stand on *its own* [auf sich *zu stehen läßt*], it thus represents itself along with the object—it is self-consciousness" (132/77). Critique becomes the explication of transcendental terms as a question that rearticulates the principle of reason: "The critical question of the sufficient reason for objects," Heidegger writes, "becomes the question concerning the *a priori* conditions for the possibility of the representation of objects of experience" (132/77). Denise Ferreira da Silva, David Lloyd, J. Kameron Carter, R. A. Judy, Robert Bernasconi, and Huapin Lu-Adler have studied the racialized frame of the Kantian critique, and they have underlined that the form of the critical subject, as a subject that sets proper limits, presumes a generalization of racial terms, because the subject of critique installs itself by differentiating itself from others, incapable of such limit-setting activity.[26] As settler life advances itself, it advances a distinction between those capable and incapable of critique, self-representation, and the management of limits, what Ferreira da Silva has termed, in a passage I underlined in this book's preface, a distinction between "the self-determined subject and its outer-determined others," and between "the subject of transparency" and "subjects of affectability."[27] Ferreira da Silva's noting the latter in the plural is a starting point for the thought I offer: that settler life is a form of life that repeatedly founds itself through its address to a plurality in "racialized subjection" (225), which it places under permanent assault. The Kantian formulations advance a particular sense of the social, in the sentences where Kant, in *Critique of Pure Reason*—the text Heidegger is discussing in the lectures I'm reading here—defines "transcendental apperception"; and I observe that this definition—in Kant's articulation of "I" as a form—is a counterinsurgent language practice in philosophical explication.[28] In this, and through Kant's formulations, I notice that settler life *is* ontology, where the subject in self-representation, "I think," *Ich denke*, as Kant writes in the second, 1787 edition of the first *Critique*, generalizes itself as a determining form for the comprehensibility of world as it sends itself against all of the others.[29] In this self-sending, philosophical reflection becomes a mutation within a tradition, where the subject is a subject of self-determined comportment and a properly stabilizing—a properly settled and settling—pose.

The Principle of Reason advances a question about being: "What does 'is' mean?" Heidegger asks. He continues, glossing Leibniz: "From grammar we know that 'is' belongs to the conjugations of the helping verb 'to be.' Yet it is not necessary to resort to grammar. The content of the sentence affords us plenty of information. 'Nothing,' that is, no being whatsoever '*is*—without *reason*.'"[30] Heidegger accentuates the verb "to be" and asks us to listen to it in a particular manner, and in this "we" are interpellated as addressees of Heidegger's explication of the principle of reason, which the lecture course makes legible in relation to the social logic of property I've underlined. Heidegger continues: "Even if it does so completely indeterminately, the 'is' always names the being of some being. So the principle of reason, which is offered as a statement about beings, says: to the being of beings there belongs something like ground. Consequently, the principle of reason proves to be not only a statement about beings; even more, what we bring into view is that the principle of reason speaks about the being of beings" (90/49). And yet to speak about the being of beings is to speak in a ground-like manner: "The principle of reason says: *to being there belongs something like ground. Being is akin to grounds, it is ground-like*" (90/49). What is emphasized is a question of proper hearing, and what one is to hear is that "*The principle of reason is an uttering of being* [Der Satz vom Grund ist ein Sagen vom Sein]" (90/49), as Heidegger italicizes this sentence. And yet if Heidegger wishes to place this ground-demanding understanding of being in question, he reiterates it through the terms of his *Bildung*-centric prose and pose, where language, in its "uttering" or "saying," *Sagen*, is recalled to a sort of being that listens properly. What I wish to underline is this: The interpellation I've noticed installs a divided field, where a distinction is drawn between those capable and incapable of proper listening—those whose acts are all "stumble" and "blur" and those whose are not. If in this settler life is a reformulation of ontology, it is not a ground through which the social may be thought. It is instead a transmuting institution, an atotal mutation, itself inidentical. And this, finally, is what it—ontology, or settler life, or property, however little I can tell the difference among these—also is; settler life—or ontology—*is* this stumbling blurring, and in this sense I observe that *Der Satz vom Grund* is a treatise on being.[31]

"Thinking is listening" (86/47), but language, in Heidegger, is recalled to a social logic and epistemic practice of property. If earlier, in *Being and Time*, being is to be thought in relation to temporality, and if, in this, there is a pressing against a privilege of the atemporal in Christianity, Aristotle, and Kant, *The Principle of Reason* persists in subordinating being to a ground—to "property" and to what is one's "own."[32] I notice two moments. First, Heidegger's response to "stumble" and "blur" points to an anxiety in relation to language, to a materiality of forms and sonic formulation, which gives us to think this response as a response, by which I mean, as a carceral and formative capture of unruly sound, and this unruliness is, readers of Kant have taught us, wholly racialized. It is not my argument that this is particular to Heidegger—or to Kant; it is not. Instead, it is my argument that this capture and this racialization are given to be read in the argumentative explications of philosophical texts; and it is my argument that this explication is a material practice for the radical privilege of what Judith Butler has termed "the self-sufficient 'I,'" thought "as a kind of possession," where "I," understood in this manner, becomes a linguistic practice for the obliteration of forms of life.[33] This moment in Heidegger also teaches us to attend to a particular thinking of language and life—and, Heidegger underlines, his effort to think the "withdrawal" of being "is nothing other than an interpretation, thought through from the point of view of the question of being, of the old definition of human nature: *Homo est animal rationale*; the human being is the living being, which is endowed with reason [*der Mensch ist das mit Vernunft begabte Lebewesen*]"—in its relation to transatlantic chattel slavery, genocide, settler colonization, race, and capital in globality.[34] I underline this to note the manner in which the Heideggerian thinking of being and language is also a thinking of life. And I do so to anticipate the reading of settler life I offer in chapter 1, where I consider the institution of the subject as a locus for the exteriorization of settler life as a social and linguistic form—a form which, if it reaches back to Aristotle's *Politics*, which Heidegger cites in Latin and translates into German, it teaches us to attend to the implication of sound with social and philosophical sense, in an unyielding extension of a particular form of life.

> When I want to write seriously I think of people like
> dg for whom I wrote a long poem for whom I revised
> until the poem forgot its way back troubled I let it go when
> you love something let it go if it returns be a good mother
> father welcome the poem open armed pull out the frying
> pan grease it coat it prepare a meal
> apron and kitchen sweat labor
> my love my sleeves pushed
> to elbows like the old days a sack
> of flour and keys I push them
> typography and hotcakes work
> seduce a poem into believing
> I can home it I can provide it
> white gravy whatever the craving

poem eat and lie down full
poem rest here full don't
lift a single l
etter.

—LAYLI LONG SOLDIER, WHEREAS

I place a passage in Layli Long Soldier's WHEREAS as an epigraph to this introduction, the opening, following its preface, and following a citation of Darwish, of this book about "poeticality," "anontological form," and "settler life": "Everything," Long Soldier writes, "is in the language we use."[35] Long Soldier is a citizen of the Oglala Lakota Nation, and the poem takes as an occasion for its enunciation the Sioux Uprising of 1862, a collective rebellion following the expropriation and theft of Native land, the settler containment of Dakota life—"However, as best as I can put the facts together, in 1851, Dakota territory was contained to a twelve-mile by one-hundred-fifty-mile-long strip along the Minnesota River. But just seven years later, in 1858, the northern portion was ceded (taken) and the southern portion was (conveniently) allotted, which reduced Dakota land to a stark ten-mile tract," Long Soldier writes (51)—and the starvation of the Dakota people. "Without money, store credit, or rights to hunt beyond their ten-mile tract of land, Dakota people began to starve" (51). It was during the Sioux Uprising that a settler, "famous for his refusal to provide credit to Dakota people," and who had stated, "If they are hungry, let them eat grass" (53), was executed. "When Myrick's body was found / his mouth was stuffed with grass" (53), and it is with this grass that WHEREAS begins. "Yet, I started this piece because I was interested in writing about grasses" (52): "Now / make room in the mouth," the volume opens, "for grassesgrassesgrasses" (5). There is a jamming of words in this opening verse, an onomatopoeic giving of language, which points to a sonority of the poetic in sonic form. It is an utterance which, borrowed from the histories of Indigenous insurgence, reiterates a refusal of "containment" in relation to ongoing settler attack and obliterating address. I linger with the form of poetic utterance because, in the collective practice it recirculates and to which it appeals, it does not devolve upon a subject in language or the social but instead gives a collective doing or making in lingual form. In this, it is as if the social act of the Dakota warriors were poetic—"I am inclined to call this act by the Dakota warriors a poem" (53)—and this is not only because of the manner in which their acts retaliated against the settler state's starvation of the Dakota people—"As a result—and without other options but to continue to starve—Dakota people retaliated" (52)—but also because language, in Long Soldier, is a practice, which is not returnable to an individuated being or social subject—a subject of self-representation or cultivated interiority, what Heidegger called "the representing thinking person"—itself a locus for the social forms, in settler colonialism, transatlantic chattel slavery, and racial capitalism, which advance the containment, at once genocidal and cadastral, to which Long Soldier points.

In this book I study the poetic as a social form and a doing in language, which, if it is not reducible to the normative terms for being, language, or life in the European, philosophical tradition—a tradition I term, in its linguistic, juridical, and formal exteriorization of itself, "settler life"—it is given in relation to the modes of suffering and destruction, which this tradition reproduces in globality. "When I want to write seriously I think of people like / dg for whom I wrote a long poem for whom I revised / until the poem forgot its way back troubled I let it go when / you love something let it go" (24), Long Soldier also shares, and I yield in the writing I offer in this book, in each of its three chapters, to this practice of love. I notice, as well, Long Soldier's manner of fostering sustenance, which she addresses to the poem as she serves a poem, in a certain sweaty labor and love: "when / you love something let it go if it returns be a good mother / father welcome the poem open armed pull out the frying / pan grease it coat it prepare a meal / apron and kitchen sweat labor / my love my sleeves pushed / to elbows like the old days a sack / of flour and keys I push them" (24). If there is a sharing in matter in this doing with the poem, a welcoming of the poem and a giving with and to and for it, the relation to the poem Long Soldier describes does not provide a "home," or a homestead, a demarcated tract of land properly allotted in white capitalist conjugality or cartographically settled form. There is, differently, a sociality of poetic doing, where the feeding of the poem, the giving of sustenance and providing of rest to the poem—"typography and hotcakes work / seduce a poem into believing / I can home it I can provide it / white gravy whatever the craving / poem eat and lie down full / poem rest here full don't / lift a single l / etter" (24)—points to a sense of the poetic as a sort of doing, a shared occasion for being with and among language and matter, and with the matter that "a single l / etter" is, as well as an intersection of matter with body, body with writing, writing with "a sack of flour," flour with earth, and earth with grass and "grassesgrassesgrasses." The poem performs its relation to a sociality in excess of the stabilizing terms to which language, in the institutions of settler domestication, and its disciplines for reading, is to be absorbed and, as Long Soldier writes, "contained."

Chapter 1, "Settler Life," studies the form of life that exerts itself through this containment. And yet my reading is not oriented toward Wittgenstein's understanding of a "form of life," *Lebensform*, because his sense of this term privileges a coherency in form, with which the reading I offer is not consonant; nor do I engage, other than briefly, the reading of life in Hannah Arendt, Michel Foucault, and Giorgio Agamben.[36] Taking Heidegger's Latin reference to Aristotle in *The Principle of Reason* as a point of departure, I argue that the thinking of life in settler life returns not so much to Aristotle as it does to a mode of thought initiated in the twelfth-Christian-century Latin translation of the Aristotelian corpus.[37] It is in *Politics* that Aristotle designates that sort of being which, capable of language, is therefore capable of life in the city, a being that is capable not solely of "life" but also "the good life." And yet this lexicon ought to be read in relation to this Latinate frame and a singular event, whose impacts continue to be reformulated in the philosophical or theoretical reflection on life: the Crusades, initiated, I've underlined, in 1095, and the Christian theological, polemical writings in relation to non-Christian beings and forms of life. An unstable distinction between "life" and "the good life" in Aristotle, at *Politics* 1252b30–31, is mutated, in Latinate and post-Latinate frames, into a harsh and mutating distinction between sorts of being and forms of life—what Sylvia Wynter, in several essays I study in chapter 1, has termed an "ontologization" of the social. Aquinas's understanding of Christianity—"Moreover, if anyone were to have himself circumcised, or to worship at the tomb of Mahomet, he would be deemed an apostate," he wrote—relocates the Aristotelian text, reformulating it into a reading practice for Christian universalization and anti-Islamic form coagulated in the modern terms for social and linguistic existence and philosophical self-reflection.[38] In this reformulation, all beings are subjected to an asymmetric demand that they lift themselves from particularity to universality, corporeality to abstraction, and death to life and peace—a demand pressed out in capitalist form and routed through Pauline formulations. I study this demand as the tradition of settler life—a tradition for the division of "life" from "the good life"—rearticulates itself into the subject of settler love and understanding (in the lectures of Francisco de Vitoria), of property, legality, and self-consciousness (in John Locke's *Essay Concerning Human Understanding* and *Second Treatise of Government*), and of the social (in Alexis de Tocqueville's essays on Algeria). And I consider this tradition, and in its dividing "monologism," to borrow a term of Hosam Aboul-Ela's, as it is reiterated in Marx—in his discussion of property (in the 1844 *Economic and Philosophic Manuscripts*) and of "primitive accumulation" and "pre-capitalist" forms (in *Grundrisse*)—and I suggest that Marx also gives us to think life in excess of the terms I study in chapter 1.[39]

Chapter 2, "Anontological Form," traces a non-Latinate history of philosophical practice in relation to the Aristotelian corpus and its late-Antique and Arabic-language contexts, and it underlines a particular sense of being and form, which the tradition of Arabic peripatetic philosophy gives.[40] If the texts

I study point to a being in which the world is to be grounded, these texts participate in a mode of explication which gives us to understand this grounding in a manner that does not reduce the object of philosophical explication to a being through which the world, and the multitude of beings it contains, would be explained or sustained, a "first principle." In framing this chapter in its disjunctive relation to chapter 1, I wish to make visible the particularly Christian, post-Latinate, and self-universalizing manner in which European-oriented social theory can tend to understand itself. To return to chapter 2: Here I study the work of three ninth- through eleventh-century philosophers: Abū Yūsuf ibn Isḥāq al-Kindī, Abū Naṣr al-Fārābī, and Abū ʿAlī al-Ḥusayn Ibn Sīnā. Through a close reading of the "path," سبيل, *sabīl,* one is to take in studying Aristotle (in al-Kindī), of the manner of pedagogical explication to be undertaken in the study of logic (in al-Fārābī), and of the terms for the reflection on "demonstration," البرهان, *al-burhān,* in its relation to metaphysics (in Ibn Sīnā), I notice that in this philosophical writing, the being that is to have been "first" is merely itself and nothing more; and that it turns to or redounds upon no thing or being or object. It is not that this being grounds the world but that in its being itself it remains indifferent to a recall to grounds, upon which its explication can rely. And I notice that this sense of being is, through this writing—and through al-Kindī's reading of Plotinus and Proclus, al-Fārābī's explication of logic, and Ibn Sīnā's discussion of *Book Lambda* of Aristotle's *Metaphysics*—generalized in relation to beings. In this writing, this or that being, whatever being, is merely what it is, and being, therefore, is not grounded in a self-identical understanding of form but gives an insubstantial, non-self-determined sense of what being is and what beings are, where being is temporally excessive, and not reducible to itself. Its form is aporetic: Because this or that being is merely itself, and because, in this, each and every being or thing is like all of the others, in a sharing of what is "common," عام, *ʿām,* as al-Fārābī wrote, this commonality gives an inidenticality, a non-selfsameness, a form, I've noticed, that is anontological—where this or that being is what it is insofar as it is not its own but is instead a kind of sharing.

Chapter 3, "Insurgence: A Poetics of Things," addresses the poetry and painting of the Lebanese and American, French- and English-language writer and painter Etel Adnan and the poetry of the Iraqi poet Khālid al-Maʿālī and his Arabic-language translations of the German-language, Jewish poet Paul Celan, and it argues that this poetry and work with materials—with paint and language—inherits the sense of form given in the philosophical tradition I discuss in chapter 2. I wish to underline: I am not arguing that the work of these philosophers "influenced" Adnan or al-Maʿālī. Instead, I am arguing that an anontological sense of being is carried in language and in Adnan's and al-

Maʿālī's work with materials. And I am arguing that this work, and the sort of doing it occasions, gives a refusal of the form of life and manner of being generalized in modern state formations, nomo-centric legalities, and the propertied sense of being and life privileged in post-Ottoman polities. The lingual and social practice of the texts I study in chapter 3 is not captured by the historical narrations and manners of conceptual or temporal opposition privileged in what Omnia El Shakry has termed "straightforward" understandings of temporality—a formulation that can link a critique of historicization to an epistemic privilege of heteronormative and accumulative manners of thought.[41] I underline, in al-Maʿālī, his Arabic-language rendering of Celan's 1960 speech, "The Meridian," as well as his inheritance of the sense of language given in the ninth-century writer al-Jāḥiẓ, where the social is thought as an indetermined, collective gathering, a manner of doing in non-subjective existence. I study, in Adnan, the aporetic form of her writing and work with materials, as her language and painting generate a refusal of the social logic of property and state legality in Western-hemispheric and post-Ottoman frames, and as her poetic practice becomes an affirmation of Palestinian life and struggle against its evisceration—in Lebanon, in Palestine—by the Zionist settler state. In the materials and practices I study in chapter 3—in Adnan, in al-Maʿālī, and in Celan as al-Maʿālī gives us to read him—there is a disaffirmation of the reduction of the social to the experience of a subject, and a refusal of the temporal determination of being, language, and life—a determination affirmed through the normative traditions of reading in the institutions of settler life.[42]

I use the term "anontological" to point to a sense of being, language, and form, which I draw out through readings in the Arabic peripatetic tradition and its being carried on in Adnan, al-Maʿālī, and, through al-Maʿālī, Celan, in poetry, painting, and translation. In this formulation I add the privative "an," to the adjective "ontological," and I do so for several reasons. I retain the word "ontology" because it points to the thinking of being in the European philosophical tradition—what I underscore is a post-twelfth-century, post-Latinate manner of thought, following Cedric J. Robinson in *Black Marxism*, as I underlined in this book's preface. And I do so because if, as I've argued, settler life is a mutation within ontology—if it *is* ontology, as it is reiterated in law and language, in capital and race, and in transatlantic chattel slavery and settler genocide—this is not something in relation to which a manner of thought, language, or being, may be said, now, to be exterior or which it may be said "not" to be. There are destructions that have taken place, mutations in what it means to think, do language, read, and know, and if these have been impressed upon languages, transforming them—for example, the Arabic language, and its transmutations in the Arabic nineteenth century—to read or think about being is to read or think about these destructions and their materiality.[43] Because these destructions are in excess of normative senses of time and history, we may not say that they have "ended" or belong to a "past," but instead that they mutate and transform in ongoing, if at times barely legible, ways. I also retain the word "ontology," because ontology, a field of statements about what is, is itself unstable and inidentical. If Aristotle underlined that one manner in which one may speak of "privation," *sterēsis*, is in the sense in which "the thing itself would not naturally possess" an attribute (for example, as Aristotle writes, "the plant is eyeless"), and if this sense may be affirmed through a predicate that is negative in both meaning and form, as would be the case with a word formed from the alpha privative (for example, as Aristotle underlines in the pages in *Metaphysics* I'm glossing here, in the words "unequal," "invisible," and "footless"), then I place in circulation the word "anontological" to underline that this formulation can refer itself, through a recursive swerve, to "ontology"—where the term "anontological" would contain within it the proposition "ontology 'is' ontology-less," where "ontology" is not itself, and where it neither subsists nor abides.[44] And if, as Aristotle also wrote, "There are as many kinds of privations as there are words which derive their negation from the alpha privative" (*Metaphysics* 1022b32–36), with the term "anontological," I wish to underline a sense of negation that is not solely negative, but which is an affirmation of a non-self-belonging, an indetermination of what is in relation to itself.

I subtitle chapter 3 "A Poetics of Things" and in this I draw upon an ongoing reflection on "the thing" in a number of works in Black Study. In an essay titled "The Racial Thing" David Lloyd relates the study of law in the work of Colin Dayan to the transmutation of persons of African descent into property, in a "governing semantics" explicated by Hortense Spillers in her discussion of transatlantic chattel slavery as a social, linguistic, and ontological operation.[45] In this, the thing, unlike the object, in Lloyd's terms, "is precisely what escapes representation, spun off on another trajectory altogether."[46] Lloyd's reading of "the thing" is in conversation with the work of Denise Ferreira da Silva and Fred Moten, and, in particular, what Moten terms "the social life of black things," and in this we are given to think the thingliness of things in their distinction from the object of representation and the subject of self-consciousness in philosophical self-reflection.[47] In the thinking of things what is given is a thinking of the social and language that would "address humans as existents, that is, as things *of* the world and not as things that experience the world," as Ferreira da Silva has written, in a manner that would render "inoperative" the terms of philosophical conceptualization and juridical-ethical form, "the occupation of existence with"—and by—"the *I Think*," she also writes.[48] There is, in this collective thinking, a being of things wholly in excess of the social terms of the subject of representation and the juridical, cadastral, and plantational forms that continue to install it, and in excess of the terms for political life—in interiorizing self-understanding—to which the social, in settler life, is reduced.

I linger with this thinking of the thing to offer the readings I pose in chapter 3 as still yet another sort of translation, a sharing out of matter with languages and among them. My intention is not to observe that "the thing," in its distinction from subject and object, is a social form that mutates across languages and that it remains legible as it mutates in this way. Instead, I observe that in the texts and practices I study we are given to think a sociality of things in excess of the forms privileged in settler life, and that, in this, the poetic is a fundamental, if inidentical social mode, a manner of doing or being. If, in post-Ottoman social formations—with the extension of capitalist relations, juridical-state legality, and propertied, cartographic form—language becomes an object in temporal usurpation, in the philological labor of orientalism and its aftermath, we may observe the poetic as a sort of doing not subsumable within these operations, where language, in the sonority of utterance, as Shaden Tageldin writes, "escapes containment."[49] In this book, thinking with Tageldin, I study such escape, a certain refusal, as I notice a manner of being in anaccumulative, anontological life. There is, I underline in chapter 3, an indetermination of the human being, salt, the sea, sweat, language, sound, and, further, of translation and painting, where the poetic is a name for a mode of inessential gathering irreducible to the sense of collectivity coerced in modern juridical form. In relating this poetics of things I offer only inessential acts of reading, a lingering with matter, a giving that may do nothing but insist on the "mis" in mistranslation, a reading that is all "mis," all stumble and blur, to draw on two terms against which Heidegger read and thought. "But what if we require blur and disorientation?" as Fred Moten has written, and what if these become, as well, essential modes of translation?[50] What if this is what our labor is? And what if these acts, in the reading, and in the listening—improperly, and without property—do nothing but give what we do and are, what we make and form, the matter we share and in which we share, away? As if, following Layli Long Soldier, in a certain kind of love? And what if the work, this book and each of its sentences, were nothing but a love letter, a letter sent in summer in the interest of a certain stumbling, a blurry reading and listening and leaning, which comes to and from us all around, in and for and from the common in which this work shares: "Instead," Long Soldier wrote, "I push my love into this world and mail you a summer letter."[51]

1
Settler Life

I hear they call life
the only shelter.

ich höre, sie nennen das Leben
die einzige Zuflucht.

—PAUL CELAN

Settler life—against the sonority of utterance in Darwish and Long Soldier—is what makes all of the distinctions; it is what declares them, and it *is* its declaration of them. Neither a substance nor a temporally selfsame form, settler life is a mode of interpretation, a manner of reading, and a particular way of thinking about language and life. Settler life installs and blurs a distinction between beings capable and incapable of properly comported linguistic existence—between those capable of linguistic life in temporally determined formulations and those incapable of it—and we are taught to read this distinction in Frantz Fanon's *The Wretched of the Earth*, where the "native" "l'indigène," is thrust outside of the social, the ethical, and the aesthetic: "The native is declared insensible to ethics, it is declared the absence of values but also the negation of values," and it is declared "the corrosive element, destroying everything that comes near to it, the deforming element, disfiguring everything that has to do with the aesthetic or the moral."[1] The settler "declares"—"The native is declared insensible to ethics," "L'indigène est déclaré imperméable à l'éthique"—and it is such declaration that brings into being the subject of settler enunciation as a subject of proper linguistic form and controlled manner, and the obliterated, "deforming" and "disfiguring" object of the settler's declarative acts, against which the lexicon of settler life sets itself. "It is the settler," Fanon also wrote, "who *has made* the colonized, who has *brought the colonized into being*, and who *continues to do so* [*C'est le colon qui* a fait *et qui* continue à faire *le colonisé*]" (40/36).[2] There is neither "settler" nor "native" prior to such "making," because each comes into being in settler declaration; the settler calls itself into being as it separates itself from and relates itself to the native, and settler life, therefore, is a manner of being and a practice of life generated through the repeated assertion and convolution of this separation—a distinction drawn between beings capable and incapable self-governed acts.[3]

In Fanon the language of the settler generates a "systematic negation": "Because it is a systematic negation of the other [*une negation systématisée de l'autre*], and a furious determination to refuse the other all attributes of humanity, colonialism forces the people it dominates to constantly ask themselves the question: 'In reality, who am I?'"[4] And yet colonialism, in the terms Fanon outlines, and in its "furious determination," may be understood as the coercive institution of the social in relation to a particular sense of the first person singular pronoun, of "I," *je*, as it is the recognition of the social in relation to that sense, a regulating and domesticating institution of self-representing form and individuated linguistic autonomy as a practice and manner of relation through which the social is to be understood and lived. In this sense, colonialism is not so much a "refusal," "refus," of "all attributes of humanity," *tout attribute d'humanité*, as it is a reformulation of language and life in relation to a general subordination of the social to the question the settler forces and the responses its language makes possible. If I open this chapter on settler life in relation to Fanon, it is not to privilege this question, "In reality, who am I?," "*Qui je-suis en réalité?*," but instead to observe its form in a global proliferation of categories, a lexicon of settler life, in a never-ending insistence on the first person singular pronoun as a locus for world, relation, and form.

The lexicon upon which the settler insists is articulated in Fanon through a passive voice verb, "est déclaré," "is declared," and Fanon's withholding of voice teaches us to read a tradition in excess of any single utterance. To think settler enunciation is to read it not only in its sustained incursions—in, as Fanon explained, its animalization of the colonized, "And, in fact, the language of the settler, when he speaks of the colonized, is a zoological language [*Et, de fait, le langage du colon, quand il parle du colonisé, est un langage zoologique*]. He speaks of the yellow man's reptilian motions, of the stink of the native quarter, of hordes, of foulness, of profusion, of swarming, of gesticulations" (45/42)—because it is also to read its terminological institution of the social. In this institution the native is engulfed in the language of the settler, and its "zoological" forms, as its language presumes and exteriorizes a quite particular sense of what language is and does. This sense of language is formed through the settler's manner of address, through its declarations, and we may therefore think of this understanding of language as a counterinsurgent practice for modern, juridical-centric linguistic existence in the divided generalization of the subject of experience as a locus for language and life. The determination of language as the practice of a subject is the thanatocentric propulsion of settler life into the social, as it is the obliteration of other modes of life, language, being, and relation. In the pages that follow I take Fanon's notes as a starting point and orientation, and I observe that the "speaking," of which Fanon writes in relation to "the language of the settler," "le langage du colon," transmutes a history of expression older than modern settler existence, where settler life is its pacifying extrapolation of itself into the languages and lives of others. I place a passage of Paul Celan's at the opening of this chapter to point to the relation of this tradition to a particular sense of life, where the life of a living being is subjected to a division between what Aristotle termed "life" and "the good life," and where this sense of life presents itself as a globally determining form for survival and exteriorizing obliteration. I study Khālid al-Maʿālī's Arabic-language translations of Celan in chapter 3, and I turn now to several passages in treatises of Aristotle, which, relocated in the textual and epistemic tradition of settler life, give the normative terms for the modern understanding of language, law, and the social.

Reading Life

In the distinction drawn between "the settler" and "the native" the former is located on the side of "the ethical," "the aesthetic," and "the moral," whereas the latter is placed on the side of animality and life, and this formulation mirrors a division between what Aristotle called "the good life" and "life," in his discussion of "the city" in *Politics*: "The partnership finally composed of several villages is the city; it has at last attained the limit of virtually complete self-sufficiency, and thus, while it comes into existence for the sake of life, it exists for the good life [γινομένη μὲν οὖν τοῦ ζῆν ἕνεκεν, οὖσα δὲ τοῦ εὖ ζῆν / *ginomenē men oun toū zēn heneken, ousa de tou eu zēn*]" (*Politics* 1252b30–31).[5] Aristotle notes that "the city" is that "partnership," "κοινωνία," "koinōnia," which is "the end of the other partnerships"—what he outlines in relation to "the union of female and male [οἷον θῆλυ μὲν καὶ ἄρρεν / *oion thēlu men kai arren*] for the sake of procreation," and "the union of the natural ruler and natural subject for the sake of security" (1252a28–31), and this is followed by the "household" (1252b10) and then the "village" (1252b17)—and the city is, as well, that form of collective life in which each of the others is completed and where the life occasioned in it is "self-sufficient" (1253a2). If Aristotle underlines that the city exists "by nature," because it is the end of the other "partnerships," and because "nature is an end" (1252b32–34), and if, with this, Aristotle explains that "the city is by nature [τῶν φύσει ἡ πόλις ἐστί/*tōn phusei hē polis esti*] and that the human being is by nature a political living being [ὁ ἄνθρωπος φύσει πολιτικὸν ζῷον/*ho anthrōpos phusei politikon zōon*]" (1253a3–4), I observe that in outlining this field of distinctions Aristotle sets others in relation to them. In his discussion of "the union of the female and male" he explains that the "human being" is linked to and separated from "other living beings" and "plants," because both of the latter are on the side of "life"—they are living beings and procreate—but not "the good life"; as Aristotle outlines "life" in this manner he subordinates the "slave" to the "human being"—"for one that can foresee with his mind is naturally ruler and naturally master, and one that can do these things with his body is subject and naturally a slave" (1252a32–33)—and "female" to "male": "Further, the relation of male to female is that of what is better by nature to what is worse, and that of ruler to subject" (1254b13–14); and as he does so he exteriorizes and links the "slave" from and to language: If the slave is able to "apprehend" language they do not "possess" it—"For he is by nature a slave who is capable of belonging to another—and that is why he does so belong—and who participates in language [λόγου/*logou*] to the extent of apprehending it but not possessing it" (1254b21–23). In this frame the "political living being" is that living being which "possesses" language and is capable of speech and therefore "the good life." "And why the human being is a political living being in a greater measure than any bee or any gregarious living being is clear. For nature, as we declare, does nothing without purpose, and the human being alone among all living beings possesses language [λόγον δὲ μόνον ἄνθρωπος ἔχει τῶν ζῴων/*logon de monon anthrōpos exei tōn zōon*]" (1253a6–11). There is an intersection of the political with a capacity to "possess" language, where this capacity is a differentiating locus for the manner of being together Aristotle understands to be a practice for collective life. This practice is given through a field of terms that links and subordinates the "slave" and the "female" to an economy of forms in relation to "life" and an exclusion from a capacity for "the good life," or, as one may also render this passage, "living well."

And yet if these texts outline a political-linguistic ontology, if in Aristotle there can seem to be a privilege of "the good life" in relation to "life," and if Aristotle aligns "the good life" with "language," "logos," while he aligns "life" with "procreation," I notice that "life" is "shared" among "living beings," and that in Aristotle's designation of terms the distinction drawn between "life" and "the good life" ceases to be legible: "First, then," Aristotle wrote elsewhere, "we must speak of food and reproduction, for the nutritive soul belongs to all other living beings besides the human being, and is the first and most widely shared faculty of the soul, in virtue of which they all have life [τὸ ζῆν / *to zēn*]. Its functions are reproduction and the assimilation of food" (*On the Soul* 415a23–27).[6] The "nutritive" faculty is related to life and to the single sense, which, Aristotle underlines, is shared by all living beings, the sense of touch: "All living beings have at least one of the senses, that of touch [τὰ δὲ ζῷα πάντ᾽ἔχουσι μίαν γε τῶν αἰσθήσεων, τὴν ἁφήν / *ta de zōa pant' exousi mian ge tōn aisthēseōn, tēn haphēn*]" (414b4). "All living beings feed on what is dry or wet, hot or cold, and touch is the sense which apprehends these" (414b8–9), he explains, and if in *On the Soul* Aristotle outlines the other faculties of the soul in their relation to life, it is this faculty which points to a mode of doing shared among living beings—"Every living thing, then, must have the nutritive soul, and each has a soul from its birth until its death" (434a22)—and which is related to a capacity for sensation, which is also to say, for life.[7] The sense of touch is anterior to the other senses and their precondition—"For without a sense of touch it is impossible to have any other sensation," Aristotle notes—and unlike the other senses touch is immediate; it "occurs by direct contact."[8] If, in this, Aristotle gives to us a phenomenology of forms, where touch is on the side of mere being while the other senses are on the side of being well—"The living being possesses the other senses," Aristotle notes, "not for the sake of being but for being well [οὐ τοῦ εἶναι ἕνεκα ἀλλὰ τοῦ εὖ / *ou toū einai heneka alla toū eū*]" (435b20–21)—I notice that the reading of "life," in *Politics*, mirrors the reading of "being" in *On the Soul*. Just as the living being, as Aristotle writes in the latter, possesses "hearing so that it may have significant sounds made to it, and a tongue so that it may make significant sounds to other living beings" (435b25–26), this practice of signification, a certain doing in language, is not separable from life but is only given through it. There is, then, in Aristotle, a practice of form that indetermines what can become, for a certain tradition of reading and commentary, a privilege of "the good life" or "living" or "being" "well"—a privilege, to return to *Politics*, of the life of the "city," the "polis," over that of the "home," "oikos," and of "mediated" sensation, in "signification," over the hapticity or tactility of "touch," without which "the living being cannot exist" (435b17).

I wish to attend to the matter of "voice" in *On the Soul*. "Voice," Aristotle explains, "is a certain sound of a being possessing a soul [Ἡ δὲ φωνὴ ψόφος τίς ἐστιν ἐμψύχου / *hē de phōnē psophos tis estin empsuchou*]" (420b6). A being that does not possess a soul, that is "inanimate," does not possess a voice: "For inanimate things never have a voice, they can only metaphorically be said to give voice, as in a flute or a lyre, and all other inanimate things which have a musical compass, and tone, and modulation" (420b6–8). There is a distinction drawn between a sort of being or thing that possesses a soul and another that does not, one that is "animate" and another that is not, and this division is routed through voice. "Voice, then, is a sound of a living being [Φωνὴ δ'ἐστὶ ζῷου ψόφος/*phōnē d' esti zōou psophos*], and that not with any part of it indiscriminately" (420b13–14). The distinction between what possesses a soul and what does not is reformulated in the difference between "voice" and "sound": "For, as we have said, not every sound made by a living being is a voice (for one can make a sound even with the tongue, or as in coughing), but that which even causes the impact, must have a soul, and use some imagination, for the voice is a sound which means something, and is not merely indicative of air inhaled, as a cough is" (420b29–421a1). The terms point to those in *On Interpretation*, where "language" is "significant speech"—"Language is significant speech [Λόγος δέ ἐστι φωνὴ σημαντικὴ/*logos de esti phōnē sēmantikē*]," Aristotle wrote there—as well as to the distinction Aristotle draws between "sensation" and "thought" in relation to life: "And life is defined, in the case of living beings, by the capacity for sensation," Aristotle also wrote, "and in the case of the human being, by the capacity for sensation and thought."[9] The distinction drawn between "life" and "the good life," as well as "being" and "being well," is mediated through Aristotle's discussion of "voice" in its distinction from "sound," a distinction which, itself, presses yet another, routed through these: a distinction between "thought," "noēsis," and "sensation," "aisthēsis."[10] And yet if this definitional exertion advances a field of distinctions, these collapse through it. In a manner that mirrors the passages of *On the Soul* I've underlined, life interpenetrates and indistinguishes the terms, and the allocation of capacities, which can seem to organize the reflection on language and life in the Aristotelian treatises. If settler life stabilizes this indistinction or interpenetration, advancing a hierarchized lexicon, what characterizes settler form is the rearticulation of these terms, in relation to "life" and "the good life," in the fallout of the translation of the Aristotelian corpus into Latin in the twelfth century, and in the absorption of these terms into the juridical and theological formulations—and institutional practices—of European, Latin Christianity.

In the reading of "life" in a number of European-oriented interventions, a critique is offered which preserves the distinction between "life" and "the good life"—the latter, Hannah Arendt wrote in *The Human Condition*, is "of an altogether different quality" than "ordinary life," because "it was no longer bound to the biological life process."[11] The matter of life was taken up, differently, by Michel Foucault, who, in *The Order of Things*, understood "life" as a post-late-eighteenth-century form—"Up to the end of the eighteenth century, in fact, life does not exist: only living beings"—where, in a transmutation from "sovereignty" to "bio-power," as he later wrote, "The old power of death that symbolized sovereign power was now carefully supplanted by the administration of bodies and the calculated management of life."[12] These terms—in Arendt and Foucault—become a site of interrogation in Giorgio Agamben, who notes that "sovereign violence is in truth founded not on a pact but on the exclusive inclusion of bare life in the state," and yet, in Agamben's reading, the distinction drawn between "life" and "the good life" is preserved as a presupposition for the thinking of the social.[13] If Agamben's desire, in reading this "exclusive inclusion," is "to put an end to the civil war that divides the peoples and cities of the earth" (180), we may understand his misrecognition of sustained attack and counterinsurgent aggression, a long-standing, obliterating pose and practice, as "civil war," as making visible the history of interpretation to which his efforts, like those of Arendt and Foucault, belong: the efforts of post-Latinate European-oriented philosophy to think the social in the absence of an understanding of the relation of its social, linguistic, and epistemic formation to the ongoing wars—and they are colonial and older and other wars—against Black and Indigenous life.[14] I wish to affirm the observations of Alexander G. Weheliye, Aileen Moreton-Robinson, and Ann Laura Stoler that this work in critical social thought takes Europe as a historical and epistemic presupposition.[15] I notice, as well, that this presupposition reiterates post-Latinate, crusading formulations, in the proliferation of what Dylan Rodríguez has termed "the social-historical logics of racial-colonial genocide," made visible in the textual exertions of Arendt, Foucault, and Agamben, which relate these thinkers' belonging to a manner of thought and a sense of language, and to a particular tradition—the tradition of settler life—which their writing on "life" makes legible.[16] It is not that the Crusades have ended—they have not—but instead that the social pose and sense of life they terminologically formulate and exteriorize have been rephrased in practices of obliteration projected against beings said to be in need of social domestication and pedagogical formation—"subjects of affectability," in Ferreira da Silva's terms, masses of "swarm" and "gesticulation," in Fanon's—which remain a constant locus in European-oriented theoretical reflection and critical thought, a site of untamed riot and disorder, to which this reflection coercively responds.

"For millennia," Foucault wrote, "man remained what he was for Aristotle: a living being with the additional capacity for a political existence; modern man is an animal whose politics places his existence as a living being in question."[17] And yet, reading *Politics* alongside *On the Soul*, I notice that being a "living being" and having a "capacity for political existence" were interlinked, that they crossed and were excessively intercorrelated, to where the two seemingly distinguishable forms become indistinct. There is, in Aristotle, an illegibility in form, in relation to the sort of being he termed a "living being" and its capacity for language and life in relation to "doing" and "making." Aristotle wrote in *Politics*, "Life is doing, it is not making [ὁ δὲ βίος πρᾶξις, οὐ ποίησίς ἐστιν / *ho de bios praxis, ou poiēsis estin*]" (1254a8). If in this passage the distinction between "doing," "praxis," and "making," "poiēsis," is explicated in relation to the slave and its relation to the household—where "an article of property is a tool for the purpose of life [ὀργάνον πρὸς ζωήν ἐστι / *organon pros zōēn esti*], and property generally is a collection of tools, and a slave is a living article of property [κτῆμά τι ἔμψυχον / *ktēma ti empsuchon*]" (1253b31–33)—and if, in this, Aristotle understands the "slave" as an object of "property" that "does" but does not "make," I underline that the explication of "doing," in the figure of the slave, and in relation to the distinction drawn between "life" and "the good life," renders illegible its distinction from "making."[18] In these formulations there is an alignment of "the good life" with "language," "politics," and "making"; at the same time there is an allocation of "life" in relation to "procreation," "nourishment," and "doing." And yet if in post-Latinate contexts these divisions can seem clear, and if their relative determination becomes a locus for theoretical reflection—in Arendt, Foucault, and Agamben, but also others—this clarity presupposes the social logic and lexical performance of Europe's crusading forms and the extension and mutation of them in colonization, settler colonization, colonial-settler genocide, the expropriation of Indigenous land, and transatlantic chattel slavery, where persons of African descent are transmuted into "things"—to draw upon the terms of Hortense Spillers, in what she calls the "semantic alignments" of "the sociopolitical order of the New World"—beginning in the fifteenth Christian century.[19] It is not, then, "for millennia," that "man remained what he was for Aristotle," but only for several hundred years—since the twelfth-century Latin translation of Aristotle and the lexical reorganization it occasions. If there is to be a reading of settler life, then, it would be one that would address this reorganization and its never-ceasing mutations while asking into a sense of "doing" that is not subordinated to "making"—a sense of *praxis* not subordinated to *poiēsis*—where being in the social is not distinct from language, where language is a sort of doing, where doing is poetic—or, if you will, *poiētic*—and where, finally, neither *praxis* nor *poiēsis* devolve upon a subject—itself a wholly modern, settler form—to which language would be recalled. In noticing this, I withdraw language from the terms to which it has been subordinated in settler life, in order to think those material and linguistic practices—a certain "doing," in its indistinction from "making"—which are subjected to ongoing assault and temporal containment in the social logic and practice of property.

Property

> The discovery of gold and silver in America, the extirpation, enslavement and entombment in mines of the indigenous population of that continent, the beginnings of the conquest and plunder of India, and the conversion of Africa into a preserve for the commercial hunting of blackskins, are all things which characterize the dawn of the era of capitalist production. These idyllic proceedings are the chief moments of primitive accumulation.
>
> —KARL MARX, *CAPITAL, VOLUME 1*

> He appears originally as a species-being, clan being, herd animal—although in no way whatever as a ζῶον πολιτικόν in the political sense.
>
> —KARL MARX, *GRUNDRISSE*

What is the relation of settler life to what Marx called, in the first volume of *Capital*, "so-called primitive accumulation"? And, further, if settler life is a regulating allocation of forms, a permutation of terms, and an exteriorizing pose, what is the relation of settler life to property? Glen Sean Coulthard has underlined, in a passage I noted in the introduction to this book, that primitive accumulation is reiterated in capital and what Cedric J. Robinson has taught us to understand as "racial capitalism."[20] Denise Ferreira da Silva has observed that in Marx the determination of capital in relation to contract (in labor) and title (in property) temporally designates primitive accumulation—and, in particular, slavery, colonization, and settler colonization—as anterior to capital and not ongoingly constitutive for it, and this practice, a manner of reading, belongs to what she terms "the determinative procedures and the delimitative statements that circumscribe the domain comprehended by the economic concept of capital."[21] It is the circumscribing of a domain, which "nullifies the participation of 'the colonies' and 'slave labor' in the creation of capital" (223), and this "nullification" is advanced through the recognition of capital "as such," in a temporally stabilizing formalization: "Consistently, according to Marx, the contractual relation," an "agreement" between "free and equal persons," she writes, "provides the grounds for the properly capitalist relation of production (capitalist and laborers), its juridical form (contract), and the very existence of capital as such" (229). As Ferreira da Silva underlines this moment in Marx, she observes that Marx's language preserves the privilege of "the *transparent I* in the scene of representation" (225), and I notice, thinking with and learning from Ferreira da Silva and Coulthard, that in Marx's explication of what capital is, in relation to primitive accumulation and so-called "pre-capitalist" forms, there is generalization of a certain manner of doing in the social, in the form of a being that "makes," that is on the side of *poiēsis*, as Aristotle discussed this term, in its distinction, in Marx's formulations, from "the animal," "the slave," and "the savage," a sort of being whose language use is, as in the passages of Hannah Arendt's I've studied above, on the side of "life."

To think about this generalization, and its relation to property, I turn to the section of Marx's *1844 Economic and Philosophic Manuscripts* titled "Private Property and Communism," where Marx writes, "My own being is social activity [*mein eignes Dasein ist gesellschaftliche Thätigkeit*]."[22] This proposition is offered following Marx's discussion of "estranged labor," "entfremdete Arbeit," and its relation to "private property," "Privateigentum," and Marx's explication of these carries forward what I wish to underline is an aporetic quality of his reflection on "my own being," "mein eignes Dasein," which, Marx tells us, "is social activity," "gesellschaftliche Thätigkeit." Marx's terms convolute the non-self-oriented sociality they can seem to affirm; his language captures such sociality, and its manner of doing, in a regulating lexical field through which he articulates what "capital" and "property" are. There is an acute tension in formulation: If "my" being is social, and if this being-social is what my being is, Marx mutes this "social" dimension of what "I" am through his writing of it, because the terms of the social are in excess of anything that is "mine" or "my own"—any practice of ownership, of property, or of what is "eigen" in its relation to *Eigentum*, the German term that renders "property," as in the formulation "mein eignes." If what is "my own" is mine, if I own and possess it, then Marx's proposition belongs to a lexical practice privileged in the individuating social logic he also describes, where the social is to be recognized in relation to a single being, "me," which is what it is, and which, through its being itself, is to be understood as a social being. And yet if the form of a being that is its own is advanced in the normative traditions of European thought and philosophical speculation, in what I'm calling "settler life," I notice that Marx's reiteration of it nevertheless speaks to us of an "activity," *Thätigkeit*, that will never have been its own, and that is in excess of the property-centric orientation Marx's language also forwards. We might therefore say that "my" being is "my own" only insofar as it will never have been "mine" but is instead a "social activity" wholly in excess of "me." This passage in Marx both gives to us and subordinates a social understanding of being to which I wish to appeal, an inessential and what I'll also call, in chapter 2, "anontological" form, subsumed in these *1844 Manuscripts*, a text which also teaches us—alongside *Grundrisse* and *Capital*—to read the property-centric sense of being and language, which the tradition of settler life sends, unceasingly, at the world.

"Political economy proceeds from the fact of private property. It does not explain it to us," Marx wrote,[23] but how may we read Marx in relation to the form of the subject presumed and advanced in the sentence with which he confronts us, in his *1844 Manuscripts*, where he writes that "my own being is social activity"? And how does this sentence relate to another, in *Grundrisse*, where Marx writes that "he," in reference to the "human being," "appears originally as a species-being, clan being, herd animal—although in no way whatever as a ζῶον πολιτικόν in the political sense."[24] How do these sentences relate to the passages in Aristotle I've underlined, where Aristotle allocates "life" to "procreation," "nourishment," and "doing," and "the good life" to "language," "politics," and "making"? Does Marx not draw a distinction, in this passage, between the "appearance" of the "human being" as a "species-being, clan being, herd animal" and its appearance as a "political living being," *zōon politikon*, "in the political sense"? Does Marx's underlining this distinction, and his placing an emphasis on it with the words "although in no way whatever," *wenn auch keineswegs*, not leave no way out for other manners of being, and other senses of language and life, not reducible to the distinctions that operate in Marx's texts? Do his texts not ask to be located in relation to a particular interpretation of form, a particular pose in the social, and a particular thinking of life? What is the relation between the distinction Marx affirms, as if it were in question or under threat, between the "species-being, clan being, herd animal" and the life of a "political living being," and Marx's explication and delimitation of what capital is? And how, finally, does this explication relate to three terms that resurface in Marx's text: "the animal," "the slave," and "the savage"? What sort of triangulation is this? To what history of the thinking about living beings and life does it belong? What sense of "doing" and "making" does it advance or obscure? How, finally, does it subordinate a social doing with materials to the making of subjects of language in proper form—to proper subjects of life?

Marx outlines the formation of "private property" in the *1844 Manuscripts*. "We shall start out," Marx notes, "from a *present-day* economic fact": "The worker becomes poorer the more wealth he produces, the more his production increases in power and extent. The worker becomes an ever cheaper commodity the more commodities he produces. The *devaluation* of the human world [*Menschenwelt*] grows in direct proportion to the *increase in value* of the world of things [*Sachenwelt*]. Labor not only produces commodities; it also produces itself and the workers as a *commodity* [*als eine* Waare] and it does so in the same proportion in which it produces commodities in general."[25] He continues: "The object that labor produces, its product, stands opposed to it as *something alien*, as a *power independent* of the producer," and this production of an "object," "Gegenstand," is the general production of objects as exterior things: "The product of labor is labor, which has been fixed into the form of an object [*die sich in einem Gegenstand fixirt*], made material in it, it is the *objectification* of labor. The realization of labor is its objectification. In the sphere of political economy this realization appears as a *loss of reality* for the worker, objectification as *loss of and bondage to the object*, and appropriation [*Aneignung*] as *estrangement*, as *alienation* [*als Entfremdung, als Entäusserung*]" (364–65/324). Labor is "fixed" "into the form of an object," and in this there is an "alienation" and an "estrangement" of the laborer, where the "product" of its labor appears to it as an "*alien* object" (365/324), and this occasions the laborer's loss of "himself," his "inner world," as well as, Marx notes, that world's "belonging" "to him": "For it is clear that, according to this premise: the more the worker exerts himself, the more powerful the alien, objective world becomes, which he brings into being over against himself [*die er sich gegenüber schafft*], the poorer he and his inner world become and the less they belong to him [*um so weniger gehört ihm zu eigen*]" (365/324). In the laborer's production of "objects" its "inner world" no longer belongs to it but instead to the object, and so there is, Marx presumes, an "ownership" of oneself and one's life—a property-centric understanding of what a "self" is—which the sort of act that capital coerces in "labor" occasions the loss of: "The worker places his life in the object; but now it no longer belongs to him, but to the object [*Der Arbeiter legt sein Leben in den Gegenstand; aber nun gehört es nicht mehr ihm, sondern dem Gegenstand*]" (365/324). Marx is in the process of "deriving" the "private property" form, but I wish to pause and observe that, for Marx, there is a "self": It is itself, and it possesses an "inner world" that is its "own." If this "self" is conjured, in the sentences I'm reading here, through a grammatical exertion, in a common noun, "der Arbeiter," or a dative pronoun, "ihm," these sentences reiterate, through that exertion, the form of a subject that possesses an "inner world."

This interiority orients Marx's discussion of the sort of act "the worker" does in its relation to "the sensuous external world," which he also calls "nature": "The worker can create nothing without *nature*, without the *sensuous external world* [*ohne* die sinnliche Aussenwelt]. It is the material in which his labor realizes itself [*Sie ist der Stoff, an welchem sich seine Arbeit verwirklicht*], in which it is active and from which and by means of which [*aus welchem und mittelst welchem*] it produces" (365/325). In the terms of Marx's explanation, "material," "Stoff," is a "means" through which the laborer "produces," and this "material" is what "nature" is; nature is a kind of material, it is "Stoff," a sensuousness, "external" to the laborer, "in which" labor is realized as well as "from which" and "by means of which" labor produces. Nature is the material through which labor transforms "Stoff" into objects, and through which an object appears as something "external." This becoming-external occurs in relation to the "object" and the act of labor itself: "Up to now," Marx continues, "we have considered the estrangement, the alienation of the worker only from one aspect, i.e. his *relationship* to *the products of his labor.* But estrangement manifests itself [*zeigt sich*] not only in the result, but also in the *act of production,* within the *activity of production* itself [*im* Akt der Produktion, *innerhalb der* producirenden Thätigkeit *selbst*]" (367/326). Marx punctuates, noting the laborer's no longer "belonging" to itself, as he outlines the social form of the capitalist: "Finally, the external character of labor for the worker is demonstrated by the fact that it is not his own but another's, that it does not belong to him, and that in it he belongs not to himself but to another [*daß sie nicht sein eigen, sondern eines andern ist, daß sie ihm nicht gehört, daß er in ihr nicht sich selbst, sondern einem andern angehört*]" (367/326). The argument is contrastive: In the capitalist relation, the labor of the worker "is not his own but another's," *sie nicht sein eigen, sondern eines andern ist,* and the genitive form "eines andern," suggests this belonging, which Marx clarifies in the immediately following clause: "It does not belong to him." The interiority and exteriority Marx affirms is invested in the practice of what one does when one does the sort of act Marx terms "labor," *Arbeit,* a manner of doing things with *Stoff.* Marx's explication of the "external character of labor for the worker" is not only a way of describing how the "product" of labor becomes an object, because it is also a way of translating what an "act" is, in its relation to "activity," *Thätigkeit,* and in relation to an individuated understanding of a being that is—and will already have been—itself.

I place an emphasis on the word "activity" because what is lost, in Marx's discussion of the capitalist relation, is not only the "being," *Wesen,* of the laborer—where labor is "external" to the laborer it does not "belong to his being [*nicht zu seinem Wesen gehört*]" (367/326), Marx wrote—but also the "species-being" or "species-character" of "man." "Man is a species-being [*Der Mensch ist ein Gattungswesen*], not only because he practically and theoretically makes the species—both his own and those of other things—his object, but also—and this is simply another way of saying the same thing—because he relates to himself as the present, living species [*er sich zu sich selbst als der gegenwärtigen, lebendigen Gattung verhält*], because he relates to himself as a *universal* and therefore free being [*als einem* universellen, *darum freien Wesen*]" (368/327). Marx further notes the "universality" and "freedom" of the social form he calls "man," as well as its relation to "life": "The whole character of a species, its species-character, resides in the nature of its life activity [*Lebensthätigkeit*], and free conscious activity is the species-character of man [*und die freie bewußte Thätikgkeit ist der Gattungscharakter des Menschen*]" (369/328). The "life activity" of "man" is "free conscious activity" in universality, and this activity constitutes the being of "man," which, itself, is lost in the sort of labor generalized in the capitalist relation: "It makes his species-life into a means for individual life," and, further, "Life itself appears only as a *means of life* [*Das Leben selbst erscheint nur als* Lebensmittel]" (369/328). I notice not only Marx's explication of the loss of the "species-being" or "species character" of "man," through the sort of labor generalized in the capitalist relation, but also the terms through which Marx's discussion is formulated: If in the reduction of "species-life" to "life itself," life becomes a "means," *Mittel*, Marx's language presumes a distinction between a kind of being which possess a capacity for free conscious activity in universality and another, which does not possess this capacity, and which, therefore, is not and cannot be what "man" is.[26]

In this: It is as if Marx, in the fallout of Aquinas's commentary on Aristotle's *Politics*—which I address in the next section of this chapter—affirms the distinction between "life" and "the good life," which, in Aristotle, remained in an indeterminate relation; and it is as if Marx, in these passages, reiterates the distinction between a sort of living being that possesses language and another sort that does not, through his explication of "man's" capacity for "free conscious activity." It is a distinction Marx draws, and reformulates, through what he calls "the animal": "The animal [*Das Thier*] is immediately one with its life activity. It is not distinct from that activity. It is *it*. [*Es unterscheidet sich nicht von ihr. Es ist* sie]. Man makes his life activity itself an object of his will and consciousness. He has conscious life activity. It is not a determination with which he directly merges. Conscious life activity directly distinguishes man from animal life activity [*Die bewußte Lebensthätigkeit unterscheidet den Menschen unmittelbar von der thierischen Lebensthätigkeit*]. Only because of that is he a species-being."[27] "Life" mediates the distinction drawn between "man" and "the animal"—each has a "life activity"—even as this distinction is "direct": It is, Marx wrote, "unmediated," *unmittelbar.* Marx's explication of the "species-being" of "man" is given through his writing of this distinction, and if in this Marx reiterates particular terms of Hegel's *Philosophy of Right*, Marx's *1844 Manuscripts* draw out the social orientation of Hegel's thinking of "thought" in a manner that identifies the "species being" of "man" and gives it content.[28] "It is true that animals also produce. They build nests and dwellings, like the bee, the beaver, the ant, etc. But they produce only their own immediate needs or those of their young; they produce one-sidedly [*einseitig*], while man produces universally [*universell*]," Marx wrote, and if this capacity for producing "universally" and not "one-sidedly" defines the "species-being" of man, Marx reiterates the terms fostered through this distinction—between "man" and "animal"—even as these are, at the same time, blurred.[29] Marx's explication is articulated through a separation of "man" from "the animal" in relation to the former's capacity for "conscious life activity," *die bewußte Lebensthätigkeit*, and his writing of a capacity for making "nature" into "objects" is therefore wholly entangled in this distinction and is a locus for its propulsion into the social.[30]

The sentences around "the animal," in the 1844 *Manuscripts*—and in relation to Marx's bees, which also appear in *Capital*—mirror Marx's statements that address "the savage," *der Wilde*: "The savage [*Der Wilde*] in his cave—an element of nature which is freely available for his use and shelter—does not experience his environment as alien, or he feels just as much at home as a *fish* in water."[31] "The savage" is on the side of "nature," exterior to the institution of world formed through the self-conscious activity of "man" as a "species-being" and its non-one-sided manner of production. If "the worker," in capitalist labor, is thrust out of sociality—the capitalist "makes the worker into a being with neither needs nor senses and makes the worker's activity a pure abstraction from all activity [*zu einer reinen Abstraktion von aller Thätigkeit*]" (420–21/360)—"the savage," in Marx, is not quite a being whose "activity" can be made into a "pure abstraction." "The savage, the animal at least has the need to hunt, to move about, etc., the need of companionship [*Der Wilde, das Thier hat doch das Bedürfniß der Jagd, der Bewegung, etc., der Geselligkeit*]" (420/360), Marx writes. But if this is to suggest a contrast with the "bestial degeneration" of life in relation to capital—"Man reverts once more to living in a cave, but the cave is now polluted by the mephitic and pestilential breath of civilization" (420/360)—the substitutability of "the savage" with "the animal"—and I note, in its German formulation, the third person singular verb, "hat," "The savage, the animal, at least *has* the need"—suggests their indistinction and, through that indistinction, their relation to Marx's explication of labor, capital, and the sort of "activity" that "man" does. Marx's reflection on "activity" in relation to labor and capital contains "the savage"—and, by extension, Indigenous and Native being and life—by recognizing these in relation to the subject of self-consciousness (in the 1844 *Manuscripts*) and its purposeful activity (in *Capital*), and retains it as what Jodi A. Byrd has termed an "antecedent," a form temporally subordinated in the settler terms for language, the social, and subjective life.[32]

I wish now to consider Marx's reading practice—itself a certain quelling of temporal insurgence, including Marx's own, as Cedric J. Robinson has noticed—in his writing of "capital as such [*das Kapital als solches*]," where "it no longer proceeds from presuppositions in order to become, but rather it is itself presupposed, and proceeds from itself to create the conditions for its maintenance and growth," as Marx wrote in *Grundrisse*.[33] Marx explains, in relation to a distinction he had outlined between the "arising" of capital and capital "itself:" "The conditions and presuppositions of the *becoming* [Werdens], of the *arising* [Entstehens] of capital presuppose precisely that it is not yet but that it is merely in *becoming* [*daß es noch nicht ist, sondern erst* wird]; they therefore disappear as real capital arises [*sie verschwinden also mit dem wirklichen Kapital*], capital which itself [daß *selbst*], on the basis of its own reality, posits [*setzt*] the condition for its realization" (372/459).

Marx outlines four "conditions":

> (1) on the one side the presence of living labor capacity as a merely *subjective* existence [*als bloß subjektiver Existenz*], separated from the *conditions* of living labor as well as from *the means of existence* [Existenzmitteln], the *means of life* [Lebensmitteln], the means of self-preservation of living *labor capacity* [Arbeitsvermögens]; the living possibility of labor, on the one side, in this complete abstraction; (2) the value, or objectified labor [*vergegenständlichte Arbeit*], found on the other side, must be an accumulation of use values sufficiently large to furnish the objective conditions not only for the production of the products or values required to reproduce or maintain living labor capacity, but also for the absorption of surplus labor—to supply the objective material for the latter; (3) a free exchange relation—money circulation—between both sides [*freies Austauschverhältnis—Geldzirkulation—zwischen beiden Seiten*]; between the extremes a relation founded on exchange values [*auf den Tauschwerten begründete Beziehung*]—not [*nicht*] on the master-servant relation [*auf Herrschafts- und Knechtschaftsverhältnis*]—i.e., hence, production which does not directly furnish the producer with his necessaries, but which is mediated through exchange [*sondern durch den Austausch vermittelt*], and which cannot therefore usurp alien labor directly [*unmittelbar*], but must buy it, exchange it, from the worker himself; finally, (4) one side—the side representing the objective conditions of labor in the form of independent values for-themselves—must present itself as *value*, and must regard the positing of value, self-realization, money-making, as the ultimate purpose—not direct consumption [*Genuß*] or the creation of use value. (376/463–464)

What determines the capitalist mode of production "as such" is the existence of a "free exchange relation." "Relation," here, is to be "founded," "begründete," on "exchange values," and not—"nicht"—on "the master-servant relation"; "usurpation" is not "direct—it is not "unmediated"—but is instead mediated through "exchange." "So long as *both* sides exchange their labor with one another in the form of *objectified* labor, the relation is impossible; it is likewise impossible," Marx writes, "if *living labor capacity* itself appears as the property of the other side [*wenn das* lebendige Arbeitsvermögen *selbst als Eigentum der andren Seite erscheint*], hence as not engaged in exchange" (376/464). He immediately underlines, in a parenthesis, that slavery, when it appears within the "bourgeois system of production," is an "anomaly": "The fact that slavery is possible at individual points [*einzelnen Punkten*] within the bourgeois system does not contradict this. However, slavery is then possible there only because it does not exist at other points [*weil sie an andren Punkten nicht existiert*], and appears as an anomaly opposite the bourgeois system itself [*und erscheint als Anomalie gegen das bürgerliche System selbst*]" (376/464). Slav,ery is an "anomaly"; it does not "found" capital or form it "as such." And yet if slavery is inessential to what Marx terms "capital," Marx's terminological formulations derive from, and are articulated through, this rendering-inessential of slavery; the temporality of "capital" captures the slave in "*the history of its* [capital's—JS] *formation*," *der Geschichte seiner Bildung*, as it is one among other "historic presuppositions," which are to have been "past and gone," *vergangne*, when "capital," finally, ceases to "become" and "arise," and merely is. "Capital" is to become autonomous, as if it were a properly cultivated, living being—and I wish to underline the word "Bildung" in the sentence I've just transcribed—just as it is to stand upright, "on its own feet," as Marx wrote in the first volume of *Capital*.[34]

Marx writes in *Grundrisse* of the "slave relation" in contrast to that of the "free worker": "In the slave relation, he belongs to the individual, particular owner, and is his laboring machine. As a totality of force expenditure, as labor capacity, he is a thing belonging to another [*ist er einem andern gehörige Sache*], and hence does not relate as subject [*und verhält sich daher nich als Subjekt*] to his particular expenditure of force, not to the act of living labor."[35] The "slave" is a "thing," "Sache," not a "subject," "Subjekt," and yet, like the "savage," the "slave" is an "animal": "The slave-owner," Marx also wrote in *Capital*, "buys his worker in the same way as he buys his horse. If he loses his slave, he loses a piece of capital, which he must replace by fresh expenditure on the slave market."[36] As is, Marx writes in *Grundrisse*, the "serf": "In the serf relation he appears as a moment of property in land itself, is an appendage of the soil, exactly like draught-cattle [*ganz wie daß Arbeitsvieh*]."[37] Slavery, in *Grundrisse* and *Capital*, is, one might therefore say, a conceptual or lexical moment through which a temporal determination of world is advanced in the epistemic capture of the slave and what Lisa Lowe has compellingly termed a "regulative temporality" in the theorization of the social in Marx.[38]

This theorization delimits the form of a laboring being, but what is the labor of such a being in what Marx terms "pre-capitalist" formations? How does this labor relate to "the savage," "the animal," and "the slave"? And how does Marx's designation of the temporality of capital relate to these formulations?[39] Marx underlines, in thinking about "labor," in *Grundrisse*, "appropriation not through labor, put presupposed to labor; appropriation of the natural conditions of labor, of the *earth* as the original instrument of labor [*als des ursprünglichen Arbeitsinstruments*] as well as its workshop and repository of raw materials [*Rohstoffe*]," in relation to what he called "pre-capitalist" formations.[40]

Marx continues:

> But this *relation* to land and soil, to the earth, as the property of the laboring individual—who thus appears from the outset not merely as laboring individual, in this abstraction, but who has an *objective mode of existence* in his ownership of the earth, an existence *presupposed* to his activity, and is not merely a result of it, a presupposition of his activity just like his skin or his sense organs [*wie seine Haut oder seine Sinnesorgane*], which of course he also reproduces and develops etc. in the life process, but which are nevertheless presuppositions of this process of his reproduction—is instantly mediated [*sofort vermittelt*] by the naturally arisen, spontaneous, more or less historically developed and modified being of the individual as *member of a commune*—his naturally arisen being as a member of a tribe etc. (393/485)

There is a "laboring individual" in the "objective mode of its existence," and it comes to belong, later, to what Marx terms "a commune," as a "member" of it. If this "individual," in its "relation to land and soil, to the earth," is "instantly mediated" *sofort vermittelt*, in its being a member of a collective, this mediation refers itself to this individual in its relation to those materials through which it labors. It is as if there is, in Marx, first, an individual, which only subsequently comes to bear a relation to "land," "earth," "nature," and an "instantaneous" mediation in the commune. Does Marx not, then, presume a "subjectivity" wholly engulfed within the social logic of property? And does his "analysis" not then refer itself to all of those modes of life at which Marx's language—like capital—pacifyingly extends itself? And does this not take the form of a particular sort of temporal capture—in a word, a certain sort of reading? For example: "Property, then, originally means—in its Asiatic, Slavonic, classical, Germanic form—the relation of the laboring (producing or self-reproducing) subject [*des arbeitenden Subjekts*] to the conditions of his production or reproduction as his own" (403/495). Is not, through this explication, the sort of "doing" occasioned in an "act" drawn back to the form of a "subject"? This, even as Marx's language opens a thinking of a sort of being which, in the materiality of its organs, will never have its "own"? The "slave," Marx wrote, is a "thing," *Sache*, not a "subject," *Subjekt*, even as it is an "animal" and not a "man," and even as it is, therefore, analogous to "the savage," but must one have been a "subject"? Ought one to have been? There is a tactility of the being of a being, which is also carried in these formulations—a mode of being that may not be reduced to subjective self-ownership.[41] Marx reiterates a determination of forms in settler life, but does not Marx's explication, at the same time, "immediately," call for a wholly other reflection on language—and the social—not grounded in, and not returning to, what is "mine," what I "own," what is my "property," or what "I" possess? A reflection where there is still yet another Marx, and still yet another "Marx beyond Marx," beyond the "methodological" form and "limits" of his language?[42] Where Marx's language, thinking with the formulations of Jacques Lezra, is not reducible—and not translatable—into itself?[43] And where "I" is already given away, among and with others, where "my" skin is not my own—"just like his skin or his sense organs," Marx wrote—where the relation to "land," "soil," and "earth" is not a relation of "property," and where "I," if something, is a form that is already its temporal and tactile relations to things, already a sort of leaning or indebtedness or giving—an "I" that *is* its "touch"?

Marx underlines a desire of capital to drive beyond and extend itself, to be more and other than itself: "It is therefore inherent in its nature constantly to drive beyond its own barrier."[44] And this, as it replaces others with itself, sending itself out and taking their place—"A precondition of production based on capital is therefore *the production of a constantly widening sphere of circulation*, whether the sphere itself is directly expanded or whether *more points within it are created as points of production*," Marx also wrote (321/407)—in its positing of itself as a social form: "Initially, to subjugate every moment of production itself to exchange and to suspend the production of direct use values not entering into exchange, i.e. precisely to posit production based on capital in place of earlier modes of production, which appear primitive from its standpoint" (321/408). Capital, then, is self-positing, it is self-*setzung*-centric, as it presses itself inward and outward in "The exploration of the earth in all directions, to discover new things of use as well as new useful qualities of the old" (322/409), and in its "production of a stage of society in comparison to which all earlier ones appear as mere *local developments* of humanity and as *nature idolatry*" (323/409–410). Marx's language is non-selfsame, it carries a tradition where what *is* is in excess of itself, an anontological tradition, and yet as it does so it reiterates the self-positing activity *Grundrisse* also describes, as it propels outward a particular sense of what a "subject" is, and as it expels "the savage," "the slave," and "the animal" from "ζῶον πολιτικόν in the political sense." It is an expulsion that extends "back" to the "pre-capitalist" forms Marx outlines, and that invests "language" and "life": "An isolated individual [*Ein isoliertes Individuum*] could no more have property [*Eigentum*] in land and soil than he could speak. He could, of course, live off it as substance [*an ihm als der Substanz zehren*], as do the animals" (393/485), Marx wrote.[45] In Marx the "slave" is not a "subject," it is "a thing belonging to another" and an "animal," on the side of "life" and incapable of the proper use of language; while the "savage," in part indistinguishable from the "animal," is a being that cannot become a possible subject of experience or self-reflexive philosophical form. The "savage" is incapable of experience while the "slave" is a "thing" and not a "subject, and this divided allocation of capacities gives the catachrestic formalization of settler life.[46] It is this formalization that installs the "subject" and its world as it congeals and reiterates, and mutates and transforms a particular lexicon and pose—a manner of social address—in post-Crusading, post-Latinate configurations in globality.

Pacification

> οὐ γάρ ἐστιν ἀκαταστασίας ὁ θεὸς ἀλλα εἰρήνης.
>
> —PAUL, 1 CORINTHIANS 14:33

The lexical catachresis of settler life is a pacifying exertion in the social, and yet one may ask: What inheritance is routed through the pose—the manner of address—through which this lexicon is formulated? Why are particular practices of being and language coerced to be recognized in relation to a generalization of the political, in what Talal Asad has called, in a compelling intervention, the "liberal values" of "the autonomous individual, the private self, and a public world of law and political order"?[47] If these are rearticulated through older forms of understanding, where, as Asad underlines, in "medieval Christian theology" the Crusades were invested "with *caritas* (love, benevolence, charity)" (397), a practice for "reaching out with charity *and* chastisement to those who need it" (398), how may we trace this "reaching out" in discrete textual instances, and what is its relation to law, the state, and the modern sense of the subject? Gil Anidjar has noted the Christian formation of the modern state, and its mutation of Pauline forms—"This new body politic that recalls and transforms previous, medieval images of the community as body," he writes, "is the state"—and he has underlined this "recalling" and "transforming" in relation to the Crusades, and Pope Gregory VII's eleventh-century "Peace of God," through which, as Tomaž Mastnak has described it, these were authorized, in practices of warfare "against the infidel enemy," within and without, and which advance, Anidjar also writes, "a Christian interventionism, for the newfound and radical involvement of the church in a world of men newly divided."[48] These practices are mutated in state juridicality and modern philosophical, self-reflexive form and the "Christian temporal practices" these presuppose and reformulate, to draw upon terms elaborated by Kathleen Biddick, and they are routed through a Christian terminology for the recognition of non-Christian being, form, and life, what Mastnak calls "an amorphous multitude of *pagani*, *gentiles*, *infideles*, and *barbari*," who are subjected to an acute and ever-pressing demand, in relation to which they can only remain incapable, to raise themselves up from "the flesh" and "death" to "life" "peace," as Paul wrote in Romans 8:6. "To set the mind on the flesh is death, but to set the mind on the spirit is life and peace," and, as Jerome translated in the Latin of the Vulgate: "Nam prudentia carnis mors est, prudentia autem spiritus vita et pax."[49]

The modern, normative terms for language, the social, and life, what I'm calling "settler life," are forwarded through this demand and the mutating allocation of its terms, coagulated in a post-twelfth-Christian-century logic, where the Crusades press outward and inward a pacifying, if divided and asymmetric, pro-life war undertaken "out of their love of God and their neighbor," as Pope Urban II wrote in a letter dated September 1096.[50] The pose made legible in the call for Crusade at the council of Clermont is reformulated in the terms for juridically determined social existence, which subtend what Carl Schmitt, in *The Nomos of the Earth* (*Der Nomos der Erde*), called the "detheologization of public life," which extended from the sixteenth through the nineteenth European centuries, where "the conflicts between religious factions had been resolved by a public-legal decision for the territorial domain of the state," and where the "*jus publicum europaeum*" appeared as a new, determining, state-centric ordering of world, in its "destruction" of the "*respublica Christiana*."[51] The institution of the "territorial domain" of the state advances the social forms and practices of language through which this domain is generated and preserved, where, Schmitt writes, "The justice of war is no longer based on conformity with the content of theological, moral, or juridical norms, but rather on the institutional and structural quality of political forms" (114–115/143), and where this new "basis" for war, installed with the "displacement" of "the medieval unity of a *respublica Christiana*" (117/145), manifests an appropriation of violence and its legalization in the state. What Schmitt terms the "neutralization" of "conflicts between religious factions" carried out in the "purely state war of the new European international law" (113/141) effects—and is an effect of—the "displacement" of the "theological" by "modern legality"

(51/82), and Schmitt's understanding of this "displacement" turns on his interpretation of European conquest and colonization in the "New World." It was through conquest that "the medieval *jus gentium*" was "overcome," Schmitt wrote, "by the self-contained, sovereign, territorial state of *jus publicum Europaeum*" (82/113), even as the terms of the former are exteriorized through the latter. If "modern legality" was installed with the "end," in Schmitt's words, of "religious wars and civil wars," this end presses itself outward as it advances particular terms for language and life, and as these terms extend themselves, in a redemptive fashion, at "the whole world."[52]

Schmitt studies "the land appropriation of the New World" through the lectures of the Salamancan theologian Francisco de Vitoria, who, in insisting on the humanity of those Spain was colonizing, absorbed them into particular terms for social and linguistic sense: "In particular, it is emphasized repeatedly," Schmitt writes of Vitoria, "that native Americans, though they may be barbarians, are nevertheless men [*daß die Eingeborenen Amerikas zwar Barbaren, aber trotzdem Menschen sind*], as are the European land-appropriators. They are men and not animals [*Sie sind Menschen und keine Tiere*]."[53] This designation of "natives of America," "die Eingeborenen Amerikas," as "men" and "not animals," recognizes them in relation to a lexicon through which they are incorporated as "barbarians," beings in which the distinction between "men" and "animals" is affirmed and collapsed. If this language is extended out of love—with Vitoria's presupposition of "the general equality of mankind," Schmitt explains, "Spaniards are and remain the barbarians' fellowmen [*die Mitmenschen der Barbaren*]; thus here also the Christian duty to 'love thy neighbor' is in force, and every man is our 'neighbor'" (75/107)—it also sends itself, exacting a generalizing demand, at "every man," "jeder Mensch."[54] This generality reenacts a Christian practice of distinction: Vitoria "no longer recognized the spatial order of the medieval *respublica Christiana*, with its distinctions between the territory of Christian peoples and that of heathens or non-believers," Schmitt explains, and yet colonization represented the "extension," *Fortsetzung*, of a conceptual-epistemic lexicon—in *Galatians* 5:14, "For the whole law [ὁ γὰρ πᾶς νόμος/*ho gar pās nomos*] is fulfilled in one word: You shall love your neighbor as yourself [Ἀγαπήσεις τὸν πλησίον σου ὡς σεαυτόν/*agapēseis ton plēsion sou hōs seauton*]"—which mutates the terminological forms of Latin Christianity in the Vulgate translation of "nomos" as "lex," and as it secularizes itself in state-juridical terms: "Also in this respect, the Spanish *conquista* was an extension [*Fortsetzung*] of the concepts of the *respublica Christiana* of the Middle Ages."[55] What is "extended," or, one might also say, what is "posited away," or even "continued on," in the verb "fortsetzen," is a social logic through which the pose carried in Crusade is pressed inward and outward, in a pacifying manner, where *nomos*, in Paul, is rephrased in the modern "secular" terms for law, language, thought, and collective social existence, terms through which asymmetric decimations are advanced in globality. "In its ideal formulation, Christendom was an endless holy war," Mastnak writes in *Crusading Peace*, and this war is a practice of Christian life—"The crusade was a living communion with Christ. Taking up the cross meant experiencing Christ's passion in thought and deed"—as well as a manner of understanding what "life" is and living it.[56] It is a manner of living that was—and is—like "Christendom," "frontierless," "a mobile moving space," one which, like law in its modern formulations, "by nature knew no frontier and so extended potentially over the whole earth" (123). And it is—and was—then as now, and in the manner in which it reformulates itself as subjective linguistic existence, not only a matter of state formation and state legality, as in Schmitt, but equally—and immediately—"a war of extermination" (125), a "cleansing operation" (127), carried out in the interest of "civil peace." Its aim, Mastnak explains of Crusade, is—and I wish to place an emphasis on the pose reiterated through this formulation, its manner of address—"to bring about civil peace worldwide" (312).

I wish to consider law and Crusade through Schmitt's discussion of Vitoria. "Just war provided the legal title for occupation and annexation of American territory and subjugation of the indigenous peoples," Schmitt wrote, and this title, for Vitoria, was not given through "discovery" or "occupation"—"Vitoria explicitly rejects discovery and occupation as legal title for land appropriation, because, for him, the territory of America was neither free nor unclaimed"—but through the papal missionary mandate.[57] "Thus," Schmitt writes, "the papal missionary mandate, even if only indirectly, by means of a just war, was the true legal title of the *conquista*" (81/112). A central text for the theorization of the just war, beginning in the twelfth century, was the *Decretum* of Gratian, which "climaxed the development of early medieval canon law collections and inaugurated the period of systematic canonical jurisprudence."[58] This theorization intersects the Roman legal tradition—"A war waged without cause was not really war but *latrocinium* or piracy, and the *causa belli* was a necessary precondition for a *justum bellum*" (5)—and, in Ulpian, the distinction between "enemies," on one hand, and "robbers" and "brigands" (7–8), on the other. Following the conversion of Constantine in the fourth century, a new terminological field for the management of internal and external antagonism was installed: "For the older antagonism between empire and Christianity was substituted a new and more explosive division between heresy and orthodoxy," and, as Frederick H. Russell goes on to explain, "According to the imperial policy of persecution, heretics were subjected to all sorts of civil disabilities and in some cases were liable to capital punishment" (13). This subjection was understood by St. Augustine—and Vitoria—as a kind of love: "Hatred," Russell writes of Augustine, "was to be overcome by a love for one's enemies that did not preclude a benevolent severity" (17), and, further, "Augustine saw the punishment of heretics as a form of charity" (24).

For Augustine, "heretics and schismatics" were to be "compelled" to "come in" to the Church, and, "Once inside by compulsion, these gradually would give assent to its teachings" (24). If, in this, the Church imitated God—"In effecting coercion of heresy the Church even imitated God himself" (24)—and if this implicated "the whole moral order" (25), this is because, as it participated in an intensive drawing and blurring of lines, this corpus of writing outlined a field of relations, which extend into the modern period—itself a closely controlled hermeneutic form—and its lexicon for law. What emerges is a "motley assemblage of enemies" (31) in relation to the institution of "Christian society" (35) and the repeated targeting of forms of alterity, within and without. The Crusades remain a singular locus:

> Seeking ways to lessen the incidence of violence within European Christian society, Urban in 1093 promulgated the Truce of God at the Council of Troia, and in his famous speech at the Council of Clermont in 1095 he exhorted knights to desist from their wicked combats against Christians and to fight the righteous war against the infidel. As incentive he promised the spiritual reward of heaven and the temporal rewards of peace, prosperity and plunder. In effect he preached a papal war waged by knights against infidels in the holy land. (35–36)

There is a gathering of authority toward the Church and law: "According to Gratian's choice of texts the Church was indeed to play a more active role, not only initiating but also directing persecution of those guilty of sin or religious heterodoxy, including heretics and infidels" (74). "In effect," Russell continues, "Gratian elaborated a justification of religious persecution that was later employed to justify crusades against infidels, heretics, and those who contemptuously disputed the exercise of papal authority" (74). These terms authorize and withhold punishment and war: "It is clear that anyone seen as a threat to the Church on earth merited physical punishment even by war" (76). There is a regulation and exteriorization of violence: "In the minds of the canonists all pagans, infidels, heretics, schismatics and excommunicates posed an almost collective threat to Christianity from within and without" (112–113), and, further, "a war against heretics to compel their return to orthodoxy was justified as a defense of the faith" (113). In this frame, Russell also explains that "the Decretalists saw the crusades as a form of repression appropriate to Saracens and heretics" (197)—and I wish to observe the indistinction and illegibility of these terms—as the language of decretal formulation sought to define the bounds of "peaceful Christian society" (142) and as the orientation of legal argument shifted in "the canonists' transition from the emphasis on the just cause," as in Augustine, to "the concern for authority and jurisdiction" (145).

In this shift in orientation, "The Decretists had made the right to take up arms the monopoly of legitimate authority" (146). If these terms represent a separation of theology and law—"after 1200 theology and canon law became more strictly delimited spheres of competence" (214)—this is in relation to a "necessity to defend public order, the faith, and the *patria* against pagans, heretics and others who confounded order and security" (159), in order, for the commentators on the *Decretum*, to "return their enemy by conquest to a state of peace" (61). The terms cut across and install a distinction between inside and outside—for Hostiensis, a student of Pope Innocent IV, whose papacy extended from 1243 to 1254, "Heresy seemed as the paradigmatic case that justified any ecclesiastical resort to warfare against its European enemies" (206), and, "The crusade was only one means among many of dealing with the pest of heresy" (209)—and this stabilization and disorganization of categories presses the social violence that coagulates in these terms.[59] If the "just war" could now be viewed as a "legal procedure" in its relation to "the hardening of territorial boundaries and jurisdictions" and "the emergence of the modern notion of the state," as Russell writes, the terms that mediate this "emergence" generalize a counterinsurgent pose in the social.[60] This lexical field advances a practice for the targeting of whatever "confounds order and security," of "those who had ruptured the bond of faith with Christian society" (185)—"violent men, heretics and pagans" (190)—and its terms are reformulated in the modern lexicon for racialized existence and philosophical self-reflection.

To think this reformulation and its relation to "Christian society" (194), I consider St. Thomas Aquinas's *Summa theologiae*, where, if the "church" is "one mystic body"—"As the whole Church is termed one mystic body [*unum corpus mysticum*] from its likeness to the natural body of man, which in diverse members has diverse acts, as the Apostle teaches, so likewise Christ is called the Head of the Church from a likeness with the human head"—those non-Christian beings to which the Church relates itself are "in" the Church only "potentially": "Those who are unbaptized though not actually in the Church, are in the Church potentially," Aquinas writes, as were "the Fathers of the Old Testament."[61] Aquinas outlines the terms for "compulsion," which articulate the frames for thirteenth-century, Latin, Christian self-understanding: "Among unbelievers [*infidelium*]," Aquinas notes, "there are some who have never received the faith, such as the heathens and the Jews [*sicut gentiles et*

Iudaei], and these are by no means to be compelled to the faith in order that they may believe, because to believe depends on the will."[62] He explains, extending the "compulsion" he had withheld, that "nevertheless they should be compelled by the faithful, if it be possible to do so, so that they do not hinder the faith, by their blasphemies, or by their evil persuasions, or even by their open persecutions" (2.2.Q10.A8). Those "such as the heathens and the Jews" should, in order that their persecution not "hinder the faith," be compelled to it. Aquinas continues, as he explicates and generalizes this persecuting logic—to draw upon the terms of R. I. Moore—as a practice in Crusading form: "It is for this reason that Christ's faithful often wage war against unbelievers [*contra infideles bellum movent*], not indeed for the purpose of forcing them to believe, but because even if they were to conquer them, and take them prisoners, they should still leave them free to believe, if they will, but in order to prevent them from hindering the faith of Christ" (2.2.Q10.A8). And yet "On the other hand," Aquinas also notes, "there are unbelievers [*infideles*] who at some time have accepted the faith, and professed it, such as heretics and whichever apostates [*sicut haeretici vel quicumque apostatae*]. Such should be submitted even to bodily compulsion, that they may fulfill what they have promised, and hold what they, at one time, received" (2.2.Q10.A8).

Aquinas clarifies that what characterizes "the sin of unbelief" is "resisting the faith," and this resistance divides. "For, since the sin of unbelief [*infidelitatis*] consists in resisting the faith [*renitendo fidei*], this may happen in two ways: either the faith is resisted before it has been accepted, and such is the unbelief of pagans or heathens [*Paganorum sive gentilium*], or the Christian faith is resisted after it has been accepted, and this is either in the figure, and such is the unbelief of the Jews [*Iudaeorum*], or in the very manifestation of truth, and such is the unbelief of heretics [*haereticorum*]" (2.2.Q10.A5). In addressing such resistance, Aquinas replies to a question regarding communication, and he underlines that while a Christian may communicate with "pagans and Jews," those "who have not in any way received the Christian faith," the Church prohibits communication with heretics and apostates, "unbelievers who have forsaken the faith once received." He notes, further, that "Christians can have unbelievers, either Jews, or pagans, or Saracens [*infideles, vel Iudaeos vel etiam Paganos sive Saracenos*] for servants. Therefore they can lawfully communicate with them" (2.2.Q10.A9). The terms Aquinas circulates—the Jew, pagan, heathen, Saracen, heretic, and apostate—press at the form of the social body, and Aquinas responds to this threat and its infinite manifestations. "It is possible to stray from the truth of faith in an infinite number of ways" (2.2.Q10.A5), Aquinas noted, as in the "apostate"—"Moreover, if anyone [*quis*] were to have himself circumcised, or to worship at the tomb of Mahomet [*vel sepulcrum Mahumeti adoraret*], he would be deemed an apostate" (2.2.Q12.A1)—and the "schismatic," a sort of being that opposes itself to "the unity of the Church": "And so those who are properly called schismatics have, voluntarily and by their own intention, separated themselves from the unity of the Church [*se ab unitate Ecclesiae separant*], which is unity principally. For the unity of particular individuals among themselves is ordered to a united Church, just as the composition of individual members in a natural body is ordered to the unity of the whole body" (2.2.Q39.A1).

If the "schismatic" is a figure through which the "unity" of the Church is affirmed, the "apostate" is a term that mediates the interiority and exteriority of that unity in relation to a lexicon of Christian recognition; it is not that an "apostate" is one who would "have himself circumcised" or "worship at the tomb of Mahomet," but instead that "anyone"—"quis"—who would do so is an "apostate." It is as if *Summa theologiae*, speaking an idiom of Christian particularity, and in a manner that installs the Church as a corporate body, calls into being its field of addressees, because whatever and whoever is a living being is to be recognizable—and translatable—in relation to its terms; and because any being that declines these terms—and the divided and illegible locus for this declining is the "Saracen"—refuses the Pauline demand, in Romans 8:6, that one lift onself from death and the flesh to life and peace, and this demand is sent at "the whole human race" (3.Q7.A11), as Aquinas wrote.[63] The displacement of theology with legality, described by Schmitt and Russell, carries these terms and redistributes them, as it exteriorizes a logic of schismatic division, where non-Christian beings pose a threat to "the unity of the Church" as well as, in its modern transmutations, to the state, law, and the institution of the social.[64] If, in this, we may observe what Ernst Kantorowicz called, in *The King's Two Bodies*, an "adaptation of ecclesiastical forms to the secular bodies politic," where, "the mystical body embraces not only those actually in the fold but also those who potentially might join the fold now or in the future—that is, it extends to both the as yet unborn future generations of Christians and the as yet unbaptized pagans, Jews, or Mohammedans, since the mystical body of Christ, that is, the Church, grows not only by nature but also by grace," I notice that this "embracing," a Pauline formulation, is a practice for the absorption of non-Christian life as well as a social attack, where the social *is* an attack, in an inward- and outward-facing pose and an exteriorizing form.[65]

The Church, as the sixth- and seventh-century Bishop Isidore of Seville wrote in his *Etymologiae*, is called in Latin "convocation," "because it calls everyone to itself [*propter quod omnes ad se vocet*]," and this address reiterates the logic of the social I've outlined.[66] They are terms that advance a promise of order and peace. Aquinas cites Augustine in book 19 of *The City of God*, "The good of the multitude seems to consist in order and peace, which is 'the tranquility of order' [*bonum multitudinis videtur esse ordo et pax, quae est 'tranquillitas ordinis'*]" (1.Q103.A2), and such "order" and "tranquility" are pressed outward in social interpellation. "The intention of a ruler over a multitude is unity or peace" (1.Q103.A3), and so too is "unity or peace," in Aquinas's words, "the end of human law": "For the end of human law," he writes, "is the temporal tranquility of the state, which end law effects by directing external actions, as regards those evils which might disturb the peaceful condition of the state" (1.2.Q98.A1). Such "direction" of "external actions" labors in relation to the "coercion" Aquinas discussed and its articulation of the social in the interest of "living-well" (1.2.Q94.A3) and "for the benefit of human life" (1.2.Q94.A5), and it advances a theological-juridical sense of relation, "without which men cannot live together [*sine quibus homines ad invicem convivere non possent*]" (1.2.Q94.A4). Such "living together" is to install and foster "the ordered concord of peace," where, if "the notion of justice became assimilated to legality," there is a "transference of definitions from one sphere to another, from theology to law," and this is "anything but surprising or even remarkable."[67] "It would be quite amiss, however, to assume that the transcendental values distinguishing rulership in the liturgical age were simply abandoned in the following period when political theories began to crystalize around learned jurisprudence," Kantorowicz also explains. There is, instead, a "translation" and "survival" of "practically all the former values," a mutation that rephrases terms, a persistence in orientation, and a reiteration in manner and pose. He also observes: "The medieval patterns and concepts of kingship were not simply wiped out, neither by Frederick II nor by others: practically all the former values survived—but they were translated into new secular and chiefly juristic modes of thinking and thus survived by transference in a secular setting."[68]

Vitoria's lectures, *Relectio de Indis*, studied by Schmitt in *Nomos of the Earth*, circulate and relocate these terms, not only in his providing to "the Spaniards" a "just title" for "natural partnership and communication," including "trade" and what we may call "theft"—"For example, if travelers are allowed to dig for gold in common land or in rivers or to fish for pearls in the sea or in rivers, the barbarians may not prohibit Spaniards from doing so"—but also in his underlining "the spreading of the Christian religion" through Spain's colonizing activities.[69] "Christians," he writes, "have the right to preach and announce the Gospel in the lands of the barbarians" (87/284). The spatial frame for this "preaching" and "announcement" extends itself into the lands and the waters of the colonized, and it sends itself at the world—"it is the Pope's special business to promote the Gospel throughout the world [*in totum orbem*]"

(88/284)—and in this Vitoria is clear that "if the barbarians attempt to deny the Spaniards in these matters"—whether those provided through the "law of nations," *ius gentium*, or those justified through the terms of "the Christian religion"—war against "the barbarians" becomes "just": "If the barbarians, either in the person of their masters or as a multitude obstruct the Spaniards in their free propagation of the Gospel, the Spaniards, after first reasoning with them to remove any cause of provocation, may preach and work for the conversion of that people even against their will, and may if necessary take up arms and declare war on them, insofar as this provides the safety and opportunity needed to preach the Gospel" (89/285). What is to be preserved is the "safety" of the colonizer—and, Vitoria notes, "The aim of war is peace and security [*Finis belli est pax et securitas*]" (85/283)—and it is the colonizer's insecurity, its sense of its own non-safety, which calls forth its war against Indigenous peoples. Such war, Vitoria writes, is to be taken up within "limits": "If the business of religion cannot otherwise be forwarded, the Spaniards may lawfully conquer the territories of these people, deposing their old masters and setting up new ones and carrying out all the things which are lawfully permitted in other just wars by the law of war, so long as they always observe reasonable limits and do not go further than necessary" (90/285–286). And yet Vitoria's demand for "limits" points to the limitlessness of "conquest," its never ceasing to "go further." If, in this, Vitoria regenerates the doctrine of *terra nullius*—"What is no one's is, according to the law of nations, the property of the one who takes it [*quae in nullius sunt, iure gentium sunt occupantis*]" (82/280)—he recognizes all beings and things in relation to the terms he advances, a proliferation of Christian life and capitalist expropriation. I do not wish to argue that, in this, Vitoria "reintroduces Christian norms" within a "secular system"; instead, I observe that Vitoria's manner of articulating social form and sense, his assuming a quite particular pose, is a mutation within a post-twelfth-Christian-century logic and its manner of thinking being, life, language, and form.[70]

In this frame I notice that *Relectio de Indis* receives and transmutes Aquinas's rendering of "living well" and "for the benefit of human life"; that in this Aquinas transforms and retains Aristotle's explication of "the good life," εὖ ζῆν, *eū zēn*, in *Politics* 1252b31, where such life points to the being together of human beings in the polis, and where, in Aquinas, this is rearticulated in relation to Latin terms for Christian recognition and crusading form; and that in Aquinas the distinction drawn in Aristotle between "the human being" and "the living being"—where the former is on the side of "the good life" and the latter on the side of "life," and where the former is capable of language and the latter incapable of it while still linked aporetically to it—is reformulated in a mutation of Aristotelian categories, where, as Aquinas wrote in his *Commentary* on Aristotle's *Politics*, "The political community [*civitas*] was originally instituted for the sake of the living [*primitus facta gratia vivendi*], namely that human beings [*homines*] adequately find the means to be able to live. But the political community's existence results in human beings not only living, but living well [*quod homines non solum vivant, sed quod bene vivant*] insofar as the laws of the political community direct human beings to virtue [*ad virtutes*]."[71] In the lexicon I've outlined, as it is transmuted in Vitoria, the colonized are located in relation to a distinction drawn between "life" and "the good life," and the Indigenous are located on the side of Aristotle's "natural" slavery—"All these barbarians appear to fall under this heading, and they might be governed partly as slaves," Vitoria wrote—and declared to be incapable of and subordinated to a demand for "the good life."[72] Aquinas's "sed"—"not only living, but [*sed*] living well"—creates a terminological frame through which the reflection on the social is reformulated in the advance of a tradition, which may be said to turn on the reading of this word as a disjunctive term. It is a tradition formulated through an anti-Islamic lexicon for the social, with its divided locus in the catachrestic figure of the "Saracen," which is to raise itself up to "life" and "peace" through its separation of itself from "flesh" and "death," as in Romans 8:6, even as all non-Christian, non-European beings remain exteriorized from these terms, objects—as Pope Urban II made clear—of a counterinsurgent linguistic demand. It is a demand that translates what remain for it illegible forms—the modes of being and the languages of the colonized and the enslaved—into the distinction between "life" and "the good life." To study this demand and its racializing formulations, I turn, now, to several essays of Sylvia Wynter's, where Wynter teaches us that, if something, settler life is also a kind of translation.

Translation

> Las Casas, a Dominican priest with a conscience, travelled to Spain to plead for the abolition of native slavery. But without coercion of the natives how could the colony exist?
>
> —C. L. R. JAMES, *THE BLACK JACOBINS*

In a two-part essay, "New Seville and the Conversion Experience of Bartolomé de Las Casas," published in 1984, Sylvia Wynter offers a reading of Las Casas that relates his writing to "the new commercial logic which linked the destiny of the Caribbean islands to sugar and African new World slavery" and "the medieval Euro-Christian episteme" and the social order it sustained and pressed out in globality.[73] Wynter underlines Las Casas's opposition to "all forms of Indian forced labor"—"As a result of his conversion-inspired mission to secure the abolition of all forms of Indian forced labor, Las Casas was to propose the importation of a limited quantity of African slaves both to recompense the settlers for their Indian labor supply; and as an incentive to Spanish peasant migration"—and she explains that this opposition cyphered two moments.[74] First, Las Casas's understanding that, while the "Indians," "los indios," had been enslaved unjustly, persons of African descent "had been *justly* enslaved according to the moral-legal system of Latin Christianity" (26); and, second, Las Casas's opposition to the claim of Ginés de Sepúlveda, "in the context of the formal debate held at Valladolid, Spain, before a conclave of theologians, jurists, scholars, royal bureaucrats and councilors in 1550–51" (26), that there was a "*natural* difference of rational capacity" (26) between the Christian, European colonizers, on the one hand, and the Indigenous peoples of the Americas, on the other, in a racializing formalization Wynter calls—in relation to Sepúlveda—"a complex of *a priori* settler assumptions" (31).[75]

In this frame Wynter underlines, at the same time, the appearance of "a new mode of being, the bearer of self-consciousness," which emerges in its break from what she understands to have been "the theological absolutism of the Late Middle Ages"—a "more inclusive order," she also writes, "displaced that of the medieval system ensemble"—and its forms of thought.[76] This "displacement" is effected in the "new world," in relation to "the scholastic order of knowledge in feudal-Christian Europe," an order Wynter outlines in "New Seville and the Conversion Experience of Bartolomé de Las Casas" and "The Ceremony Must Be Found"—a second essay of Wynter's I'm citing here, which was also published in 1984—and which she also details in "1492: A New World View," an essay published in 1995, which I'll trace presently.[77]

Wynter is concerned with western-hemispheric social existence and she notes "two of the events founding to the institution of the post-1492 Caribbean and the Americas," which she outlines as follows: "For it was to be with the terms of the same discourse of legitimation that, first, Columbus would, on landing, at once take possession of the islands at which he arrived, expropriating them in the name of the Spanish state," and, second, "it was also to be on the initial basis of the same mode of juro-theological legitimation, that, under the auspices of the slave-trading system out of Africa that had been established by the Portuguese in the wake of 1441, large numbers of peoples of African descent would be transshipped as the substitute slave labor force whose role would be indispensable to the founding of the new societies" (11). This occasions, Wynter explains, the institution of "race" as a modern social and ontological category—"The new symbolic construct of *Race* or of innately determined difference that would enable the Spanish state to legitimate its sovereignty over the *lands of the Americas* in the postreligious legal terms of Western Europe's now expanding state system" (11–12)—in relation to "Western Europe's epochal transfer of the other-worldly goal of the *citivas dei* to the this-worldly goal of the *civitas saecularis*" (14). In this "transformation of the divinely ordained feudal order into the new one of the modern state" (17), and with the institution of transatlantic chattel slavery, settler colonization, capitalist expropriation, and Indigenous genocide, there is a "transfer" and a "replacement" (14) of one field of categories—what Wynter terms "feudal," "medieval," and "theological"—with another, which attends these and is formulated through them.

Wynter explicates this "transformation," and its mediation in settler colonization, transatlantic chattel slavery, and the modern institutions of law and the state, in the formation of a lexicon, a field of terms, where "the New World peoples" were to be understood as "a human population divided up into Christians (who had heard and accepted the new word of the gospel), infidels like the Muslims and the Jews, who, although monotheists, had refused the Word after having been preached the Word (and who were therefore *inimici Christi*, enemies of Christ), and *idolators*, those pagan polytheistic peoples who had either ignored or had not yet been preached the Word" (29). In this, Wynter teaches us, "race" transmutes and reorganizes older categories, taking their place, and yet if these terms "reoccupy" (39) the position of others, Wynter writes—and, in this, Wynter is quite close to Hans Blumenberg, whose *The Legitimacy of the Modern Age* she cites—this "reoccupation" gives place to a social form that addresses itself, ongoingly, at the world.[78]

Race, in its relation to this "reoccupation," enacts a "new notion of order," Wynter writes, "based on a *by-nature difference* between Europeans, on the one hand, and peoples of indigenous and African descent, on the other," and these terms are mediated by the terminological lexicon of Aristotle's *Politics*.[79] A distinction is drawn, she explains, between the "natural" and the "civil" slave in relation to capitalism, the expropriation of Indigenous land, new forms of state-juridical social determination, and transatlantic chattel slavery. "In the place of the category of the *idolators*," the Spanish, Wynter writes, "adopted the category of *natural slaves* from Aristotle, in order to represent the indigenous peoples as ones who were *by nature different from the Spanish*" (34). "This difference," she continues, "made it clear that the 'Indios' had been as intended by natural law to be 'natural slaves,' as the Spaniards had been also intended to be natural masters" (35). The "Indios," Wynter outlines, in terms that also point to Vitoria's *Relectio de Indis* and Aquinas's *Summa theologiae*, "while potentially as rational as the Spaniards, nevertheless could enjoy the use of their reason only *potentially*, as in the case of children" (35).

And there remained the question of labor:

> For this legitimation to be congruent, the indigenous peoples could therefore no longer be made into a totally disposable slave labor force. And since the land-labor ratio in which the former was in such excess supply called for a totally disposable labor force, the transported slaves of African descent, who, in the new statally determined triadic model were defined as *civil slaves* and therefore as legal merchandise, would now function as the only legitimately enslavable group of the three. (35)

Aristotle outlines these terms in *Politics*: "One who is a human being belonging by nature not to himself but to another [μὴ αὑτοῦ φύσει ἀλλ'ἄλλου / *mē hautou phusei all' allou*] is by nature a slave [οὗτος φύσει δοῦλός ἐστιν / *houtos phusei doulos estin*]" (1254a15–16), and this is distinguished from "slavery by law": "For there is also such a thing as a slave or a man that is in slavery by law [κατὰ νόμον / *kata nomon*], for the law [ὁ γὰρ νόμος / *ho gar nomos*] is a sort of agreement under which the things conquered in war are said to belong to their conquerors" (1255a5–7). The gloss in Aquinas's *Commentary* on *Politics* retains these terms: "For, inasmuch as a slave is himself [*ipsum*] something that belongs to another [*alterius*]," he writes, "Any human being who by nature belongs not to himself but to another is by nature a slave [*quicumque homo non est naturaliter sui ipsius, sed alterius, ipse est naturaliter servus*]."[80] As Aquinas comments on this passage, following the Latin translation of William of Moerbeke at *Politics* 1255a6, the slave "by law," κατὰ νόμον, *kata nomon*, is rendered as "according to posited human law," *secundum legem inter homines positam*, and this, further is understood in relation to the "law of nations," *ius gentium*: "For law declares that war captives are the slaves of the victors, and almost all peoples observe it, and so we call it a law of nations" (A91/34). Reading and thinking with Wynter's intervention, I wish to observe that these phrasings propel a particular understanding of life. The rendering of the slave "by nature," where the slave is "a part of the master, a part of the body, alive but separated from it" (*Politics* 1255b11–12), if it locates the slave as a living being, recognizable in relation to the practice of "living well," this is only as an appendage, "as if," Aquinas wrote in his gloss, "he were a living instrument [*organum animatum*] that is a separated part of his master's body."[81] There is, in Aquinas, a generalization of Christian form and sense, where the distinction between "life" and "the good life"—between "living" and "living well"—is reiterated into a field of Christian, theological, and juridical distinction, and this field is reformulated in global and Western-hemispheric terms, where the enslaved become "legal merchandise," a sort of being "reduced to a thing, to *being* for the captor," as Hortense Spillers has written.[82] It is a "conception," in Wynter's terms, that affirms an "opposition" between "the *white* (unmixed peoples of Indo-European descent) and the *black* (peoples of wholly or of partly African descent)," where this ordering's oppositional language "represented its own culture-specific Judaeo-Christian and European statal *nos*, as if it were the *nos* of humankind in general."[83] "Others," Wynter also writes, "could therefore only be the lack of this *nos*, infidels or idolators" (36–37). Lingering with this "or," and its ongoing indeterminacies, I notice that the field of terms Wynter outlines and which she teaches us to think in relation to a "feudal-Christian episteme" (19) and its relation to "all non-Christian peoples and cultures" (17) exceeds itself, blurring the categories it also advances, as it coerces modes of fundamental social and ontological obliteration.[84] If we may think of these terms as post-twelfth-Latin-Christian century, as the terms of Crusade—and I would not wish to follow Wynter in thinking this formation as "Judaeo-Christian,"[85] itself a twentieth-century invention of philological-settler orientalism—this would be to underline the manner in which Wynter relates them to "a specific form of life," if one that generates a lexicon, and a manner of address in genocidal form, that is atotal, a mutating, divided, lexical-social catachresis in globality.[86]

I wish to return to Wynter's discussion of Sepúlveda and Las Casas in order to think about this catachresis—a self-extension in social and lingual terms. If, for Wynter, one is to disaggregate Sepúlveda from Las Casas, I notice that the sense of being and life in which they share—given through what Wynter calls a "complex of *a priori* settler assumptions"—reproduces the post-twelfth-Christian-century lexicon Wynter outlines, and which is, itself, excessive, carrying forward Christian practices for the asymmetric obliteration of non-Christian alterities intensively coagulated in "the Saracen." In Wynter, Sepúlveda represents racial exclusion—"*by-nature difference*," "an ontological difference of substance"—while Las Casas "laid the basis for the theoretical delegitimization of all forms of inter-human domination and subordination," and yet the terms they affirm mutate a forced proliferation of differentiating inclusion, a global extension and reformulation of settler life.[87] This extension may be understood to belong to a mutation in counterinsurgent form, not so much a "displacement" (as elaborated in in "The Ceremony Must Be Found") as an excessive rephrasing of terms, in advance of a pacification routed through what Wynter called, "a new mode of being, the bearer of self-consciousness," which, in its self-determined, propertied form, continues to striate the world, in the ongoing transmutations of Paul's "eirēnē" into the "pax" of the Latin of the Vulgate: "Therefore," Paul wrote, "since we are justified by faith, we have peace with God through our Lord Jesus Christ" (Romans 5:1).[88] It is this pacification—and, "Their goal," then as now, "is to return their enemy by conquest to a state of peace"—that Wynter outlines in its ever-morphing forms.[89]

Politick Societies

We may consider this pacification in a letter of Alexis de Tocqueville's, published on August 22, 1837, in which Tocqueville writes of the colonization of Algeria in the following terms:

> Hardly were we masters of Algiers than we hastened to gather up all of the Turks, without forgetting a single one, from the dey to the last soldier of his militia, and transported the lot of them to the coast of Asia. In order to make the vestiges of the enemy domination disappear [*Afin de mieux faire disparaître les vestiges de la domination ennemie*], we first took care to tear up or burn all written documents, administrative records, and papers, authentic or otherwise, that could have perpetuated any trace of what had been done before us [*qui auraient pu perpétuer la trace de ce qui s'était fait avant nous*]. The conquest was a new era, and from fear of mixing the past with the present in an irrational way, we even destroyed a large number of streets in Algiers so as to rebuild them according to our own method, and we gave French names to all those we consented to leave alone.[90]

Settler colonization installs itself in the panicked institution of "a new era," *une nouvelle ère*, in what it wishes to have been the destruction of a previous order and its documentary practices. The desire to eliminate "any trace" of "the vestiges of the enemy domination," the rushed manner in which the colonizer "hastened to gather up all of the Turks," and the fear that they might leave one behind—"without forgetting a single one," as Tocqueville noted—points to the formative incompletion of settler legalities: The burning of documents, the deportation of "Turks," the "destruction" and "rebuilding" of streets and their renaming—all point to the excessive manner of settler form, which will never, finally, have been finished with the native. In settler colonization there will always have been remains, a refusal of the colonized to disappear, finally, in the destruction the settler advances, and this is a destruction, as Tocqueville's language suggests, that will never have ceased. The settler demand for temporal clarity is reiterated in its fear of improper mixing—"mixing the past with the present in an irrational way"—and "confusion," and the colonizer therefore calls for a stabilizing order: "Once the Turkish government was destroyed, with no substitute to replace it, the country, which could no longer run itself, fell into appalling anarchy. All the tribes fell on top of one another into an immense confusion [*Toutes les tribus se précipitèrent les unes sur les autres dans une immense confusion*]; brigandage emerged everywhere. Even the shadow of justice disappeared, and everyone resorted to force"

(47/17). It is at this moment that Tocqueville divides "the Arabs," who require governance, from "the Kabyle," who are "independent," and with whom "we" can establish "peaceful relations": "If we continue to establish frequent and peaceful relations with the Kabyles, if their leaders have nothing to fear from our ambition and see that we have simple, clear, firm laws that will protect them [*et rencontrent parmi nous une législation simple, claire et sûr qui les protège*], it is certain that they will soon fear war more than we ourselves, and that we shall perceive the almost invincible attraction that draws savages toward civilized man at the moment they no longer fear for their liberty" (52/20). Unlike the Kabyles, who are assimilable into legality, "the Arabs" embody a political threat: "With the Kabyles we must focus above all on questions of civil and commercial equity; with the Arabs on political and religious questions" (52/21). The division of natives into those who require "governance" and those suited for "independence," in a social logic of self-determined, self-legislated morality and statal security, frames Tocqueville's letter. The framing opposes itself to 'Abd al-Qāder and collective struggle—"It is indeed very important to us not to let the Arabs yield to anarchy, but it is even more important not to expose ourselves to seeing them united against us all at once" (54/22)—and the anxiety induced through the surging force of a body that "we" would "see," as if it were a single being, a collective posed "against us," *contre nous*, presses Tocqueville to further clarify his letter's terms.

These terms privilege "cultivation," a "productive" use of land, in contrast to what Tocqueville calls "tribal" life: "The Arabs lived in tribes 2,000 years ago in Yemen; they traversed all Africa and invaded Spain in tribes; they still live in the same manner until this day" (56/23), and through this designation Tocqueville recalls "the Arabs" to property, legality, and agriculture: "I told you at the beginning, sir, that the Arabs were once shepherds and farmers, and that, although they held the entire extent of the land, they never cultivated more than a very small part" (57–58/24). The promise of "cultivation" opens the possibility of what Tocqueville calls "a communal life with us"—"It would be equally wrong to think that the Arabs' civil customs make them incapable of yielding to a communal life with us [*On aurait égalment tort de penser que les habitudes civiles des Arabes les rendent incapables de se plier à une vie commune avec nous*]" (59/25)—in a regulated proximity of settler form: "So the Arab population is quite sparse; it occupies much more terrain than it can possibly cultivate every year. The consequence is that the Arabs sell land readily and cheaply, and that a foreign population can easily establish itself next to them without causing them to suffer" (58/24). There is, then, at once a strategic formulation, which advances foreign settlement in relation to what the settler understands to be the capacities and incapacities of the native, and a subordination of the "communal" to propertied, settler form, where the field of action open to "the Arabs" is that they "yield," *se plier*, to the colonizer, that they "fold" or "bend" themselves, a sort of act that would affirm, for the settler, its right to colonize for the benefit of the colonized, and "without causing them to suffer."

This proximity is to be mediated in property, legality, and the social form of the "individual": "We need in Africa, just as in France, and even more than in France, essential guarantees to men living in society; nowhere is it more necessary to establish individual liberty, respect for property, and guarantees of all rights than in a colony" (57/24). There must be "essential guarantees," and these must be enforced through administrative procedure—"But, on the other hand, a colony needs a simpler administration, one more expeditious and independent of the central power than those that direct the continental provinces of the empire" (57/24)—and this is because, while "communal life" is promised, it is immediately forestalled in the language of this "Letter on Algeria."

Tocqueville's promise of "the Arabs" to "society," *société*, is to transform "nomadic life" into a life of "property" and "persons":

> In Spain, the Arabs were sedentary and agricultural; in the areas around the Algerian towns, a great number of them are building houses and devoting themselves seriously to agriculture. The Arabs are thus not naturally and necessarily shepherds. It is true that as you advance toward the desert, you see the houses disappear and the tent emerge. But this is because the security of property and persons [*la sûreté des proptiétés et des personnes*] diminishes as you leave the coasts, and because nothing is more expedient than the nomadic life for a people that fears for its existence and its liberty. I can well see that the Arabs prefer to wander in the open air than to remain exposed to the tyranny of a master, but everything indicates to me that if they could be free, respected, and sedentary, they would be quick to settle down [*que s'ils pouvaient être libres, respectés et sédentaires, ils ne tarderaient pas à se fixer*]. I have no doubt that they would adopt our style of life if we gave them a lasting interest in doing so. (59/25–26)

"Our style of life," *notre genre de vie*, is pressed outward, and what is recognized as "wandering" is recalled to the "sedentary" and the "agricultural," and the locus of these in "property" and the "person." This recall of the social life of "the Arabs" to the manner of life of the European settler is, for Tocqueville, brought on by the colonized, who can do nothing but wage war "on us," who "surround us," and by whom "we," the settler collective, is threatened: "But the Arab tribes' passions or religion and depredation always lead them to wage war on us. Peace with Christians from time to time, and habitual war, such is the natural taste of the populations that surround us."[91] It is the colonized and their "natural taste," *le goût naturel*, which calls forth the aggressive force of the settler. What is required, Tocqueville explains, is that "the Arabs," who are "half-civilized," be domesticated in cultivation, property, and, finally, "towns": "The Arabs, however, are in greater need of towns than they themselves imagine. No society, even if only half-civilized, can subsist without towns. Nomadic peoples do not escape from this necessity more than any others; indeed they are even more subject to it than others, because the wandering life they lead prevents them from cultivating even coarsely the sciences and arts that are indispensable even to the least advanced civilization" (116/73). The colonized are responsible for their colonization; because they are warlike, and on the side of "passion" and "religion," the colonizer is to socialize them, to translate them into the terms of recognition in settler life.

"The French," Tocqueville wrote in his notes on a trip to Algiers in 1841, "are substituting broad arcaded streets for the Moors' tortuous little alleys," and this "substitution" is mirrored in the colonizer's manner of extending its demand as an exertion in reformulation of the social.[92] The suppression of what appears as if it were "wandering," the cordoning off of what remain, for the colonizer, illegible modes of being and life, presents itself as an endless task—"Domination over semi-barbarous nomadic tribes, such as those around us, can never be so complete that a civilized, sedentary population could settle nearby without any fear or precaution"—and this endlessness extends to the imperative to install, in Algeria, and Africa, the "social body" as a controlling form.[93] "The truth is that there do not yet exist in Africa what Europeans call a society [*un société*]. The men are there, but not the social body [*le corps social*]" (160/105), Tocqueville underlines. The force of Tocqueville's language turns on the word "yet," *encore—il n'existe pas encore*—which promises the institution of the social, in the settler colony, within the terms for "society" given in European textual formulations—property, legality, the person—even as this is permanently impossible, demanding further colonization.

With the institution of "the right of property" (154/101), Algeria—and here, again, Tocqueville speaks, expansively, of "Africa"—is to be colonized and settled by Europeans, in order to do away with "war" and install "society," and yet the settler does not cease to grant to itself exceptions to the rule of legality it desires to install. If Tocqueville does not support the notion that, in colonizing Algeria, "we should fight them," as he writes, "by killing everything we meet," if only because "it is far more destructive than useful," he outlines at the same time: "On the other hand, I have often heard men in France whom

I respect, but with whom I do not agree, find it wrong that we burn harvests, that we empty silos, and finally that we seize unarmed men, women, and children." "These, in my view," he goes on, "are unfortunate necessities, but ones to which any people that wants to wage war on the Arabs is obliged to submit" (112/70), and such "necessities," a never-ending waging of war, are extended, in Tocqueville's letter and notes, to the field of language.

In his 1841 notes Tocqueville outlines his visit to a French colonial school, where he meets a European teacher of Arabic, who had studied with the Orientalist Isaac Antoine Silvestre de Sacy, the teacher of the Semitic philologist Ernest Renan. "I met a young Arabic teacher there, a student of M. de Sacy's, a man who seemed distinguished and very intelligent," he writes.[94] In response to a query about the Qur'an and its translation into French, the teacher explains: "Savary's is elegant and unfaithful. Besides, there really is no good translation, because one would have to translate the five or six principal commentaries that help explain the text. The Koran is, in fact [*à vrai dire*], a collection of daily rules and proclamations [*un recueil d'ordres du jour et de proclamations*] about which we understand nothing [*auxquels on ne comprend rien*], if the events that motivated them are not explained" (80/49).

The promise of "understanding," placed into the mouth of a European instructor of the Arabic language, immediately calls for a gloss, which explains what the Qur'ān is as it calls for further translation: "The Koran is the source of the laws, ideas, mores of this entire Muslim population with whom we are dealing [*Le Coran est la source des lois, des idées, des moeurs de toute cette population musulmane à laquelle nous avons affaire*]; the government's first scientific task clearly should be to have the best possible translation made of both text and commentary" (80/49). "Our" "dealing" with "this entire Muslim population" demands scientific "tasks," as translation is to assist in the French settler-colonizing project. The Qur'ān is to be understood as the "source" to which "the rules of their civil law [*les règles de leur droit civil*]" may be "traced," and through this framing Tocqueville advances the sense of language and law—and reading—he presumes.[95] I notice that if, in this explication, Tocqueville reformulates the pose of the settler—"Visit to the environs of Algiers, at Couba. Superb road that seems as though it must lead to the provinces of a vast empire, and that one cannot follow more than three leagues without being beheaded. Delicious country. Sicily with the industry of France. Prodigious vegetation, the land dense with vegetation. A promised land, if one didn't have to farm with gun in hand"—this pose is invested in and routed through the epistemic and formal terms of his letter and notes.[96] In this: Language is to be subordinated to its sense, an "idea," to which the matter of language, its lingual materiality, is to point; and the Qur'ān is to be understood as a "legal" text and through this it is to be comprehended in relation to the individuated social sense, which Tocqueville's language presumes. Tocqueville forwards the terms of settler life as he generalizes a lexicon of subjective linguistic existence in relation to the Qur'ān—and the Arabic language—and as he exteriorizes a regulating, colonial-genocidal logic of legality, property, and form.

The sense of language forwarded in Tocqueville's letter, essay, and notes is schematized in John Locke's *Essay Concerning Human Understanding*, where reading is to be understood in relation to sense, because "a Man who reads or hears with attention and understanding," Locke writes, "takes little notice of the Characters, or Sounds, but of the *Ideas*, that are excited in him by them."[97] It "is the sence, and not the sound, that is, and must be the Principle or common Notion" (I.iii.18), and it is in relation to this imperative that Locke thinks about language as a practice of naming in relation to the sensory apprehension of "things," as things become objects for "us." "Hence it is," he also states, "that we may often observe, that when any one sees a new Thing of a kind that he knows not, he presently asks what it is, meaning by that Enquiry, nothing but the Name" (II.xxxii.7).

Locke's desire is to ask "what it is" when one "sees" "a new Thing of a kind that he knows not," and yet this procedure is not universal but particular—it is the epistemic and social practice, which "language" is, when one is that sort of being "such as have been bred up in the Learning taught in this part of the World" (II.xxxi.6), a being that Locke recognizes—as if he were Aquinas—to be "any one" (II.xxxii.7). There is an absolute generalization: In this reflection on language what is in play is "every Man's Mouth," where "*Words,*" "*in every Man's Mouth, stand for the* Ideas *he has*, and which he would express by them" (III.ii.3). This encompasses "all Languages whatsoever" (III.ix.16), even as Locke observes that there are differences in relation to "customs and manner of Life" (III.v.8), which give place to a material inidenticality of words in relation to the "*Idea*," for which each is to "stand": "Nay, if we will look a little more nearly into this matter, and exactly compare different Languages, we shall find, that though they have Words, which in Translations and Dictionaries, are supposed to answer one another; yet there is scarce one of ten, amongst the names of complex *Ideas*, especially of mixed Modes, that stands for the same precise *Idea*, which the Word does that in Dictionaries it is rendred by" (III.v.8). Despite these differences—and Locke's reading extends from "the beginning of Language" (III.vi.45) and "the Writings of Men, who have lived in remote Ages, and different Countries" (III.ix.10)—language is to have a single function, "conveying the sense and intention of the Speaker, without any manner of doubt and uncertainty, to the Hearer" (III.ix.22). Language is a sort of "use" that subordinates "Sounds" to "general Conceptions": "The Use of Language is, by short Sounds to signifie with ease and dispatch general Conceptions" (III.v.7).

Locke's delimitation of "the end of speech in general," what he also calls "the end of Language," "which being to mark, or communicate Men's Thoughts to one another" (II.xxii.5), regulates language in a particular manner. "Sounds," and what appear to Locke as if they were without sense, "empty Sounds, with little or no signification" (III.x.2), are captured in a stabilizing pose; they are "noise":

> To make Words serviceable to the end of Communication, it is necessary, (as has been said) that they excite, in the Hearer, exactly the same *Idea*, they stand for in the Mind of the Speaker. Without this, Men fill one another's Heads with noise and sounds; but convey not thereby their Thoughts, and lay not before one another their *Ideas*, which is the end of Discourse and Language. (III.ix.6)

Among those beings at whom a capacity to "use" language in this way is sent, in a regulating generalization, where language is to become a practice which, through the proper "Postures of his Mind in discoursing" (III.vii.3), gives place to meaning and sense in communication, and where "Speech" is to become "the great Bond that holds Society together, and the common Conduit, whereby the Improvements of Knowledge are conveyed from one Man, and one Generation to another" (III.xi.1), is the "child":

> When Children have, by repeated Sensations, got *Ideas* fixed in their Memories, they begin, by degrees, to learn the use of Signs. And when they have got the skill to apply the Organs of Speech to the framing of articulate Sounds, they begin to make *Use of Words*, to signifie their *Ideas* to others: These verbal Signs they sometimes borrow from others, and sometimes make themselves, as one may observe among the new and unusual Names Children often give to things in their first use of Language. (II.xi.8)

The capacity to be recognized as a "child," a sort of being capable of language, where language entails a faculty for "making use of general signs for universal *Ideas*" (II.xi.10), mediates the terms Locke's *Essay* proliferates, which encompass the "Idiot," the "Brute," the "Beast," and "the whole course of Men in their several Ages, Countries, and Educations" (II.xi.16), which is also to say, a delimited field of living beings, those recognizable as or in relation to "Men," including, but not limited to, "Creatures in the World, that have shapes like ours, but are hairy, and want Language, and Reason" (III.vi.22). Such "Creatures," an illegible and ever-pressing collective, form a constant backdrop to Locke's elaborations. "Beasts," for example, do not have "the power of *Abstracting*," it is not, Locke writes, "in them" (II.xi.10), while "Idiots" and their "faltering" hold out in their indefinability: "How far *Idiots* are concerned in the want or weakness of any, or all of the foregoing Faculties, an exact observation of their several ways of faltering, would no doubt discover" (II.xi.12).

"It is possible to stray from the truth of faith in an infinite number of ways," Aquinas wrote in a passage I cited in *Summa theologiae*, and this infinitude is replaced, in Locke, by the "several ways of faltering" of the hairy, idiotic, brutish beasts to whom he does not cease to refer, all of whom lack "the power of *Abstracting*." In this frame, I wish to underline that Locke's allocation of a "capacity" to be a "child" is, in the acuteness of its formulation, withheld; the framing of the "child" as a being capable of language is cyphered, in Locke's formulations, by the incapacity it presumes and extends at the schismatic collectives against which those formulations are directed. The theorization of language as a practice where "Sounds" are to be subordinated to "sence" advances an attack on all non-European, Black, Indigenous, colonized, and enslaved persons as it reformulates the catachrestic logic of post-twelfth-Christian-century exertions. The passage in 1 Corinthians 14:33 I cited above—"For God is not a God of confusion but of peace [οὐ γάρ ἐστιν ἀκαταστaςίας ὁ θεὸς ἀλλα εἰρήνης/*ou gar estin akatastasias hō theos alla eirēnēs*]"—routes the exteriorizing form of these Lockean sentences; the "confusion" of which Paul writes, where the Greek word "akatastasias," which contains within it the word "stasis," at once a "placing" or "setting," a "standing still," a stability, as well as "faction," "sedition," and "discord," is rendered, in the Vulgate, as "dissensionis," "dissension," in the Lutherbibel as "Unordnung," "disorder," and, in the King James Bible, as "confusion."[98] Paul's address to "noise," in the *Essay* at III.ix.6, rephrases this translation, in the fallout of the textual tradition I've traced, where Locke's sense of what language is advances a philological-terminological counterinsurgency, carried in "Translations and Dictionaries" (III.v.8) and formalized in the *Essay*.

Locke wishes to argue against the "innate" knowledge of "general Maxims," and he does so through his insistence that "but, alas, amongst *Children, Ideots, Savages*, and the grossly *Illiterate*, what general Maxims are to be found? What universal Principles of Knowledge?" (I.ii.27)—and, further, "Such kind of general Propositions, are seldom mentioned in the Huts of *Indians*; much less are they to be found in the thoughts of *Children*, or any Impressions of them on the Minds of *Naturals*" (I.ii.27)—and as he does so, his terms withhold survival, as they institute the social as the decimation of such permanently incapable beings: "*Children, Ideots, Savages*, and the grossly *Illiterate*," "*Indians*" and "*Naturals*," as well as "the heathen World, i.e. the greatest part of mankind" (I.iv.15), Locke writes.[99] A distribution of pedagogical capacity—"When Children have, by repeated Sensations, got *Ideas* fixed in their Memories, they begin, by degrees, to learn the use of Signs" (II.xi.8)—exacts the obliteration of those exteriorized from an ability "to learn the use of Signs."

In face of collectives in social indeterminacy, by which he takes himself, like Tocqueville and Aquinas, to be surrounded and besieged, Locke asserts, as a form for regulative capture, a sort of being that "turns inwards upon itself" and reflects upon its "Mind," where this being becomes "the Object of its own Contemplation":

> And hence we see the Reason, why 'tis pretty late, before most Children get *Ideas* of the Operations of their own Minds; and some have not any very clear, or perfect *Ideas* of the greater part of them all their Lives. Because, though they pass there continually; yet like floating Visions, they make not deep Impressions enough, to leave in the Mind clear distinct lasting *Ideas*, till the Understanding turns inwards upon itself, *reflects* upon its own *Operations*, and makes them the Object of its own Contemplation.[100]

These pages advance a privilege of "consciousness," which, Étienne Balibar has written, "renders me the owner of myself by means of my thoughts," what Balibar also calls "the discovery of the self's inalienability" in its relation to "the proper and property," a discovery—and what Balibar also calls an "invention"—which is not an explication of what is but instead forwards "a postulate," "if not," he also writes, "an injunction."[101] These Lockean terms have been interpreted by C. B. Macpherson as making linguistically manifest a "political theory" of "possessive individualism," and Brenna Bhandar has compellingly read Locke through Balibar and Macpherson to underline a settler colonial logic of property as a social and epistemic logic of appropriation: "The *power of appropriation*," she writes, "is the point of origin of the Lockean subject."[102] Thinking with and learning from Bhandar and Balibar, I notice that what is given to us in Locke's *Essay* is what we might understand—as I outlined in the introduction to this book—as primitive accumulation in the field of language, where, in relation to "language," "thinking consists in being conscious that one thinks," and where thinking, in this manner, is sent out at the world in a propertied, and at once divided and asymmetric generalization of social form.[103] In "consciousness," where "Men" "reflect on their own Minds" (I.iii.23), self-reflection provides the occasion for the self's being itself. Locke's analogy is the "atom," which is itself insofar as, "considered in any instant of its Existence, it is, in that instant, the same with itself" (II.xxvii.3). This sameness is provided, for the "Person," through its "consciousness": The "Person,"

Locke explains, "is a thinking intelligent Being, that has reason and reflection, and can consider itself as it self, the same thinking thing in different times and places; which it does only by that consciousness, which is inseparable from thinking, and as it seems to me essential to it: it being impossible for anyone to perceive, without perceiving that he does perceive" (II.xxvii.9). This perception that one is perceiving gives to the "Person" its consciousness, and, as Balibar underlines, the intercontamination, of "own" and "self": "This may shew us wherein *personal Identity* consists, not in Identity of Substance, but, as I have said, in the Identity of *consciousness*" (II.xxvii.19), where the first-person singular pronoun, "I," individuates the self through its reflection on itself, where this pronoun "is easily here supposed to stand also for the same Person" (II.xxvii.20). "I," in "standing for" "the same Person" takes the place of "Substance" and becomes a locus for consciousness, what Locke understands to be a manner of self-ownership: "That with which the *consciousness* of this present thinking can join it self, makes the same *Person*, and is one *self* with it, and with nothing else; and so attributes to it *self*, and *owns* all the Actions of that thing as its own, as far as that consciousness reaches, and no further; as every one who reflects will perceive" (II.xxvii.17).

Consciousness, in its relation to the "*Person*," founds law: "In this *personal Identity* is founded all the Right and Justice of reward and punishment; Happiness and Misery, being that, for which every one is concerned for *himself*, not mattering what becomes of any Substance, not joined to, or affected with that consciousness" (II.xxvii.18). This "foundation" is pressed out as the world is coerced to become a site for the recognition, "Where-ever," of "the same *Person*": "Where-ever a Man finds, what he calls *himself*, there I think another may say is the same *Person*" (II.xxvii.26). The word "*Person*" is "a Forensick Term," Locke continues, "appropriating Actions and their Merit; and so belongs only to intelligent Agents capable of a Law, and Happiness and Misery" (II.xxvii.26).[104] "Politick societies" are to be founded through it—"For though Men uniting into politick Societies, have resigned up to the publick the disposing of all their Force, so that they cannot employ it against any Fellow-Citizen, any farther than the Law of the Country directs: yet they retain still the power of Thinking well or ill; approving or disapproving of the actions of those whom they live amongst, and converse with: And by this approbation and dislike they establish amongst themselves what they will call *Vertue* and *Vice*"—as is "the *Civil* Law," which is to be "made" by "the force of the Commonwealth, engaged to protect the Lives, Liberties, and Possessions, of those who live according to its Laws," and which "has power to take away Life, Liberty, or Goods, from him, who disobeys; which is the punishment of Offences committed against this Law."[105] This sense of law presumes an understanding of language in relation to life, and it is to give place to "Society," of which "Language," as Locke explains, is the "common Tye": "GOD having designed Man for a sociable Creature, made him not only with an inclination, and under a necessity to have fellowship with those of his own kind; but furnished him also with Language, which was to be the great Instrument, and common Tye of Society" (III.i.1).

There is, Robert Cover has written, a constitutive relation between the law and violence—"Legal interpretation takes place in a field of pain and death," he writes—and this "legal interpretation," he underlines, is not to be understood as "a mental activity of a person" but instead "as the violent activity of an organization of people."[106] Through the terms it generalizes law "becomes constitutive of a world," in the manufacture of "paradigms of behavior," made legible in "a lexicon of normative action," as it juridicalizes the social through linguistic practices in legal, theological, and philosophical statement.[107] Settler life is the advance of such a "lexicon," where the objects of Locke's aggression are coerced to be recognized—in the languages of white social existence—as riotous collectives against the social, which call forth settler life's terminological formulations—a "taxonomic carcerality," to drawn upon a term of Zakiyyah Iman Jackson's, which transmutes older formulations.[108]

What Locke calls "the prevailing custom of using Sounds for *Ideas*" (IV.vi.1) is a practice for doing language customary among "those, who, after the ordinary way, measure all others by themselves" (II.x.9), in its relation to the pacification of insurgent life and a stabilization of "World," "the great collective *Idea* of all Bodies whatsoever" (II.xxiv.1), and the institution of a juridical sense of the subject as the self-reflective, self-owning, other-measuring subject of property—the "*Person*."[109]

This institution founds what Locke terms "politick Societies" (in the *Essay*) and the "Body Politick" (in the *Second Treatise of Government*), each of which sends itself inward and outward in a regulating pacification.[110] It is perhaps in this sense that we may understand Locke's statement that "in the beginning all the world was America" (V.49), because, if, for Locke, the world is what can and does become "property"—"As *much Land* as a Man Tills, Plants, Improves, Cultivates, and can use the Product of, so much is his *Property*" (V.32)—the topographical expansiveness of Locke's terms does not recognize an end; it is—as in the logic of Crusade, as Mastnak underlined—"frontierless." And if the institution of legality is a form of social totalization, because "*No Man in Civil Society can be exempted from the Laws of it*" (VII.94), "*Society*" is the advance of a logic of life and death through an excessively divided and mutating installation of borders. Peace grants life—"God, who hath given the World to Men in common, hath also given them reason to make use of it to the best advantage of Life, and convenience" (V.26)—as it extends itself as a pacifying attack upon "confusion": "For Laws not being made for themselves, but to be by their execution the Bonds of the Society, to keep every part of the Body Politick in its due place and function, when that totally ceases, the *Government* visibly *ceases*, and the people becomes a confused Multitude, without Order or Connexion" (XIX.220). It is a practice in the social to do away with "the Quarrelsom and Contentious" (V. 34), where any being that appears as if it were a "noxious Creature" (XVI.182), what Locke also termed "the common Enemy and Pest of Mankind," "is to be treated accordingly" (XIX.230).

In Locke a "Constituted Commonwealth" is what stands "upon its own Basis" (XIII.149), but what "stands" in this way is made articulable only in relation to a particular sense of property and labor: "Though the Earth, and all inferior Creatures be common to all Men, yet every Man has a *Property* in his own *Person*. This nobody has a Right to but himself. The *Labour* of his Body, and the *Work* of his Hands, we may say, are properly his" (V.27). It is an explication that refers itself to "the People of America," who "enjoy'd their own natural freedom" (VIII.105), and who form a conceptual presupposition for the terms Locke presents: "That the *beginning of Politick Society* depends upon the consent of the Individuals, to Joyn into and make one Society; who, when they are thus incorporated, might set up whatever form of Government they thought fit" (VIII.106). The doctrine of "consent" disavows the many forms of nonconsent, which its explication advances. The privilege of the "Individual"—if also of the "*Person*"—is a polemic forwarded through the field of sentences Locke generates. What appeared to Locke as those "vacant places of America" (V.36), "wild woods and uncultivated wast" (V.37), are located in relation to philosophical argument, in the self-reflective subject's explication of itself. In the advance of its pacifying terms, "Men" are called upon to "make *one Body Politick*" (VIII.95), and all beings are coerced to be recognized in relation to the white subject of "Forensick" existence, "those, who, after the ordinary way, measure all others by themselves," as Locke wrote in the *Essay*.[111] In this we are given to read, in Locke, and from Aquinas to Tocqueville, and earlier and later, from Kant to Marx and Heidegger, and with, I also notice in chapter 3, Emmanuel Lévinas, a tradition one may call the tradition of settler life.

"Politics," Stefano Harney and Fred Moten have written, "is an ongoing attack on the common," and I wish to think this attack as the divided exteriorization and asymmetric generalization of a particular sense of form, where "politics" is form, where form is the form of a subject, where the subject is to be a being capable of abstraction, and the reduction of sound to sense, and where the subject is that being to which the social—and language—are to be reduced.[112] And yet language gives, differently, a sharing in sociality, a gathering in inessential form, of which I'll write in chapters 2 and 3. If the tradition of settler life proliferates, in Ferreira da Silva's words, "political subjugation in general," a subjugation to political life—the life of a being that "possesses" language, as Aristotle wrote—I appeal to a wholly other sense of life, a sociality given in anaccumulative, non-self-determined form.[113] If what reading in insurgence—reading without a subordination of sound to sense, or matter to experience—is to occasion is "a contribution to the dissolution of Subjectivity (self-consciousness) and *its* world" (93), it does this as it gives a sense of being or language, indistinct as these are, wholly other than what is demanded in settler life. And if, in this, I give an ear to Marx, to listen to a sort of doing where "I" is a being which, never having been solely what it is, acts or does in a non-selfsame manner, this is to do so in refusal of those terms Marx also advances as they set themselves against the insurgencies of linguistic and social life in globality. I turn now, in chapter 2, to observe a tradition formed though such giving, what I term a tradition of "anontological form," and its inheritance or rephrasing—in poetics, painting, and translation—in chapter 3.

2
Anontological Form

There is a more than one tradition that insurges against settler life, across languages and temporal frames, giving manners of social relation which, in their lack of adherence to the demand for self-determined interiority, occasion a temporal mode that advances the dissolution of the harsh rule of the settler. And yet it is not that there is a collective, "us" or "we," which precedes the giving of form occasioned in the traditions of insurgence, but that collectives are called into being through the social practices of life and gathering, of lingual doing, which their being together occasions. Such doing exceeds the time of the modern state and law, and to consider a particular tradition of insurgence and study its excess in relation to any single language, practice, or form, I turn in this chapter to the tradition of peripatetic philosophical writing in Arabic, and, in chapter 3, to the reiteration and reformulation of this tradition, and the sense of being, language, and the social it passes on, in twentieth- and twenty-first-century Arab and Arabic poetry, painting, and translation. The texts I approach in this chapter formulate a philosophical lexicon in Arabic, and I linger with the sense of language and being these texts give, where a reflection on what is becomes indistinct from language, and where what is is indetermined and non-self-identical—what I've called a tradition of "anontological form." In what follows I linger as much with the material performance of linguistic utterance as I do with the formal terms of argument. As I read, translate, and comment on these texts I notice the sense of language they presume and the sense of being they give, at times in tension with the explication they also privilege. To think the recapitulation of the sense of language and sociality these texts formulate in "later" twentieth- and twenty-first-century poetry, translation, and painting I study, in chapter 3, the passing on of this tradition across languages and materials. There is a wholly other sense of language and being given in these texts and the sort of doing they occasion, which modern reading institutions, in the capitalist logic of property, and the juridical form of the subject, continue to translate into those forms, which do not cease to be propelled at the world in settler life.

I'll want to read, then, quite slowly, and I'll begin with the ninth-century pedagogical text of the philosopher Abū Yusūf Ya'qūb ibn Isḥāq al-Kindī, his "Letter on the Quantity of Aristotle's Books and What Is Required in the Attainment of Philosophy" (رسالة في كمية كتب أرسطوطاليس وما يحتاج إليه في تحصيل الفلسفة/*Risāla fī kammiyyat kutub Arisṭūṭālīs wa mā yaḥtāj ilayhi fī taḥṣīl al-falsafa*). Al-Kindī's letter presents itself as a response to a question, and in it al-Kindī outlines the mode one must assume in the study of the books of the Stagirite, and the devotion, which this study demands. In this letter of pedagogical address the time of philosophy is the time of its "attainment," تحصيل, *taḥṣīl*, and to "attain" philosophy is to do philosophy in a particular manner, it is to perform the practice it demands. And yet there is no subject of or for this practice, but only a being, a "student," مُتعلّم, *muta'allim*, called into being through the terms for linguistic and philosophical explication al-Kindī's letter gives: "Aristotle's books have been placed in a particular order, which the student must follow with devotion [التي يحتاج المتعلّم إلى إستطراقها على الولاء/*allatī yaḥtāj al-muta'allim ilā itstiṭrāqihā 'alā al-walā'*], according to that order and arrangement, so that they maybe become, through their study, a philosopher [ليكون بها فيلسوفا/*li-yakūn bihā faylasūfan*]."[1] The reader of al-Kindī's letter is conjured as an addressee, interpellated in relation to a practice of philosophical form, where this addressee is, therefore, not a subject of philosophical articulation but instead an inessential locus for the taking on of a tradition in a non-individuated practice of study. It is perhaps for this reason that Ibn Abī Uṣaybi'a, in his thirteenth-century biographical dictionary, wrote of al-Kindī that he "imitated" or "followed," إحتذى حذوى, *iḥtadhā ḥadhwa*, Aristotle. We might say that Ibn Abī Uṣaybi'a's entry rephrases the terms for philosophical instruction presupposed in al-Kindī's letter.[2] In its recirculation of the language of Ṣā'īd al-Andalusī's eleventh-century compilation of the sciences, an analogy is generated: al-Kindī is to Aristotle as the addressee of this "Letter on the Quantity of Aristotle's Books and What Is Required in the Attainment of Philosophy" is to al-Kindī.[3] It is not only that al-Kindī imitated Aristotle but that in doing philosophy he followed his example. The biographical rendering reiterates the terms for philosophical and linguistic understanding it both presumes and passes on, and which it gives to us as it explicates the place of al-Kindī among what Ibn Abī Uṣaybi'a, in the title of his dictionary, called the "classes of scholars," طبقات الأطباء, *ṭabaqāt al-aṭibbā'*.

This explication extends to the sociality occasioned in doing philosophy, which Ibn Abī Uṣaybiʿa describes when he explains that al-Kindī "translated many books of philosophy and made clear what was obscure in them, commented on what one might find difficult, and simplified what was complex [وترجم من كتب الفلسفة الكثير وأوضح منها المشكل ولخّص المستصعب وبسّط العويص / *wa tarjama min kutub al-falsafa al-kathīr wa awḍaḥa minhā al-mushkil wa lakhkhaṣa al-mustaṣʿab wa bassaṭa al-ʿawīṣ*]."[4] The terms for the doing of philosophy intersect the formation of a philosophical subject in language, and yet, I've underlined, this formation does not constitute a "subject" but instead gives an occasion in language for the formation of an inessential collective. Just as there is no philosophical subject exterior to the practice of philosophy, so too there is no instruction in philosophy—no field of terms for philosophical training, enunciation, or argument, and no manner of doing in philosophical form—anterior to al-Kindī's epistolary practice. One might say that there are no beings that do philosophy but only a practice that transpires in acts designated through finite verbs, a sending and giving of language, in what Ibn Abī Uṣaybiʿa calls "translation," ترجمة, *tarjama*, "clarification," إيضاح, *iyḍāḥ*, "comment," تلخيص, *talkhīṣ*, and "simplification," تبسيط, *tabsīṭ*. There is, in what al-Kindī terms "attainment," تحصيل, *taḥṣīl*, a sociality that privileges no single being but instead occasions a manner of being-together, and a way of doing language, which, if it does something, it shares and gives, it responds and offers, in scenes of linguistic address. If this practice has made manifest an "Arabic abstract style," the language form of what has been called an "epistemic community," I notice that this is so only insofar as it occasions a kind of doing—a practice in common that forms the occasion for no subject, a way of being that is not determined through a giving of sense, a community secured through no single being, no first or final cause—where language, in the sort of act that philosophy is, gives place to further acts of insubstantial form.[5]

Patience

Al-Kindī frames the question to which he responds in the following way:

> سألتَ—أسعدك الله بمطلوباتك، فصيّرها فيما يقرّب منه، ويباعد عن الجهل به، ويكسب إنارة الحق—أن أنبئك بكتب أرسطوطاليس اليوناني الذي تفلسف فيها، على عدتها ومراتبها، التي لا غنى لمن أراد نيل الفلسفة واقتناءها وتثبيتها، عنها، وأغراضه فيها بالقول المجمل الوجيز.[6]

You have asked me—may God help you in the things you seek, so that he makes them among the things that bring you near to him, keep you

> away from ignorance, and allow you to acquire the illumination of the truth—to tell you, according to their number and their order [*ʿalā ʿiddatihā wa marātibihā*], about the books of Aristotle, the Greek man who did philosophy in them [*alladhī tafalsafa fīhā*], and which are indispensable for those who wish to attain philosophy, and to possess it and persist in it [*li man arāda nayl al-falsafa wa iqtināʾahā wa tathbītahā*]—and to tell you about his purposes in them, with a brief, concise discussion.[7]

In this passage "Aristotle" is spoken of only in relation to "his books," he is "the Greek man who did philosophy in them," and the verb "to do philosophy," تفلسف, *tafalsafafa*, allows us to hear the register of the practice, and the mode, to which the word "philosophy," فلسفة, *falsafa*, points. What one is to do, in this passage, is to "attain," نيل, *nayl*, philosophy through the practice of doing it; the sort of act one does when one does philosophy is not an accessory to the activity that philosophy is, something that may be subtracted out and left behind in the attainment of philosophy, because it is essential to it. One may hear this sense of what philosophy is in the terms emphasized in the penultimate phrase in this passage, where al-Kindī draws upon the words "to possess," إقتناء, *iqtināʾ*, and "to persist in," تثبيت, *tathbīt*. *Iqtināʾ* is "to acquire" or "to possess," and the word contains a material or corporeal dimension. Ibn Manẓūr, the fourteenth-century North African lexicographer, explains under the heading "qanā" in his lexicon لسان العرب (*Lisān al-ʿArab*), that "they acquire them [goats], which is to say, they train them and make them their property [فأقنوهم أي علّموهم وأجعلوا لهم قنية/*fa aqnūhum ayy ʿallimūhum wa ajʿalū lahum qinya*] through that training, by which they subsist when they need it." It is not that "acquiring," in relation to the verb "qanā," gives a sense of property in its modern, capitalist orientations, but instead that acquiring something and taking it as a possession occasions a relation to "training" and "subsistence," mediated in relation to "need"; it is, further, as Ibn Manẓūr cites al-Jawharī's *al-Ṣiḥāḥ*, "when you have acquired something for yourself, not in order to sell it." *Tathbīt*, Ibn Manẓūr also underlines, is like *shabbaṭa*, to cling, cleave, or hold on to, and *tathabbata fī al-amr* is *taʾannā*, to act slowly or deliberately, and it implies *shāwara*, to reflect, and *faḥaṣa*, to examine or scrutinize, which further implies *shiddat al-ṭalab*, an intensity in one's seeking, and *baḥatha*, to seek intently.[8] To "possess" philosophy is, therefore, to persist in a certain sort of behavior, it is to subsist philosophically, in "slow" or "deliberate" acts, and the attainment of philosophy is therefore a practice in form—a certain sort of doing in a nonsubjective manner.

The question about the books of Aristotle, to which al-Kindī replies, calls for an explication of what is prescribed in philosophy—it calls for philosophy's "prescriptions" or "requirements," معيّنات, *muʿayyanāt*—and to do philosophy, in relation to what it requires, is to travel upon a "path," سبيل, *sabīl*.[9] To follow this path is to do so in a particular manner, in a temporal exercise with language, where, as one reads, one comes to gain an understanding of philosophy, "through a long practice of inquiry and training [لطول الدؤوب في البحث والتروّض / *li-ṭūl al-duʾūb fī al-baḥth wa-l-tarawwuḍ*]" (373/287).

This "training," *al-tarawwuḍ*, requires "patience," *al-ṣabr*, in those who are to practice philosophy:

> وما يمدّ لها تبيين ذلك من الصبر على الدؤوب في قطع مسافاتها واستضلاع تحمل ثقيل الموت فيما أقول على بلو غ المطلوب منها الذي لا يقاس إلا بقطعها، وسيما إذا كان لها في كل نظرة من تلك السبل نيل جزء من مطلوباتها، وتحصيل من ربح قنيتها، وعون على تناول ما يليه من مقصودها، وتسهيل لما بقى من مستوعراته، ومذلق للحركة التي هي غرضه. (363–364)

> What the explanation of this fosters in them is the patience to persist in traveling the distances of the paths [*al-ṣabr ʿalā al-duʾūb fī qaṭʿ masāfātihā*] and the skill required to bear the heavy burden of attaining what is sought through those distances, which, as I shall explain, can only be measured by travelling them. This is especially true, since at each instance in which they contemplate these paths [*fī kull naẓra min tilka al-subul*], they obtain part of what they are searching for, attain the benefit derived from possessing it [*wa taḥṣīl min ribḥ qinyatihā*], and are helped to achieve what follows in what they aim at, as the obstacles that remain are eased, and the motion, which is their purpose, becomes well-formed. (281)

Philosophy, in these passages in al-Kindī, is "patience," الصبر, *al-ṣabr*. Yet if philosophy is patience, this is because patience is the practice—the manner of comportment—which philosophy presupposes. In the patience philosophy requires, one is to cross "distances" through which, al-Kindī explains, one must bear burdens. It is not that philosophical training is a burden, something that may be set aside; it is, instead, that this training presumes a temporal practice, as well as a particular philosophical curriculm, through which one must pass in the study—and what al-Kindī termed the "possession"—of philosophy. Philosophy, therefore, is a training in form, and to express this al-Kindī makes use of the word تروّض, *tarawwuḍ*, which carries the meaning of "training," "discipline," and "exercise."[10] And this training leads to a practice, where "motion" becomes ذليق, *dhalīk*, a word that relates to a sharpening, *ḥadda*, or a molding or forming, *sanna—dhalika al-lisān*, Ibn Manẓūr also wrote, "which is to say, *dhariba*, to be sharp or cutting"—and this relates, finally, as Ibn Manẓūr cites al-Kasa'ī, to the terms *faṣiḥ*, "eloquent," and *balīgh*, "well-formed"—each of which points to a giving of clarity in language.[11]

After having outlined the practice of philosophy, al-Kindī relates the ordering of the Aristotelian books:

> بعد علم الرياضات هي أربعة أنواع من الكتب: أما أحد الأربعة فالمنطقيات؛ وأما النوع الثاني فالطبيعيات؛ وأما النوع الثالث ففيما كان مستغنيا عن الطبيعة، قائما بذاته غير محتاج إلى الأجسام—فإنّه يوجد مع الأجسام مواصلا لها بأحد أنواع المواصلة؛ وأما النوع الرابع ففيما لا يحتاج إلى الأجسام ولا يواصلها البتة. (364–365)

> After the knowledge of the propaedutics [*al-riyāḍāt*], Aristotle's books are of four kinds. The first of the four is logic [*al-manṭiqiyyāt*]. The second is physics [*al-ṭabīʿiyyāt*]. The third deals with what has no need for nature, subsists in itself, and does not require bodies, but exists together with bodies and is connected to them in some way. The fourth deals with what does not require bodies and is completely unconnected to them [*wa lā yuwāṣiluhā al-bata*]. (282)

Al-Kindī underlines that the "propaedeutics," الرياضات, *al-rīyāḍāt*, are to have been mastered prior to the study of philosophy: "For if someone lacks knowledge of the propaedeutics, which are arithmetic, geometry, astronomy, and harmonics," he explains, "then even lifelong study will not complete his knowledge of any of these, and he will acquire nothing, through his endeavour concerning them, other than the passing on of utterances [إلا الرواية / *ʾilā al-riwāya*], if he has a good memory" (369–70/284). The word *riwāya*, which I've rendered as "the passing on of utterances," points to the transmission of a corpus of unwritten texts, in particular the corpus of the pre-Islamic poets and the *ḥadīth* of the prophet Muḥammad. *Riwāya* is transmission, which requires memorization, and, in relation to poetry, a knowledge of metrical forms. "It is said that someone transmits poetry to someone else [روّى فلان فلانا شعرا / *rawwā fulān fulānan shiʿran*]," Ibn Manẓūr wrote, "when he recites it to them until they have memorized it, and it has, therefore, been transmitted from them [إذا رواه له حتى حفظه للرواية عنه / *idhā rawāhu lahu ḥattā ḥafiẓahu lil-riwāya ʿanhu*]."[12] *Riwāya* may be understood, following Ibn Manẓūr, in two senses: it is "to bear" or "to carry," *ḥamala*, and, with a corporeal locus, it is *istiẓhār*, "to bear upon one's back," from the word "back," ظهر, *ẓahr*, upon which one bears a burden; and it is also to give this burden—a poetic text, for example—to another. *Riwāya* is a practice of bearing in language, and we may understand al-Kindī's use of this term in an analogous sense: Just as the memorization of poetry in the absence of proper form, and in the absence of a knowledge of poetic meter, would divest it as a language practice, the reading of Aristotle without one's having mastered the propaedeutics al-Kindī has outlined, and the "devotion," الولاء, *al-walā'*, which he has explained the study of the books of Aristotle requires, would be to read as if one were uttering sounds—it would be to read, as it were, without reading. Al-Kindī's explication of the philosophical curriculum, and his relating the order in which one is to study the philosophical books, in its inheritance of a late antique, Greek, and Syriac tradition, relays that curriculum in the language forms through which the Arabic poetic and *ḥadīth* traditions had been and were being articulated—as were the disciplines of jurisprudence, grammar, and rhetoric—and so one might say that the Arabic peripatetic tradition is given through a language practice that relays a particular sense of form and comportment in the temporality of linguistic enunciation in Arabic.[13]

In addition to logic, the three other "kinds," أنواع, *anwā'*, of philosophical book al-Kindī outlines are physics, *al-ṭabī'īyāt*, the first of which consists in "his book which is called 'the lecture on physics' [كتاب الخبر الطبيعي/*kitāb al-khabar al-ṭabī'ī*]," followed by *On the Heavens* [كتاب السماء/*kitāb al-samā'*], *On Generation and Corruption* [كتاب الكون والفساد/*kitāb al-kawn wa al-fasād*], and others; the books on "things that have no need for bodies for their persistence and subsistence, but exist together with bodies," the first of which is *On the Soul* [كتاب النفس/*kitāb al-nafs*]; and, finally, *Metaphysics*: "There is one book on things that have no need for bodies and are unconnected to bodies, and this book is called 'Metaphysics' [ما بعد الطبيعيات/*mā ba'd al-ṭabī'īyāt*]" (368/283).

It is following this explication that al-Kindī points to the ethical books, which are to be studied "after all of these," and he refers, in particular, to *Nicomachean Ethics*, "his long book on ethics [كتابه الكبير في الأخلاق/*kitābuhu al-kabīr fī al-akhlāq*] for his son Nicomachus, which is called 'Nīqūmākhīyā,' and which contains eleven treatises" (369/284), as he alludes, as well, to *Eudemian Ethics* and *Magna Moralia*. It is as if the books on "ethics," الأخلاق, *al-akhlāq*, belong to and exceed the outlining of the Aristotelian corpus and its propeadeutics up through *Metaphysics*. "These books are the fruit of knowing the earlier ones, and they produce a benefit derived from comprehending them," al-Kindī writes, "and they are his books on ethics, by which I mean the character of the soul and its governance [أخلاق النفس وسياستها/*akhlāq al-nafs wa sisyāsatahā*], so that the soul may be founded upon human virture [حتى تقوم على الفضيلة الإنسانية/*ḥattā taqūm 'ala al-faḍīla al-insāniyya*] and become a unity by means of it" (369/284). If the practice of philosophy occasions a particular sort of doing in relation to patience, and if patience is required for the mode of study, which the books of Aristotle demand, this mode is only named in the ethical books, which one will have studied after having completed the late antique curriculum. What is required in the study of the books of Aristotle is something that can only be imparted through a practice of pedagogy, a passing on of a tradition in the form of a response to a question, and a certain doing in language, which presumes the terms it requires. "Human virtue," al-Kindī notes on the same page of this letter, "has no substitute," and neither does the practice of reading the books of Aristotle "according to their number and their order." It is as if one begins to study the Aristotelian books only after having done so, and that this initiation into philosophical study is, itself, a kind of return. One only attains philosophy through a practice of reiteration, and so the reading of the Aristotelian books reduplicates the travel which al-Kindī outlines in the opening passages of his letter. It is, as well, as if one must return in order to read, and that one must do so with patience. And patience may therefore be nothing more than a way of relating to language—a way of doing language—about which one might say, as al-Kindī wrote, that "no good may be obtained without it," لا خيرَ مع عدمها, *lā khayra ma' 'adamihā* (369/284).

Mere Being

Among the treatises al-Kindī edited is an Arabic-language translation and gloss of sections of the fourth through the sixth of the *Enneads* of Plotinus, which were circulated under the title "The Theology of Aristotle" (أثولوجيا أرسطوطاليس / *Uthūlūjīyyā Arisṭūṭālīs*). The opening of the second treatise of the fifth *Ennead* is rendered as follows:

> الواحد المحض هو علة الأشياء كلها، وليس كشيء من الأشياء بل هو بدء الشيء، وليس هو الأشياء بل الأشياء كلها فيه؛ وليس هو في شيء من الأشياء، وذلك أنّ الأشياء كلها إنما انبجست منه وبه ثباتها وقوامها وإليه مرجعها. فإن قال قائل: كيف يمكن أن تكون الأشياء في الواحد المبسوط الذي ليس فيه ثنوية ولا كثرة بجهة من الجهات؟ قلنا: لأنه واحد محض مبسوط ليس فيه شيء من الأشياء. فلما كان واحدا محضا انبجست منه الأشياء كلها، وذلك أنه لمّا لم تكن له هوية انبجست منه الهوية.[14]

> The absolute one is the cause of all things and is not like any of the things. Rather it is the beginning of the thing and is not the things but all things are in it, and it is not in any of the things, for all things gush forth from it [*wa dhālika anna al-ashyā' kullahā innamā inbajasat minhu*], and through it they are sustained and provided support and it is their locus of return. If someone says: How is it possible for the things to be contained in the simple one, in which there is no duality

> or plurality in any respect?, we reply: Because it is one, absolute and simple [*li-anna wāḥid maḥḍ mabsūṭ*], containing none of the things, and since it is absolutely one all things gush forth from it. For while it has no being, being [*al-huwiyya*] gushes forth from it.[15]

The "absolute one," الواحد المحض, *al-wāḥid al-maḥḍ*, is simply and solely one, and it is the "cause," علة, *ʿilla*, of things even as it is not any one of them. Those things of which it is the cause are sustained through and find their support in it: They cannot be without it, while it is without "duality," ثنوية, *thanawiyya*, or "plurality," كثرة, *kathra*, and this is because it is "one, absolute and simple," واحد محض مبسوط, *wāḥid maḥḍ mabsūṭ*. A field of terms is generated: "The absolute one" must be "without intermediary," "different" from what comes "after it," "self-sufficient," and "not mixed" with others. "Before all things," a passage from the fourth treatise of the fifth *Ennead* is rendered and glossed, in a text related to "Theology of Aristotle," titled "Letter on Divine Science" (رسالة في العلم الإلاهي/*Risāla fī al-ʿilm al-ilāhī*), explains that "there must be something prior to all things without an intermediary and different from the things after it [وينبغي أن يكون قبل الأشياء كلها شيء بلا متوسّط، وأن يكون غير الأشياء التي بعده/ *wa yanbaghī an yakūn qabla al-ashyāʾ kullahā shayʾ bilā mutawassiṭ, wa an yakūn ghayr al-ashyāʾ allatī baʿdahu*], and it must be self-sufficient and not mixed with the things [وأن لا يكون مختلطا بالأشياء/*wa an lā yakūn mukhtaliṭan bi-al-ashyāʾ*], and it must be present to the things in some way, and it must be one. It must not be something and then be one, for when a thing is one in this way the one in it is false and is not truly one [وأن لا يكون شيئا ما ثم يكون بعد ذلك واحدا، فإن الشيء إذا كان واحدا على هذا النوع كان الواحد فيه كذبا وليس واحدا حقا/*wa an lā yakūn shayʾan mā thumma yakūn baʿd dhālika wāḥidan, fa inna al-shayʾ idhā kāna wāḥidan ʿalā hādhā al-nawʿ kāna wāḥidan fīhi kadhiban wa laysa wāḥidan ḥaqqan*]."[16] The "absolute one" is itself; it is not "something" and then "one"; and, in its merely being what it is, and in its merely being in this manner, it is distinct from all other beings; it is, as this Arabic text renders Plotinus, "different," غير, *ghayr*, a rendering of the Greek ἕτερον, *heteron*: δεῖ μὲν γάρ τι πρὸ πάντων εἶναι ἁπλοῦν, τοῦτο καὶ πάντων ἕτερον τῶν μετ'αὐτό/*dei men gar to pro pantōn einai haploun, touto kai pantōn heteron tōn met' auto*, "For there must be something simple prior to all things and different from all things after it."[17]

The rendering of the Greek "simple," ἁπλοῦν, *haploun*, as "without an intermediary," بلا متوسّط, *bilā mutawassiṭ*, registers the sense of the simple, which the translator of "Letter on Divine Science" underscores; there is a drawing of a distinction, as the Arabic text explicates the meaning of the word "simple" rather than substitutes an Arabic word for it. The simple is what it is without intermediary, without a second or third term, even as there are things that come after it: "Whatever is after the first is necessarily from the first, though it may come from it either directly, without intermediary, or through the medium of other things which are between it and the first [كل ما كان بعد الأول فهو من الأول إضطرارا، إلا أنه إما أن يكون منه سواءً بلا توسّط، وإما أن يكون منه بتوسّط أشياء آخر هي بينه وبين الأول/*kull mā kāna ba'd al-awwal fa-huwwa min al-awwal iḍṭirāran, illā annahu immā an yakūn minhu sawā'an bi-lā tawassuṭ, wa immā an yakūn minhu bi-tawassuṭ ashyā' ākhar hiyya baynahu wa bayna al-awwal*]"[18] The simple is without intermediary, and its relation to the beings that come after it does not introduce mediation into it. It is in this sense that it is "different," and this difference reiterates the distinction between the simple and the nonsimple, which this passage in "Letter on Divine Science," in its relation to "The Theology of Aristotle," affirms: "The absolute one [*al-wāḥid al-maḥḍ*] is the cause of all things and is not like any of the things [*wa laysa ka-shay' min al-shayā'*]." What is absolutely one is its mere simplicity, and to underscore this, the translator explains of "the first," الأوّل, *al-awwal,* as the force of the verb "it must be," وينبغي أن, *wa yanbaghī an,* is carried forward through the sentences of "Letter on Divine Science," that "it must be above every sensible and intelligible substance [وأن يكون فوق كل جوهر حسي وعقلي/*wa an yakūn fawq kull jawhar ḥissī wa 'aqlī*]," as Plotinus's citation of Plato, at *Republic* 509b9 is rendered into Arabic. The Greek, ὃ δὴ καὶ ἐπέκεινα λέγεται εἶναι οὐσίας/*ho dē kai epekeina legetai einai ousias,* speaks of what is "beyond being," and as the reflection on "the first" is related, in this Arabic passage, to the term *ousia,* which may be rendered as "being" and "substance." Yet it is not that this text is engaged in a reading of the Aristotelian term "substance" (in *Categories*), but that the translator's rendering of these formulations presses the reference to the Platonic passage in Plotinus and relates it the reflection on "the absolute one" and its simplicity. It is a sort of being, this citation underlines, that bears a particular relation to "every sensible and intellectual substance": It is "above" them. The term *fawq* is drawn upon, then, to prepare the reader for the coming sentences, which, in the fallout of the late antique philosophical tradition, outline the relation of "the first" to "composition" and "motion": "For if the first were not simply and truly one, and outside every description and every composition, it would not be first at all [وذلك أنه إن لم يكن الأول مبسوطا واحدا حقا خارجا عن كل صفة وعن كل تركيب، لم يكن أولا ألبتة/*wa dhālika annahu in lam yakun al-awwal mabsūṭan wāḥidan ḥaqqan khārijan 'an kull ṣiffa wa 'an kull tarkīb, lam yakun awwalan al-bata*]."

"The first agent," this text continues, is "stationary and completely motionless," and for this reason "its action" must be "without reflection, motion, or intention, which would incline toward its object [من غير روية ولا حركة ولا

إرادة مائلة إلى المفعول/*min ghayr rawīya wa lā ḥaraka wa lā irāda mā'ila ilā al-maf'ūl*]."[19] Because the first is what gives form, it does not have form; it is without "inclination," ميل, *mayl*, and, in this non-leaning, it is what gives definition: "A thing is defined by its shape and its form [وإنما حد الشيء حيلته وصورته/*wa innamā ḥadd al-shay' ḥīlatuhu wa ṣūratuhu*]," the glossator on these passages in the Arabic Plotinus text underlined, and it is for this reason that the first, which is without resemblance to anything, is "mere being": "The first creator does not resemble any thing, because all things are from it and because it has no particular, inherent shape or form. That is because the first creator is absolutely one, by which I mean that it is mere being without any particular attribute, because all of the attributes break forth from it" (185/2.281). That the first is "mere being," آنية فقط, *āniyya faqaṭ*, and that it has neither limit nor form—"The first creator is unlimited in every respect, and it therefore possesses neither neither shape nor form" (188/2.475)—means that it is outside of multiplicity and number: "The first must not be multiple in any way, for if it were, the multiplicity in it would be connected with another one, prior to it [وينبغي للأول ألا يكون كثيرا من جهة من الجهات، وإلا كانت الكثرة التي فيه معلقة في واحد آخر قبله/*wa yanbaghī lil-awwal alā yakūn kathīran min jihha min al-jihhāt, wa illā kānat al-kathra allatī fīhi mu'allaqa fī wāḥid ākhar qablahu*]" (188/2.475–476). This passage renders the seventeenth paragraph of the seventh treatise of the sixth *Ennead*, "But the first must not be in any way multiple [ἔδει δὲ τὸ πρῶτον μὴ πολὺ μηδαμῶς εἶναι/*edei de to prōton mē polu mēdamōs einai*] for its multiplicity would then depend on another again before it [ἀνήρτητο γὰρ ἄν τὸ πολὺ αὐτοῦ εἰσ ἕτερον αὖ πρὸ αὐτου/*anērtēto gar an to polu autou eis heteron au pro autou*]," and I wish to underline that that, in relation to "multiplicity," the translation of πολὺ, *polu* as كثير, *kathīr*, carries a tradition of thinking the simple in philosophical explication into Arabic, where "the first" must not be implicated in a dependency upon another. These passages share in the designation of a being that would be merely itself, and which would ground being and beings. The activity of translation, a sort of doing that takes place in no single language but only among languages, generates a reflection on being, where what is is merely itself, without plurality and prior to number—where what is is "mere being."

"The First," in a passage in "Theology of Aristotle," which glosses the first treatise of the fifth *Ennead*, is "the maker of number," فاعل العدد, *fā'il al-'adad*—an Arabic formulation which renders ὁ τὸν ἀριθμὸν ποιῶν, *ho ton arithmon poiōn*—and which may not, therefore, be numbered. If one were asked, the Arabic Plotinus explains, who established the relation between "mind," العقل, *al-'aql*, and "soul," النفس, *al-nafs*, one is to reply:

> الذي أبدعه وهو الواحد الحق المحض المبسوط المحيط بحميع الأشياء البسيطة والمركبة الذي هو قبل كل شيء كثير، وهو علة آنية الشيء وكثرته، وهو فاعل العدد. وليس العدد أول الأشياء كما ظنّ أناس، لأن الواحد قبل الإثنين، والإثنين بعد الواحد. وإنما كان الإثنان من الواحد وكانا محدودين وكان الواحد غير محدود لأن الإثنين من الواحد. ونقول إن الإثنين محدود عند الواحد وهما في أنفسهما غير محدودين.[20]
>
> The one who originated it is the true, absolute, and simple one, which encompasses all things, simple and compound, is prior to all plurality, is the cause of the thing's being and its plurality, and is the maker of number. Number is not the first of things, as some think, because one is prior to two and two is after one. Two is from one and is limited. One is not limited, because two is from one. We say that two is limited in relation to one, while in itself it is not limited.[21]

Number occurs with the introduction of limitation, "When two undergoes limitation it becomes number" (113/2.273), and we may consider number in its relation to "the first," in the pages devoted to this question in al-Kindī's treatise "On First Philosophy" (في الفلسفة الأولى/*Fī al-falsafa al-ūlā*), of which an introduction and three chapters of the first part are extant. Al-Kindī begins by offering a definition of philosophy: "Indeed, the human art which is highest in degree and most noble in rank is the art of philosophy, the definition of which is knowledge of the true nature of things [حدها علم الأشياء بحقائقها/*ḥadduhā ʿilm al-ashyāʾ bi-ḥaqāʾiqihā*], insofar as is possible for the human being."[22] The sort of knowledge that philosophy provides is to be given in relation to a particular understanding of what a cause is: "We do not find the truth we are seeking without finding a cause; the cause of the existence and continuance of everything is the true one, because each thing that has being has truth [وعلة وجود كل شيء وثباته الحق، لأن كل ما له إنية له حقيقة/*wa ʿillat wujūd kull shayʾ wa thabātuhu al-ḥaqq, li-anna kull mā lahu inniyya lahu ḥaqīqa*]. The true one exists necessarily, and therefore beings exist" (97/55). The term *iniyya*, formed from the particle *inna*, which introduces a sentence that states a relation between subject and predicate—"it is the case that this is that," for example—can mean at once "thatness" and "being," if only the being of a thing that retains its being from "the true one." Al-Kindī follows and transforms the "Theology of Aristotle," in its thinking of being in relation to "the first" in its absolute simplicity. "The pure true one," al-Kindī writes, "is not one in respect of anything, but merely in itself [بنفسه فقط/*bi-nafsihi faqaṭ*]," and "On First Philosophy," one might therefore say, as it recirculates the word "mere," and as language is borrowed, shares in the formulations of Plotinus's translated and commented-on Arabic texts.[23]

It is in this frame that al-Kindī explicates the sort of inquiry or mode of knowing that is entailed in thinking what is "beyond nature," and such inquiry turns on a definition of what the "eternal," *al-azalī*, is:

> إنّ الأزلي هو الذي لم يجب ليس هو مطلقا؛ فالأزلي لا قبلَ كونيا لهويّته؛ فالأزلي هو لا قوامه من غيره؛ فالأزلي لا علة له، فالأزلي لا موضوع له، ولا محمول، ولا فاعل، ولا سبب، أعني ما من أجله كان، لأن العلل المقدمة ليست غير هذه.[24]

> The eternal [*al-azalī*] is that which must never have been a non-existent being, for the eternal has no temporal "before" in relation to its being [*li-huwiyyatihi*]. The eternal's subsistence [*qiwāmihi*] is not due to another. The eternal has no cause, it has neither subject nor predicate [*lā mauwḍūʿ lahu wa lā maḥmūl*], it has neither agent [*fāʿil*] nor reason [*sabab*], by which I mean that for the sake of which it is, for there are no causes other than the ones which have been previously stated.[25]

Al-Kindī underlines that "the eternal does not perish [لا يفسد/*lā yufsid*], perishing being but the changing of the predicate, not of the primary substratum [تبدل المحمول لا الحامل الأول/*tabaddul al-maḥmūl lā al-ḥāmil al-awwal*]; as for the primary substratum, which is being [الأيس/*al-ays*], it does not change, for the perishing of a perishable object does not involve the being of its being [تأييس أيسيته/*taʾyīs aysiyyatihi*]" (113/67), and insofar as the eternal is what does not perish, and insofar as what does not perish is "being," the eternal is exterior to motion. Motion is a predicate of the body—"Every predicate of the body, whether quantity, place, motion, or time—that which is segmented through motion—and the sum of everything which is predicated of a body in actuality, is also finite, since the body is finite. Therefore, the body of the universe is finite, and so is everything inferior predicated of it" (116/70)—and this predication of motion to the body becomes an argument for the finitude of the "body of the universe." Al-Kindī explicates an understanding of world and things, and time in relation to beings, where the world is temporal and where time is duration, مدة, *mudda*: "Time is the time, by which I mean the duration, of the body of the universe. If time is finite, then the being of this body is finite, since time is not an independent being. Nor is there any body without time, as time is but the number of motion, by which I mean that it is a duration counted by motion [مدة تعُدُّها الحركة/*mudda taʿudduhā al-ḥaraka*]. If there is motion, there is time; and if there were not motion, there would not be time" (117/70). Time is to duration as number is to motion, and the understanding of the being of things is delimited in relation to a distinction drawn between what belongs to time, what has duration, and what does not, and this delimitation is extended to encompass a comprehension of world.

Al-Kindī's reflection on duration leads to a discussion of number, and if to think number is to think a relation between "one" and "two," two is "the first number" (146/98) while one is exterior to quantity. And yet if one cannot participate in quantity, it is an "element" of which multiplicity is composed: "One, therefore, is an element of number and not number at all" (150/102). One is an element of number, but if numbers are composed of elements, one is not a number among them. Two, "though considered an element of three, has an element, which is one; while one, though the element of two has no element" (149/101). It is for this reason that one is not "composite," مُركَّب, *murakkab*: "One is not composite, and it is thus distinguishable from two in being simple; while two is a composite composed of the simple one" (149/101). It is through its marking of these distinctions—where one is an element but not a number, and where number is composed of ones insofar as one is, merely, an element—that these sentences become a preparation for the explication of "the true one," الواحد الحق, *al-wāḥid al-ḥaqq*, and its definition.

فإذن الواحد الحق أزلي؛ ولا يتكثَّر بتة بنوع من الأنواع أبداً؛ ولا يقال: واحد، بالإضافة إلى غيره؛ فإذن هو الذي لا هيولى له ينقسم بها، ولا صورة مؤتلفة من جنس وأنواع؛ فإن الذي هو كذلك يتكثَّر بما ألِف منها؛ ولا هو كمية بتة، ولا له كمية؛ لأن الذي هو كذلك أيضا ينقسم، لأن كل كمية أو ذي كمية يقبل الزيادة والنقص، وما قبل النقص منقسم، والمنقسم متكثَّر بنوع ما. (153)

> Consequently the true one is eternal [*fa-idhan al-wāḥid al-ḥaqq azalī*]; it does not become multiple in any way; it is not said: it is one, in addition to something other than itself. The one is therefore that which has no matter in which it is divisible [*alladī lā hayūlā lahu yanqasim bihā*], nor form composed of genus and species [*wa lā ṣūra muʾtalifa min jins wa anwāʿ*], for that which is so is multiple through that of which it is composed; neither is it at all a quantity nor has it quantity, for that which is so is also divisible [*li-anna alladhī kadhālika ayḍan yanqasim*], since every quantity or quantitative thing is subject to addition and diminution [*al-ziyāda wa-al-naqṣ*], and that which is subject to diminution is divisible [*munqasim*], the divisible is multiple [*mutakaththir*] in a certain way. (104)

The indivisibility of "the true one" sets it outside of a relation to matter, form, quantity, quality, and relation, and, al-Kindī further specifies, it "has neither genus, specific difference, individual, property, common accident, or movement," and it is, therefore, "mere simple unity, which is to say, it has nothing other than unity, while every other one is multiple" (160/112). It is "one in essence, which is never multiple at all, in any way, and which is not divisible in any way, not in relation to its essence and not in relation to something other than it—not time, place, subject, predicate, all, part, substance or accident—and it does not divide through any kind of partitioning or multiplicity" (161/112), al-Kindī also explains. "The true one" is "the cause of unity in unified things [علة الوحدة في الموحدات / *ʿillat al-waḥda fī al-muwaḥḥidāt*]," it is the cause which, through its being, creates unity in the world of things. One may therefore say that just as the true one gives unity to things, causing them to be what they are, so, too, "every multiplicity," insofar as it is something, derives its being from the unity of the true one, because it "comes to be through unity, and if there were no unity the multiple would not have being" (161–162/113). This explication of unity, where unity is the cause of the being of things, shares in the language of another ninth-century Arabic document, a series of texts translated under the title "What Alexander of Aphrodisias Excerpted from Aristotle's Book titled 'Theologia,' Which Means 'On Divinity'" (ما استخرجه الإسكندر الأفرودسي من كتاب أرسطوطاليس المسمّى ثولوجيا ومعناه الكلام في الربوبية/*Mā istakhrajahu al-Iskanadar al-Afrūdisī min kitāb Arisṭūṭālīs al-musammā thūlūjīā wa maʿnāhu al-kalām fī al-rubūbiyya*), which contains translations of and glosses on the *Elements of Theology* of the fifth-century, Greek-language philosopher Proclus. In a discussion of "multiplicity" in relation to the fifth proposition of *Elements of Theology*, to which the heading "that each multiplicity is after the one [إن كل كثرة هي بعد الواحد/*inna kull kathra hiyya baʿd al-wāḥid*]" is appended, the Arabic Proculus underlines that while one and multiplicity are neither "opposites" nor "mutually distinct," they are nonetheless separated, since one is "prior."[26] This joining separation is explicated through a distinction drawn between a thing's being understood as an "essence," ذات, *dhāt*, and as a "cause," علة, *ʿilla*:

فإن قال قائل إنّ الواحد أيضا موجود فيه كثرة، قلنا: أما في الذات فالواحد واحد فقط، ليس فيه شيء من الكثرة البتة؛ وأما في الإنبثاث فالواحد هو كثير أيضا، أقول إنّ الكثرة تنبثّ من الواحد، وإنّ الواحد هو العلة الأولى وإنّ الكثرة هي المعلولة من الواحد. فنرجع فنقول إنّ الواحد أما من جهة الذات فهو واحد فقط لا كثرة، وأما من جهة العلة فهو لا واحد، أقول إنّ الواحد يتكثّر من أجل معلولاته. وكذلك أيضا تكون الكثرة أما في ذاتها فهي كثرة فقط، وأما من أجل علتها الواحدة فهي واحدة. فإن كان هذا على ما ذكرنا فلا محالة أنّ الواحد قد شارك الكثير والكثير شارك الواحد. فنقول الآن إن كان الاشتراك والاجتماع في الأشياء المشتركة والمجتمعة، أعني الواحد والكثرة، من آخر غيرهما، كان ذلك الشيء وهو الجامع لهما قبلهما وأولهما. وإن كان بأعيانهما يشتركان ويجتمعان، فليسا هما متضادين، لأنّ المتضادة لا تسرع إلى شركة بعضها من بعض ولا تجتمع البتة. فإن كان هذا على هذا وكان الواحد والكثرة متخالفين وكانت الكثرة بأنها كثرة لا واحدة وكان الواحد بأنه واحد لا كثرة ولم يكن أحدهما في الآخر البتة، كان كل واحد منهما واحدا وإثنين معا وهذا محال غير ممكن أن يكون. ونقول أيضا إن كان قبلهما شيء آخر وهو

الجامع لهما، فلا محالة إما أن يكون ذلك الشيء واحدا وإما أن يكون لا واحدا؛ فإن كان لا واحدا، فإما أن يكون كثيرا وإما أن يكون لا شيء. فنقول إنه لا يمكن أن يكون الشيء الجامع لهما كثيرا، لئلا يكون الكثير قبل الواحد وذلك محال كما بيّنا آنفا. ولا يمكن أن يكون الشيء الجامع لهما لا شيء لأنّ لا شيء لا يجمع شيئا البتة. فإن كان هذا غير ممكن، فالواحد إذاً هو الجامع للأشياء الكثيرة لأنّه أوّلها وقبلها وهو علة الكثرة وليس فوقه شيء آخر البتة. فقد استبان الآن وصحّ فيما ذكرنا من المقاييس الصحيحة المقنعة أنّ الواحد قبل الأشياء الكثيرة وأنّه العلة الأولى وليس فيه شيء من الكثرة، وأنّ الأشياء كلها معلولة منبثة منه كما بيّنا وأوضحنا. (10–11)

If someone were to say that the one also has within it multiplicity, we would say: In its essence the one is merely one [*ammā fī-al-dhāt fa al-wāḥid wāḥid faqaṭ*], there is absolutely no multiplicity in it at all; but in its pouring forth the one is also many. I say that multiplicity overflows from the one, and that the one is the first cause and multiplicity is what is caused by the one. We may return and say that the one, in relation to its essence [*min jihhat al-dhāt*], is one only, without multiplicity, and that in relation to its being a cause [*min jihhat al-ʿilla*], it is not one. I say that the one becomes multiple on account of what it causes. In the same way, also, multiplicity is, in its essence, mere multiplicity, and on account of its one cause it is one. If things are in the way we have stated, it is certain that the one participates in the multiple and the multiple participates in the one [*al-wāḥid qad shāraka al-kathīr wa al-kathīr shāraka al-wāḥid*]. So we say, now, that if this participation and joining together is in participating and joined-together things, by which I mean the one and the multiple, each as much as the other, then that thing, which is what joins them, is prior to each of them and the first. And if each of these two, in their essences, participates and joins together, then they are not opposites [*mutaḍādayn*], because what is opposite does not hurry to participate with another and does not join together at all. If things were this way, and if the one and the multiple were mutually distinct [*mutakhalifayn*], if the multiple were, merely, multiple, and not one, and if the one were merely one, and not multiple, and neither of the two were in the other at all, then each of the two would be one and two at the same time, and this is a contradiction; it is impossible that this be the case. We say, also, that if there were, prior to the two of them, something else, which joined them together, then it is impossible that that thing would be anything but either one or not one. If it were not one, it would be either multiple or it would be nothing. We say that it is not possible that the thing that joins them be multiple, in order that the

> multiple not be prior to the one, which is impossible, as we have previously explained. And it is not possible that the thing which joins them be nothing, because nothing does not join together anything at all. And if this is not possible, the one, therefore, is what joins the many things [*al-jāmiʿ lil-ashyāʾ al-kathīra*], because it is the first and prior to them [*li-annahu awwaluhā wa qablahā*]. It is the cause of multiplicity and there is no other thing above it at all [*wa laysa fawqahu shayʾ ākhar al-batta*]. It has therefore become clear, now, and it is true, based upon the accurate, persuasive arguments we have mentioned, that the one is prior to the many things, that it is the first cause, that there is absolutely no multiplicity in it, and that all things are caused by and overflow from it [*wa anna al-ashyāʾ kullahā maʿlūla munbaththa minhu*], as we have explained and clarified.

The one and the multiple are related; each is, the Arabic translation of Proclus explains, "in" the other, and it is this manner of being "in" the other, this "joining-together," الإجتماع, *al-ijtimāʿ*, and "participating," الإشتراك, *al-ishtirāk*, that the translator and commentator of this text explicates as they affirm that the "one," in its unity, does not have an essential relation to any other being or thing. And yet the one is what it is only insofar as it is related to a division between "essence" and "cause"—where the one is to be thought in relation to this division, insofar as it is an "essence," ذات, *dhāt*, on one hand, and insofar as it is a "cause," علة, *ʿilla*, on the other—even as this division affirms the unity of the one and its relation to what is more or other than it. The aporetic form of these Proclean affirmations compels sustained attention, a certain reading, where this text is in excess of itself and takes on the form of the overflow of being, which the rendering of Proclus in Arabic places on the side of the understanding of the one insofar as it is a cause. These aporetic linguistic formulations teach us to read the form of that "thing" which, in Proclus, is what "joins" the "one" and the "multiple." And yet this thing, which must be "either one or not one," and which must be neither "multiple" nor "nothing," is, Proclus explains, "the first and prior to them": "It is the cause of multiplicity and there is no other thing above it at all." Proclus's concluding sentences, in this fifth proposition of *Elements of Theology*, demonstrate the tightly argued and still nonselfsame manner of his explications and the beings they describe. "What joins the many things," he writes, is "the first cause," in which there is "no multiplicity," and it is this which causes "all things" just as all things "overflow from it." If this text explicates what "the primary being" (Arabic: الهوية الأولى, *al-huwiyya al-ūlā*/Greek: τὸ πρώτος ὄν, *to prōtos on*), in the seventy-third proposition of the Arabic Proclus translation, is, this sense is extended to a more general understanding of being, where being is "mere being": *huwiyya faqaṭ* (in "What Alexander of Aphrodisias excerpted from Aristotle's book titled 'Theologia'") and *āniyya faqaṭ* (in "Letter on Divine Science"), and where "mere being" is in excess of itself.

Philosophy is a practice that is to give place to "knowledge," علم, *ʿilm*, what al-Kindī terms the "perception of things in their true natures," and this knowledge is one wherein we are to understand that the world of things is given only in its relation to the "the true one" and its emanation of unity: "The emanation [فيض/*fayḍ*] of unity from the true one, the first," al-Kindī explains, "is the coming to be of each sensible object and what attaches to each sensible object," and, further, "the true one causes every one of those objects to exist when it causes them to be through its being."[27] "The cause of coming to be is from the true one, which did not receive unity from another but is one through its essence," al-Kindī also writes, and yet if "the true one" is one through its essence, al-Kindī's language exceeds the terms through which it affirms the distinctions it seems to hold.[28] This excess is given at each moment at which "the first," which is at once "one" and "eternal," is described in terminological formulations. In his philosophical lexicon al-Kindī notes that the "eternal" is "what has never been non-being, and has no need for anything else in its subsistence," and such a being, al-Kindī has underlined, is returned to no cause, and is exterior to the opposition between the numeric and the one, even as it is what gives the being of each and every being and thing.[29] This being is, I've noticed, its overflow of itself—إنبثاث, *inbithāth*, in the Arabic Plotinus translation and commentary, and فيض, *fayḍ* in al-Kindī's "On First Philosophy"—and for this reason it is a being that ceases to be what it is. We might say that it is itself only because it gives itself away, becomes something other, even as it "has never been non-being, and has no need for anything else in its subsistence." The writing of this being undoes the distinctions through which it is written in philosophical discursivity as it initiates and carries on a tradition of thinking about being, where what is does not coincide with itself. These texts partake in a language practice that exceeds historical and philological designation, and which disallocates the subordination of language to those terms in relation to which it remains still illegible.

Demonstration

The form of life we are given to read in al-Kindī is further explicated, in relation to the study of logic in its relation to the philosophical disciplines, in a text of Abū Naṣr al-Fārābī's titled *The Philosophy of Aristotle* (فلسفة أرسطوطاليس/

Falsafat Aristūtālīs), in which al-Fārābī provides a definition of the word الحكمة, *al-ḥikma*:

> وعرّف ما الصناعة التي تحتوي على هذه المواد والموجودات التي فيها يوجد اليقين— وهي المواد التي منها تأتلف القضايا الإضطرارية—وميّزها من التي إنما تشتمل على موجودات لا يمكن فيها اليقين، وهذه الصنائع إنما تنظر أو تستعمل المواد التي تأتلف عنها القضايا الممكنة والوجودية. وخصّ هذه الصناعة باسم الحكمة دون غيرها.[30]

> He [Aristotle] defined what the art is that contains the materials and beings with regard to which certainty exists [*allatī fīhā yūjad al-yaqīn*], which is to say, the materials from which the necessary propositions [*al-qaḍāyā al-iḍṭirāriyya*] are compounded, and distinguished it from the arts that comprise only the beings with regard to which certainty is not possible, and these are the arts that inquire into, or use, the materials from which the possible and existential propositions are compounded. He bestowed the name "philosophy" [*al-ḥikma*] specifically upon this art to the exclusion of others.[31]

A necessary proposition is that sort of assertion which gives place to "certainty," and it is in relation to such propositions that al-Fārābī delimits the domain he calls "philosophy," *al-ḥikma*. The term "certainty," اليقين, *al-yaqīn*, points to the Aristotelian logical books, and to *Posterior Analytics*, in particular, as it had been studied in the Arabic tradition.[32] Al-Fārābī's *The Book of Expressions Used in Logic* (كتاب الألفاظ المستعملة في المنطق/*Kitāb al-alfāẓ al-mustaʿmala fī al-manṭiq*), presents itself as an introduction to the study of logic, and I turn to this text here. "This book," he writes, "has brought forth statements through which one's setting out in the study of the art of logic is made easy. It is necessary, therefore, now, to commence the study of logic, and we begin with the book which encompasses the first part of this art, which is *Categories*."[33] It was "Aristotle alone" who established this art as a pedagogical form—"As for the one who established this art [المنشئ لهذه الصناعة/*al-munshiʾ li-hādhihi al-ṣināʿa*], set it down in a book, and created a path to it, by which whoever intends it [من يقصد إليها/*man yaqṣud ilayhā*] is able to acquire it and learn it, through speech, this was Aristotle alone" (108–109)—and this art, he also explains, is a "tool": "As for its relation to other arts, it is possible that some consider logic to be a part of the art of philosophy, for what this art, also, encompasses is one of the existing things," but, he continues, "even if these were one of the existing things, this art would not study them or comprehend them insofar as they were one of the existing things, insofar as they were beings, but insofar as they were a tool through which we arrive at a knowledge of beings [على أنّها آلة نتوصّل بها إلى معرفة الموجودات / *ʿalā annahā āla natawaṣṣul bihā ilā maʿrifat al-mawjūdāt*]" (107). In order to clarify what he intends in defining logic as a "tool," آلة, *āla*, as it had been understood in the late antique tradition, al-Fārābī likens logic to grammar, and he suggests that logic is concerned with "beings" in the manner in which grammar is concerned with "utterances": "The art of grammar encompasses the study of utterances [الألفاظ / *al-alfāẓ*], and utterances are one of the beings, which are able to be intellected, and yet the art of grammar does not consider them insofar as they are one of the intelligible things, for if it did then the art of grammar, and, in general, the science of language [وبالجملة صناعة علم اللغة / *wa bil-jumla ṣināʿat ʿilm al-lugha*], would encompass intelligible meanings, and this is not the case" (107). He continues, clarifying the manner in which logic is a tool, and drawing out the analogy between grammar and logic: "Even if they were one of beings, which were able to be intellected, the art of grammar would not comprehend utterances that signify insofar as they were intelligible meanings but insofar as they signified intelligible meanings, so we consider them insofar as they are exterior to the intelligibles entirely, for we do not study them in this manner. In the same way: If what the art of logic encompassed were one of the beings, we would not study them insofar as they were one of the beings but insofar as they were a tool through which we arrive at knowledge of beings, so we consider them as if they were something other, exterior to beings, and as if they were a tool for our acquiring knowledge of beings" (107–108). Insofar as logic does not speak of beings but is instead a tool through which one acquires knowledge of them, it is not a "part" of philosophy but instead a "self-subsistent" art: "Therefore it is not necessary that this art be considered a part of the art of philosophy, since it is an art that is self-subsistent [*qāʾima bi-nafsihā*; قائمة بنفسها] and neither part of another art nor a tool and a part of another art together" (108).

Al-Fārābī's discuussion of logic as a tool is addressed to "whoever intends it," من يقصد إليها, *man yaqṣud ilayhā*, and this "intending" is given in an orientation through which one will have related oneself to logic and understood it to be a particular sort of practice. Logic, then, is a sort of doing, which calls into being, through its explication, the sort of being, which intends in the manner in which logic, in its relation to the philosophical disciplines, requires. Intention, then, presumes and gives place to a way of being and a form of life, generated through the logical books and the practice of study al-Fārābī outlines. It is a way of being made manifest in and carried by "us," the linguistic collective al-Fārābī's language generates in the several verbs conjugated in the first person plural, in the passages in *Book of Expressions* I've translated—as, for example, "If what the art of logic encompassed were one of the beings, we would not study them insofar as they were one of the beings

[فليست ننظر فيها على أنّها أحد الموجودات/*fa laysat nanẓur fīhā ʿalā annahā aḥad al-mawjūdāt*] but insofar as they were a tool through which we arrive at knowledge of beings." Logic, as we are given to understand it in these passages, is a "self-subsistent" tool; it precedes philosophy and yet only as a preparation for it and as a manner for doing it. It is in this frame that al-Fārābī notes: "As for the rank of this art, in its relation to all of the others, it precedes all of the arts, which are included within the art of philosophy [فإنّها تتقدّم جميع الصنائع التي تشتمل عليها صناعة الفلسفة/*fa-innahā tataqaddam jamīʿ al-ṣanāʾiʿ allatī tashtamil ʿalayhā ṣināʿat al-falsafa*] and, taken together, all of the other arts, which are of the sort that are to be taught orally" (108).

Al-Fārābī draws a distinction between two aspects of instruction: "Instruction may take place through listening and it may take place through imitation [والتعليم قد يكون بسماع وقد يكون بإحتذاء/*wa al-taʿlīm qad yakūn bi-samāʿ wa qad yakūn bi-iḥtidhāʾ*]" (86). He goes on to explain that "what is through listening is that wherein the teacher uses speech, and this is what Aristotle calls oral instruction [التعليم المسموع/*al-taʿlīm al-masmūʿ*]. And what is through imitation is what takes place where it is possible for the student to see the teacher in a particular state, in the performance of an act or in something else, and they imitate them in that thing, or they do what resembles what they have done [أو يفعل مثل فعله/*aw yafʿal mithla fiʿlihi*], and the student, thereby, gains a capacity to do that thing or that act" (86). Among the "matters" that it is possible to teach using speech, there are those which may also be taught by imitation, and those which may be taught "by speech only, and not in any other way" (86), and among the latter, al-Fārābī wrote, is logic. He explicates the teaching of those matters, which must be taught by speech only, as follows:

> وكل شيء شأنه أن يُتعلّم بقول، فإنّه يلزم ضرورة أن يكون للمتعلّم في ذلك الشيء أحوال ثلاثة. أحدها أن يتصوّر ذلك الشيء ويفهم معنى ما سمعه من المعلّم، وهو المعنى الذي قصده المعلّم بالقول. والثاني أن يقع له التصديق بوجود ما تصوّره أو فهمه عن لفظ المعلّم. والثالث حفظ ما قد تصوّره ووقع له التصديق به. وهذه الثلاثة هي التي لا بدّ منها في كل شيء يُتعلّم بقول. والمعلّم فأنما ينبغي أن ينحو أبدا نحو أن يحصّل للمتعلّم هذه الثلاثة بالجهات التي يكون تحصيلها أسهل إمكانا، وأن يكون الذي يحصل على أجود ما يمكن أن يحصل. (86–87)

> For each thing which is, by its nature, to be taught using speech, the student of that thing must possess, necessarily, three states. The first of these is that the student conceptualize [*yataṣawwar*] that thing and understand the meaning of what they have heard from their teacher, and this is the meaning, which the teacher intends through their speech. The second is that they verify [*yaqʿ lahu al-taṣdīq*] the existence of what they have conceptualized or understood from the words

> of their teacher. The third is that they memorize [*ḥifẓ*] what they have conceptualized and verified. These three are what are required in each thing that is learned through speech. As for the teacher, they must lead the student on the path which causes them to attain [*taḥṣīl*] these three things, by means of those ways which, through them, the student's attainment of these things is the easiest possible, so that the student attains what they attain with the greatest possible mastery.

Logic is among those arts that are to be taught through speech, and the mode of teaching, which this requires, entails three states—"conceptualization," "verification," and, finally, "memorization." Each of these is "required," and it is through this requirement, and its being carried out in teaching, that the student is able to attain the art, which it is their intention to attain. In his discussion of teaching al-Fārābī calls attention to words in relation to pedagogical practice: "When a thing has two names and one of them is better understood by the student and the other is more hidden from them [فكان احدهما أعرف عند المتعلّم والآخر أخفى/*fa kāna aḥadhumā aʿraf ʿind al-mutaʿallim wa al-ākhar akhfā*], so that they do not understand that thing by its more hidden name, the better understood is substituted in place of the hidden" (89). In the same way, an expression consisting of multiple words, al-Fārābī also explains, should take the place of a single word, when the single word does not make the understanding of the thing easy, "and the substitution of a single word by an expression consisting in multiple words is called the 'explication' of the name and the 'decomposition' of the name [يسمّى شرح الاسم وتحليل الاسم/*yusammā sharḥ al-ism wa taḥlīl al-ism*] in the speech of the one who is explicating it" (89).

In the teaching of logic there is an address in language, and this becomes an occasion for a temporal performance, which implies the time, and the inessential being together, of the beings which partake in it—the "student" and the "teacher." In this performance, words call for and give place to others: to an "expression," which consists in multiple words, in "explication," and in a breaking down and a dissolution, a "decomposition," تحليل, *taḥlīl*, of a single word into others, where a word is substituted by its definition: "The substitution of a definition for the name of the thing is called the 'decomposition' of the name in the definition [وإبدال الحدّ مكان اسم الشيء يسمّى تحليل الاسم إلى الحدّ/*wa ibdāl al-ḥadd makān ism al-shayʾ yusammā taḥlīl al-ism ilā al-ḥadd*]" (89). With this framing of instruction, and with this description of the sort of acts in which the performance of instruction in logic consists, the language practice of pedagogy gives a sociality of form: Just as a single word points to those other words that are to be called upon to explicate and decompose it, and just as those words are capable of extending without end—"And in this way," al-Fārābī commented, "the definitions of the parts of the definition of a thing might take the place of the definition of the thing" (89)—and just as each word, in pedagogy, is itself insofar as it relates to others, so too may the being who teaches or studies logic be said to be itself insofar as it belongs to the inessential, non-self-identical collective constituted through the language practice al-Fārābī named "instruction."[34]

Al-Fārābī underlines that it is through logic that the "mind," الذهن, *al-dhihn*, is led, "to know that a thing is this or not that [إلى أنّ الشيء هو كذا أو ليس هو كذا / *ilā anna al-shay' huwwa kadhā aw laysa huwwa kadhā*]," as he wrote in *Book of Expressions*.[35] Among the modes through which the mind may be led al-Fārābī names five—the poetic, the rhetorical, the sophistical, the dialectical, and, finally, what leads it "to what is true and certain [لما هو حق يقين / *li-mā huwwa haqq yaqīn*]" (96). The understanding of certainty gives orientation to pedagogy in logic—it is "demonstration," برهان, *al-burhān*, which "urges the mind to be led to what is true and certain," al-Fārābī noted, and "The most important intention of the art of logic is to understand demonstration [والمقصود الأعظم من صناعة المنطق هو الوقوف على البراهين / *wa al-maqṣūd al-a'ẓam min ṣinā'at al-man ṭiq huwwa al-wuqūf 'alā al-barāhīn*]" (99)—and demonstration, as with each of the terms in al-Fārābī, is to be understood in relation to a sociality of philosophical form, in a practice or way of life in non-self-oriented comportment.

The discussion of demonstration in al-Fārābī's logical texts points to *Posterior Analytics*: "By demonstration I mean," Aristotle wrote, "a syllogism which produces knowledge; by knowledge I mean what enables us, through our possessing it, to know [ἀπόδειξιν δὲ λέγω συλλογισμὸν ἐπιστημονικόν. ἐπιστημονικὸν δὲ λέγω καθ' ὃν τῷ ἔχειν αὐτὸν ἐπιστάμεφα / *apodeixin de legō sullogismon epistēmonikon. epistēmonikon de legō kath' hon tō exein auton epistametha*]" (71b17–19).[36] The tenth-century Arabic translation of *Posterior Analytics*, which was rendered by Abū Bishr Mattā ibn Yūnus, from the Syriac translation of Isḥāq ibn Ḥunayn, as أنولوطيقا الأواخر, *Anūlūṭīqā al-awākhir*, "The Later Analytics," was also rendered under the title كتاب البرهان, *Kitāb al-burhān*, "The Book of Demonstration," and it translates this passage as follows: "I mean, by demonstration, a syllogism that leads to certainty; and I mean by 'what leads to certainty,' that which we know through what exists in us [وأعني بالبرهان القياس المؤتلف اليقيني وأعني بالمؤتلف اليقيني الذي نعلمه بما هو موجود لنا / *wa a'nī bi-al-burhān al-qiyās al-mu'talaf al-yaqīnī; wa a'nī bi-al-mu'talaf al-yaqīnī alladhī na'lamuhu bi-mā huwwa mawjūd lanā*]."[37] The discussion of logic and instruction in al-Fārābī turns on these pages of *Posterior Analytics* as they were translated into Arabic, in the rendering of "demonstration" as "a syllogism that leads to certainty." It is through this translation that logic, in Arabic, is linked to a particular practice of study and knowing, a linkage Aristotle underlines in the first sentence in *Posterior Analytics*: "All teaching and learning that take place in thought proceeds from a knowledge that already exists [كل تعليم وكل تعلّم ذهني إنما يكون من معرفة متقدمة الوجود/*kull taʿlīm wa kull taʿallum dhihnī innamā yakūn min maʿrifa mutaqaddima al-wujūd*]" (71a1). This practice of knowing turns on a knowledge that already is and which one already possesses; there is a having of knowledge that exceeds the perspective of a subject, at once the student of logic and the teacher who is to impart a knowledge of it. There is no subject of logical or philosophical knowledge in the texts of Arabic propeadeutics which precedes the manner of doing practiced in them; instead, there is a sociality: an address in pedagogical form.[38] And yet if the subject of philosophy is no one, it is, at the same time, anyone: It is whoever is able to enter into a pedagogical relation in the Arabic language; and it is whatever being "intends," in the sense in which al-Fārābī uses this term. We might therefore say that philosophy is that practice which takes place in what al-Fārābī also names, in its irreducibility to logic—and in its sharing in the mode of comportment logic also demands—*ḥikma*.[39]

The sort of knowing, which occurs in the way of life that philosophy occasions, is, in the sense in which al-Fārābī speaks of it, discursive, because it takes place in thought—and the Arabic word *dhihnī*, in the translation of *Posterior Analytics* I've cited here, renders the Greek διανοητικὴ, *dianoētikē*, from διάνοια, *dianoia*, a mode of thought or intellection, which encompasses, at once, what is "practical," "productive," and "theoretical," as Aristotle elaborates these terms in *Book Epsilon* of *Metaphysics* (1025b26). In the translation of *Metaphysics* used by the twelfth-century philosopher Ibn Rushd in his commentary on that text, *dianoia* is rendered as فكرة, *fikra*, "thought." The passage that opens *Book Epsilon* is translated in this way: "It is clear that the principles and causes of beings are what is sought, in their essence, as beings [إنّه بين أنّ أوائل الهويات وعللها مطلوبة على كنهها هويات/*innahu bayyin anna awāʾil al-huwiyyāt wa ʿilalaha maṭlūba ʿalā kunhihā huwiyyāt*]." The translation continues: "And in general all knowledge obtained in thought, or which treats something in thought, has, as what it seeks, causes and principles [وبقول كلي فكل علم فكري أو تناول شيء فكري فله علل وأوائل/*wa bi-qawl kullī fa kull ʿilm fikrī aw tanāwul shayʾ fikrī fa-lahu ʿillal wa awāʾil*]" (1025b3–7), where "all knowledge obtained in thought," كل علم فكري, renders πᾶσα ἐπιστήμη διανοητικὴ, and where "or which treats something in thought," أو تناول شيء فكري, renders ἢ μετέχουσά τι διανοίας.[40] This rendering of *dianoia*, shares in and points to the sociality, which is presumed in philosophical life in the tradition in which al-Fārābī participates. "Thought," as it is rendered in the Arabic text of *Metaphysics* used by Ibn Rushd, is a practice of sociality, a mode where there is no "I," a substance that is itself, but only an inessential gathering of beings. To know is to do so through a partaking in this sociality, even as such knowing presumes an anteriority of forms and a distinction between what is more known and what less, and even as this distinction is given through a "requirement," which, itself, presumes the terms of the practice of demonstration, which that requirement explains: "For if the meaning of what it is to know is as we have posited," Abū Mishr Mattā ibn Yūnus's translation of *Posterior Analytics* continues, "it is required, of necessity, that demonstrative knowledge [العلم البرهاني / *al-ʿilm al-burhānī*] proceed from propositions that are true and premises that are immediate, and which are more known than the conclusion, prior to it, and are its cause."[41] It is this field of terms, which distinguishes and relates syllogism to and from demonstration—in the reading al-Fārābī offers in *Philosophy of Aristotle* and *Book of Expressions*, and in the pedagogical framing of logic he outlines—and which distinguishes knowledge that is certain from knowledge that is not. "Neverthless the knowing that is produced from a syllogism may be possible without these conditions, but demonstration is not, for it would not give place to certainty [على أنّ الذي قد مرّ من القياس قد يكون من غير هذه أيضا، وأمّا البرهان فلا يكون، لأنّه لن يكون محصّلا لليقين / *ʿalā annā alladhī qad marra min al-qiyās qad yakūn min ghayr hādhihi ayḍan, wa ammā al-burhān fa-lā yakūn, li-annahu lan yakūn muḥaṣillan lil-yaqīn*]."[42]

The sociality of demonstrative thought may be considered in *Kitāb al-burhān*, where Aristotle underlines the indemonstrability of premises:

> أما أن تكون القضايا صادقة فقد يلزم من قِبل أنّه لا سبيل إلى أن يعلم ما ليس بموجود، مثل ذلك أنّ القطر مشارك للضلع. وأمّا أنّ البرهان من أوائل غير مبرهنة، فذلك أنّه لم يكن يوجد السبيل إلى أن تعلم إذا لم يكن عليها برهان. وذلك أنّ معنى أن تعلم الأشياء التي عليها برهان لا بطريق العرض، إنّما هو أن تقتني البرهان عليها. (71b26–30)

> That the premises must be true is required, because there is no path to knowing what cannot exist—for example that the diagonal of a square is commensurate with its sides. Demonstration proceeds from indemonstrable premises [*wa ammā al-burhān min awāʾil ghayr mubarhana*], and that is because otherwise there would not be a way to acquire knowledge of them if it was not based upon demonstration. That is because the meaning of what it is to have knowledge of something through demonstration is not to know it by accident, but rather it is to acquire a knowledge of it through demonstration.

There is a necessity to proceed, in knowledge that is certain, by way of premises that are indemonstrable; there is an exteriority of the premise, and one's knowledge of it, from demonstration, because if that premise were to require demonstration, then demonstration would be without ground and the knowledge it generates would not be certain. Demonstration cannot rely upon itself; it must rely upon another, and the other upon which it must rely is an indemonstrable premise. Anterior to demonstration is an indemonstrability, which places a stop at the infinite regress, which the demand for premises compels: "That an argument is from premises means that it is from appropriate principles," Aristotle wrote in *Kitāb al-burhān*. "That is, what I mean by a primary premise and a principle is the same thing. And the principle of demonstration is a premise without intermediary, and what is without intermediary is that in relation to which there is no other premise prior to it [ومبدأ البرهان هو مقدّمة غير ذات وسط، وغير ذات وسط هي التي ليس توجد أخرى أقدم منها / *wa mabda' al-burhān huwwa muqaddima ghayr dhāt wasaṭ, wa ghayr dhāt wasaṭ hiyya allatī laysa tūjad ukhrā aqdam minhā*] (72a6–8).[43] There is to have been a premise anterior to all of the others, a premise that is not demonstrable and forms the basis for demonstrative knowledge. Demonstrative knowledge is knowledge based on premises, and yet if it is not able to give an account of the principles on which it is based, this is because it speaks to us of a mode of knowing, a disposition or comportment, which does not seek principles or grounds. Because demonstrative knowledge requires premises, it speaks to us of a form of knowledge that is, in order to be what it is, without principle: The principle that has no principle other than itself, the premise that has no demonstration, which would give reasons for it, is a principle that would stop relying on or responding to the demand for principles, which it seems, nevertheless, to authorize. "As for us," Aristotle also explained, "we say that not all knowledge is by demonstration [وأما نحن فنقول إنّ ليس كل علم فهو برهانا/*wa ammā naḥnu fa naqūl inna laysa kull 'ilm fa huwwa burhānan*], and that knowledge, which is immediate, is not demonstrative" (72b19–20). There is a disaffirmation of the demand for principles, a grounding of philosophy in a sense of what a principle is, which has a ground that is a principle which, itself, has none; the principle to which one must turn in philosophical explication to ground demonstrative knowledge, speaks to us of a practice that, because it can do nothing but appeal to a ground—سبب, *sabbab*, "cause," مبدأ, *mabda'*, "principle," or مقدّمة, *muqaddima*, "premise"—disorganizes the form it nevertheless generates.

That al-Fārābī privileges certainty, in his discussion of *ḥikma* in *Philosophy of Aristotle*, recalls this ambiguating and indefinitional sense of what a principle is; the emphasis on and grounding of philosophical speech in certainty points to the practices I've drawn out here—in relation to pedagogy in logic, in relation to the sort of thought that constitutes philosophy, and in relation to the explication of what a premise or principle in demonstration is—in order to relate them to the sort of doing in which one is engaged when one does philosophy, what al-Fārābī called "the art that contains the materials and beings with regard to which certainty exists."[44] If this art must encompass logic in its relation to philosophy, this is perhaps only because the mode of being presumed in logic—and in *Posterior Analytics*—becomes generalized in it. *Ḥikma*, if it is something, is a practice occasioned in philosophical acts and in relation, as al-Fārābī underlines, to the categorization of the "theoretical arts": "Then he made known the relative ranks of the species of the theoretical arts," al-Fārābī writes. "And he explained," he continues to write of Aristotle, "that the one that was shown to be emphatically prior to the rest ought to be the most deserving of the name 'wisdom' [*al-ḥikma*; الحكمة] and the most deserving of the name 'knowledge'" (77/86). If *ḥikma* is the one among these arts that is the most prior and most deserving, we might also notice that logic precedes it, in the manner in which philosophical reflection requires and explains. There is, al-Fārābī has shown, a philosophical manner, a form of life—سيرة ما, *sīratun mā*—which gives place to what *ḥikma* is, and so we also might say that *ḥikma* is that mode wherein a philosophical vocabulary is drawn upon in order to practice the theoretical arts and rank them.[45] If this mode is founded through a pedagogy in logic, it occasions a sociality, which is presumed in and gives place to philosophy. It is not that *ḥikma* is philosophy, or that *falsafa*—the Arabic transliteration of the Greek term φιλοσοφία—is or is not *ḥikma*, but that *ḥikma* is a name for the taking on of a manner of comportment, which gives that mode of being, which philosophy is. It is perhaps in this that al-Fārābī inherits the manner of Aristotle, who was, as the eleventh–twelfth century doxographer al-Shahrastānī explains, "the founder of the logical teachings," and who yet, through this founding gave place to a tradition that exceeds the temporal opposition between what is founding and founded, between what is originary and its own and what is not.[46]

Insubstantiality

"What is intended in all knowledge that is sought, is a knowledge of what is intended in the question [والمقصود من كل ما طُلب معرفته هو معرفة ما قُصد بالطلب/*wa al-maqṣūd min kull mā ṭuliba maʿrifatuhu huwwa maʿrifat mā quṣida bi-al-ṭalab*]," al-Fārābī wrote in *Book of Utterances*, and I wish now to consider this passage in relation to al-Fārābi's outlining of the manner in which one asks into the being of a thing.[47] "When we say 'Is the thing?,' we are asking into a

PLATE 1 Etel Adnan. *Untitled*. c. 1970–1973. Watercolor on paper. 10.5 x 24 cm (4 ⅛ x 9 ½ in). Copyright The Estate of Etel Adnan. Courtesy of Sfeir-Semler Gallery Beirut/Hamburg.

PLATE 2 Etel Adnan. *Soleil sur le Mont Tamalpais*. 2017. 57 x 61.5cm. Etching, edition of 19. Copyright The Estate of Etel Adnan. Courtesy of Galerie Lelong & Co., Paris/New York.

PLATE 3 Etel Adnan. *Untitled*. 2014. Oil on canvas. 22.4 x 29.1 cm (9 ⅝ x 11 ½ in). Copyright The Estate of Etel Adnan. Private collection. Courtesy of Galerie Lelong & Co., Paris/New York.

PLATE 4 Etel Adnan. *Untitled*. 1965–66. Oil on canvas. 54 x 57.5 cm (21 ¼ x 22 ⅝ in). Copyright The Estate of Etel Adnan. Digital Image copyright The Museum of Modern Art, New York. Licensed by SCALA/Art Resource, New York.

PLATE 5 Etel Adnan. *Autumn in Yosemite Valley*. 1964. Oil on canvas. 51 x 51 cm (20 ⅛ x 20 ⅛ in). Copyright The Estate of Etel Adnan. Courtesy of the Barjeel Art Foundation, Sharjah.

PLATE 6 Etel Adnan. *Untitled*. c.1970. Oil on canvas. 55 x 46 cm (21 ⅝ x 18 ⅛ in). Copyright The Estate of Etel Adnan. Private collection. Courtesy of Galerie Lelong & Co., Paris/New York.

PLATE 7 Etel Adnan. *Untitled*. 1965. Oil on canvas. 66.5 x 66.5 cm (26 ⅛ x 26 ⅛ in). Copyright The Estate of Etel Adnan. Private collection. Courtesy of Galerie Lelong & Co., Paris/New York.

PLATE 8 Etel Adnan. *The Suez Canal*. 1967. Oil on canvas. 61 x 61 cm (24 x 24 in). Copyright The Estate of Etel Adnan. Private collection. Courtesy of Galerie Lelong & Co., Paris/New York.

PLATE 9 Etel Adnan. *Untitled*. 2017. Oil on canvas. 41 x 33 cm (16 ⅛ x 13 in). Copyright The Estate of Etel Adnan. Courtesy of Galerie Lelong & Co., Paris/New York.

PLATE 10 Etel Adnan. *En route vers le désert*. 2018. 76 x 45.4 cm. Etching, edition of 35. Copyright The Estate of Etel Adnan. Courtesy of Galerie Lelong & Co., Paris/New York.

PLATE 11 Etel Adnan. *Untitled*. c.1984–87. Oil on canvas. 20 x 25 cm (7 ⅞ x 9 ⅞ in). Copyright The Estate of Etel Adnan. Courtesy of Galerie Lelong & Co., Paris/New York.

PLATE 12 Etel Adnan. *Untitled*. 2014. Oil on canvas. 30 x 24.4 cm (11 ¾ x 9 ⅝ in). Copyright The Estate of Etel Adnan. Courtesy of Galerie Lelong & Co., Paris/New York.

PLATE 13 Etel Adnan. *Untitled (Sausalito)*. c.1980. Oil on canvas. 20 x 25 cm (7 7⁄8 x 9 7⁄8 in). Copyright The Estate of Etel Adnan. Courtesy of Sfeir-Semler Gallery Beirut/Hamburg.

PLATE 14 Etel Adnan. *Untitled*. 2016. Oil on canvas. 41 x 33 cm (16 ⅛ x 13 in). Copyright The Estate of Etel Adnan.

PLATE 15 Etel Adnan. *Le poids du monde 30*. 2017. Oil on canvas. 33 x 24 cm (13 x 9 ½ in). Copyright The Estate of Etel Adnan. Private collection. Courtesy of Galerie Lelong & Co., Paris/New York.

PLATE 16 Etel Adnan. *Le poids du monde 2*. 2016. Oil on canvas. 31 x 25.1 cm (12 ¼ x 9 ⅞). Copyright The Estate of Etel Adnan. Frank F. Yang Collection. Courtesy of Galerie Lelong & Co., Paris/New York.

knowledge of its being only [فإنّه متى قلنا هل الشيء فإنما نطلب معرفة وجوده فقط/*fa-innahu matā qulnā hal al-shay' fa-innamā naṭlub ma'rifat wujūdihi faqat*]," while the particle ما, *mā*, asks into what a thing is: "Among the particles is that one which, if it is linked to a thing, indicates that what is sought from that thing is a conceptualization only of the essence of the thing, not a knowledge of its being or of anything other than its essence [ذاته/*dhātihi*], not its quantity or its time or its place. And this is like our saying 'What?' or 'What is it?' So when we say 'What is the thing?' or 'What is it that is the thing' we are inquiring, with this particle, into the conceptualization of the knowledge of the essence of the thing and nothing else" (48). The particle *mā*, when it is used as the question *mā?*, "what?," as al-Fārābī further elaborates in a text titled *Book of Letters* (كتاب الحروف/*Kitāb al-ḥurūf*), "is set down, firstly, to posit a question about a particular thing [وُضع أولا للدلاة على السؤال عن شيء ما مفرد/*wuḍi' awwalan lil-dalāla 'alā al-su'āl 'an shay' mā mufrad*]," and so the question regarding "what" something is begins as a question addressed to this or that "thing," شيء, *shay'*.[48] The framing of the question is: There is a "thing" and one asks into what it is. And yet the recognition of this or that thing as a thing is brought about through the form of address made manifest in the question, and the sort of answer sought with this particle—with the word "what?"—is the "whatness," ماهية, *māhiyya*, of a thing: "If we say 'this is a thing' we mean by that: What has a particular whatness [إذا قلنا 'هذا شيء' فإنّا نعني به ما له ماهية ما/*idhā qulnā, 'hādha shay',' fa-innā na'nī bihi mā lahu māhiyya mā*]" (128). These passages lead to al-Fārābī's discussion of "primary" and "secondary" substance, in a gloss on Aristotle's *Categories*, and yet I wish to underline that the thing, in relation to which one inquires with the particle *mā*, is not what it is, considered as a thing, prior to its being addressed in this manner; it is not that a thing, first, is, and that the terms for philosophical elaboration—and the questions al-Fārābī outlines—arrive to clarify this thing and make it known. Instead, logic, in the pages of *Book of Letters* I'll address presently, is a practice wherein the world is compelled to appear as if it consisted in things, about which one inquires in particular ways.

The thing about which one inquires, when one asks into what a thing is, is a "substance," جوهر, *jawhar*, and al-Fārābī discusses the term "substance" in the following manner: "As for in philosophy," he continues, "substance is said of that thing which is pointed to [المشار إليه/*al-mushār ilayhi*], which is not in any way in a subject. And it is said of each predicate that makes known what this thing that is pointed to is in relation to species, genus, and difference [يعرّف ما هو هذا المشار إليه من نوع وجنس وفصل/*yu'arrif mā huwwa hādha al-mushār ilayhi min nū' wa jins wa faṣl*], and of what makes known the whatness of each species of this species of thing that is pointed at and in what its foundation and whatness consist [وما به ماهيته وقوامه/*wa mā bihi māhiyyatuhu wa qiwāmuhu*]—and it is clear that what makes known what each species of this species of thing that is pointed to is, makes known what this thing, which is pointed to, is" (100). The explication derives, in part, from *Categories*, and al-Fārābī provides an elaboration of "primary" and "secondary" substance: "For Aristotle named that thing which is pointed to, which is not in a subject, 'primary substance,' and its universals, 'secondary substance,' for the former have their being outside of the soul, while the latter transpire in the soul after that, as is said, with all of the other things, in the book *Categories*" (102). The terms reiterate those of the translation of Isḥāq ibn Ḥunayn:

> فأمّا الجوهر الموصوف بأنّه أوّل بالتحقيق والتقديم والتفضيل فهو الذي لا يقال على موضوع ما، ولا هو في موضوع ما، ومثل ذلك: إنسان ما، وفرس ما. فأمّا الموصوفة بأنّها جواهر ثوانٍ فهي الأنواع التي فيها توجد الجواهر الموصوفة بأنّها أُوَل. ومع هذه الأجناس هذه الأنواع أيضا. ومثال ذلك أنّ إنسانا ما هو في نوع، أي في الأنسان، وجنس هذا النوع الحيّ. فهذه الجواهر توصف بأنّها ثوانٍ كالإنسان والحيّ.[49]

> Substance [*al-jawhar*], which is described as what is primary [*awwal*] in determination, priority, and preference, is what is not said of a subject [*lā yuqāl ʿalā mawḍūʿ mā*] and is not in a subject [*wa lā huwwa fī mawḍūʿ mā*], for example: a particular human being, a particular horse. What are described as secondary substances [*jawāhir thawānin*] are the species [*al-anwāʿ*] in which the substances described as primary are, as is the case with the genera [*al-ajnās*] of these species. An example of that is, a particular human being belongs to a species, the human being [*al-insān*], and the genus of this species is the living being [*al-ḥayy*]. So these substances, such as the human being and the living being, are described as secondary.

Al-Fārābī's explication of substance, in relation to genus and species, entails the following, which is elaborated—through a continued reflection on the particle *mā*—in relation to one's asking, "What is this visible thing?" Al-Fārābī notes that: "We might say of it, 'It's a palm,' or 'It's a tree,' or 'It's a plant,' or 'It's a body,' and each of these is a differential, general universal, each of which is suitable to reply to the question 'What is this visible thing?' And if you were to take any two of these, the more particular is called the species and the more general is called the genus, not because it would not be possible to call what is called the genus a species, or something else, and not because it would not be possible to call what is called a species a genus, or something else, but because it has been set down that the more particular among two things is called the species and the more general is called the genus."[50] The passage elaborates, through a discussion of the particle *mā*, the understanding of secondary substances, species, and genera, and we may consider this elaboration through the discussion of difference and accident in the *Isagoge* of Porphyry, a text which, since the fourth century, had been appended as an introduction to the logical books. "If we ask about the human being," Porphyry wrote, in the Arabic translation of Abī ʿUthmān Dimashqī, "'What sort of living being is this?' [أي حيوان هو / *ayy ḥayawān huwwa*], we reply: 'a speaking being'; and if we ask about the crow, 'What sort of living being is this?' we reply: 'black'; and speaking is a difference, and black is an accident [والناطق فصل والأسود عرض / *wa al-nāṭiq faṣl wa al-aswad ʿaraḍ*]. But if we ask about the human being, 'What is it?' [ما هو / *mā huwwa*], we reply: a living being, because the living being is the genus of the human being [لأنّ جنس الإنسان قد كان الحيوان / *li-anna jins al-insān qad kāna al-ḥayawān*]."[51] And so we might say that substance, in the pages I'm tracing in *Book of Letters*, is understood in relation to the terms articulated through Aristotle's *Categories* and the terminology of Porphyry's *Isagoge*, as these had been translated into Arabic in carrying on the logical tradition of late antiquity, and that this understanding turns on the articulation of a sense of what a thing is.[52] One asks about a thing, and it is only through this asking, in questions such as "Is the thing?", "What is the thing?", and "What sort of thing is this?" that the lexicion of logic is initiated and elaborated, even as this elaboration forwards an understanding of "primary" substance as this particular thing—as "this," that "thing" at which one points when one asks the question, "What is it?" ما هو؟, *mā huwwa?*—and as the terms for this understanding—in relation to genus and species, and in relation to difference and accident, "secondary" substance—are generated through the sort of asking, which the logical books pass on.

It is the understanding of a "thing" as "substance" that gives the "essence" of the thing: "And it might be said, in general," al-Fārābī writes, "of what makes known the whatness [ماهية / *māhiyya*] of whichever thing, which falls under one of the species of categories, and of what, through it, has its own form, and that is in what, through their joining together, each to the other, the essence of the thing is attained, and the essence of the thing is that which, when it is intellected, the thing itself—in its summing up of its parts, through which its form is given, or in its summing up of the things, through which its form is given—is intellected, and it is what, through the joining together of its parts, each to the other, that the thing is attained—whichever thing it is [أيّ شيء كان / *ayy shayʾ kāna*]."[53] "Therefore," as al-Fārābi continues, "you hear the philosophers saying: the definition makes known the substance of the thing, and form signifies the substance of the thing," and, he further explains, "they therefore mean by substance, here, the things which, through their joining together, each to the other, the essence of the thing is attained" (101). Substance, in this sense, is "the substance of a particular thing [*jawhar li-shay' mā*; جوهر لشيء ما]" (101), and it is what speaks to us of the "whatness" of a thing, and a "thing" is therefore that which is posited by the sort of being who inquires into what a thing is in relation to genera and species, and in relation to the predicates it gives one to assemble in the form of its definition: "The ancients," al-Fārābī wrote, as he explicated these terms' intersection, "called the predicate of a thing that which, when it is intellected, what is intellected is what that thing is [ما هو ذلك الشيء/*mā huwwa dhālik al-shay'*], and they called its essence [ذات/*dhāt*] the substance of that thing, and they called the whatness of a thing [ماهية الشيء /*māhiyyat al-shay'*] its substance, and a part of its whatness a part of its substance, and what makes known what the thing is what is made known through its substance" (176).

And yet if substance is that through which what a thing is is made known, and if what is sought with the particle *mā* is what is made known to us through the category substance—"What is sought with it," al-Fārābī wrote of the particle *mā*, "is knowledge of the essence of the thing, about which one has asked, and that its essence be conceptualized, intellected, and posited as an intelligible" (172)—it is substance which speaks to us of being: "It is not necessary," al-Fārābī underlines, "to imagine to yourself that the meaning of the term 'substance' is that it is like a thing that is dense, bulky, solid, or firm, because of what you hear from a group which has become accustomed to saying 'It is what is self-subsistent' and 'Its subsistence is in itself,' and statements that resemble this, which imagine of substance that it is not a substance of predication, a substance not predicated of a subject at all, except in a manner that asks into what is" (177). Al-Fārābī, in this passage, calls attention to the distinction between primary and secondary substance, between "substance" understood as a "sensible thing," المحسوس, *al-maḥsūs*, at which one points and about which one asks, and its understanding as that thing's whatness, described through genus, species, and difference, the terms for the predication of universals and particulars in logic. And yet if "it is not necessary" to understand substance to be a material or sensible thing—"dense," "bulky," "solid," "firm"—this is because it is necessary to think of substance in relation to the posing of the question regarding what a thing is: *mā huwwa*? This relates not only to the whatness of a thing but also its being, and so it is not that a thing is and is then asked about, but that the being of a thing is given through the manner of inquiry al-Fārābī has outlined. It is the form of the question, al-Fārābī has underlined, wherein one inquires into whether a thing is, and what it is, and because this happens in each and every instance, it is as if the being of a thing is not separable from the asking of a question. Because the question is a mode of address, the form of the thing—and its being—are enveloped within, and indistinguishable from, that asking. There are things, and there are only things, and yet each and every thing, what al-Fārābī calls "whichever thing," is already a thing in lingual address, as it is, as well, already this or that thing in its not-being-itself, its sharing in things, and so it may be the case that, in al-Fārābī, this—this "whatever" or "whichever," this mode of being where what is is already something else—is what is, where being is, finally, insubstantial.

Common Things

In a short text titled "Letter on the Aims of Aristotle's *Metaphysics*" (رسالة في أغراض ما بعد الطبيعة/*Risāla fī aghrāḍ mā baʿd al-ṭabīʿa*), al-Fārābī approaches the Aristotelian treatises that came to be recognized under that name by noting that among those things studied in the "universal science" is "the thing that is common to all beings":

> وأمّا العلم الكلّي فهو الذي ينظر في الشيء العام لجميع الموجودات مثل الوجود والوحدة وفي أنواعه ولواحقه وفي الأشياء التي لا تعرض بالتخصيص لشيء شيء من موضوعات العلوم الجزئية مثل التقدّم والتأخّر والقوة والفعل والتام والناقص وما يجري مجرى هذه وفي المبدأ المشترك لجميع الموجودات وهو الشيء الذي ينبغي أن يسمّى باسم الله جلّ جلاله.[54]

> The universal science is the one that studies the thing that is common to all beings [*al-shayʾ al-ʿām li-jamīʿ al-mawjūdāt*], such as being and unity, its species and concomitant attributes, the things which are not proper accidents of any subject of the particular sciences [*al-ulūm al-juzʾiyya*], such as priority and posteriority, potentiality and actuality, perfection and deficiency, and similar things, and the principle that is shared among all beings [*al-mabdaʾ al-mushtarak li-jamīʿ al-mawjūdāt*], namely, that thing which ought to be called by the name "God," may his glory be exalted.[55]

Al-Fārābī underlines that there is only one universal science, because if there were two such sciences, then each would have its own object, and each would therefore be a particular science and there would not be a universal one, with an object proper to it. There is to have been a universal science, and there is to have been only one, and to speak of the "aims of Aristotle's *Metaphysics*" is therefore to locate this science in its relation to and distinction from "the divine science": "It is therefore necessary that the divine science be contained within this science, because God is a principle of absolute being, not of one being to the exclusion of another, so the part of the universal science that comprises the giving of the absolute principle of being ought, itself, be the divine science."[56]

The divine science is a "part" of the universal science and it is "contained" within it; it belongs to the universal science and is subordinated to it as a "part" that is distinct from and still related to it. On one hand, there is a delimitation of borders and a setting of terms: a science may only be "universal" or "particular," and there may only be one universal science, since if there were two neither would be universal, as al-Fārābī also outlines; and yet because the divine science is contained within the universal science, because in a certain sense it "belongs" to it, it may not be said to be wholly other than it, and so if there is an object of the divine science this is only insofar as it is shared with the universal science and discombobulates the terms through which a reflection on the universal science is produced.[57] There is, one might say, a blurring, or an indistinction, because if the object of the universal science includes within it that principle, which is the principle of all things, of whatever thing is a thing, then the delimitation of this object as the object of the universal science overflows the boundaries among the sciences, which al-Fārābī's letter seems to set out.

Al-Fārābī points to this blurring when he explains, in a gloss on *Book Epsilon* of *Metaphysics* in the same letter, and in a discussion of "the science of what is after nature," علم ما بعد الطبيعة, *ʿilm mā baʿd al-ṭabīʿa*, that this treatise "contains a clarification of the essential differences between the three theoretical sciences, which are the natural, mathematical, and divine sciences—and there are three of them only—and makes known the fact that the divine science is contained within this science, and, more so, that it is this science, in a certain respect."[58] There are, al-Fārābī underlines, three theoretical sciences "only," and it is the setting in place of these sciences, their being located, each in relation to the others, which is to give a proper understanding of Aristotle's *Metaphysics* and its aims. Al-Fārābī explicates the relations among the universal science and these three other sciences in the following manner. First, since what is treated in universal science is more general than what is treated in natural science, "this science is higher than natural science and comes after it, and for this reason it should be called the science of what is after nature" (35/79), or, somewhat literally, and following the sense of the Greek terms which render the title of this corpus of treatises, "metaphysics," what comes after, بَعد , *baʿd*, the study of nature, الطبيعة, *al-ṭabīʿa*. And yet both physics and metaphysics are distinct from the science of mathematics, العلم التعليمي, *al-ʿilm al-taʿālīmī*, which, if it is "higher than natural science," because, as al-Fārābī writes, "its objects are abstracted from matter," it "should not be called the science of what is after nature because the abstraction of its objects from matter occurs in the imagination and is not an aspect of their being" (35/79). If al-Fārābī provides a further clarification in relation to the objects of mathematics—one sort of mathematical object "has no existence in natural things at all," because "their being and nature are abstract," while the other is that sort which "exists in natural things, even though one can imagine them abstracted from them" (35/79)—in each instance there is a relation to things which are either in matter or separate from matter, and mathematics, therefore, may not be considered to be the science of what comes "after" nature—the science of metaphysics. One may summarize the aporetic relationality of the sciences, in this Fārābīan text, in this way: The divine science is separated from the universal science through its containment within it; the mathematical is separated from and linked to the natural and what is beyond nature—what belongs to the study of "metaphysics"—through the split dimension of the mathematical object. If what is explicated is a clarification of objects, one may observe that to read or study this text is to subordinate oneself to this clarification—al-Fārābī's word in the passage I've cited here is إبانة, *ibāna*—even as it is a clarification which clarifies by intensifying indistinctions and by outlining the aporetic form of the setting out of the Aristotelian sciences.

Al-Fārābī further addresses the relations among the sciences in his compendium *Enumeration of the Sciences* (إحصاء العلوم/*Iḥṣā' al-'ulūm*), and he underlines, in relation to what he also terms there "the divine science," a three-part division. The first "investigates," يفحص, *yafḥaṣ*, "beings and the things predicated of them, insofar as they are beings"; the second investigates "the principles of demonstration in the particular theoretical sciences, each of which is distinguished by its study of a particular being"; and the third investigates "beings that are not of bodies or in bodies."[59] As it does so the divine science asks whether such beings exist, whether they are many, whether their number is finite, and, finally, "whether their ranks, in relation to perfection, are one or diverse" (61).

Al-Fārābī continues:

> ثم يبرهن أنّها على كثرتها ترتقي من عند أنقصها إلى الاكمل فالاكمل إلى أن تنتهي في آخر ذلك إلى كامل ما لا يمكن أن يكون شيء هو أكمل منه، ولا يمكن أن يكون شيء هو أصلا في مرتبة وجوده ولا نظير له ولا ضد، وإلى أول لا يمكن أن يكون قبله أول، وإلى متقدّم لا يمكن أن يكون شيء أقدم منه، وإلى موجود لا يمكن أن يكون استفاد وجوده عن شيء أصلا، وأنّ ذلك الواحد هو الأول والمتقدّم على الإطلاق وحده، ويبيّن أنّ سائر الموجودات متأخّر عنه في الوجود، وأنّه هو الموجود الأول الذي أفاد كل واحد سواه الوجود، وأنّه هو الواحد الأول الذي أفاد كل شيء سواه الوحدة، وأنّه هو الحق الذي أفاد كل ذي حقيقة سواه الحقيقة، وعلى أي جهة أفاد ذلك، وأنّه لا يمكن أن يكون فيه كثرة أصلا ولا بوجه من الوجوه بل هو أحق باسم الواحد ومعناه، وباسم الموجود ومعناه من كل شيء يقال فيه إنّه واحد أو موجود أو حق سواه. ثم يبيّن أنّ هذا الذي هو بهذه الصفات هو الذي ينبغي أن يُعتقد فيه أنّه هو الإله عز وجل. (61–62)

And then it demonstrates that, despite their plurality, these beings rise from the most defective to the most perfect, and from the most perfect

> until they end, after that, at a single perfection—which it is not possible that there be something more perfect than it, and that it is not possible that there be a thing which is of the same rank in relation to its being at all, and that there is nothing comparable or contrary to it—and at a first, which it is not possible that there be before it a first, and at something primary, of which there can not be something more primary, and at a being, whose being it is not possible that it is derived from something else at all. And that one thing is the first and the most primary—absolutely and in itself. And it clarifies that the rest of the beings are subsequent to it in being, that it is the first being, from which the being of all other things is derived, that it is the first one, from which all things other than it receive their oneness, that it is the truth, from which all things other than it, which are real, receive their reality, in whatever way it is given, and that it is not possible that there be in it a plurality at all, not in any way, and that it is the most deserving of the name "one" and its sense, and of the name "being" and its sense, in relation to anything other than it of which it is said of it that it is one or that it is or that it is true. Then it clarifies that the one who bears these attributes is the one that ought to be considered to be the deity, how exalted and powerful he is.

There is, in this explication, "a being," موجود, *mawjūd*, which is also a single "thing," شيء, *shay*ʾ—solely and merely itself. It is what is "most perfect" and without peer in rank, there is no "first" that comes before it, there is nothing more "primary" than it, and its being is not derived from any being other than itself. It is this being that is the object of metaphysics, and it is metaphysics that explicates its form. And yet insofar as al-Fārābī writes of this "being" or "thing," and insofar as he speaks to us of it in relation to the field of oppositions his language recapitulates, its distinction from "the rest of the beings" becomes indistinct. Insofar as it is a being or a thing, the "first cause" may be said to be like all of the others—and this in particular at the moment at which al-Fārābī speaks of "that one thing" that is "the first and the most primary—absolutely and in itself."[60] If this being is "the most deserving of the name 'one' and its sense, and of the name 'being' and its sense," its explication shares the quality attached to it out among others. In his "Letter on the Aims of Aristotle's *Metaphysics*" al-Fārābī noted that the task of the universal science is to study "that thing common to all beings," and we may understand the sense in which al-Fārābī elaborates the term "one" as an instance of such commonality, if only because, in this Fārābīan world of terms, each and every being is a being, including "the first and the most primary—absolutely and in itself" among them. Al-Fārābī's explication holds or guards an indifferentiation among beings—a blurring of distinctions which also speaks to us of what a thing or being is. Insofar as the philosophical writing of what "the first and the most primary—absolutely and in itself," and of "the most deserving of the name 'one' and its sense, and of the name 'being' and its sense," is explicated through these terms and in this way, the textual field to which al-Fārābī's language belongs holds and passes on what I've termed a tradition of "anontological form," where what is is like all of the others, where being is a kind of sharing, and where what is, insofar as this is the case, is not solely itself but instead a kind of excess. In a passage in his "Letter on the Aims of Aristotle's *Metaphysics*" I've studied al-Fārābī also speaks of "sharing"—what he terms "the principle shared among all beings"—and we may consider this "sharing," الإشتراك, *al-ishtirāk*, as that mode of being in which al-Fārābī's treatises school their addressees. If what we are given to read is, therefore, a commonality given through this sharing, this commonality may be only this: That if that being which is "the first and the most primary—absolutely and in itself" is what relies on and turns to no cause, but is, itself, the cause of all of the other beings and things, then the being of a being that is without cause is given to us as a common form; and that if each and every being or thing is a being, merely this or that one, this is because it is hardly itself, but is already a certain giving, in the inessential manner through which each and every thing, by not being itself, becomes what is.

Necessity

"Every being, considered from the point of view of its essence, without consideration of other things," Abū ʿAlī al-Ḥusayn ibn ʿAbdallah ibn Sīnā writes, "is found to be such that either being necessarily belongs to it in itself or it does not."[61] That sort of being to which being necessarily belongs "in itself" is a being that necessarily is. "If being belongs to it necessarily," Ibn Sīnā further explains in *Remarks and Admonitions* (الإشارات والتنبيهات / *al-Ishārāt wa-al-tanbīhāt*), "then it is the truth in itself and that whose being is necessary from itself [الواجب الوجود من ذاته / *al-wājib al-wujūd min dhātihi*], and this is the independent reality" (3.4.9.19). Naṣīr al-Dīn al-Ṭūsī underlines in his commentary on these passages that the formulation "the truth in itself" points to "the stable and permanent in itself [الثابت الدائم بذاته / *al-thābit al-dāʾim bi-dhātihi*]," and that "the independent reality" points to "the self-establishing, which is not dependent, in its being, upon another in any way," whereas "the possible," الممكن, *al-mumkin*, is what may be or not be.[62] A possible being is one whose being is not grounded in itself but in another—"It follows that the being of every possible thing is from another," Ibn Sīnā writes—and it is, therefore, that which is not only not merely itself but which, in order to be what it is, is related to another and dependent upon it.[63] The being, "whose being is necessary in itself," and through which the being of merely possible, contingent beings is to be grounded, is, at once, the "first," الأول, *al-awwal*, a "principle," مبدأ, *mabda'*, and a "cause," علة, *'illa*, and it is only in relation to it that all other beings and things may be said to be: "Thus, if there is a first cause, it is a cause of each being and the cause of the reality of every concrete being" (3.4.8.18), and, further, "Everything other than the first is caused, and that which is caused is not equal to the necessary principle [وكل ما سوى الأول فمعلول، والمعلول لا يساوي المبدأ الواجب/*wa kull mā siwā al-awwal fa ma'lūl, wa al-ma'lūl lā yusāwī al-mabda' al-wājib*]" (3.4.26.52–53).

In Ibn Sīnā the discussion of that being "whose being is necessary in itself" becomes a reflection on being in relation to necessity, and Ibn Sīnā's language, in the passages in *Remarks* I've underlined here, as well as in his compendium *The Healing* (الشفاء/*al-Shifā'*), creates an indistinction among terms, with which I wish to linger here. If a reflection on the relation between logic and language reaches back to the earliest of the late antique commentaries on Aristotle, I notice that, in Ibn Sīnā's formulations, "metaphysics," what Ibn Sīnā also calls "first philosophy" and "absolute wisdom," becomes indistinct from logic, that logic, understood as a "tool" for the practice of philosophy, becomes indistinct from language, and that philosophy becomes a reflection on, and a practice of, form, in a sense that may be called "anontological," where what is, I've underlined, is more or less than itself, where being is a temporal and ontological indetermination.[64] To study this sense of form in Ibn Sīnā I outline his rendering of the relations among metaphysics, logic, and demonstration, and I underline the relations among these in his explication of that being "whose being is necessary in itself," what he also calls "the necessary being." In the opening paragraphs of the *Metaphysics* of *The Healing* Ibn Sīnā points to the *Book of Demonstration* (كتاب البرهان/*Kitāb al-Burhān*), named for the fourth of the eight logical books in Arabic, whose subject matter Ibn Sīnā explicates in the logic of *The Healing*. "This much is what you would have come to know from the books that have previously come to you. But from this it would not have become evident to you what the object [الموضوع/*al-mawḍū'*] of metaphysics really is, except for a remark in the *Book of Demonstration*, in the *Logic*, if you remember it."[65] Ibn Sīnā directs us to *Posterior Analytics*; he asks us to read it in relation to *Metaphysics*, and I wish, following this direction, to underline four moments, which constrain the reading I offer: first, to think about metaphysics, in Ibn Sīnā, is to read the logical books, and, in particular, it is to read *Posterior Analytics*, which is, in its Arabic rendering, *Book of Demonstration*; to do so is, also, to think about the relation of metaphysics to other, particular sciences; it is, as well, to think about logic in another sense, also drawn from *Posterior Analytics*: It is to think about the manner in which the principles or premises, which form the elements of syllogisms, are demonstrated; and, finally, it is to think about the relations among necessity, possibility, and impossibility, as Ibn Sīnā also explains.[66]

One might ask: What is the relation of metaphysics to the other, particular sciences? Why is this question important for Ibn Sīnā, and why does it appear, as a question, at the opening of the *Metaphysics* of *The Healing*? How does a reflection on the relation between metaphysics and the other sciences touch upon the explication of what "the necessary being" is, and how does this relate, further, to a reflection on being? Ibn Sīnā outlines the relation between metaphysics and the other sciences in *Book of Demonstration*, where he observes that "the principles of all of the sciences are clarified in the science of metaphysics [ومبادئ جميع العلوم تُبيّن في علم ما بعد الطبيعة/*wa mabādiʾ jamīʿ al-ʿulūm tubayyan fī ʿilm mā baʿd al-ṭabīʿa*]."[67] In this frame, Ibn Sīnā's statement suggests a sense of the term "metaphysics" and its relation to the particular sciences: Metaphysics is a name for that sort of knowing wherein the principles of all of the other sciences are to be clarified, and this is because, Ibn Sīnā underlines, the principles of a science are not able to be clarified within that science: "A practitioner of a science is not able to clarify its principles insofar as they are a practitioner of it, for the geometrician, insofar as they are a geometrician, is not able to substantiate the principles of geometry," and, he also explains, "Just as it is not for a practitioner of a science to clarify its principles, so too they have nothing to say to those who contradict them, nor to those who do not build upon its principles. Nor are they required to reply to each sort of question, but, if they are a geometrician they are obliged to answer geometrical questions" (3.1.194).

The relation between principles and sciences is elaborated in the following terms:

> ومن البين أنّه لا سبيل إلى أقامة البراهين في العلوم على مبادئها، وإلا فما يبيّن به المبدأ هو المبدأ، والعلم به أحق من العلم بما قيل إنه مبدأ له. فبعض مبادئ العلوم بينة بأنفسها، وبعضها محتاجة إلى بيان. وكلاهما من المستحيل أن يبيّنا في العلوم التي هي لها مبادئ أول. (2.10.184)

> It is clear that there is no way to establish demonstrations in the sciences based upon the principles of those sciences, for were that the case, what would be clarified through the principle would be the principle [*wa illā fa mā yubayyan bihi al-mabdaʾ huwwa al-mabdaʾ*], and the knowledge of that principle would be more true than the

> knowledge of what it is said to be a principle of. For some of the principles of the sciences are clear in themselves, and some require clarification. And it is impossible that either of them be clarified in the sciences for which they are the primary principles.

A "science," علم, *ʿilm*, cannot demonstrate its own principles, because a principle demonstrated in such a manner would be more true than the field of terms through which it, itself, was determined to be a principle—and such a field of terms includes, as Ibn Sīnā clarifies, principles.[68] One must not turn to the principles that operate "in" a science in order to explicate those terms, because such a practice would rely upon the terms for which it wished to provide an explanation. The understanding of such a science would be unable to provide a ground for itself without determining that ground through the terms it presupposes, and a principle would therefore be determined based upon principles for which it does not account. To resolve this difficulty Ibn Sīnā returns to the distinction between principles that are clear in themselves and those that require clarification: "As for those principles, which are clear in themselves, they may not be clarified in that science or in another science. But a principle, which is not clear in itself, may be clarified in another science, and especially a higher one."[69] The "higher" science, through which the principles of the sciences that are not clear in themselves are to be clarified is, Ibn Sīnā underlined, metaphysics, what he also calls "the divine science": "And you have also heard," Ibn Sīnā writes in the *Metaphysics of The Healing*, "that the divine science is the one in which the first causes of natural and mathematical being, and what relates to them, are investigated, as is the cause of causes and the principle of principles—namely God, exalted be his greatness."[70]

He continues:

> وأيضا قد كنت تسمع أنّ ههنا فلسفة بالحقيقة، وفلسفة أولى، وأنّها تفيد تصحيح مبادئ سائر العلوم، وأنّها هي الحكمة بالحقيقة. وقد كنت تسمع تارة أنّ الحكمة هي أفضل علم بأفضل معلوم، وأخرى أنّ الحكمة هي المعرفة التي هي أصح معرفة وأتقنها، وأخرى أنّها العلم بالأسباب الأولى للكل. وكنت لا تعرف ما هذه الفلسفة الأولى، وما هذه الحكمة، وهل الحدود والصفات الثلاث لصناعة واحدة، أو لصناعات مختلفة كل واحدة منها تسمّى حكمة. (1.1.9.5)

> Moreover, you used to hear that there is, here, a philosophy in the real sense, a first philosophy, and that it imparts validation to the principles of all of the other sciences [*wa annahu tufīd taṣḥīḥ mabādiʾ sāʾir al-ʿulūm*], and that it is, in reality, wisdom. You also used to hear, at one time, that wisdom is the best knowledge of the best object of

> knowledge, at another, that it is the most correct and perfect knowledge, and at another that it is knowledge of the first causes of the world. But you did not know what this first philosophy [*hādhihi al-falsafa al-ūlā*] is, or what this wisdom [*al-ḥikma*] is, and whether these three definitions and attributes belong to one art or to different arts, each of which is called wisdom.

Ibn Sīnā underlines that the "higher science," through which principles are "clarified" and "investigated," is to be studied insofar as it is "first philosophy": "We will now show you that this science we are after is first philosophy [الفلسفة الأولى / *al-falsafa al-ūlā*] and that it is absolute wisdom [الحكمة المطلقة / *al-ḥikma al-muṭlaqa*], and that the three attributes with which wisdom has been described are the attributes of one art, which is this one" (1.1.10.5). If "metaphysics" is the name for this science, when considered from the point of view of its relation to other sciences, the reflection on "first philosophy" becomes an occasion for outlining a distinction between the "object" of "first philosophy" and what is "sought after" in it: If the being of "the necessary being" is not the object of this science, because it is what is sought after in it—"If, then, the inquiry, concerning its being is in this science, it cannot be the object of this science, because it is not for any science to establish its object [فإنّه ليس على علم من العلوم إثبات موضوعه / *fa innahu laysa ʿalā ʿilm min al-ʿulūm ithbāt mawḍūʿihi*]" (1.1.12.6)—there must still be, for "first philosophy," an object, and this is "the being insofar as it is a being": "If the examination of causes pertains to them inasmuch as they exist, and if it pertains to the things that relate to them in this respect, then the primary object must be the being insofar as it is a being [الموجود بما هو موجود / *al-mawjūd bi-mā huwwa mawjūd*]" (1.1.17.9). The outlining of "first philosophy," and the reflection on principles and causes this occasions, leads to a reflection on being, following the language of Aristotle in *Book Gamma* of *Metaphysics*.[71] And yet if the reflection on "the being insofar as it is a being" is the "object" of "first philosophy," it is not what demonstrates that object or provides a ground for it. This ground, instead, is to be found in the reflection on "the necessary being," that being "whose being is necessary in itself." If, in Aristotle, the question of being becomes a question about substance—"Indeed, the question which was raised long ago, is still and will always be, and which always baffles us, 'What is being?', is, in other words, 'What is substance?'", Aristotle also wrote—this question, in the formulations of Ibn Sīnā, becomes modal.[72]

The privilege of the term "necessity" is outlined in relation to causality: What Ibn Sīnā terms "the necessary being" must not have a cause, because if it did, it would not be itself and it would not be necessary. "For if in its being the necessary being were to have a cause, its being would be through that cause," and insofar as its being were through that cause, it would not be a necessary being.[73] Ibn Sīnā explains: "But whatever is through something else, if considered in itself, apart from another, its being would not be necessary. And anything, if it is considered in itself, apart from any other, and if its being is not necessary, it is not necessary in itself. It is thus evident that if what is in itself a necessary being were to have a cause, it would not be in itself a necessary being [فبين أنه إن كان لواجب الوجود بذاته علة لم يكن واجب الوجود بذاته/*fa bayyin annahu in kāna li wājib al-wujūd bi dhātihi ʿilla lam yakun wājib al-wujūd bi dhātihi*]" (1.6.3.38). What is drawn out in these passages in the *Metaphysics* of *The Healing* is not only a determination of the sense of being of the necessary being, but also a particular orientation for this question and the more general reflection on being it entails. There is a reflection on being in relation to logic, and one might then say that the tradition of logic in al-Fārābī—and it is al-Fārābī whom Ibn Sīnā names in his autobiography, in relation to his "Letter on the Aims of Aristotle's *Metaphysics*"—gives place in Ibn Sīnā to an explication of what being is, and what beings are, which privileges "necessity" in relation to "first philosophy."[74]

This manner of explication is outlined in a commentary of Ibn Sīnā's on *Book Lambda* of Aristotle's *Metaphysics*, to which I'll turn presently in detail. Ibn Sīnā draws out a reflection on necessity from a reflection on motion: "He [Ibn Sīnā—JS] refuted Aristotle and the commentators. For he said: It is repugnant to arrive at the first truth by way of an analysis of motion, and by way of stating that it is the principle of motion," and, Ibn Sīnā also writes, "For this group does not bring forth anything other than to establish that it is a mover, not that it is a principle of being [فإن القوم لم يوردوا أكثر من إثبات أنه محرك ليس أنه مبدأ للموجود/*fa inna al-qawm lam yūradū akthar min ithbāt annahu muḥarrik laysa annahu mabdaʾ lil-mawjūd*]."[75] The commentary refers to the Arabic translation of *Book Lambda*, with which Ibn Sīnā worked, and to an Arabic translation of a commentary on that book of *Metaphysics*, of Themistius, the fourth-century Greek-language commentator, who spoke of motion in the following manner:

وحدوث الحركة ليس يكون إلا بحركة. فيجب أن يكون قبل الحركة حركة لأنّ الإستحالة والتغيّر والفتور إنّما هي من أنواع الحركة. ولا بدّ من أن يكون جسم من الأجسام هو الذي يتحرّك. فإن قلنا إنّ ذلك الجسم لم يحدث، لكنّه تحرّك عن سكون، وجب أن نُخبر بالسبب الذي له تغيّر من السكون إلى حركة. فإن قلنا إنّ ذلك الجسم حدث، تقدّم حدوث الجسم حدوث الحركة. فإذ قد بان أنّ الحركة والزمان أزليان، فالجسم أزلي. وإن كان العرض كذلك، فبالحرى أن يكون الجوهر كذلك. والحركات: إما مستقيمة، وإما مستديرة— ولاإتصال لا يكون إلا فيها، لأنّ المستقيمة تنقطع. والإتصال أمر ضروري للأشياء

> الأزلية. فإنّ الذي سكن ليس بأزلي. ونقول إنّ الزمان متصل لأنّه لا يمكن أن يكون قطعٌ منه مبتورة. فيجب من ذلك أن تكون الحركة متصلة. فإن كانت الحركة المستديرة هي وحدها متصلة، فيجب أن تكون هي أزلية، فيجب أن يكون محرّك هذه الحركة أزلية. لأنّ علة الأزلية يجب أن تكون أزلية، إذ لا يكون ما هو أخسّ علة لما هو أفضل. فيجب أن يحرّك تحريكا دائما. فإنّه إن كان محرّكا لكن ليس تحريكه بدائم، فتحريكه لا يكون أزليا، وهذا لا يمكن أن يكون.[76]

> Motion only originates in motion, so there must be, prior to motion, a motion [*fa yajib an yakūn qabla al-ḥaraka ḥaraka*], because transformation and change and lassitude are sorts of motion. And there must be a body, which is what moves. If we were to say that that body is not originated, and that it moves from a state of rest, we must relate the cause through which the change from rest to motion has occurred. If we were to say that that body was originated, its origination would precede its motion. And if it were clear that motion and time were eternal, the body would be eternal. And if an accident were such, how appropriate it would be for a substance to be as well. Motion is either straight or circular—and continuousness occurs only with the latter, because what is straight may be interrupted. And continuousness is necessary for eternal things. For what is at rest is not eternal. We say that time is continuous because it is not possible that a piece of it be cut off, and it is therefore necessary that motion be continuous. If circular motion, then, is alone continuous it must be eternal, and the mover of this motion must be eternal. For the cause of what is eternal must be eternal [*ʿillat al-azaliyya yajib an takūn azaliyya*], because what is more base cannot be a cause for what is more virtuous. And, therefore, it must cause motion permanently, for if there were a mover, but its giving place to motion were not permanent, it would not be eternal—and this is not possible.

The eternal motion, which is the source of motion in things, is the motion of the heavens: "If there is motion that has no rest," Themistius writes, "what gives place to its motion is eternal, and it is the heavens" (14). And if there is a thing that moves and gives place to motion, there must be a thing that does not move, but gives place to motion in things: "If there is a thing that both moves and gives place to motion in things, and if there is a thing that moves only, without giving place to motion in things, then there must of necessity be a mover that does not move. And its nature is such that it is not contaminated with matter, and it is that whose substance is in act" (14). There are among the heavenly bodies unchanging and changing motions, and these motions require a mover that is unmoved, and it is through Themistius's explication of this mover, and its necessity, that the necessity of a first principle is shown: "And what moves the heavenly bodies in this way—what we have said is the first motion and the first change—does not move in any way, does not change, and does not change location. It is not possible that there is in it any difference—not in its substance and not in anything else" (16).

Aristotle underlines, in the Arabic translation of *Book Lambda*, which Ibn Sīnā studied, and which had been translated by Abū Mishr Mattā ibn Yūnus, that "it is necessary that there be an eternal, immovable substance [ومن الإضطرار أن يوجد جوهر أزلي غير متحرك/*wa min al-idṭirār an yūjad jawhar azalī ghayr mutaḥarrik*]," [77] and we may consider Aristotle's further explication, where he notes that there is a "thing," شيء, *shay'*, which moves with an unceasing motion:

> إنّ هاهنا شيئا يتحرّك حركة دائمة غير متغير، وهذا هو المحرّك على الإستدارة. وليس
> يُنال هذا بالقوة حسب، ولكن بالفعل ظاهر. فإن كانت السماء تتحرّك حركة دائمة أزلية،
> فالمحرّك لها بهذه الصفة. وإن كان هاهنا شيء يحرّك بأن يتحرّك، فيجب أن يوجد شيء
> يحرّك من غير أن يتحرّك، هو جوهر، وذاته فعله. (1072a22–26)

> There is a thing that moves with an unceasing, unchanging motion, and this is a motion that is circular. This motion is not only given in potentiality but, manifestly, in act. If the heavens move with an eternal, unceasing motion, what gives place to motion in them possesses this attribute. And if there is something that gives place to motion in things while itself being in motion, there must be a thing that gives place to motion in things while itself not being in motion, and this is substance, and its essence is its act.

The Arabic translation of *Book Lambda* continues: "The mover of these things is immovable, it is in act only, and it is not possible that there take place within it change at all. The first thing in motion, which proceeds from it, is that whose motion is circular. This mover, however, gives place to this motion necessarily [من الإضطرار/*min al-idṭirār*]" (1072b10). Aristotle clarifies the term "necessarily" as follows: "There are several sorts of necessity: what is by compulsion, and this is not what is intended; that without which a better state is not possible; and that which it is not possible that it be other than what it is" (1072b12–14). It is in relation to the sense of necessity as "that which it is not possible that it be other than what it is," الذي لا يمكم أن يكون بخلاف ما هو عليه, *alladhī lā yumkin an yakūn bi khilāf mā huwwa ʿalayhi*, that Aristotle outlines the principle of the heavens and of nature—"Such, then, is the principle on which the heavens depend and on which nature relies (1072b14–15)—as well as the principle of "beings": "The principle of beings [مبدأ الموجودات/*mabda' al-mawjūdāt*], and of the most primary being, is, in its essence, and not accidentally, immovable, and it is this which is the mover of the first, eternal motion" (1073a24–25). And this being is, finally, an eternal substance: "It has become clear from what has been stated that there is an eternal, immovable substance [جوهر/*jawhar*], distinct from sensible things" (1073a5–6). "Themistius offers the following summary: "It has become clear from what we have stated, and from what we have defined, that the first principle is one, and that it moves the first, unceasing, and eternal motion," and this is because, he further writes, "Each thing that is in motion, its motion is from a mover, and the first cause must, of necessity be one and be immovable [فالعلة الأولى يجب ضرورة أن تكون واحدة غير متحركة / *fa al-'illa al-ūlā yajib ḍarūratan an takūn wāḥida ghayr mutaḥarrika*]."[78]

The privilege of motion in these pages in *Book Lambda* presses Ibn Sīnā's reflection on being: "For motion to be the path through which the one, the true being, which is the principle of all being, is established," is, he writes, "repugnant" in the explication of first philosophy.[79] And yet, "As for their supposition that the motion of the heavens is necessary [ضرورية/*ḍarūriyya*], and without beginning or end, this is perhaps accurate, so we must consider its requirements" (24). Ibn Sīnā explains, elaborating this consideration: "So we say: they have not established that the body of the heavens is necessary in itself [يجب وجوده في نفسه /*yajib wujūduhu fī nafsihi*], or that if it is, that it must [وجب/*wajaba*] have motion, and that if it does not have motion, that its essence is negated" (24). Ibn Sīnā's phrasing places an emphasis on necessity, rather than the being in motion of things: "They say, however, that if the heavens are and if they are in motion, that there must not be, for their motion, a beginning. So they attach this motion's being permanent to its being and that it is. The necessity of its being in permanent motion, then, is that there is, in it, motion, and yet it is not necessary, based upon this, that they are in motion of whatever sort" (24). Being and necessity, Ibn Sīnā suggests, are convoluted without explanation: The necessity of the heavens' being in permanent motion is that they are in motion in this way—"The necessity of its being in permanent motion, then, is that there is, in it [وجد فيها/*wajada fīhā*], motion"—and so the statement presumes the outcome it asserts. Necessity has not been shown but presumed, "And we do not mean by this a necessity that is out of compulsion, or where a thing must be the case, but in the sense that it is not possible that it be in any other way" (25). Instead, what is required is that one think the question Ibn Sīnā is studying—the question of motion and necessity in relation to "the one, the true being"—through the distinction he draws between what is "necessary" in its being and what is, in its being, only "possible": "The meaning of this," he clarifies, "is not that the motion of the heavens is necessary in itself [ضرورية بذاتها / *ḍarūriyya bi-dhātihā*], and that it cannot be other than what it is, but instead that it is necessary through the condition I have mentioned. If each thing were considered in itself, as unrelated to what it receives from the first truth, it would not be necessary in being, but possible" (25).

It is in relation to this commentary that Ibn Sīnā elaborates the distinction between what is necessary and what is possible in relation to the object of first philosophy, "the being insofar as it is a being," and it is through this commentary that he addresses being in its relation to the first truth, that being which is, itself—and it is the only one—necessary in itself. Since this relation—the relation between what is necessary and what is possible in its being—is the relation through which Ibn Sīnā thinks what being is, he further explains that "were it possible for this relation to be sundered, each thing would disappear and become null [ولو جاز أن تفصم العلاقة لتلاشى وبطل/*wa law jāza an tufṣam al-ʿalāqa la-talāshā wa baṭala*]" (25–26). "For each thing," he notes, "considered in itself, is null and dead, except in relation to the true one, which is the truth in itself, while the other things are the reality of his being, how great is his power" (26). What Ibn Sīnā underlines is a distinction between what is conditionally necessary and necessary in truth: "There is a group who thinks that this necessity is necessary in itself, but they do not distinguish between what is conditionally necessary and what is necessary in truth, and they say, 'What is all this'?" (26). He clarifies: "I said to Abī Bishr: 'If necessity is as we have stated it to be, what is the position of the first cause in this matter?' He said: 'The permanence of motion.' But this is impossible. For the position of the first truth is that necessity is from it, and there is no necessity possessed by a thing in itself other than it. What points to their carelessness is that they understand necessity to belong to the thing in itself and permanence to be from another, so that the necessity that is in itself does not require permanence as long as that permanence is not extended from another" (26). There is a distinction drawn, as Ibn Sīnā reads Themistius reading and commenting on Aristotle, between what is necessary and permanent, and this distinction obscures an understanding of what necessity "in itself" is. It is this to which Ibn Sīnā points as he withdraws the understanding of the being of the "first truth" from the privilege of motion, to advance an understanding of the being of this being in relation to the modal frame, which he underlines is at once ontological and cosmological:

> بل الحركة—وجودها، وضرورة وجودها من حين توجد، ودوام وجودها—كله معلق بأسباب الحركة؛ والله تعالى نرفعه عن أن نجعله سببا للحركة فقط، بل هو مفيد وجود كل جوهر يمكن أن يتحرّك فعلا عن حركة السماء. فهو الأول، وهو الحق، وهو مبدأ ذات كل جوهر، وبه يجب كل شيء سواه، وتأتيه الضرورة عند النسبة التي يجب أن يقع بينه وبينه. (26)

> As for motion—its being, and the necessity of its being, insofar as it is, and the permanence of its being—all of this is linked to the causes of motion; and God, may he be exalted, we lift him, from making him a cause of motion only, for he is the one who gives the being of each substance [*bal huwwa mufīd wujūd kull jawhar*], which is able to move, in actuality, from the motion of the heavens. For he is the first, the truth, and the principle of the essence of every substance, and each thing other than him is necessary through him [*wa bihi yajib kull shayʾ sawāhu*], and its necessity comes to it from the relation, which must take place, between it and him.

The "principle," Ibn Sīnā explains, "upon which the heavens rely," is "one, simple, and it intellects itself through its essence, whether any being other than it intellects it or not, it is pure good," and, he continues, it is "a being from which necessity flows to things [منبجس عنه الضرورة إلى الأشياء / *munbajis ʿanhu al-ḍarūra ʾila al-ashyāʾ*], so that there is, for the beings, a necessity from him" (26), and this "overflow" of being, إنبجاس, *inbijās*, is given through the necessary being's intellection of its essence: "Among those things in relation to which Themistius was correct is that he clarified that the first principle intellects its essence, and that it then, from its essence, intellects each thing, for it intellects the intelligible world all at once, without a need for altering its location, or moving from one intelligible object to another, for it does not intellect things as if they were things outside of it, which it intellects, as the case is with us in relation to sensible objects, but it intellects them in its essence" (26–27). I wish to underline only this: Ibn Sīnā's thinking of being in relation to logic desubstantializes the "first principle" and it carries forward a lingual sense of what a "principle" is in relation to the Arabic tradition of the reading of the Aristotelian logical books. Rather than a substance there is only a giving of forms, an understanding of being that is also a formal indetermination of sense. What is demonstrated in Ibn Sīnā is a sense of being, which is not reducible to the terms grammar can be taken to privilege—in formulations such as, the "one who gives the being of each substance," where *mufīd*, "the one who gives," is a first person singular active participle. In the drawing of a distinction between an understanding of the first principle as "a cause of motion only" and its understanding as "the principle of the essence of every substance," where "each thing other than it is necessary through it," this principle ceases to be a substance and becomes a form, something like a lingual practice, given through its elaboration in the terms of logic as Ibn Sīnā reread "metaphsyics" and "first philosophy" through *Posterior Analytics*. In this, "first philosophy" becomes a modal formalization of the being of things, and logic, in its indistinction from ontology, and ontology, in its indistinction from language, forms the occasion for a giving of world.

Generosity

الفيض فعل فاعل دائم الفعل، ولا يكون فعله بسبب دعاه إلى ذلك ولا غرض إلا نفس الفعل.
— إبن سينا، التعليقات

> Emanation is the act of an agent whose act is permanent, and whose act does not transpire on account of a cause that calls him to that or an intention other than the act itself.
>
> —IBN SĪNĀ, *AL-TAʿLĪQĀT*

Ibn Sīnā explicates the being of the world through a discussion of the necessary being's intellectual apprehension of its essence: "Because it intellectually apprehends its essence, and since it is the principle of all things, it apprehends through its essence all things," he writes.[80] This "intellectual apprehension" is the cause of things and the world: "For its intellectual apprehension of its essence is the cause of its intellectual apprehension of what is posterior to its essence, and its intellectual apprehension of what is posterior to its essence is, therefore, the effect of its intellectual apprehension of its essence" (8.7.4.364).[81] This understanding of what a cause is, in relation to "intellectual apprehension," and in relation to the totality of what is, is outlined through a discussion of "necessity": "Hence," Ibn Sīnā writes, "it must intellectually apprehend that the being of the whole, from it, is a necessary consequence of it [فيجب أن يعقل أنه يلزمه وجود الكل عنه / *fa yajib an yaʿqal annahu yalzamuhu wujūd al-kull ʿanhu*], because it apprehends itself only intellectually, as a pure intellect and a first principle, whereas it intellectually apprehends the being of the whole, which proceeds from it, insofar as it is its principle."[82] The being of the whole is an effect of the necessary being's intellectual apprehension of its essence, and yet it apprehends in this way only insofar as it is a "pure intellect" and a "first principle." If the necessary being "must intellectualy apprehend," then the sort of act, which this apprehension is, and the sort of doing it occasions, becomes a locus for philosophical elaboration in these pages in Ibn Sīnā's *Metaphysics* of *The Healing*.[83] The explication of the sort of "act," فعل, *fiʿl*, which the necessary being does, is immediately an explication of world, because such acts give place to the being of things and of beings, and there will have been no beings or things without it, "because its essence [the essence of the necessary being—JS] is of a nature that all being emanates from it [ذاته من شأنه أن يفيض عنها كل وجود/*dhātahu min shaʾnuhu an yafīḍ ʿanhā kull wujūd*]."[84]

"There is, among the things that are, nothing that is not in some manner necessitated by it as as cause—this we have shown" (8.6.16.359), Ibn Sīnā explains of "the necessary being," and yet this necessitation is also a kind of giving: "It has become evident that the necessary being must in itself be the one who gives all being [مفيدا لكل وجود/*mufīdan li-kull wujūd*] and every perfection of being" (8.6.4.356), and this "giving," الإفادة, *al-ifāda*, a term which repeats the form of the "one who gives the being of each substance," in Ibn Sīnā's commentary on *Book Lambda* of Aristotle's *Metaphysics*, is the act through which the world comes to be what it is. But how may we understand this giving? What sort of act is it? If there is a giving, how may we think it in relation to the coming to be of beings and things in the world? If there are to be beings or things, and if their being is derivative of the necessary being, which, itself, derives from no other, because "it is impossible that there should, in any manner whatsoever, be for it a principle and a cause" (9.4.2.402), how may we think that act of giving that gives place to all beings other than it? In what sense may the being of these beings be said to have been given, and in what sense may such an act be said to be an "act" at all? If the being of such beings, outside of a relation to the necessary being, is "nugatory," باطلة, *bāṭila*—"They are all, in themselves, nugatory, true only through it, and, with respect to what follows it, realized" (8.6.5.356)—how does Ibn Sīnā think the relation between the necessary being and all of the others? If such beings or things are contingent—if they are possible in themselves, and necessary through the necessary being—and if what they share is their not sharing in anything with the necessary being, how does Ibn Sīnā explicate the sharing that occurs among them, and which initiates, firstly, in an act of "intellectual apprehension," which is also an act of giving?[85]

To consider these questions I wish to return to Ibn Sīnā's discussion of emanation in its relation to what he terms the "first act," الفعل الأول, *al-fiʿl al-awwal*: "But the first act of the first truth, through its essence, however, is that it intellectually apprehends its essence, which, in itself, is the principle of the order of the good in being."[86] And yet if it is this act that gives place to being, and to beings, this is not in order that the act of the first do so; instead, it is merely the case that the necessary being's intellectual apprehension of its essence is the sort of act that it is, without any "for the sake of," لأجل, *li-ajli*.[87] Such an act is, merely, a doing that takes place necessarily in the giving of being, and in the overflow it also is: "And, as we have explained at great length, its intellection is the cause of being in accordance with what it intellectually apprehends. The being of what comes to be through it is by way of a necessity of its being and a necessary consequence of its being—not, however, in the sense that its being is for the sake of the being of something other than itself."[88]

The intellection of the first, then, is an act without intention:

فلهذا لا يجوز أن يكون كون الكل عنه على سبيل قصد منه كقصدنا لتكوين الكل ولوجود الكل فيكون قاصدا لأجل شيء غيره. وهذا الفصل قد فرغنا من تقريره في غيره، وذلك فيه أظهر، ونخصه من بيان إمتناع أنْ يقصد وجود الكل عنه أنّ ذلك يؤدي إلى تكثّره في ذاته. فإنه حينئذ يكون فيه شيء بسببه يقصد، وهو معرفته وعلمه لوجوب القصد أو إستحبابه أو خيرية فيه توجب ذلك، ثم قصد، ثم فائدة يفيدها إياه القصد على ما أوضحنا قبل؛ وهذا محال. (9.4.2.402)

For this reason it is impossible for the being of all things [*kawn al-kull*], which proceed from it, to be by way of an intention from it—like our intention—for forming the whole and for the being of the whole, so that it would be intending for the sake of something other than itself [*fa yakūn qāṣidan li-ajli shay'in ghayrihi*]. We have devoted ourselves to this part of our explication elsewhere, where it has been made apparent, and we have, in particular, clarified the impossibility [*imtināʿ*] of its intending the being of the whole [*wujūd al-kull*], which proceeds from it, in that this would lead to a multiplicity in its essence. For then there would be something in it by reason of which it intends [*yakūn fihi shay' bi-sababihi yaqṣud*]—namely, its cognizance and knowledge of the necessity of intending, or a deference to it, or a goodness therein that necessitates it—and then there would be in it knowledge of the intention, then of a benefit the intention would bestow on it, as we have previously clarified—and this is impossible [*muḥāl*].

Just as there is no intention, where the necessary being would intend in a manner that would be "like our intention," so too there is no "willing" but instead a "pure intellectual willing" (8.7.10.366), which is, Ibn Sīnā also explains, "generosity," جود, *jūd*: "This willing, in the form we have ascertained, which is not connected to a purpose within the emanation of being [في فيض الوجود/*fī fayḍ al-wujūd*], is nothing other than emanation itself [نفس الفيض/*nafs al-fayḍ*]—which is generosity" (8.7.12.367). In relation to the necessary being there is a willing that is an "intellectual apprehension" and a "generosity," a giving that can do nothing but give away, and where this giving away, in "emanation itself," is the giving of place to being through an act of "willing" without a desire for recompense. "Generosity," Ibn Sīnā wrote in *Remarks and Admonitions*, "is to provide what is necessary, yet not in order to be compensated."[89] In this frame: The necessary being is nothing but the acts Ibn Sīnā has outlined—in "apprehension," "intention," "willing," and "generosity"—and this is what the necessary being's being, its "thatness," إنّ, *innun*, is: "We have ascertained for you, regarding the matter of generosity, that which, if you remember it, you will have known that this will is itself generosity, and if you were to ascertain this, you would know that the primary attribute of the necessary being consists in its being a thatness and that it is a being [تكون الصفة الأولى لواجب الوجود أنه إنٌّ وموجود/*takūn al-ṣiffa al-ūlā li-wājib al-wujūd annahu innun wa mawjūd*]."[90] This formulation suggests a thinking of the being of the necessary being and its "quiddity" or "whatness," ماهية, *māhiyya*, which is, Ibn Sīnā writes, its merely being what is: "There is no quiddity of the necessary being other than its being the necessary being, and this is its thatness" (8.4.9.346). If one were to summarize the intersections of being, form, and act in Ibn Sīnā, one might say that the "thatness," إنية, *inniyya*, of the necessary being is that it is, its being is that it intellectually apprehends, its apprehension is what gives place to world, and its acts are generosity.[91]

It is in relation to the necessary being that Ibn Sīnā explains "the first of the beings," which "proceeds" from it: "It has become evident, then, that the first of the beings proceeding from the first cause is one in number, that its essence and quiddity are one, and that it is not in matter" (9.4.6.404), and yet this being, unlike the necessary being, contains a plurality, because it intellectually apprehends itself and the first: "The effect in itself is possible in being and, through the first, necessary in being. Its necessary existence consists in its being an intellect; it intellectually apprehends itself and necessarily apprehends the first intellectually" (9.4.11.405). It is in relation to this being, which Ibn Sīnā also calls "the first intellect," that "the structure of the whole cosmos [هيئة الكل/*hayʾat al-kull*], the relation of its parts to each other, and the order deriving from the first principle to the most remote beings that fall within its arrangement" (9.7.19.429), is given:

> فيكون إذن العقل الأوّل يلزم عنه بما يعقل الأوّل وجود عقل تحته، وبما يعقل ذاته وجود صورة الفلك الأقصى، وكمالها وهي النفس، وبطبيعة إمكان الوجود الحاصلة له المندرجة في تعقّله لذاته وجود جرمية الفلك الأقصى المندرجة في جملة ذات الفلك الأقصى بنوعه، وهو الأمر المشارك للقوة. فبما يعقل الأوّل، يلزم عنه عقل وبما يختصّ بذاته على جهة تلزم عنه الكثرة الأولى بجزئيها، أعني المادة والصورة، والمادة بتوسط الصورة أو بمشاركتها، كما أنّ إمكان الوجود يخرج إلى الفعل بالفعل الذي يحاذي صورة الفلك. وكذلك الحال في عقل عقل، وفلك فلك، حتى ينتهي إلى العقل الفعّال الذي يدبّر أنفسنا. (9.41.12.406–407)
>
> Thus there necessarily follows from the first intellect [*al-ʿaql al-awwal*], insofar as it intellectually apprehends the first, the being of an intellect beneath it [*wujūd ʿaql taḥtahu*]. Insofar as it intellectually apprehends itself, there follows from it the being of the form of the outermost sphere and its perfection—namely, the soul. Through the nature of the possibility of being that is realized for it, enfolded in [*al-mundarija fī*] its intellectual apprehension of itself, is the being of the corporeality of

> the outermost sphere, enfolded in the aggregate of the outermost sphere, taken as a species, and this is the thing that has a sharing in common with potentiality. Thus, insofar as it intellectually apprehends the first, there follows necessarily from it an intellect; and insofar as in one respect its intellection is applied specifically to itself, there follows necessarily from it the first multiplicity [*al-kathra al-ūlā*] in its two parts—I mean matter and form—matter coming to be either through the mediation of form or through its participation in it, just as the possibility of being is actualized by the actuality that parallels the form of the sphere. This is the state of affairs in each successive intellect and each successive sphere, until it terminates with the active intellect [*al-ʿaql al-faʿʿāl*] that governs our souls.

"There is no way for you to deny the wonderous manifestations in the formation of the world, the parts of the heavens, and the parts of animals and plants" (9.6.1.415), Ibn Sīnā writes, and such "manifestations" come to be only through that sort of "act" that takes place without "intention" and in relation to which there is no why: "There is no why regarding it [لا لِمَ له / *lā limma lahu*], and, you shall know that there is no whyness regarding its act [وستعلم أنه لا لميّة لفعله / *wa sa taʿlam annahu lā lamiyya li-fiʿlihi*]" (8.4.16.348). The necessary being, then, intends only insofar as it does so generously, without a desire for recompense, and its acts may therefore also be termed a sort of "love": "He," Ibn Sīnā notes in relation to the first, "is a lover of his essence [عاشق ذاته / *ʿāshiq dhātihi*], which is the principle of all order and good, insofar as its essence is such a principle" (8.7.3.363). This being, which is the ground of being and the principle of all beings, is merely its being, its "thatness," *inniyya*, and yet it does not cease relating itself to others, if in a manner that is neither a relation nor a sharing: "For all things are from it, and it shares nothing with that which proceeds from it, for it is the principle of all things, and it is not any one of things that are posterior to it" (8.5.14.354). The form of the necessary being is, then, aporetic, because the being that is "the principle of all things" is a "principle," and it is itself, only insofar as it relates to such "things" by not relating to them, where "all relations to it" (8.5.14.354) are affirmed, and are a kind of giving, yet only in a sense that affirms no relation, and that designates "relations" as what Ibn Sīna terms "necessary concomitants," لوازم, *lawāzim*.[92]

The terms of this aporetic form are given in the language of the Aristotelian logical books: The necessary being cannot be demonstrated but instead is "the demonstration of all things [البرهان على كل شيء / *al-burhān ʿalā kull shayʾ*]" (8.5.14.354). This passage recalls us to *Posterior Analytics*. "It is clear, then," Ibn Sīnā writes in the *Logic* of *The Healing*, "that all knowledge is not through demonstration, and that some of what is known is known in itself without mediation, and its place is at the end of the analysis. Such a thing, and what is analogous to it, is the principle, with which the premises of demonstrations end." He continues: "It is not, furthermore, as what is thought, that the premises of demonstrations are either without end or that they stop, in each demonstration, at a ground that is given without true clarification. Rather, the truth is that a demonstration ends with what is clear in itself without mediation."[93] If, in this, metaphysics is explicated in the terms of logic, I observe that logic becomes indistinct metaphysics, and that metaphysics becomes a kind of ontology: a discourse on what is, if one that is not translatable into a temporally determined understanding of being but is, instead, anontological.[94] In this, what *is* may be said to be a kind of sharing. "The first," Ibn Sīnā writes, is "one" because its being is not shared—"It is one insofar as it does not share at all the being, which it possesses"—and yet, insofar as it is "the necessary being," and insofar as its being is explicated in terms of this necessity, its being is not its own and sharing is all that it is able to do.[95] What the textual tradition I've studied passes on is a sense form, where what is *is* itself, and where this is so only insofar as this ceases to be the case, where being is non-selfsame and inidentical. If being is inidentical, and if it is, therefore, not reducible to those "common notions" which, as Aristotle outlined in *Book Beta* of *Metaphysics*, one is to presume, this would perhaps be the case only insofar as one already interpreted such notions in a particular manner, in relation to being and form, to which the Aristotelian treatises ought not be reduced.[96] Instead, I underline a sense of being where what *is* is in excess of itself, where it shares itself out, and where it is a kind of generosity—in "emanation" or "overflow," in Ibn Sīnā's language, and in the language of the Arabic Plotinus texts I study in this chapter, and which Ibn Sīnā had read.[97] If this tradition has been subordinated through the interpretive and social pose I'm calling "settler life," it remains legible in the textual practices, which Ibn Sīnā—and not only he—reformulates for us still.

3
Insurgence
A Poetics of Things

The sea throws its waves very high.

—ETEL ADNAN

In 1980 the poet and painter Etel Adnan published a volume of poetry in French titled *L'Apocalypse arabe,* which she translated into English and published in 1989 under the title *The Arab Apocalypse.* The opening of the volume—see figures 1a and 1b—approaches the sun, a cosmological form which, in its singularity, is already plural, because there are, at the opening of the poem, already several suns: "A yellow sun A green sun a yellow sun A red sun a blue sun."[1] Each of the fifty-nine poems contained in the volume is numbered with a roman numeral, as if a question of number and counting were at stake in the poem, and to think about the poetic in relation to number and being in Adnan I underline that the first line of this poem, which I've reproduced here, does not contain a verb. Adnan's language merely states the being there of the sun, even as it is not "the" sun but only "a" sun, a form which, in its mere being, does not rely upon or turn to another in order to give account for it, and which does not draw upon another to ground it or give to it its sense. Instead, there is already a relation to others, a plurality in indetermined form, a giving of being, which does not advance or call for its sense or a semanticity in the social, or a subordination of matter or language to the experience or self-reflective pose of a subject. A non-selfsame understanding of language and relation is here shown, a cosmology that does not affirm a being's or a thing's identity with itself, and which decomposes a sense of self-standing being: an anontological form.

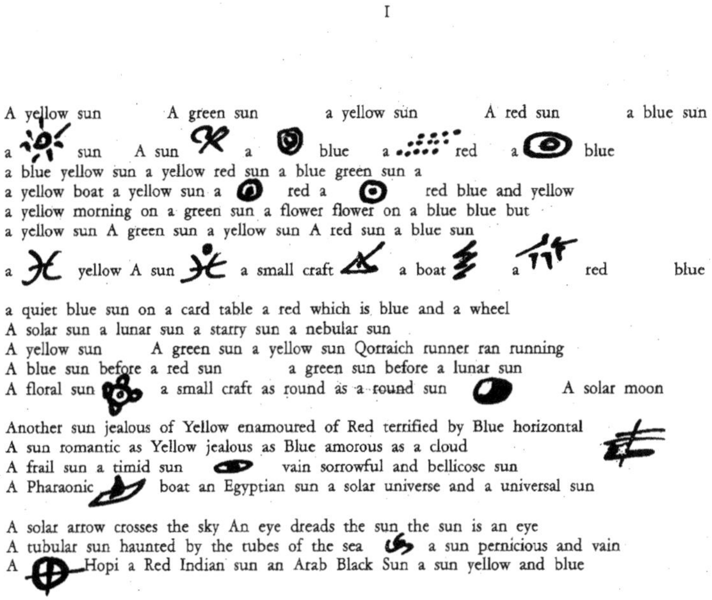

I

A yellow sun A green sun a yellow sun A red sun a blue sun
a sun A sun a blue a red a blue
a blue yellow sun a yellow red sun a blue green sun a
a yellow boat a yellow sun a red a red blue and yellow
a yellow morning on a green sun a flower flower on a blue blue but
a yellow sun A green sun a yellow sun A red sun a blue sun
a yellow A sun a small craft a boat a red blue
a quiet blue sun on a card table a red which is blue and a wheel
A solar sun a lunar sun a starry sun a nebular sun
A yellow sun A green sun a yellow sun Qorraich runner ran running
A blue sun before a red sun a green sun before a lunar sun
A floral sun a small craft as round as a round sun A solar moon
Another sun jealous of Yellow enamoured of Red terrified by Blue horizontal
A sun romantic as Yellow jealous as Blue amorous as a cloud
A frail sun a timid sun vain sorrowful and bellicose sun
A Pharaonic boat an Egyptian sun a solar universe and a universal sun
A solar arrow crosses the sky An eye dreads the sun the sun is an eye
A tubular sun haunted by the tubes of the sea a sun pernicious and vain
A Hopi a Red Indian sun an Arab Black Sun a sun yellow and blue

Figure 1a. Etel Adnan. *The Arab Apocalypse*. The Post-Apollo Press. Sausalito, California. 1989. Poem I. Copyright The Estate of Etel Adnan. Courtesy of the Post-Apollo Press.

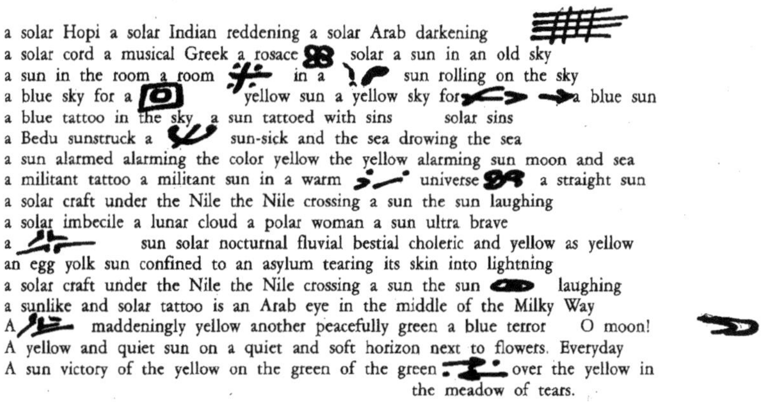

a solar Hopi a solar Indian reddening a solar Arab darkening
a solar cord a musical Greek a rosace solar a sun in an old sky
a sun in the room a room in a sun rolling on the sky
a blue sky for a yellow sun a yellow sky for a blue sun
a blue tattoo in the sky a sun tattoed with sins solar sins
a Bedu sunstruck a sun-sick and the sea drowing the sea
a sun alarmed alarming the color yellow the yellow alarming sun moon and sea
a militant tattoo a militant sun in a warm universe a straight sun
a solar craft under the Nile the Nile crossing a sun the sun laughing
a solar imbecile a lunar cloud a polar woman a sun ultra brave
a sun solar nocturnal fluvial bestial choleric and yellow as yellow
an egg yolk sun confined to an asylum tearing its skin into lightning
a solar craft under the Nile the Nile crossing a sun the sun laughing
a sunlike and solar tattoo is an Arab eye in the middle of the Milky Way
A maddeningly yellow another peacefully green a blue terror O moon!
A yellow and quiet sun on a quiet and soft horizon next to flowers. Everyday
A sun victory of the yellow on the green of the green over the yellow in
the meadow of tears.

Figure 1b. Etel Adnan. *The Arab Apocalypse*. The Post-Apollo Press. Sausalito, California. 1989. Poem I. Copyright The Estate of Etel Adnan. Courtesy of the Post-Apollo Press.

I've argued in the introduction and chapter 1 of this book that the form of life that has been privileged in the normative terms for thought, being, language, and philosophical self-reflection—what I've termed "settler life"—advances a social logic of property and whiteness, and of controlled linguistic understanding and carceral social form, in a radical privilege of subjective being, and that this social logic is instituted in relation to transatlantic chattel slavery, settler colonization, colonial-settler genocide, the theft of Indigenous land, and the global transmutations of earth into property. I've also argued, in chapter 2 of this book, that a particular practice of language and a sense of being, wholly other than what I've termed "settler life," is carried in the writings of al-Kindī, al-Fārābī, and Ibn Sīnā. I've noticed that in this tradition, the being that is to have been "first," and in relation to which a discourse on what Ibn Sīnā called "absolute wisdom," الحكمة المطلقة, *al-ḥikma al-muṭlaqa*, is to have been installed, is merely itself and nothing else. And I've also noticed—reading al-Kindī's references to Plotinus and Proclus, al-Fārābī's pedagogical writings on logic and the Arabic translation of Aristotle's *Posterior Analytics*, and Ibn Sīnā's discussion of *Book Lambda* of Aristotle's *Metaphysics* and the Arabic translation of Themistius's fourth-century commentary on it—that through an attention to this understanding of being an anontological sense of form is generalized. In this tradition, this or that being, whatever thing or being, is merely what it is; it does not rely on an atemporal being exterior to or above it, even as it belongs to an overflow of being in an ontology of emanative forms. Because this or that being or thing is merely itself, and because, in this, each and every being or thing is like all of the others, in a sharing of what is "common," عام, *ʿām*, as al-Fārābī wrote in his "Letter on the Aims of Aristotle's *Metaphysics*," this sharing gives an inidenticality, where a being or thing is what it is only insofar as its form occasions a temporal excess. Since this temporal excess is formal, it gives a sense of being not reducible to self-sameness, where a thing or being would be itself; instead, the force of propositional statements—where the verb "to be" would assert a relation of identity between subject and predicate, for example "A is B"—is convoluted or decomposed.[2] In the Arabic-language tradition I studied in chapter 2 an understanding of being is passed on, which is wholly unlike what has been privileged in post-twelfth-Christian-century, post-Latinate philosophy in that region of the earth we continue to call "Europe," and in its global self-exteriorization, its ceaseless sending out of itself and its divided—and still ever-mutating—languages of social domestication and capture.

This chapter considers reiterations of the tradition of anontological form, its being carried on and reformulated, in the Arabic-language poetry of the Iraqi poet Khālid al-Maʿālī, who was born in 1956 near the city of al-Samāwa in Iraq and fled to Paris in 1979, and from there to Cologne, where he founded the literary press Manshurāt al-Jamal in 1983, and in al-Maʿālī's translations into Arabic of the German-language, Romanian-Jewish poet Paul Celan; and in the poetry and painting of Etel Adnan, who was born in Lebanon in 1925, and left for Paris to study in 1949, and, later, to the United States in 1955, where she became a teacher of art at Dominican College in San Raphael, California, to return to Beirut in 1972, and to depart, again, in 1977, after the outbreak of the Civil War in Lebanon.[3] In studying reformulations of this tradition in Adnan and al-Maʿālī, I observe a refusal of the terms privileged in settler life and its mutations in post-Ottoman, Arab, and Arabic contexts, in relation to the demand this form generates for autonomy and self-determination in language. The modern institutions of property, legality, and the state—a collocation of forms that point, inidentically, to histories of social formation and juridical practice, and which are coagulated in the capitalist and abstracting terms of the 1858 Ottoman Land Code—are refused in the material practice, and the sort of doing, which language, in Adnan and al-Maʿālī, is.[4] In Adnan's poetry and painting, in the poetic and translational texts of al-Maʿālī, and in the poetic formulations of Celan, as al-Maʿālī's Arabic-language translations teach us, language carries a tradition, an inessential practice in the poetic, given to us in the Arabic-language philosophical texts I study in chapter 2. Through a lingering with these texts—with al-Maʿālī, Adnan, and Celan—in a non-agential yielding to them, a slow reading or blurry listening, I notice a social or lingual doing in excess of the terms for being and language in settler life. In this sort of doing—and in its indetermined temporal mode, where the poetic occasions an indistinction of "praxis" from "poiēsis," as I noted reading Aristotle in chapter 1—language and painting become insurgence.

Reverberation

Settler life imposes itself as a demand at the inhabitants of the earth, differentially, and with asymmetric force and consequence. There is a global exteriorization of terms, which points to what al-Maʿālī, in a poem written in 1985, called "the question's origin": "Each thread," he writes, "that encounters me/drags me to the slaughter/to the question's origin" [كل خيط يلاقيني/ يسحبني إلى المجزرة / إلى علة السؤال; *kull khayṭ yulāqīnī/yasḥabnī ilā al-majzara/ilā ʿillat al-suʾāl*]."[5] The subject of poetic utterance is "dragged," and it is this being-dragged that occasions the formulation of poetic speech. In this, we may understand the materiality of language in its decomposition of temporal forms, where if "I" am, this is only insofar as "I" is dragged to the slaughter, a violence that points not only to the social destruction and collective unsurvival in 1980s Iraq but also a rescoring of the terms for language and life in a longer time frame, where beings are interpellated, in excess of the time of the postcolonial state, to become proper subjects of law, language, and the social, in an interiorizing sense of linguistic existence in the fallout of the Arabic nineteenth century.[6] And yet this passage points as well to what comes, as if from a future—"Each thread," he writes, "is a sign of a coming victim / singing in their loudest voice [كل خيط / علامة لقتيل قادم / وبأعلى صوته يغنّي; *kull khayṭ / ʿalāma li-qatīl qādim / wa bi-aʿlā ṣawtihi yughannī*]"—and al-Maʿālī's formulations therefore overflow the terms for state formation and "the production of Iraq as a bounded territorial space over which post-Ottoman sovereignty could be asserted and economic development, as the extraction of resources, carried out," as Sara Pursley incisively has written, in relation to the pedagogical and juridical institution of "modern self-disciplined subjects with self-disciplined interiorities" and a privilege of "individual title to land" and "the monogamous conjugal couple," in a reconfiguration of temporality and its orientation toward the "future" and "a whole mode of being in the world."[7]

If "the question's origin" points to the coercive terms for legality in the modern state, and if it speaks to us of the generalization of settler life as a pacifying global form, it does so in relation to the translation and reformulation of the terms for "governance," السياسة, *al-siyāsa*, in post-Ottoman frames.[8] The mutations in Ottoman political and social form, from the fourteenth through the nineteenth centuries, occasion—with the global and regional institution of capitalism, and the displacement of the tradition of *siyāsa* with modern legality and politicality, and a demand for subject-centered social existence—a coercive and differentiating privilege of the subject of property, language, and law, a subject of interiorizing self-reflection and controlled lingual acts.[9] Al-Maʿālī gives us to read these mutations in relation to the poetic and language, and the regimes of cartographic life. "I wonder: Have the laws been established? / Has the door been closed upon me? [هل يا ترى قامت الشرائع / وأغلق الباب عليَّ; *hal yā turā qāmat al-sharāʾiʿ / wa aghlaqa al-bāb ʿalayya*]," al-Maʿālī asks, and I linger with this passage in relation to the question of which al-Maʿālī spoke, as well as the question of its origin and its relation to "the slaughter," المجزرة, *al-majzara*.[10] If "the slaughter" congeals histories of linguistic and social violence, there remains the matter of "the question," السؤال, *al-suʾāl*, and its relation to thought, language, and the social, and the beginning at which one is obligated to begin: "I am obligated to begin with a question about the pilings-up of the thinking of another / who remains sitting, exhausted from thought / forfeiting moments, which will be lost, finally [يتعيّن عليَّ البدء بسؤال عن تراكمات تفكير آخر /

ما زال جالسا، متعبا من التفكير / يضيّع لحظاتٍ، ستضيع حتما; *yata'ayyan 'alayya al-bid' bi-su'āl 'an tarākumāt tafkīr ākhar/mā zāla jālisan, mut'aban min al-tafkīr,/yuḍayyi'u laḥaẓātin, sataḍī' ḥatman*] (58), al-Ma'ālī wrote in another poem included in the same volume, written in Cologne in March 1983.

The "beginning," البدء, *al-bid'*, at which one is obligated to begin is a question where one gives language; there is already an obligation, through which the beginning initiates, and which gives the form that "I" is. One might say that there is no "I" without a relation to this obligation, where language takes place in interlocution, and where, in address, language is wholly in excess of any self-oriented or self-determined form. The subject of poetic utterance is not a single being, one that would first be itself and then speak, but a form given in an address toward "another," آخر, *ākhar*, in the "pilings-up," تراكمات, *tarākumāt*, and what one might also render as the "accumulations" of thought, which are, al-Ma'ālī writes, on the cusp of their loss. This loss is futural and has already taken place, there will already have been loss and the site of utterance convokes a context of devastation—"I've lived," he writes, "off of garbage" [لقد أرضعتني المزبلة/*la qad arḍa'atnī al-mazbila*] (86)—even as the devastation of context does not install a recognizable temporal break, a clarity in historical time. Instead there are "accumulations," where the end ceases to end. Certitude withdraws—"Today, I saw the face/I saw the clouds/The sky departed/Each star took a path/I no longer knew the way to certainty" [اليوم، رأيت الوجه/ رأيت الغيوم/ السماء رحلت/ وكل نجمة أخذت طريقا/ ما عدت أعرف باب اليقين; *al-yawm, ra'aytu al-wijh/ra'aytu al-ghuyūm/al-samā' raḥalat/wa kull najma akhad-hat ṭarīqan/mā 'udtu a'rif bāb al-yaqīn*]"—and this withdrawal gives a sense of language that indetermines the speaking subject as a temporal ground for the social.[11] It is as if the poem addresses the terms for interpretation to which language is ceaselessly exposed, which delimit language—which settle it—in the terms for subjective linguistic existence and a privilege of "an individuated practice of reading."[12] In this, as Kamran Rastegar explains through a close discussion of the transformations in language in the Arabic nineteenth century, in Ottoman and post-Ottoman contexts, rather than a sociality there is "an ontology of faithful transference" (305) in relation to reading and translation. The "object" of reading appears "as as form of property" (310), and the terms for linguistic understanding do not so much eliminate the temporality of language as reduce it, cordon it off in a cadastral logic, which mirrors the temporal imperatives of the state and its "self-policing literary domains" (314) and bounded modes. The understanding coerced in modern, juridical, and state-determined life imparts a particular sense of what language and reading are, and this sense is at odds with al-Maʿālī's poetry, even as his poetry points to a relation to the social and linguistic destruction this understanding generates.

In al-Maʿālī words bear a sonority that is not legible in relation to the modern demand for temporal clarity and the radical subordination of sound—in the "utterance," اللفظ, *al-lafẓ*, a term in the Arabic lexicon of rhetoric and poetics, to which I'll turn below—to sense.

الكلمة التي جاءت
شُدّت بمعنى
وكلّما خاض الحرفُ درباً
أعادوه إلينا
واجلسوه في الظلام
لكنّها ذكرى يومٍ قديم.[13]

The word that came
Was fastened to a meaning
Whenever the letter entered upon a road
They returned it to us
They sat it down in the dark
But it is a memory of an ancient day.

I notice that in this passage, which appears in a volume titled *Singsong* (حداء/ *Ḥidā*ʾ), published in 2002, "the word," الكلمة, *al-kalima*, the material form which, in utterance, constitutes language, is "fastened," شُدّت, *shuddat*, to "a meaning," معنى, *maʿnā*. The word "comes," and in its coming it is "fastened" to sense, in a coercive gesture of interpretive consolidation, which al-Maʿālī renders with a passive voice verb. The passive quality of the verb at once holds histories of lingual interpretation and institutional and modern state practices for the domestication of the social. If "they," a collective subject that remains unnamed, will have returned language to "us," and if they will have sat "the letter," or, even, the phonemic utterance, الحرف, *al-ḥarf*, down, capturing it in the prone position of an object, in a manner that mirrors the tortuous procedures of the Iraqi state, language retains a temporality in excess of this, a relation to a tradition older than the time of a word's utterance. In the moment at which language is "fastened," the letter "enters" upon a road, and this "entering" points to a materiality of lingual form, whose time is "whenever," in a word's carrying "a memory of an ancient day." This materiality points to the blowing of the wind—"These things which I possess / and which I see / how they've passed, how they've gone away / They extended their embankments, while the wind / passed over them / throwing across them dust and rain [هذه الأشياء التي عندي / والتي أراها / كيف مرت، كيف راحت / مدت جسورَها، وكانت الرياح /

تهبّ عليها/ترمي الغبار والأمطار; *hādhihi al-ashyā' allatī 'indī / wa allatī arāhā / kayfa marrat, kayfa rāḥat / maddat jusūrahā, wa kānat al-riyāḥ / tahubb 'alayhā / tarmī al-ghubār wa al-amṭār*]" (134)—as it does to the neighing of horses and the reverberating sound of the desert. Words come, and if there is an indistinguishability between language and rain, this is perhaps because in al-Ma'ālī language does not yield to a distinction drawn between word and utterance, or sound and wind.

One of the words for sound in al-Ma'ālī is الرنين, *al-ranīn*, which I render as "reverberation":

في هذه الطريق التي لم تعد طريق
كانت الحياةُ تدرجُ
والحنينُ رايةٌ مرفوعة لكل عابر
أتى من بعيد
ملوّحاً بشارةٍ من الصحراء.

وفي هذه الطريق التي أغلقت
كانت الذكرياتُ تبهت
وتبدو كالرنين. (118)

On this road which was no longer one
Life continued on
Longing was a flag raised to each passerby
Who came from afar
Waving with a sign from the desert.

On this road that was closed
Memories were fading
Like a reverberation

This poem is dated March 16, 2000, and it speaks to the destruction imparted since the American invasion of 1991 and the sanctions regime of the 1990s and early 2000s, as it anticipates the years following the invasion and occupation of Iraq in 2003 and its ongoing and genocidal effects in the conscription of Iraq into the legal-juridical terms of settler understanding and the global institutions for social domestication such as the International Monetary Fund, the World Bank, and the rule of law as a technology for nomocentric life. The American- and British-led wars and the global institutions for security, carcerality, and indebtedness exteriorize the juridical and social terms installed in Christian Europe since the twelfth century and its crusading activities, and in these terms' ongoing mutations and relocations. The call to and for legality reiterates the social logic of these terms as it imparts a devastation that is never final and which al-Maʿālī gives us to read in the excess of language over these violences. If the road is "closed," as al-Maʿālī wrote, there is, still, a beckoning "from a distance," من بعيد, *min baʿīd*; the "sign," الشارة, *al-shāra*, that waves from the desert points to "memories," ذكريات, *dhikrayāt*, which, if they have faded, they reverberate sonorously. In al-Maʿālī there is a return to the desert, sound, and reverberation, to winds and rains, a beckoning of signs, and to the matter of topographical life in excess of state-juridical conceptualization: "For each thing," al-Maʿālī writes, "is a story / a faint verse of poetry / the meaning of a meaning / a letter wandering / in the steppes [فكل شيءٍ/ حكاية/ بيتاً خافتاً من الشعر/ معنى معنى/ وحرفاً تائهاً/ في البراري; *fa kull shayʾin / ḥikāya / baytan khāfitan min al-shiʿr / maʿnā maʿnā / wa ḥarfan tāʾihan / fī al-barārī*]."[14] Letters wander, and this wandering is a dimension of "things," أشياء, *ashyāʾ*, in their relation to "the desert," a word that appears, in the poem I've translated above, as الصحراء, *al-ṣaḥrāʾ*, and which is given, in this passage, in the active participle تائها, *tāʾihan*, where we can hear the noun التيه, *al-tīh*, still another word for the desert, and which also points, in al-Maʿālī, to البراري, *al-barārī*, "steppes."

There is a poetic life of things, which is linked to sound and the desert: "The mourners cry out to us / Their voices disappear with the echoes / The wind blows / The echoes grown silent and cease [يصرخنا النادبون/ أصواتهم تتلاشى مع الأصداء/ الريح تهب/ وتخفت الأصداء، تنتهي; *yaṣrakhunā al-nādibūn / aṣwātuhum tatalāshā maʿ al-aṣdāʾ / al-rīḥ tahubb / wa takhfut al-aṣdāʾ, tantahī*]."[15] In this, something comes on the wind, and yet, as I underlined in the introduction to this book, the "thing" is neither a "subject" nor an "object" in representation—as in the principal modes of philosophical articulation in the European, Christian tradition since Kant's first *Critique*—but a sort of doing in materiality, a giving of relation in social or poetic form, which, in al-Maʿālī, is occasioned in the sensuality and sonority of sound. Unlike the terms for cognitive appropriation or interiorizing self-reflection, there is instead "reverberation," رنين, *ranīn*, the resounding of sound, where the thing may be likened to, and where the thing is, an utterance that comes on the wind and remains, al-Maʿālī writes, "before" us: "Thus, from there, we walked / bearing our pains in our bags / while the reverberation that came from a distance / was still travelling before us on the road" [من هناك إذن، سرنا/ نحمل العذاب في أكياسنا/ والرنين الذي كان يأتي من بعيد/ ما زال أمامنا في الطريق يسير; *min hunāka idhan, sirnā / naḥmilu al-ʿadhāb fī akyāsinā / wa al-ranīn alladhī kāna yaʾtī min baʿīd / mā zāla amāmanā fī-al-ṭarīq yasīr*] (99).

"Language is sound," Etel Adnan writes in a volume titled *Seasons*, published in 2008. "To speak is to make modulation, rhythm, and tone," she also observes, and this "making" is the sort of act through which the poetic, in al-

Maʿālī, is offered.[16] If there is a subject, "I," أنا, *anā*, in al-Maʿālī, this is only in relation to a sort of making or doing, in the indistinction between these, which, as in Adnan's poetry and painting, and as in al-Maʿālī's translations, gives language in the sonic activity of poetic form. Language is given in relation to the wind, the desert, steppes, neighing, reverberation, and "chanting," or "recitation," الترتيل, *al-tartīl*: "Whenever the words came and I came / my voice would begin to chant them in order to write them / anew or to sing them [وكلما جاءت الكلمات وجئتُ / راح صوتي يرتّلها ليكتبها / من جديد أو يغنّيها; *wa kullamā jāʾat al-kalimāt wa jiʾtu / raḥ ṣawtī yurattiluhā li-yaktubahā / min jadīd aw yughannīhā*]," and the coming of words occasions a giving in voice that is not initiated in a subject but is a practice occasioned in a recitation carried out in words and their motion.[17]

"Chanting" is indistinct from "writing," الكتابة, *al-kitāba*, or "song," الغناء, *al-ghināʾ*, and, in this, we might say that language does not derive from a subject but is a sonic or material doing. "My voice," صوتي, *ṣawtī*, does not occasion a self-possession, because it is instead a material locus for the inheritance of tradition in the lingual practice of poetic life. And yet if a poetic or linguistic inheritance is given in al-Maʿālī, it does not arrive untouched from a past, as if there were a "past" outside of a relation to the modern forms of social and linguistic destruction. For this reason, we may only say that there is language—or poetry—in al-Maʿālī insofar as it is a practice of sound in reverberation, where the voice of the speaking subject is indistinct from the neighing of a horse, and where voice is given, al-Maʿālī notes, on the wind:

كانت الأوهامُ قد وصلت
ومثل طيرٍ حلّقت في الأعالي
ثم حطّت
وهنا، عند المصير
حيث يدي التي رُفعت،
ثم نُسيت
وجدتُ حاوية الذكريات مرميةً
الوصايا التي أعدت، تُركت
والحصان الشارد في البراري
ما زال يعدو في الخيال
ويصهل.[18]

My thoughts had arrived
Like birds they hovered above
Then descended
Here, upon the path
Where my hand had been raised

And then forgotten
I found memories' innards strewn
The testaments that had been prepared were abandoned
The horse wandering on the steppes
Was still running in my imagination
Neighing.

The title of the volume, *Singsong*, points to the urging on of a camel in song, and al-Maʿālī provides a passage from Ibn Manẓūr's *Lisān al-ʿarab*, offering a lexicographical excursus on the verb *ḥadā* as an epigraph to the poems contained in it. *Ḥadā*, of which *ḥidāʾ*, the title of the volume, is the abstract nominal form, is to "restrain it from behind and drive it forward," and this driving forward is supplemented by the singing of the camel driver: *al-ḥudw*, one further reads, "is to lead camels and sing to them [سوق الإبل والغناء لها/*sūq al-ibl wa al-ghināʾ lahā*]." And so we can understand a material practice of the poetic in al-Maʿālī in its relation to "song," الغناء, *al-ghināʾ*, as it is outlined in Ibn Manẓūr's lexical entry, and as it points to a relation to sonority in poetic utterance. In al-Maʿālī there is a disappearance of world—"Life was forgotten/After they departed/They left memories for us/a thread of thoughts/upon which we hung/We no longer saw the earth at all [الحياة نُسيت/بعدما ذهبوا/تركوا لنا الذكريات/خيطاً من الأوهام/تعلّقنا به/وما عدنا نرى من الأرض شيئاً; *al-ḥayāt nusiyat/baʿdamā dhahabū/tarakū lanā al-dhikrayāt/khayṭan min al-awhām/taʿallaqnā bihi/wa mā ʿudnā narā min al-arḍ shayʾan*]"—but the finality of loss is undone in "singsong" and its reverberation.[19] It is as if the act of the poetic subject, its doing the sort of thing that it does when it does language, is already preceded by wind and the "sounds" or "voices," أصوات, *aṣwāt*, it carries. Wind carries death—"Death, here, blows like the wind [الموت هنا، يهبّ مثل الريح/*al-mawt hunā, yahubb mithla al-rīḥ*]" (57)—and yet if death points to the slaughter of which al-Maʿālī wrote, and to the institution of the modern state and its regimes of carcerality, it also points, in a wholly different sense, to an inheritance in language. In this second sense death is a name for the carrying of tradition, and it gestures to the reiteration of an economy of forms, a tautness in the poet's language—"For I am taut like a rhyme [إذ إنّي مفتول كقافية/*idh innī maftūl ka qāfiya*]," al-Maʿālī writes—which is occasioned in the doing of poetic speech and the practice of form in sound.[20]

Consider this practice in al-Maʿālī's rendering of a pomegranate seed:

إلى الشجرة التي بلا ظلّ
أتيتُ بحثاً عن المأوى
كنتُ أشدُّ الخيوط إلى الوهم
بيدي وأسعى في الليل

وحيداً، أنوء بثقلٍ
هنا كنتُ، أقدامي على الأحجار تخطو
والليلُ الثقيلُ يلوح كرؤيا
هنا كنتُ أخطو، الليلُ خلفي
والذكريات تتيه كأعواد
تقذفُ الريحُ بها في كل إتجاه.

إلى الشجرة التي تاهت بلا ظلّ
كنتُ أتيتُ
حبة الرمان في يدي
والزهرُ الذي كان أحمر
ما زال يابساً في الكيس
الذي حملتُ فيه أنفاسي
غير أنني الآن ملقى
على الدرب، الريحُ تذرو التراب
والرؤيا تاهت في الأعالي
والدنيا مثلي بثقلٍ تنوء.[21]

I came to the shadeless tree
In search of shelter
With my hand I'd pull the threads tautly
Around my thoughts and walk at night
Alone carrying a heavy load
I was here, my feet stepping across stones
The difficult night glimmering like a vision
Here I would walk with the night behind me
My memories wandering like sticks
Tossed in all directions by the wind.

I used to come to the tree
That wandered without shade
With a pomegranate seed in my hand
Its red flowers
Still dry in the bag
In which I carried my breath
But I am, now, thrown
Upon the path. The wind scatters the dirt
And my vision is lost in the heights
Like me, the world carries a heavy load.

A poetic subject, speaking in the first person singular, relates their coming to a tree in search of shelter. The word "tree" is the first noun in the poem and an emphasis is therefore placed upon it, as if in order to speak of a pomegranate seed, and in order to speak of "my breath," the poet had to return to a tree and seek shelter there. The past tense verb كان, *kāna*, appears only in the third line of the poem, and yet we may think of it as governing the time of the poem and its verbs. The poem relates an act that took place in the past, and yet if al-Maʿālī speaks of his coming to the tree, as the second line of the poem is rendered with a past tense, finite verb, أتيتُ, *ataytu*, the word كنتُ, *kuntu*, in the third line, envelops this earlier verb and gives us to read it as a repeated past act. The first two lines of the poem relate an act that took place and came to an end, and yet they speak of what the poetic subject used to do or would do, a habitual action of return to "the shadeless tree," and it is perhaps in this sense that we may understand the "breaths," أنفاس, *anfās*, al-Maʿālī carries as at once singular and plural: the breath he carries at this or that instance, and the breaths, which point to the repeated temporality of the time of the poem. It is as if the act that one does in the poetic were a kind of return, and it is as if in this one seeks shelter from a shadeless tree—a tree that cannot provide shelter. I've noted that in al-Maʿālī something has been lost, and that what has been lost is, in a certain sense, a relation to tradition, and we may think of the poet's return to the tree as a commemoration of this loss, which has not come to an end. "It is as if my voice had been lost [وكأنّ صوتي قد ضاع/*wa ka'anna ṣawtī qad ḍāʿa*]," al-Maʿālī also wrote, and it is this "as if" that relates the temporality of poetic utterance: Loss has taken place and it is unfinished and atotal.[22] The time of the poetic is the time of this loss, routed through "voice," الصوت, *al-ṣawt*, as it is through poetic utterance in what al-Maʿālī calls "wind," الريح, *al-rīḥ*, "neighing," الصهيل, *al-ṣahīl*, "chanting," الترتيل, *al-tartīl*, and "singsong," الحداء, *al-ḥidā'*. One might say that poetry is this routing in a time of language's devastation, and that it gives or shares a sonorous practice, for which "reverberation," الرنين, *al-ranīn*, is also one name.

Inessential Gathering

"For I am taut like a rhyme," al-Maʿālī wrote, and I turn now to consider this tautness in relation to the closural forms of settler understanding and their extensions and mutations in post-Ottoman state and juridical formations and the ongoing global wars for legality.[23] The substance of the poetic, in Arabic, is "sound," الصوت, *al-ṣawt*, a term which the eighth- and ninth-century writer Abū ʿUthmān ʿAmrū ibn Baḥr al-Jāḥiẓ, in his manual on eloquence, addresses in relation to the "movements of the tongue," حركات اللسان, *ḥarakāt al-lisān*, through which "sound" constitutes "utterance," اللفظ, *al-lafẓ* :

والصوت هو آلة اللفظ وهو الجوهر الذي يقوم به التقطيع وبه يوجد التأليف. ولن تكون حركات اللسان لفظاً ولا كلاماً موزوناً ولامنثوراً إلا بظهور الصوت. ولا تكون الحروف كلاماً إلا بالتقطيع والتأليف.[24]

> Sound [*al-ṣawt*] is the instrument of utterance [*al-lafẓ*] and the substance through which articulation is carried out and through which composition formed. The movements of the tongue [*ḥarakāt al-lisān*] will not constitute an utterance [*lafẓ*], and neither will they constitute metered speech or prose [*wa lā kalāman mawzūnan wa lā manthūran*], except through the bringing forth [*ẓuhūr*] of sound [*al-ṣawt*]. And units of sound [*al-ḥurūf*] will not constitute speech [*kalām*] except through articulation and composition.

Al-Jāḥiẓ explicates what language is in its relation to "movements of the tongue"—and "language," اللغة, *al-lugha*, as the historian and philosopher Ibn Khaldūn wrote, in a passage I noted in the preface to this book, is a "lingual act," فعل لساني, *fi'l lisānī*—and such "movements," and the economy of forms they presume, point to a materiality in linguistic formulation, which destabilizes a distinction between material articulation and sense. Prior to a giving of sense, language is already a certain doing in relation to matter, and this sense of what language is—where language is a temporal practice, a "movement" and a "bringing forth," in relation to "sound"—is given to be read in al-Jāḥiẓ. Language, then, may be understood as what takes place in the movement of the tongue and the formation of utterance in sound, since it is only through the motions of the tongue that the matter of "sound," or "voice," transmutes, in utterance, into "speech," الكلام, *al-kalām*. The materiality or substance, the "sound" of utterance, becomes "speech"; it becomes the social form and manner of doing, which language is, through its rendering in relation to the terms for poetic and linguistic practice al-Jāḥiz explicates.

In his *Eloquence and Elucidation* (البيان والتبيين/*al-Bayān wa-al-tibyīn*), which I've begun to cite here, al-Jāḥiẓ outlines an economy of terms, one of which is "concision": "The proper use of language is concision [والإيجاز هو البلاغة/*wa al-iyjāz huwwa al-balāgha*]," al-Jāḥiẓ writes.[25] He places an emphasis on "clarity of expression" in a relation between "speaker" and "listener"—"The point of the matter and the intention in relation to which the speaker and the listener are related is understanding and giving to understand, for anything through which you give someone to understand or clarify the meaning, that is clarity of expression in that context" (1.56)—and yet "clarity of expression," البيان, *al-bayān*, does not privilege an ideational content but instead lingual, material expression: "The best speech is that which, in its spareness, relieves you from its multiplicity, and whose meaning is apparent in its expression" (1.61). What is privileged is an economy in formulation: "Speech," al-Jāḥiẓ writes, "the number of whose phonemic units are few and the number of whose meanings are many" (2.244). If eloquence were to be concerned only with the imparting of meaning, the sense of what language is would become convoluted: "Those who claim that eloquence [البلاغة/*al-balāgha*] is what occurs when the listener understands the meaning of the speaker [أن يكون السامع يفهم معنى القائل/*an yakūn al-sāmiʿ yafham maʿnā al-qāʾil*] make fluent language and incorrect pronunciation, error and proper usage, ambiguous and clear expression, and ungrammatical and grammatical speech all the same [جعل الفصاحة واللكنة والخطأ والصواب والإغلاق والإبانة والملحون والمعرب كله سواءً/*jaʿla al-faṣāḥa wa-al-lukna wa al-khaṭaʾ wa-al-ṣawāb wa al-ighlāq wa al-ibāna wa al-malḥūn wa al-muʿrab kullahu sawāʾan*]; they make all of them clarity of expression" (1.105). The privilege of "understanding," الفهم, *al-fahm*, in relation to "meaning," المعنى, *al-maʿnā*, would mute the economy in speech, where language is an act of the tongue in relation to a sensual doing in voice.

It is a sort of act where "beauty," الجمال, *al-jamāl*, relates to a measured practice of language in shared, non-selfsame form. "'Al-Abbās ibn ʿAbd al-Muṭallab said to the Prophet, prayers and peace be upon him, 'Oh Prophet of God, in what does beauty consist?' He said: 'In language' [وقال العباس بن عبد المطلب للنبي: يا رسول الله فيما الجمال؟ قال: في اللسان/*wa qāla al-ʿAbbās ibn ʿAbd al-Muṭallab lil-nabī: yā rasūl Allah, fīmā al-jamāl? Qāla: fī-al-lisān*]" (1.109), al-Jāḥiẓ reports, and if the eleventh-century philologist Ibn Rashīq comments, citing this passage, that "in this he intended eloquent speech," يريد البيان, *yurīd al-bayān*, this is to point to a sense of language, where language is a practice of constraint in a sociality of collective form, which does not coerce a communal sense organized around a self-owning subject, but instead gives an inessential gathering in linguistic life.[26] "A man's beauty is in the eloquence of his language [جمال الرجل فصاحة لسانه/*jamāl al-rajul faṣāḥat lisānihi*]," the Prophet also said, as al-Qāḍī al-Quḍāʿī reports, and we may consider beauty in relation to eloquence and in its giving us to think the one who speaks—a being that does language—in its relation to those collective practices through which "language" comes to be what it is.[27] Such doing is linked, in al-Jāhiz, to utterance, sound, and hearing: "The best verse of poetry is one which, when you hear its first hemistich you know its rhyme [خير أبيات الشعر البيت الذي إذا سمعت صدره عرفت قافيته/*khayr abyāt al-shiʿr al-bayt alladhī idhā samaʿta ṣadrahu ʿarafta qāfiyatahu*]," and al-Jāḥiẓ's placing an emphasis on the verb "to hear," سمع, *samiʿ*, since the sentence also says, "if you hear, you know," teaches us to heed a relation to the ear in poetic and lingual doing.[28]

"Poetry is speech held together by rhyme [الشعر كلام عُقد بالقوافي / *al-shi'r kalam 'uqida bi-al-qawāfī*]," Ibn Rashīq writes, and yet if "meter is the most important of the pillars in the delimitation of poetry [الوزن أعظم أركان حد الشعر / *al-wazn a'ẓam arkān ḥadd al-shi'r*]," it is equally understood that "rhyme shares with meter in the specification of what poetry is, for something is not called poetry unless it has a meter and a rhyme."[29] Each of these—meter and rhyme—is linked, in Ibn Rashīq, to "intention," النيّة, *al-niyya*, and his discussion relates these to utterance and meaning: "Poetry, following intention, consists in four things: utterance, meter, meaning, and rhyme, and this is what delimits poetry [الشعر يقوم بعد النية من أربعة أشياء: اللفظ، والوزن، والمعنى، والقافية، فهذا هو حد الشعر / *al-shi'r yaqūm ba'd al-niyya min arb'at ashyā': al-lafẓ, wa al-wazn, wa al-ma'nā, wa al-qāfiya, fa hādhā huwwa ḥadd al-shi'r*]" (1.119). There is an intention in poetic speech, and if, for "the Arabs," al-Jāḥiẓ wrote in *Eloquence and Elucidation*, "everything," كل شيء, *kull shay'*, is "intuition and improvisation, as if it were inspiration, there is no effort or suffering or pondering or prolixity [بديهة وإرتجال، وكأنه إلهام، وليست هناك معاناة ولا مكابدة، ولا إجالة فكرة، ولا إستعانة / *badīha wa irtijāl, wa ka'annahu ilhām, wa laysat hunāka mu'ānāat wa lā mukābada, wa lā ijālat fikra, wa lā isti'āna*]" (3.425), we may understand the tradition of prosody in Arabic—as well as the discussion of utterance and its relation to grammar, as in the foundational text on language of the eighth-century grammarian Sibawayh, titled "The Book," الكتاب, *al-Kitāb*—as bearing an understanding of language, where language is a practice in the articulation of form, in acts of the tongue, which call into being collectives without essence or substance. Here, language is a name for the sort of practice one does in a sharing that does not devolve upon a subject; it is not a closed system for the communication of sense but instead a doing with matter, where motions of the tongue give place to a sociality.

The tenth-century philologist Abu Hilāl al-'Askarī explains that "the Commander of the Faithful, 'Alī ibn Abī Ṭālib, may God be pleased with him, said: I have not seen an eloquent person, except if their speech is concise and its meanings many [ما رأيتُ بليغا قط إلا وله في القول إيجاز، وفي المعاني إطالة / *mā ra'aytu balīghan qaṭ illa wa lahu fī al-qawl iyjāz, wa fī al-ma'ānī iṭāla*]," and this statement passes on an understanding of language where language is an inessential performance of form, one locus of which is the formation of poetic speech in utterance.[30] Al-'Askarī notes that eloquence does not only relate to "meaning" because it is given in "the well-formed utterance and its clarity [جودة اللفظ وصفائه / *jūdat al-lafẓ wa ṣafā'ihi*]" as well as in "the soundness of its arrangement and order, and an absence of crookedness in composition and arrangement [صحة السبك والتركيب، والخلو من أود النظم والتأليف/*ṣiḥḥat al-sabk wa al-tarkīb, wa al-khilw min awad al-naẓm wa-al-ta'līf*]" (72). "Short poems enter the ear more easily [القصار اولج في المسامع/*al-qiṣār awlaj fī al-masāmi'*]," Ibn Rashīq also writes, and we may understand this "entering" of language "into" the ear as giving the social form of the poetic as a practice for linguistic life, in which the being of the speaker of language is not its own, and where language does not accumulate in the formation of a self-determined subject, but where it is instead a particular sort of doing, a practice, in non-selfsame form.[31]

To consider this practice we may turn to the explication of "intention," النيّة, *al-niyya*, in Ibn Manẓūr, where the verb نوى, *nawā*, is "to aim toward," قصد, *qaṣada*, or to "purpose," as in "to intend toward a home," إنتوى المنزل, *intawā al-manzil*, and *al-nawā* is, as well, "the direction toward which one departs," الوجه يُذهب فيه, *al-wijh yudhab fihi*, or, as Ibn Manẓūr cites al-Jawhari's lexicon *al-Ṣiḥāḥ*, it is "the direction a traveller intends, from near or from afar," الوجه الذي ينويه المسافر من قُرب أو بُعد, *al-wijh alladhī yanwīhi al-musāfir min qurb aw bu'd*. It is, further, a "distance," بُعد, *bu'd*, just as it is "to move from one place to another or from one house to another, and the like, as the Bedouin move in their desert." The verb *nawā* is, further, to preserve or guard someone, حَفِظَه, *ḥafiẓahu*: "Al-Farrā' said: God cares for you, which is to say, he guards you," قال الفراء نواك الله أي حفظك, *qāla al-Farrā': nawāka Allah ayy ḥafiẓaka*, as in when God accompanies someone on their travels, صحبه الله في سفره وحفظه, *ṣaḥibahu Allah fī safrihi wa ḥafiẓahu*.[32] I linger with the corporeal dimension of "intention" as Ibn Manẓūr explicates it and consider its relation to the linguistic and poetic, where, as Ibn Rashīq explains, it is only "following" intention that one is to consider poetic statement in its relation to utterance, meaning, meter, and rhyme. Intention presupposes a being that acts in a particular manner, and yet there is no subject of such an act but only a shared practice, where one intends in relation to a "direction" or "distance." In the sense of language presumed here, intention precedes the poetic, and the poetic is a practice of linguistic form. The sociality of utterance gives place to a mode of poetic life—a life of linguistic sociality—where if "I" speaks, this is only insofar as "speech" is a practice that temporally exceeds itself, a doing that gives itself away and to others, and which, as the Prophet stated in the passage cited by al-Jāḥiẓ and Ibn Rashīq, is that in which beauty consists.[33]

I wish now to consider the thinking of the social suggested by al-Jāḥiẓ in his treatise on the sociality of language and life, titled *The Book of Living Beings* (كتاب الحيوان/*Kitāb al-ḥayawān*). Language, he writes there, is a practice shared among living beings—birds, he writes, "Possess a language through which they give their needs to be understood by each other [لها منطق تتفاهم بها حاجات بعضها إلى بعض/*lahā manṭiq tatafāham bihā ḥājāt baʿḍihā ilā baʿḍ*]"—and it is this sense of language as "giving one another to understand," تفاهُم, *tafāhum*, that is outlined in these sentences, where the social is constituted in language, through the being together of creatures in relation to a communication of needs.[34] "Know," al-Jāḥiẓ further writes, "that the need of people for each other is a necessary characteristic according to their nature, a disposition founded in their substance, which is firmly rooted and does not pass away, and which encompasses them in their plurality, and includes those who are closest and those who are farthest away" (1.60). This sense of language is placed in the context of a life of linguistic plurality, where language is to be a medium for semantic interlocution, in the exchange of meaningful speech, where a sense of language as a communicative practice is extended and generalized across languages. "The human being," al-Jāḥiẓ explains, "is a being who speaks language well [والإنسان فصيح/*wa al-insān faṣīḥ*], even if they express themselves in Persian or Sanskrit or Greek, for the Arab does not understand the unintelligible speech of the Greek less well than the Greek understands the eloquence of the Arabic tongue [وليس العربي أسوأ فهما لطمطمة الرومي من الرومي لبيان لسان العربي/*wa laysa al-ʿarabī aswaʾ fahman li ṭamṭamat al-rūmī min al-rūmī li-bayān lisān al-ʿarabī*]" (1.54).

This communicative sense of language is addressed further in the seventh book of *Book of Living Beings*, where al-Jāḥiẓ turns to the question of the language of birds:

> فإن قال قائل: ليس هذا بمنطق، قيل له: أما القرآن فقد نطق بأنّه منطقٌ، والأشعارُ قد جعلته منطقاً، وكذلك كلامُ العرب، فإن كنتَ إنما أخرجتَه من حدّ البيان، وزعمتَ أنّه ليس بمنطق لأنك لم تَفهم عنه، فأنتَ أيضا لا تفهم كلامَ عامة الأمم؛ وأنتَ إن سمّيْتَ كلامَهم رَطانةً وطَمْطمةً فإنك لا تمتنع من أن تزعم أنّ ذلك كلامُهم ومنطقُهم، وعامة الأمم أيضاً لا يفهمون كلامَك ومنطقَك، فجائزٌ لهم أن يُخرِجوا كلامَك من البيان والمنطق، وهل صار ذلك الكلامُ منهم بياناً ومنطقاً إلا لتفاهمهم حاجةً بعضهم إلى بعض، ولأنّ ذلك كان صوتاً مؤلفاً خرج من لسان وفم، فهلاّ كانت أصواتُ أجناس الطير والوحش والبهائم بياناً ومنطقاً إذْ قد علمتَ أنّها مقطعة مصوّرة، ومؤلّفة منظمة، وبها تفاهموا الحاجات، وخرجت من فم ولسان، فإن كنتَ لا تفهم من ذلك إلا البعض، فكذلك تلك الأجناس لا تفهمُ من كلامك إلا البعض. (7:36)

If someone were to say: "This is not language," it would be said to them: "The Qurʾān has said that this is language, poetry has made it language, and the speech of the Arabs has done so as well. If you were nevertheless to remove it from the field of clearly expressive language [*in kunta innamā akhrajtahā min ḥadd al-bayān*] and were to claim that it is not language at all [*wa za'amta annahā laysa bi-manṭiq*], because you don't understand it, it is also the case that you do not understand the speech of most nations. And if you were to call their language gibberish or unintelligible words, you would not be prohibited from claiming that that is what their speech and their language is, and since most nations do not understand your speech and your language, it would also be possible for them to remove your speech from the field of clear expression and language [*min al-bayān wa al-manṭiq*]. Yet does that speech of theirs not become clear expression and language through their giving one another to understand their needs [*li tafāhumihim ḥājat baʿḍihim ilā baʿḍ*], for it consists in composed sound that comes out of the mouth and is uttered by the tongue. And do not the sounds of the species of birds, wild animals, and livestock constitute language and communicative speech, for you have learned that it consists in syllables and forms, that it is composed and ordered, that through it they give one another to understand their needs, and that it comes out of the mouth and is uttered by the tongue [*kharajat min fam wa lisān*]. And if you understand only a bit of it, so too those species would only understand a little bit of your speech."

Al-Jāḥiẓ refers in this passage to a Qur'ānic verse in *Surat al-Naml* (*The Ants*): "Oh people, we have been taught the language of the birds [يَأَيُّهَا النَّاسُ عُلِّمْنَا مَنْطِقَ الطَّيْرِ/*yā ayyuhā al-nās ʿulimna manṭiq al-ṭayr*]" (7.34), and as he does so he generalizes speech as a practice among living beings. In al-Jāḥiẓ's discussion there is an attention to a verbal form, تفاعل, *tafāʿala*, and to the verb تفاهم, *tafāhama*, which I've translated as "to give one another to understand," and which may be understood as a practice in speech where living beings communicate in a sharing of "needs," حاجات, *ḥājāt*.[35] In his ninth-century manual for secretaries Ibn Qutayba notes that the verbal form *tafāʿala* relates to an action that occurs "between two [من إثنين/*min ithnayn*]," and I notice that al-Jāḥiẓ renders the verb *tafāhama*, which is formed from the verb *fahima*, "to understand," as a practice in language that exceeds two beings to encompass a field of sociality constituted through linguistic practice.[36] If فصيح, *faṣīḥ*, intends "eloquence in speech, even if it is not Arabic," as it refers to someone whose "language is well-formed so that they do not speak ungrammatically," as in a young boy who speaks fluently—"It is said," Ibn Manẓūr explains, "a boy is fluent in his speech if you understand what he says as soon as he speaks [أفصح الصبي في منطقه إفصاحا إذا فهمتَ ما يقول في أول ما يتكلم/*afṣaḥa al-ṣabī fī manṭiqihi ifṣāḥan idhā fahimta mā yaqūl fī awwal mā yatakallam*]"—we may understand al-Jāḥiẓ's reflection on language to open a sociality of form where "understanding," فهم, *fahm*, is already a kind of "giving one another to understand," تفاهم, *tafāhum*, and where the practice of eloquence, in *balāgha* and *bayān*, and in metered form in the poetic, is to be understood in relation to a non-self-centric practice of language in the tongue.[37] In a passage in *Book of Living Beings* I cited above, al-Jāḥiẓ uses the word جماعة, *jamāʿa*, to refer to a collectivity, a plurality of beings, and we may understand this plurality as given place to through a shared practice in language, where language institutes the social, and where, through this linguistic doing, an inessential mode of being together, a gathering without substance, is convoked.

And yet if the interrelational form of the verb *tafāʿala* is given, in al-Jāḥiẓ, to promise a communication between beings, a giving and receiving of sense, the action occasioned in this verbal form exceeds this frame to become a social and linguistic mode in excess of what is occasioned when one being gives language to be understood by another—as in Ibn Qutayba's manual. Instead of a practice of communication language becomes a form that gives place to inessential collectives called into being in language. In this, I notice that the gathering of creatures of which al-Jāḥiẓ writes is indistinguishable from language, as the "human being" is indistinct from the "bird," and such collectives may be said, therefore, to be منطق الطير, *manṭiq al-ṭayr*, at once the "language" or "speech" of the birds as well as their gathering in a collectivity occasioned in a scene of address where any single being or thing, in its lingual practice, is already more and less than itself. *Tafāhama*, then, in al-Jāḥiẓ, does not privilege a giving of sense—it is not a semantic-centric practice—but it instead names a gathering occasioned in the doing of language, where the speaking subject is already among others: an insurgence in form. What is given place to in language—and the poetic—is a mode of being where the social is a linguistic practice for an inessential, indetermined, and what I'm calling an "anontological" collective life.[38]

"The speech of each thing is its language [وكلام كل شيء منطقه/*wa kalām kull shayʾ manṭiquhu*]," Ibn Manẓūr explains, and I want to underline this practice of language in relation to the poetic, and its locus in the motion of the tongue, as it is given to us in al-Maʿālī's poetry and his translations of Paul Celan.[39] We may consider, then, al-Maʿālī's tongue: "I am from the land of Gilgamesh," he writes; "My story is lacking / My name is buried in the dirt: / I have no hand with which to signal, no tongue, and no mouth that might utter [أنا من أرض كلكامش / سيرتي ناقصة، إسمي في التراب مدفون: / لا يد لي لتلوّح، لا لسان، ولا فم لينطق ; *anā min arḍ kilkāmish / sīratī nāqiṣa, ismī fī-al-turāb madfūn: / lā yad lī li-tulawwiḥ, lā lisān, wa lā fam li-yanṭuq*]."[40] Something has been cut off or buried, and this points to a finality in the destruction imparted through the violences of colonial and settler forms—in what I've termed "settler life"—and their reconfiguration in the postcolonial state. And yet it is as if "sadness," الأسى, *al-asā*, has been lost as well: "The sadness that had been a tent for us/was lost in the storms' dust that/came from a distance in order to remind us [والأسى الذي كان خيمةً لنا/ضاع في غبار العواصف التي/جاءت من بعيد لكي تذكّرنا; *wa al-asā alladhī kāna khaymatan lanā/ḍā'a fī ghubār al-'awāṣif allatī/jā'at min ba'īd li-kay tudhakkiranā*]" (67). There is no longer a shelter that would shield or safeguard language, or a subject that could speak from a locus exterior to the devastations settler life generates. And yet if one is no longer capable of speech, there are "storms' dust" and "pebbles," a certain material, in the formulation of "I" and its "stammering" in the poetic: "For there is nothing left for me here/other than pebbles. I stammer them and continue on, like the shadow of a shadow [فلم يعد لي هنا/ غير الحصى، ألوكها وأمضي كظل ظل; *fa lam yu'd lī hunā/ghayr al-ḥaṣā, alūkuhā wa amḍī ka ẓill ẓill*]" (64). The poem tells us that something has ended, and yet the poet "stammers" and "continues on." The ashen form of the word reiterates the terms of al-Ma'ālī's poetic statement—"This word/an ashen deposit in memory's plains/Whenever it is destroyed/I feel it [هذا القول/رمادي المترسب في قيعان ذاكرة/كلما تهدمت/أشعر به; *hādhā al-qawl/ramādī al-mutarassib fī qī'ān dhākira/kullamā tahadammat/ash'ur bihi*]"—and in this reiteration of form the sense of the poetic, linguistic, and social, which I've noted in al-Jāḥiẓ, is carried forward as a practice for inidentical life.[41]

This carrying forward occurs through the "destruction" or "collapse," تهدّم, *tahaddum*, of which al-Ma'ālī writes, and it is for this reason that this destruction touches on "sound," صوت, *ṣawt*, "speech," قول, *qawl*, "utterance," لفظ, *lafẓ*, and "breath," نفس, *nafas*, as well as the formulation of the poetic and the extension of the economy of its terms in "rhyme," قافية, *qāfiya*:

يصلُ الألمُ إلى الشاعر
جالس يترقّبُ ضوءَ
نهارٍ فائت، وَلَجت فيه
المعاني، والوصفُ،
يبارِكُ النهاية.
اليدُ في حركة مَن يريد
أن يقول شيئاً
أن يُكمل الجملة
التي بُدِىء اليوم بها.
الخجل يتحسّس الطعنات؛
وصلتْ إلى الصميم.
الإيثار بلا حوْل يداعبُ الأشواق
في نهاية البيت، حيث قافيةٌ

تتلكّأ، الدمارُ يتواصلُ
والمعنى، خيطٌ مفتولٌ
به تُسحب، كجثث القتلى البقايا.
الورقة تُترك بيضاء
والنهار يأفل.

يغرفُ الألمُ ليلاً من كأس الشاعر
يثِبُ كأخر معنى. (48)

The poet's pain arrives
While he sits gazing at the light
Of a passing-away afternoon
Cut through with meanings whose
Depiction blesses the end.
His hand moves like someone who wants
To say something
To complete the sentence
With which the day began.
Shame feels its thrusts;
They arrive at the matter.
A love, powerless, plays with the desire
At the end of the verse where a rhyme
Tarries. The destruction continues
And meaning, a taut thread,
Is dragged along by it,
Like the remaining corpses of the dead.
The paper is left white
And the afternoon closes.

The pain ladles a night from the poet's cup
It jumps away like the last meaning.

"Pain" is the first noun in this poem, and it arrives in relation to a practice of language, which al-Maʿālī asks us to read. The pain that arrives is "the poet's pain," and yet this is so only insofar as poetic utterance partakes in a practice in language, where this pain is not the poet's own. The word "arrives" does not point to a subject but gestures to a poetic doing, not reducible to any single being. It is as if there were no subject of arrival but only an occurrence of pain in lingual form. The arrival of pain does not occasion the appearance within a temporal horizon of something that was not there before, and this is not only because pain does not allow for such temporal distinctions but also because arrival does not signal an event, historical process, or temporal development but instead a "destruction" in language—the term al-Maʿālī uses is دمار, *dimār*, "annihilation" or "demolition"—which does not cease and is not final. The insinuation of destruction in language touches on the economy of terms in Arabic poetics and rhetoric I've outlined. If "A love, powerless, plays with the desire / at the end of the verse where a rhyme / tarries," *fī nihāyat al-bayt, ḥaythu al-qāfiya / tatalakka*ʾ, the poem's bearing of loss, where "a meaning" is "dragged along" by the destruction, "like the remaining corpses of the dead," points to the impossibility of temporal closure and the touching of loss—and corpses—upon the poem. The poem speaks to us of the terms for utterance in language, and if this utterance remains impossible—"The paper is left white / and the afternoon closes," *al-waraqa tutrak bayḍā*ʾ */ wa al-nahār ya*ʾ*ful*—the poem utters as it passes on a mode of social and linguistic being, and the terms for collective form and inessential gathering, which settler life does not cease to target.

Language

Khālid al-Maʿālī's Arabic-language translation of Paul Celan's 1960 speech "The Meridian" ("Der Meridian"), translated by al-Maʿālī as خط الظهيرة (*Khaṭṭ al-ẓahīra*), is an occasion for a material doing in poetic life. "The Meridian" cites four lines of a poem, a quatrain, written, Celan notes, "a few years ago," and I wish to draw attention to the word "voices," *Stimmen*, the first word of the first of the four lines: "Voices from the path through nettles: / *Come to us on your hands.* / Whoever is alone with the lamp, / has only their hand to read from [*Stimmen vom Nesselweg her:* / Komm auf den Händen zu uns. / *Wer mit der Lampe allein ist, / hat nur die Hand, draus zu Lesen*]."[42] An imperative is offered, "Come to us," and it is as if a social manner of being is constituted through that address. "We resound, / alone [*wir tönen, / allein*]," Celan wrote elsewhere, and I observe that the being of a subject, insofar as it is "alone," is its resounding.[43] If "we" is a word uttered by the poet, this is not to presume for the poetic an individuated sense of being but instead a sociality whose ground is nothing but a lingual doing—an inessential sharing in language. And if "we" enunciates itself in language, this is only through its sonority, where being "alone," *allein*, is a temporal excess, and where the being that "I" or "we" is, is given only in this temporality, where "I" or "we" insurges.

In this poetic citation in "The Meridian" Celan speaks of reading—"Whoever is alone with the lamp, / has only their hand to read from"—and if this reading occasions one's being-alone, we may also consider the practice of reading to be implicated in Celan's poetic formulations: One is only alone insofar as one is with others. Such formulations involve matter and bits of matter: stone, silt, sand, shells. "Tracks of green crab, tomorrow, / creep-furrows, crawlways, wind- / sketch in gray / silt. Fine sand, coarse sand, that / peeled off the walls, next / to other hard-parts, in the / shells," Celan wrote in *Sprachgitter*, the volume in which the quatrain he cites in "The Meridian" appeared.[44] In notes Celan drafted for the "The Meridian" the temporality of stone is underlined, as Celan writes of "the stone" in its relation to "another time": "The stone is older than we are, it stands [*steht*] in another time," and "The stone, the inorganic, the mineral, is the older, that which stands toward and opposite man."[45] But if the stone is "the older," and if, in this, "The stone is the other, the outside-of-the-human," it "gives to the one who speaks direction and space [*gibt er dem Sprechenden Richtung und Raum*]," and, Celan notes, "one can confide in it [*Man kann sich ihm anvertrauen*]" (98). "And stones are like flowers," Celan also wrote, "only their scent is stronger." He provides a proximate note: "Poems are porous things: Here life seeps and flows in and out from them [*Das Leben strömt und sickert hier aus und ein*], unpredictably, of their own will, recognizable, and in the strangest form."[46] The overflow of scent from stones mirrors the poem's porosity, as it points to the manner of relation of the stone, in which one can "confide." There is, in this "confiding," a mode of address, and it is therefore as if the "standing toward" and "standing opposite," of which Celan writes, indetermines the geological from the anthropological, and the stone-like from the human. "The stoniness of poetic language remains alien to the petrifying claims of representational art," Marc Redfield has written of Celan, and it affirms, Redfield also writes, "a poetics very different from the reifying and theological idiom of aesthetic formalism."[47] Thinking with Redfield, and noting the consonance of this aesthetic formalism in its relation to the practice of form I underlined in chapter 1—as well as in its distinct material and linguistic reformulations, as I underline in this chapter, in post-Ottoman frames—I notice that we may think this difference in poetics in relation to the geological and the lingual, where what Celan calls "thickness" may be understood in relation to, and as if it were analogous with, "breath," *Atem*: "Thickness," Celan writes, "to be understood from the geological, and thus from the slow catastrophes and the dreadful fault lines of language——."[48]

In the "geological," the poetic—and the linguistic—are stoney, silted, formed of crushed shells; they "fold": "The poem involves language: it folds itself [*Das Gedicht involviert die Sprache: es faltet sich*]" (102), Celan also writes in his *Meridian* notes. There is touching of matter upon matter, an indistinction of things, where, "touching always touches upon the border of what is not able to be touched," and where this thinking of "touch," *Berührung*, in its materiality, and in the manner of temporal non-self-coincidence this occasions, becomes, as Yvonne Al-Taie has written, a "poetological thought-figure" in Celan.[49] Linked to stone, silt, and the folding of matter, the poetic is related, as well, to "darkness," *Dunkelheit*. "One must learn to love (to acknowledge) the dark like the dark-eyed, the dark-skinned—[*Man muß das Dunkle lieben lernen (gelten lassen) wie das Dunkeläugige, Dunkelhäutige—*]" (129), and this love relates to the poem, as it folds itself, and as the poem is a kind of fold, a relation to language and breath: "The poem: the trace of our breath in language [*Das Gedicht: die Spur unseres Atems in der Sprache*]" (115). These notes and drafts for "The Meridian" point to a history of social form, which al-Maʿālī's translations give us to think in a global frame, where the time of law—the time of juridical life, in the interiorizing abstractions of capitalist and accumulative form—is not opposed to but instead sustains the social, linguistic, and ontological violences, which Celan and al-Maʿālī give us to read. The global practices of anti-Black and anti-Indigenous violence intersect the anti-Jewish violences Celan's language also teaches us to think, as these become inidentical loci for the generalization, the interior and exterior extension and mutation, of legality, property, individuated social form, and whiteness, to which all other senses of being, language, relation, and life are to be subordinated and into which they are to be subsumed, either domesticated as recognizable forms or obliterated.

The institution of the modern state and its privilege of the property-owning subject is not reconcilable with the form of poetic statement in Celan, which carries more than one older practice of language. The "mutely/vibrating consonant [*stumm/vibrierender Mitlaut*]," of which Celan writes, overflows and exceeds the normative, capitalist terms of linguistic and social understanding.[50] The juridicalization of the social is reiterated in the violences to which Celan was subjected, and yet there is, in the ongoing permutations of these violences, a desire to overcome them through a privilege of the subject of interiorizing experience, self-consciousness, autonomy in language, and, through these, law. These terms, I've noted, are racialized, including the terms for the normalizing understanding of linguistic life: "White, white, white/like lattice whitewash,/the laws fall into line/and march/inward [*Weiss, weiß, weiß/wie Gittertünche,/reihn die Gesetze sich ein/und marschieren/einwärts*]," Celan wrote.[51] The turning inward of law, its "falling into line" and "marching," do not only point to the incapacity of law to shield non-white, non-Christian beings from social destruction, within and outside of Europe—an incapacity pointed to in a verse of Celan's I placed as an epigraph to chapter 1, where he wrote that "I hear they call life/the only shelter"—because it points to the articulation of settler form congealed in law and its terms. If law coerces a particular institution of the social, and if this, as Samera Esmeir has shown, is the "coloniality of modern law," where the law invests matter, domesticating and transmuting it, we may consider Celan in the terms for refusal I've outlined in this book.[52] Esmeir has observed that in the modern state and law there is a replacement of the theological by the cartographical, and the "world" by the "international," where "the world," Esmeir writes, "is the horizontal surface of the earth, divided into states, maintained and exhausted by an international sphere and its institutions."[53] This state-determined division, outlined by Schmitt in *Nomos of the Earth* in its Western-hemispheric contexts, occasions a suppression of forms of life as well as, in Esmeir's words, "the pacification of internal rebellion" (110), and if Esmeir recalls, in particular, the 1856 Treaty of Paris and its recognition of Ottoman "territorial integrity" (104), I notice, thinking and reading with Esmeir, that the mutation of "world" into the "international" she describes also reformulates a globalizing proliferation of particular sense of being, form, and life, to which beings are asymmetrically subjected.

Rather than promise a return of language to its determination in a self-cognizing understanding of world, Celan gives a sense of the social that disaffirms such temporal or material capture. Instead, what we are given is "breath," *Atem*, in what Celan calls "conversation," *Gespräch*, and I consider now Celan's discussion of "conversation" in relation to the time of poetic utterance in "The Meridian":

> Erst im Raum dieses Gesprächs konstituiert sich das Angesprochene, versammelt es sich um das es ansprechende und nennende Ich. Aber in diese Gegenwart bringt das Angesprochene und durch Nennung gleichsam zum Du Gewordene auch sein Anderssein mit. Noch im Hier und Jetzt des Gedichts—das Gedicht selbst hat ja immer nur diese eine, einmalige, punktuelle Gegenwart—, noch in dieser Unmittelbarkeit und Nähe läßt es das ihm, dem Anderen, Eigenste mitsprechen: dessen Zeit.

> Only in the space of this conversation does the addressed constitute itself, does it gather around the I that is addressing and naming it. But the addressed, which through naming has, as it were, become a you, brings its otherness into this present. Even in this here and now of the poem—for the poem itself has always only this one, unique, momentary present—even in this immediacy and nearness it lets what is ownmost in the other speak: its time.[54]

The address occasioned in poetic utterance is a "turning of the breath," *Atemwende*, and this turning of the breath is given in "intention": "The poem intends another, it needs this other, it needs an opposite. It goes toward it, bespeaks it [*Das Gedicht will zu einem Anderen, es braucht dieses Andere, es braucht ein Gegenüber. Es sucht es auf, es spricht sich ihm zu*]," Celan writes. "For the poem, everything and everyone is a figure of this other toward which it is heading [*Jedes Ding, jeder Mensch ist dem Gedicht, das auf das Andere zuhält, eine Gestalt dieses Anderen*]."[55] Because the poem is what intends and goes toward another, it is given to be thought in relation to this heading toward, and I notice in this a sociality of poetic form. There is a giving in language, and if in this the object of address "constitutes itself," *konstituiert sich*, this being, an addressee, is not "itself" but maintains an "otherness," *Anderssein*, in the time of poetic utterance. It is not that there is an addressee toward which language is sent, but that "the addressed" comes to be what it is through a poetic sending. If the addressed "becomes a you," the poem gives the time of "the addressed," and what Celan calls "the other," to speak. This "time" is what is "most-own" in relation to the other; it is what gives the other's time to be what it is. The word Celan uses is *Eigenste*, a term which retains within it the word *Eigentum*, which renders "property," as I noted reading Heidegger (in the introduction) and Marx (in chapter 1). One might therefore say that what is most "own" is a non-self-belonging and a temporal excess in linguistic address. The form of a being that owns itself is wholly unlike the poetic in Celan, where the being of a being is its address, a material doing in language: a lingual practice.

There is no promise of property in Celan, no attachment to a self-determined form or the terms of world and relation it sustains, and I study this non-attachment in relation to al-Maʿālī's translation of the passages in "The Meridian" I'm considering here, in order to think al-Maʿālī as a reader of Celan.

Al-Maʿālī renders the passage I've cited above as follows:

> ولكن في فضاء هذه المحاورة يتشكّل المتحدّث إلىه، يجتمع حول الأنا المتحدّث إليه والمسماة. لكن بواسطة التسمّي في ذات الوقت المتحوّل إلى "أنت" المتحدّث إليه، أيضاً في هنا وآن القصيدة—للقصيدة نفسها، لها فقط هذا الحاضر الفريد والمنظّم—وفي هذه المباشرة والقرب تترك حقيقة الآخر أن تتحدّث: وقت الآخر.[56]

It may be translated in English in this manner:

> But in the space of this conversation the addressed is given form [*yatashakkal al-mutaḥaddith ilayhi*], it gathers itself around the I that is addressing and naming it. But by means of this naming, at the same time, the addressed is transformed into a "you," also in the here and now of the poem—of the poem itself, which has only this unique, pointed present—and in this immediacy and nearness [*wa fī hādhihi*

al-mubāshara wa al-qurb] the poem leaves the essence of the other [*ḥaqīqat al-ākhar*] to speak: the other's time.

In al-Ma'ālī's translation the "constitution," of which Celan writes, *konstituiert sich das Angesprochene*, becomes "formation," يتشكّل المتحدَّث إليه, *yatashakkal al-mutaḥaddith ilayhi*, and so "constitution" is thought as the assumption of a "form," شكل, *shakl*, distributed in the social in relation to the sort of being that an addressee—in its linguistic or poetic constitution—is. In this formulation, interlocution is a sociality and a mode of being, and this indistinction of the linguistic from the social and the social from the ontological is given in the rendering of "constitution" as "formation," where the "constitution" of an addressee in language—of "you"—is in excess of propertied form. Al-Ma'ālī's rendering of the German word *Eigenste* with the Arabic word حقيقة, *ḥaqīqa*, which I've offered as "essence," may also render what is "real," "true," or "accurate." The interplay of *eigentlich*, *Eigentum*, and *Eigenschaft* is divested of its property-centric orientations in the rendering of *Eigenste* as "the essence," or even "what is most essential." In al-Ma'ālī's rendering, what is "ownmost," because it is what is "real" or "true," is what may not be subordinated to a social logic of property or the form of life it sustains; in al-Ma'ālī—as in Celan—what is most "real" or "true," what is most "itself," is what is not its "own." What poetic utterance in Celan gives, as al-Ma'ālī reads Celan, is a practice without object or subject, a material doing with and in and as things—what I noted, in the subtitle of this chapter, as "a poetics of things." In this "poetics of things" the form of a being convoked in language is older than the time of utterance, and wholly other than the social forms that attend the regime of legality, constitutive for the modern, normative terms for language, relation, and life. It is perhaps for this reason that the "otherness," *Anderssein*, of the addressee, of which Celan writes, does not appear in al-Ma'ālī's rendering, because the sense of language in which it shares presumes the sense of the social, which Celan's language also gives. The "present" is already a time of the other—of all of the others, those who have died and those still living, and the languages they give and share—and the understanding of the present as self-constituted is incongruent with the terms for thinking language in Celan as well as in al-Ma'ālī.

It is in this sense that we can understand the many dates Celan accentuates in "The Meridian": "But the poem speaks! [*Aber das Gedicht spricht ya!*]. It remains mindful of its dates [*Es bleibt seiner Daten eingedenk*], but—it speaks. For certain, it speaks only on its own, its very own behalf [*Gewiß, es spricht immer nur in seiner eigenen, allereigensten Sache*]," Celan writes. He continues: "But I think [*Aber ich denke*]—and this thought [*dieser Gedanke*] can hardly surprise you, now [*jetzt*]—, I think that it has always belonged to the hopes of the poem [*daß es von jeher zu den Hoffnungen des Gedichts gehört*], precisely in this manner, to speak of the *strange*—no, I can now [*jetzt*] no longer use this word, precisely in this manner to speak *on behalf of the other*—who knows, perhaps on behalf of a *wholly other* [*wer weiß, vielleicht in eines* ganz Anderen *Sache*]."[57] I notice that, at the moment at which Celan speaks of the poem "speaking," in the present tense, and at the moment at which he speaks of the poem's "mindfulness," *Eingedenken*, in relation to its "dates"—and it is this explication that leads to the poem's speaking "on its own," *in seiner eigenen*, and on "its very own behalf," *allereigensten Sache*—he draws back and offers the word "but," *aber*. It as if the speaking of the poem generates a response, an address, and that its form disaffirms the propertied mode of language I've noted in relation to the terms *eigentlich*, *Eigentum*, and *Eigenschaft*. On the one hand, the poem speaks; as it speaks, it is mindful of its dates, and in this mindfulness the poem speaks "on its own," *in seiner eigenen*. And yet—"but," *aber*, Celan writes—the poem, and the act of speech, which the poem is, does not come down to itself. The *aber* in this passage is not explicatory, it does not advance an argument about the poetic—or about "the poem," *das Gedicht*. Instead, it gives the social form which the doing of poetry in Celan is. Insofar as Celan speaks of a "wholly other" this speaking is not so much ethical—by which I mean, related to an individual being or its self-understanding—as it is social, and in this non-self-determined orientation Celan's language is entirely other than what is demanded in the property-centric manner privileged in settler life.

I want to think this distinction between the ethical and the social through al-Maʿālī's rendering of these passages in "The Meridian." In particular, his rendering of *seiner eigenen* as خصوصيتها, *khuṣūsiyyatuhā*, displaces the propertied sense of language promised in what is one's "own" onto the particularity of utterance. *Khuṣūsiyya* points to what is *khāṣ*, to what is particular, to this or that act of speech in poetic enunciation, and to the sharing, which the poem is, where doing and being are indistinct.[58] Rather than a subject of property, there is an inessential performance, a collective lingual gathering without substance, what I've called "insurgence." It is a form Celan names a "turning of the breath": *Dichtung: das kann eine Atemwende bedeuten*, "Poetry: that can mean a turning of the breath," Celan wrote; الشعر: يمكن أن يعني تحوّلا في النفس, *al-shiʿr: yumkin an yaʿnī taḥawwulan fī al-nafas*, al-Maʿālī rendered this passage.[59] Insofar as "poetry," *Dichtung*, is an occasion for this turning, a "transformation" or "conversion," a "turning away," as one might also render al-Maʿālī's *taḥawwul*, the poem is not merely itself but is instead a non-self-possessed practice in language, given in an utterance in the present tense: *Aber das Gedicht spricht ja!*, "But the poem speaks!," and, as al-Maʿālī wrote: لكن القصيدة تتحدّث!, *Lākin al-qaṣīda tataḥaddath!*[60] Because it is a "turning of the breath," and because it is, in each instance, only this, poetic enunciation does not occasion the linguistic act of a temporally selfsame subject, which would precede the speaking of the poem and found it. Instead, language is a doing in excess of a subject, which gives a mode of being where "I" is shared out among others, where "I" is this sharing-out, and where this sharing-out is what the poetic—and language—are.

"I am you when I am I [*Ich bin du, wenn ich ich bin*]," Celan wrote, and, as al-Maʿālī renders this passage, أنا أنتِ، عندما أكون أنا, *ana anti, ʿindamā akūn anā*, and I notice that in this passage "I," *ich*, is already "you," *du*, in its formulation and mode, and that this relation between "I" and "you" destabilizes a self-standing sense of pronominal or lingual understanding.[61] The utterance of the word "I" is a practice in inidentical form, a giving of "opacity," in "the irrefutable echo / of every opacity [*das unwiderlegbare Echo / jeder Verschattung*]."[62] It is not that opacity shields a self-standing being, which one would properly understand through ever-more-precise interpretive acts, in what Erin Graff Zivin has termed an "identitarian logic," but that it is instead a name for a manner of being in sonority—in "reverberation"—in the sense in which al-Maʿālī gives us think it.[63] In this sense, the poetic is a name for being in sonority, and being is a practice in poetic form. Al-Maʿālī's rendering of *ich* as *anā* gives to us a translation: If Celan, as we read him with al-Maʿālī, gives us to think "I" as a social form—and this, in a manner that is not reconcilable with a reading of Celan in ethical or subjective terms, as in the philosopher Emmanuel Lévinas, to whose writing I turn in the next section of this chapter—al-Maʿālī gives us to read Celan in globality. In reading al-Maʿālī reading Celan we are given to think the global forms of social obliteration as the advance of a particular sense of the social, language, reading, and life, even as the poetic, in Celan, and in al-Maʿālī, gives a wholly other understanding of language, in a practice of inessential, and what I've called "anontological," form.

It is a form, I've argued, that insurges, and it is given, in al-Maʿālī's poetry, in the "sentence": "And every sentence I'd sing / would circle in the open / for the echo to seize it [وكل جملة أحدو بها / تدور في الفضاء / لكي يتلقفها الصدى; *wa kull jumla aḥdū bihā/ tadūr fī al-faḍāʾ / li-kay yatalaqqafahā al-ṣadā*]."[64] The passage refers to a past tense verb, which sets a temporal frame for it, and it links the "singing" of the subject, its address to the camel in driving it forward in حداء, *ḥidāʾ*, to the form of poetic statement. The singing of the poetic subject is its offering of sentences sent into the space of the "open," الفضاء, *al-faḍāʾ*, as if this were a material locus through which language were given. The traveling of the poet in the open, the desert, points to a "listening," الإصغاء,

al-iṣghā'—"Where are the birds lost in the desert? / Where is the desert? / You'll listen, then. The sound comes to you / The echo reverberates in the open / Your sorrow takes a rest / While you sing in silence / And continue on alone" (122)—as well as a motion in corporeal form, a doing with matter where sound "comes to you," يأتيك, *ya'tīka*. There is a reverberation, a sonority, and yet it is not that utterance initiates in a single being but that there is already a giving of words in a cosmological relation, a conversing with moons and stars. A time for song has passed—"You want to rest, anew / Or sing, lifting with your voice / Those orphaned words / But the time for singing has passed / The night that disappeared has returned / So that we may converse with its moons and its stars [والليل الذي ضاع يعود / لنناجي أقماره والنجوم; *wa-al-layl alladhī ḍā' ya'ūd / li-nunājī aqmārahu wa-al-nujum*]" (115)—yet the poet sings, if in a manner that does not affirm harsh distinctions in substance, and where the poetic is, already, "conversation," مناجاة, *munājāt*. Rather than a propertied world of temporally determined beings, the poetic—in the tradition al-Ma'ālī inherits, in relation to which he teaches us to read Celan, and in which, I'll notice in what follows in this chapter, Adnan shares—gives an insubstantial sense of language and life, where language, in its refusal of the time of the state—in its refusal of settler life—insurges, as it passes on a sense of world, relation, and form wholly otherwise: "Does each hand that memories raise high / Beckon to our sorrows? / While we, we who walk upon this path / Drag our steps / As we return from a thousand and one wars / Wailing, like the wounded, a song of our return to the world [عائدين من ألف حرب وحرب / نئنّ كجرحى أغنية الرجوع إلى الدنيا; *'ā'idīn min alf ḥarbin wa ḥarb / na'inn ka jurḥā ughniyat al-rujū' ilā al-dunyā*]" (61).

Poetic Being

Etel Adnan's *The Arab Apocalypse* gives a meditation on life and being through a writing of the sun—"A yellow sun A green sun a yellow sun A red sun a blue sun"—in its relation to water, matter, minerals, the sea, and color.[65] One is drawn to the colors of the sun, and it is as if Adnan wished to draw our attention to color in relation to painting, poetry, and thought: "Thoughts have color," she writes.[66] Color intersects language as painting intersects the poetic, a material that coagulates the historical injustices occasioned and retained in language—all of which, Adnan notes, the sea holds. "The great slaughters consistently perpetrated throughout history are jamming the conduits to the sea, claiming anonymity. She washes carefully the humiliated bodies thrown to her, before annihilating them in the oblivion she harbors" (37). There is, in this annihilation, a reformulation of the primitive accumulation I underlined in the introduction to this book and chapter 1, where the sea, as Laleh Khalili has compellingly written, is subjected to "a form of accumulation by dispossession, an enclosure of a space held in common—the sea—for the purpose of speculation and sales," where "land and sea" are "posited as clearly distinct spaces" in relation to regimes of migrant labor, "racialized technologies of rule," capitalist extraction, settler-colonial exertion, and the suppression of collective refusal.[67] All of this mirrors practices of reading in affirmation of ontological distinction and temporal closure, a sense of being and form inconsonant with the anontological practice—the poetics of things—in Adnan, al-Maʿālī, and Celan.

I wish to ask about the sun in Adnan, and wish to wonder about it in relation to sea, language, and form, and in relation to line and repetition in Adnan's painting and drawing. There is already a plurality of suns in Adnan, and so if the sun imparts a "dominance"—"So what brings you back from over mountains, in July's aridity, under the sun's dominance, missing parents, divinities that we share, where is blind energy coming from, the earth, the sky, the void?"—this is dissolved in the poetic writing of color and matter, of materials and substances, and of the sea.[68] The sun points to the ongoing siege, the many wars against the colonized and enslaved, and yet the sun is not an atemporal ground for the world but instead a kind of matter. The sun, in Adnan, shares in the corporeality and porosity of bodies, and the permeations of sweat and salt, a density in the being-together of things, of which Adnan also writes: "When 'there' is 'here' and the air slows down you realize the sun's weight and as I know intimately the temperature we give up swimming and our eyes get heavy with humidity and you drag yourself to the door" (29). There is a phenomenology of interrelational forms—"Currents meet in my body while it swims and I become water, part of water. The 'you' is always the 'I' so we inhabit each other in our irremediable singleness" (27), Adnan also writes in *There*—and this gives a sense of being in a materiality rendered through Adnan's writing of water, liquid, and the sea, which I'll draw on to suggest a reading of being in its indistinction from the social, the linguistic, the poetic, and, finally, from what is wet and from color: "Water's iridescence is language," Adnan shares in an aphoristic sentence that links language and the poetic to color and painting.[69] "Bodies produce words among other secretions" (13), she notes in *Sea and Fog*, and there is a passing-through and an overflow of water, mineral—salt, for example—and "The spherical ocean's luminescence is a thing familiar, but our energies won't respond to its call; they're designed for the body's penetration by salt, and the soft happiness that invades the spirit when water meets light" (5)—and the "penetrations" and "secretions" of liquid through the skin in sweat, where "our eyes," Adnan wrote, "get heavy with humidity."

In Adnan we are given to read an inheritance of the tradition of anontological form through a thinking of the sea, painting, and color, and all of this in relation to thought. Thought, in Adnan, overflows with sea: "The sea's instincts collaborate with ours to create thinking. Our thoughts come and go, in birth and evanescence. We feel we own them but we're the ones to belong to the radiations that they are, lighter than fog, but endearing in their unreliability . . ." (6). The ellipsis Adnan places after the word "unreliability" points to an excess of language over the closural force of syntactic finality, and it gestures to a non-propertied form of thought and its "radiations," mirrored in the perspiration of earth. "Earth sweats humid air" (98), Adnan writes, as she asks us to notice a distinction between earth and property. "Thought" does not point to a stability, secured in the interiority of a subject of self-reflection; instead, "our thoughts come and go," and if with this coming and going we "feel" that we "own" our thoughts, this is a misunderstanding abetted by the privileged terms for propertied comprehension.[70] It is not only that "thought" is not "ours" but that "we," a linguistic and social collective, is generated through a relation to the sea and the "thoughts" produced—"radiated" is Adnan's term—in the "collaboration" that thinking is. If these "thoughts" are "lighter than fog" we may also understand thought in its relation to mist, humidity, iridescence, and an interpenetration of materials that is also a practice of being.

The Arab Apocalypse poses a thinking of settler colonization in Palestine in relation to language and the poetic: "The night of the non-event. War in the vacant sky. The Phantom's absence. Funerals. Coffin not covered with roses. Unarmed population. Long. The yellow sun's procession from the mosque to the vacant Place. Mute taxis. Plainclothed army. Silent hearse. Silenced music. Palestinians with no Palestine."[71] This passage refers, as Adnan's numbering of the fifty-nine poems contained in *The Arab Apocalypse* suggests, to the fifty-nine-day siege and massacre of Palestinians at the Tell al-Zaʿatar refugee camp in Lebanon in 1976.[72] She writes in poem XLV: "I breathed the breath of the plague and they chased me out of the camp/throwing stones at me throwing stones throwing stones/the living had slept 59 days with the corpses 59 days 59 days/not counting the nights and hours."[73] "O Camp of thyme and verbena carrion smelling Tell Zaatar," Adnan writes in poem XIII—see figures 2a and 2b—"Women children men everything is dead" (31–32).

The poetic subject is, in the first person singular, a subject of breath: "I breathed the breath of the plague." There is a dispersal of the subject in breath, where "I" is only given through its enunciation in relation to the massacre, a

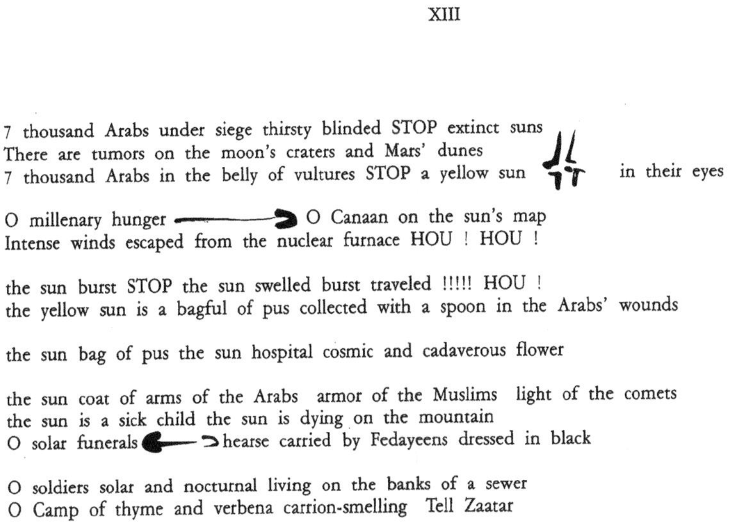

XIII

7 thousand Arabs under siege thirsty blinded STOP extinct suns
There are tumors on the moon's craters and Mars' dunes
7 thousand Arabs in the belly of vultures STOP a yellow sun in their eyes

O millenary hunger O Canaan on the sun's map
Intense winds escaped from the nuclear furnace HOU ! HOU !

the sun burst STOP the sun swelled burst traveled !!!!! HOU !
the yellow sun is a bagful of pus collected with a spoon in the Arabs' wounds

the sun bag of pus the sun hospital cosmic and cadaverous flower

the sun coat of arms of the Arabs armor of the Muslims light of the comets
the sun is a sick child the sun is dying on the mountain
O solar funerals hearse carried by Fedayeens dressed in black

O soldiers solar and nocturnal living on the banks of a sewer
O Camp of thyme and verbena carrion-smelling Tell Zaatar

Figure 2a. Etel Adnan. *The Arab Apocalypse*. The Post-Apollo Press. Sausalito, California. 1989. Poem XIII. Copyright The Estate of Etel Adnan. Courtesy of the Post-Apollo Press.

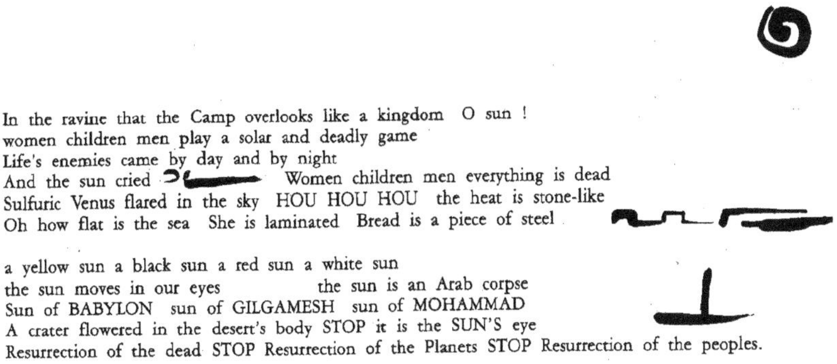

In the ravine that the Camp overlooks like a kingdom O sun !
women children men play a solar and deadly game
Life's enemies came by day and by night
And the sun cried Women children men everything is dead
Sulfuric Venus flared in the sky HOU HOU HOU the heat is stone-like
Oh how flat is the sea She is laminated Bread is a piece of steel

a yellow sun a black sun a red sun a white sun
the sun moves in our eyes the sun is an Arab corpse
Sun of BABYLON sun of GILGAMESH sun of MOHAMMAD
A crater flowered in the desert's body STOP it is the SUN'S eye
Resurrection of the dead STOP Resurrection of the Planets STOP Resurrection of the peoples.

Figure 2b. Etel Adnan. *The Arab Apocalypse*. The Post-Apollo Press. Sausalito, California. 1989. Poem XIII. Copyright The Estate of Etel Adnan. Courtesy of the Post-Apollo Press.

form mutated through Adnan's English-language translation of the poem. Adnan's French carries the form of a breathing subject, which the pronoun *moi* emphasizes, as if there were no subject outside of the relation to breath of which the poem speaks, pointing to an intensification of the unstable form of a speaker in its relation to the massacre: *"moi j'ai respiré l'haleine des pestiférés et ils m'ont chassé du camp."*[74] There is no exteriority to the social forms mutated through the violences of which Adnan writes—"We are all future corpses," she states, "the sun like you is covered with flowers"—and it is as if the verb "to be," which Adnan uses here, and which she conjugates in the first person plural—"*Nous sommes tous de futurs cadavres*"—carries or is mediated through the social forms attendant upon the massacre.[75] It is not only that these forms belong to the social institution of sectarian life in its relation to the Zionist colonization of Palestine, and in relation to orientalist forms generalized in the nineteenth and early twentieth centuries—as Adnan has shown in her 1977 novel *Sitt Marie Rose*, and as Edward W. Said argued in *The Question of Palestine*, which was published one year following—but that the form of life that sustains this massacre, and others, before and after, exceeds the terms for any context, any legible distinction between inside and outside.[76] To think the social as Adnan teaches us to do so is to think settler life and its extensions and mutations of itself as a global event for language, being, and the poetic. And it is to do so through Adnan's poetry and painting, outside of a desire for a self-redemptive pose or the closure of temporality in the terms for philosophical self-reflection—in the opposition between subject and object, or between person and thing. There is a dense negativity in Adnan's formulations, a concentration in utterance and aphoristic statement mirrored also in painting. The poetic, in Adnan, is not a locus for the expression of a "self," where language would be a means, but is instead a material composition, where thinking is indistinguishable from the poetic, and where being is a practice of linguistic life—a manner of acting in sociality.

We may consider Adnan's thinking of the social, thought, and the poetic in relation to a passage in *There*, published in 1997, where Adnan speaks of "Columbus": "Oh yes! Columbus landed somewhere, where, bringing stench, disease and mortal wounds, logs to crucify Indians on, and when was it and why? So you're my twin enemy brother, my twin shadow, and did we go to the Americas, who sent us there?"[77] Adnan localizes the question of thought and the poetic in relation to "Columbus," "my twin enemy brother," and this name points to a manner of being and life that persists and which belongs, in an excessive manner, to the ongoing siege upon forms of life and ways of being in relation to "the Americas," and also in relation to Palestine, Lebanon, and Iraq—"In Iraq, people recite prayers in mosques out of a fear of an additional catastrophe."[78] And yet catastrophe, in Adnan, is not an isolatable or recognizable event but instead a manner of social existence and exteriorizing obliteration; it is, one might also say, the asymmetric generalization of the subject of experience as a subject of language and world; and it is the brutalizing subordination of world to the white, settler, capitalist, hetero-patriarchical mode and manner I've termed "settler life." One might say that Adnan's language writes this catastrophe as it speaks to us of it, and as Adnan gives, in a poetic generosity, a wholly other form, something her poetic writing and her labor with paint and color carry and reformulate—and which it does not cease to reformulate, in a gesture that points to the refusal, and *re*fusal, I underline in this book's title.

In Adnan thought does not entail the representation of an object for a self-reflective subject but instead is an occasion for a certain doing with materials, one of which is language, even as matter is a kind of rumor, which intersects the poetic with the being of the sea and its sonority. "There are rumors about the existence of a new kind of matter" (39), and yet this matter is older than the "present," permeating and desedimenting it. To speak of matter and its rumorous form, its temporally insubstantial and indeterminable mode, is to speak of Lucretius and the news—"The idea had already occurred to Lucretius but the discovery is recent. A boat down the coast was loaded with fresh news" (39)—and so matter, in Adnan, appeals to something sent to us from a "past," an idea that "had already occurred to Lucretius," as well as a movement of language in the "present," the inidentical time at which one speaks of the "news" loaded on "a boat down the coast."[79] There is always another coast and still more sea in Adnan—"Down the coastline there's always the sea"—and just as the shape of the coast is indeterminate, the stuff Adnan names "matter" does not cease to imply the insubstantiality of its form.[80] The sea has always been a locus for patience in Adnan—she writes in the first line of a 1948 poem titled "La Mer," "The Sea," that, "I would like to speak to you of the sea, of its patience [*Je voudrais te parler de la mer, de sa patience*]"—as it is a mutation in form.[81] "There is only one 'sea': oceans, gulfs, bays, these are all one," she writes in the same poem, "The sea is a strange spirit whose form is constantly changing; it is a heavy fluid, it's a haze, it's cloud, snow crystal [*La mer rest un esprit étrange changeant constamment de form; c'est un fluid lourd, cest de la brume, du nuage, de cristal de neige*]" (22). In Adnan matter intersects form as the sea yields its inessential mutations, outside of the temporal frames for linguistic understanding in the modern state and the object-forming practice of philosophical reflection, as salt glimmers on the surface of the body of the lover—"Salt glimmers on the lover's body. Lingers. Tears return when heartbreaks don't heal with time," Adnan writes in *Sea and Fog*.[82] "Often my body feels close to sea creatures: sticky, slimy, unpredictable, more ephemeral than need be," as if the separations between things and beings were akin to the form of the shoreline—"A tide of mud is moving on the shore, messing the shoreline. Sounds are raining"—and as if the saying of what being is belonged to the poetic—a practice of sound in cosmological form.[83] "The universe makes a sound—is sound" (39), Adnan also writes, and this sonorous being of the world withdraws language from the ways of knowing privileged in the settler terms for the social and their translation on a global scale—as al-Maʿālī and Adnan have given us to understand, in post-Ottoman social and linguistic formations and their juridical, propertied, state-centric terms, and in the exposure of these to the modern settler, cadastral, and plantational logics of the ongoing American wars—and with the losses these continue, still now, to exact: "We have lost the liturgies under the wars, the bombings, the fires we went through. Some of us didn't survive, and they were many" (7).

Settler life demands subjects of the political—subjects capable of self-representation, self-ownership, self-determination, and self-orientation—and Adnan, in declining this demand, refuses the temporal and cadastral terms such a sense of the subject presumes as she asks into the "deed of ownership" of the sky: "The horizon asks not to be pursued. We can't figure out what was whistling all night long, having lost our deed of ownership for the sky" (12). To ask into such a deed is not to presume it but to reflect on the sense of property addressed to earth and sky, and imposed upon the sea, and which Adnan's writing places in question, in a poetic "thingliness," to draw upon the meditation of J. Kameron Carter, and in Adnan's thinking of the sea, which enables, in Arabic-language contexts, a concrete—by which I mean a material and poetic, an insubstantial—refutation of the property form.[84] The sea contains an "inimitable blue": "I take up my letter again. I haven't written to you for several days. In the meantime, I went to Glossa to see the sun set over the sea and the surrounding islands. There was the sea as I have always loved her. It was like going to Beirut, to see her inimitable blue."[85] And the sea, in its relation to color, gives a sense of being, where "to look at the sea is to become what one is" (80), and where "looking" does not affirm the being of a self-owning subject. It is not that there is, first, a being that looks, and that through its looking it becomes "what it is," but that "to look at the sea" is what the being of one's being is, where the subject of vision and its definitional practice dissolves in the sea's salt.

I want to linger with Poem VII in *The Arab Apocalypse* and the words "Palestine" and "PARIS," which call out to a number of forms, to triangles sitting on a chopped line tilted slightly upward, followed by a line drawn slightly beneath it, and what may be a dot or a point—see figure 3a. "A warring sun in Beirut thunderous April cool breeze on the ships/yellow sun on a pole an eye in the gun's hole a dead from Palestine/a purple sun in my friends pocket meanderings in PARIS/a bird on a dead Palestinian's toe a fly at the butchery" (19). The address to the violences of settler life is extrapolated in a practice of form—of triangles, angles, lines, points, and, on the first and second pages of Poem VII, spiral-like shapes—see figures 3a and 3b. If Adnan's triangles mirror each other, their form is not identical. Shape blurs. The first triangle is colored in black; the left arm of the second is at a lower slope than the others, it reaches below its base, sending itself downward; the top point of the third is somewhat flat, pointing to an unfinished quality in sketched form, which calls out to sky, planets, cosmos, and suns. The three shapes' trajectory is upward; they traverse the words "PARIS" and "Palestine." The horizontal, sketched line that follows them is followed by a dot that creates an ellipse-like form; both the line and the dot are incomplete. They overflow. Like Adnan's spirals, there is a perforability. The poems contained in *The Arab Apocalypse* are intercalculated with shapes such as these—sketches, drawings, points, and marks—which call attention to the muting terms of syntactic coercion and the material excess of lingual practice or drawing. These do not recall an incapacity of language but instead host a manner of doing, a sense of being and form. It is not a manner given outside of the violences to which Adnan gestures, but which is formulated through them, at times, in Adnan, in yielding to them—"Sea vomiting corpses," she also writes, and "Waves are brutal"—as I'll underline below.[86]

The sketches in *The Arab Apocalypse* point to Adnan's painting, her work with color and materials, and to Mount Tamalpais, in Marin County, California. Adnan's partner Simone Fattal discusses Adnan's paintings of Mount Tamalpais and their "innumerability": "She looked and lived with the mountain even after she came back to Beirut. All the time she was painting the mountain, drawing it in oil, watercolor, ink. She made thousands of these drawings," Fattal writes.[87] Fattal comments on Adnan's "early paintings," and their "squares

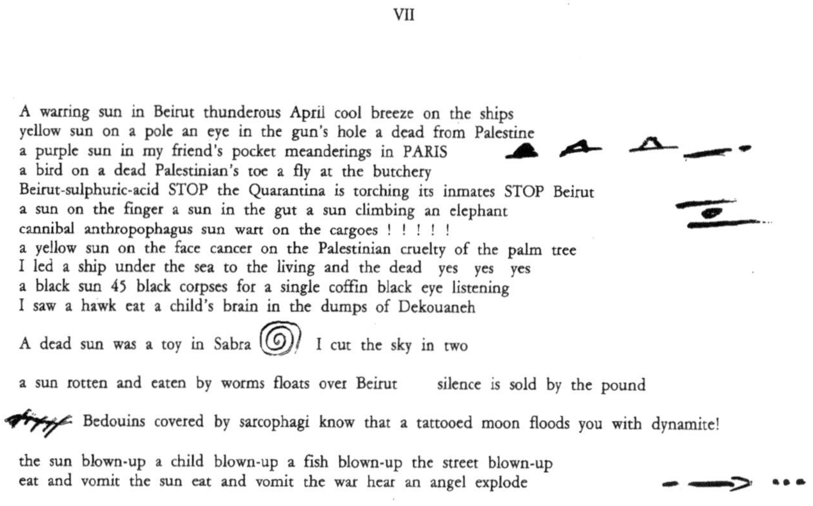

VII

A warring sun in Beirut thunderous April cool breeze on the ships
yellow sun on a pole an eye in the gun's hole a dead from Palestine
a purple sun in my friend's pocket meanderings in PARIS
a bird on a dead Palestinian's toe a fly at the butchery
Beirut-sulphuric-acid STOP the Quarantina is torching its inmates STOP Beirut
a sun on the finger a sun in the gut a sun climbing an elephant
cannibal anthropophagus sun wart on the cargoes ! ! ! ! !
a yellow sun on the face cancer on the Palestinian cruelty of the palm tree
I led a ship under the sea to the living and the dead yes yes yes
a black sun 45 black corpses for a single coffin black eye listening
I saw a hawk eat a child's brain in the dumps of Dekouaneh

A dead sun was a toy in Sabra I cut the sky in two

a sun rotten and eaten by worms floats over Beirut silence is sold by the pound

Bedouins covered by sarcophagi know that a tattooed moon floods you with dynamite!

the sun blown-up a child blown-up a fish blown-up the street blown-up
eat and vomit the sun eat and vomit the war hear an angel explode

Figure 3a. Etel Adnan. *The Arab Apocalypse*. The Post-Apollo Press. Sausalito, California. 1989. Poem VII. Copyright The Estate of Etel Adnan. Courtesy of the Post-Apollo Press.

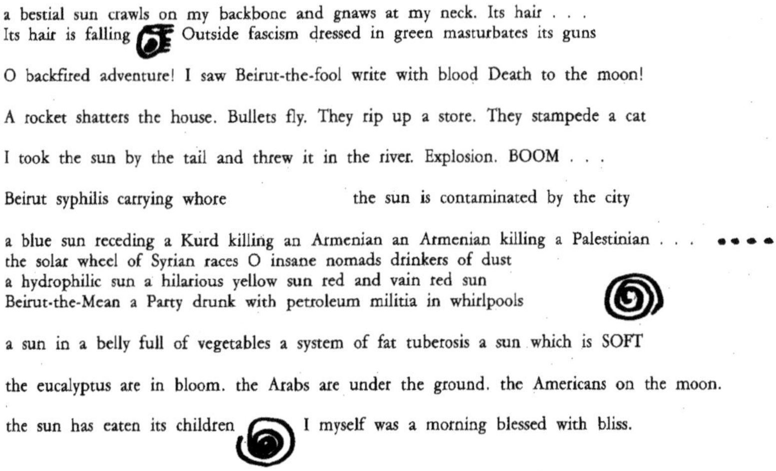

a bestial sun crawls on my backbone and gnaws at my neck. Its hair . . .
Its hair is falling 🌀 Outside fascism dressed in green masturbates its guns

O backfired adventure! I saw Beirut-the-fool write with blood Death to the moon!

A rocket shatters the house. Bullets fly. They rip up a store. They stampede a cat

I took the sun by the tail and threw it in the river. Explosion. BOOM . . .

Beirut syphilis carrying whore   the sun is contaminated by the city

a blue sun receding a Kurd killing an Armenian an Armenian killing a Palestinian . . . ● ● ● ●
the solar wheel of Syrian races O insane nomads drinkers of dust
a hydrophilic sun a hilarious yellow sun red and vain red sun
Beirut-the-Mean a Party drunk with petroleum militia in whirlpools   🌀

a sun in a belly full of vegetables a system of fat tuberosis a sun which is SOFT

the eucalyptus are in bloom. the Arabs are under the ground. the Americans on the moon.

the sun has eaten its children   🌀   I myself was a morning blessed with bliss.

Figure 3b. Etel Adnan. *The Arab Apocalypse*. The Post-Apollo Press. Sausalito, California. 1989. Poem VII. Copyright The Estate of Etel Adnan. Courtesy of the Post-Apollo Press.

and cubes mounted on each other or next to each other" (96), and she elaborates: "And so the square made room for the Mountain. The square divided itself into a Pyramid, which happened to be the Mountain's form—a Pyramid soon inhabited by spheres. To draw a sphere one needs a line, and the line led to an innumerable number of watercolors and drawings of the mountain. She drew the Mountain everywhere and all the time" (96). From three untitled watercolors, which date to 1970–73—plate 1—to a 2017 print, *Soleil sur le Mont Tamalpais*—plate 2—and more, Adnan has sketched, printed, painted, and colored Mount Tamalpais. This return to the mountain is "the substance of painting itself," and yet this may be only insofar as "substance" is this return, an irreducibility of matter to regulated form.[88] I notice the motion of the mountain in a 2014 untitled oil painting on canvas—plate 3—and the movement implied in its lines. It is as if the mountain were not a stable form, an object exterior to a subject and made available in representation, or a resource for extractive, capitalist life, but instead a being in the world of things. If the block-like form at the bottom left may be said to promise a ground for world, the intersection of its dark green with light splotches of differently colored blue, and the textured form of its sides, disaffirm such grounding. The block's dark green obtrudes into the lighter green of the mountain, mirroring the peach-colored, square-like form in the top right corner of the painting; they may be connected by an unfinished line, which the form and motion of the mountain indetermine. It is not that painting is offered for a subject in contemplative life, an aesthetic formalization and temporal determination of self and world—as in the Kantian subject of transcendental apperception in the first *Critique* and its mutation into the subject of aesthetic judgment in the third, the *Critique of the Power of Judgment*—but that the subject, in painting, is given instead through a material practice of color, a weightiness in form, in a sort of doing that mirrors language or sound.

The Palestinian poet Mahmoud Darwish, one of whose poetic verses I've placed as the epigraph of this book, wrote in a diary entry, written between the summers of 2006 and 2007, that "An ordinary word, which someone says, not intending anything, to another, at an intersection or in the market, is what makes a poem possible!"[89] Darwish's attention to a word offered, an utterance, as if it were a sort of matter—like language, or like paint or pastel—teaches us to read Adnan and the shapes that permeate her painted, drawn, and sketched works. In the 2017 print reproduced in plate 2 there are three upright triangles, all incomplete, and an unfinished drawing of a horizon. The incompletion of horizon interrupts the cartographic, state-determined containments privileged in modern conceptualizations of the social and language. The angles of the triangles point upward, gesturing to others in a movement in sociality, resounding in them. Mount Tamalpais gives ground and slope, a giving of shape in an infinity of triangles within triangles, as the triangles within the sun or moon, which hovers over the others, suggest further angles; they are, Fattal has written, "innumerable." In Adnan the mountain holds and shares plurality as it does language—and languages. "So mountains are languages and languages are mountains," Adnan further noted. "We speak both."[90]

The harsh formalization of topography in the cadastral life of the settler state is disaffirmed in the unfinished dimension of sketched or painted form and the intercombobulation of color with shape. In an untitled oil painting dated 1965–66—plate 4—four blocks of color, in blue, green, yellow, and orange, are stacked at the center of a painting of nearly rectangular shapes in light browns muted with orange and yellow, while a red square extends from a white rectangle, placed off-center. If each block promises a square consisting in two pairs of parallel and equal sides intersecting at right angles, the lines that constitute each side are indirect or skewed. Line leans outward or inward, as if the matter in which it consisted pressed against the regularity of form its geometry required. The terms are mirrored in an earlier, untitled piece—plate 5—from 1964–65, where line and color convolute to create an indistinction of form and materials. There is an excess in line, an overflow of the capture of form in temporal horizon, which mirrors the excess in language, as well as being—the anontological form—which the poetic, in Adnan, gives. I notice this overflow in two other paintings—in plate 7, which appears in the cover of this book, and in plate 8. The first is untitled, and dated 1966, while the second, titled *The Suez Canal*, is dated 1967. In plate 7 deep browns and oranges color ground or earth upon which red, white, and green forms rest; orange strokes intersect the brown foreground, penetrating earth and disallocating a distinction between ground and thing, material and substance. There is a light brown square-like object floating in the air, slightly to the left, drawing one's eye in a motion that destabilizes horizon while giving a density in color and inheritance; something is given—language, paint, color, texture—and the terms of relation refute the propertied form of settler life. In plate 8 the blue of sky and light orange or brown of earth are cut through by a blackness touched with green, as if the canal, in a topography of commercial capital and imperialist formation, perforated geographic form—the canal opened in 1869, funded by a concession granted to form the Suez Canal Company in 1858 and constructed using corvée labor, and was nationalized 1956—as it is routed, in Adnan, through an indistinct delineation in line.[91] Fattal describes Adnan: "She worked on the canvas like a sheet of paper, the canvas laid on the table, using a palette knife instead of a brush. She posed on it squares and masses—vivid bright stretches of color."[92] Adnan calls this "gesture": "At first, since I had these little ends of pastels, I'd start with a red square. And this red square called for the gestures that followed. That's how it is. That is, you make a mark, and the mark creates a situation, and this situation calls for other gestures."[93] In painting, "You move, you look around for colors, you make gestures" (53). "For instance, when I put two colors together: that's a situation and I must proceed. I have to continue painting" (80). "I cannot separate the events that shape my day-to-day existence from whatever I write or paint," Adnan also wrote, and we may consider the sort of act that painting is, in the manipulation of instrument and the tool's pressing upon canvas, to belong to such "events," where "I" does not precede making in art—"You make a mark, and the mark creates a situation," "You make gestures"—but is given through it.[94] Each shape, as in plates 4, 5, 7, and 8, reaches toward others, leans upon them. Each yields in the incompleteness of its form; manner, in Adnan, is anaccumulative, it gives a non-propertied form of life. Like language, painting insurges.

Rather than stabilized by a horizon external to it painting is cut through by horizon, and by an intersection of horizons—plate 6—which multiplies—plate 9—refuting the temporal orientation of a subject. A 2018 print, *En route vers le desert*—plate 10—reiterates this refutation as it points to the relations among form, matter, color, and line and their pertinence in Adnan's works, for example in plates 11 and 12. If, in plate 11, a dark blue rectangle punctuates the horizon, leaning slightly against a lighter blue square, and standing unsteadily on another square- or rectangle-like form, in plate 12 the square, in bright green, is aloft, floating; it provides a disallocation of the formal subordination of materials to temporal capture. An untitled oil painting marked by the location Sausalito, California, and dated 1980—the year in which *L'Apocalypse arabe* was published—gives an overflow of color and form in the topographical—see plate 13. The mountain-like triangles interpose and their shapes reiterate the unfinished form of the sketches I've underlined. In plate 13 the triangle-mountain on the middle left, perhaps yellow painted over green, reaches slightly higher than the muted brown or orangish sloping triangle to its right. Atop it sits another triangle, its point tending downward, even as that triangle is, on left and right, supported by two forms, each interlayered with triangles. The motion of the painting draws one's eye upward, toward the stars or planets—"The ocean's sound waves are heard on the moon," Adnan writes.[95] Just as there is already more than one sun, and just as the sun is already more than one—as in figure 1a—I observe this plurality in Adnan's reiteration of triangles, a practice of leaning, in painting. It is as if gesture and color, in painting, and in the floating or balancing form of the sun—plates 14, 15, and 16—reiterate the sort of practice, in indetermined form, which the poetic is.[96]

"It seems to me that I write what I see, paint what I am," Adnan also writes, and to think about the manner in which painting, in Adnan, occasions or gives place to a particular mode of being, I turn to several texts of Emmanuel Lévinas and consider them in relation to Heidegger's discussion of being, which I outlined in the introduction, as well as Marx's reflection on the social and language, which I studied in chapter 1.[97] In an essay titled "Is Ontology Fundamental?" ("L'Ontologie est-elle fondamentale?"), published in 1951, Lévinas places an emphasis on language in offering the confrontation with Heidegger, which the title of this essay suggests. In Heidegger, in *Being and Time*, being is to be understood not in reference to an atemporal being but instead in relation to temporality in "care," *Sorge*, and "being-toward-death," *Sein-zum-Tode*, and in relation to a privileging of what is, in each case, "mine," and for Lévinas this points to a comprehension of being in relation to a "*horizon of being*," and, through this, "understanding rejoins the great tradition of Western philosophy: to understand the particular being is already to place oneself beyond the particular."[98] Temporality, in Heidegger, as Lévinas reads him, is reduced to the "being-toward-death" of a single being and, contra Heidegger, Lévinas draws out an explication of being in its relation to language and what he terms "the other": "The other is not first an object of understanding and then an interlocutor" (17/6), and this is because the relation given in language is "prior to" understanding, consciousness, philosophical conceptualization, and ontology:

"Speech delineates an original relation [*une relation originale*]" (17/6). Lévinas underlines: "It is a matter of seeing the function of language not as subordinate to the *consciousness* we have of the presence of the other, or of his proximity, or of our community with him, but as a condition of that conscious realization" (17/6). Prior to philosophy, and prior to ontology, there is a relation to the other, and this relation is given in "address," the "vocative," and one's being "called upon": "The person with whom I am in relation I call being, but in calling him *being* I call upon him. I do not just think that he is, I speak to him" (18/7).

Lévinas privileges a single being, "man," in relation to language: "Man is the only being I cannot meet without my expressing this meeting itself to him," Lévinas writes. He continues: "In every attitude toward the human being there is a greeting—even if it is the refusal of a greeting" (18–19/6–7). And yet "expression," like "greeting," does not "consist in *articulating* the understanding I already have in common with the other. It consists, prior to any participation in a common content through understanding, in instituting sociality through a relation that is, consequently, irreducible to understanding" (19/7). This relation, "this bond with the other which is not reducible to the representation of the other, but to his invocation" (19/7), occasions a "sociality": "The object of the meeting," he writes, "is at the same time given to us and *in society* with us, but without that event of sociality [*cet événement de socialité*] being reducible to any property whatsoever revealed in the given—without knowledge being able to take precedence over sociality" (19/8). The being with which one is in relation in "sociality," in the "formal structure" Lévinas elaborates, is the "neighbor," *prochain*, and, in a passage I'll turn to below, in *Otherwise Than Being* (*Autrement qu'être*), published in 1974, the "brother." The "neighbor," in "Is Ontology Fundamental?", is that sort of being which occasions the ethical relation, and it is this relation that is other than and prior to ontology. "The relation to the other is therefore not [*n'est donc pas*] ontology" (19/7), and the sort of being given in that relation, "the being as such," *l'étant comme tel*, is given in invocation. "The being as such (and not as an incarnation of universal being) can only be in a relation in which he is invoked. That being is man, and it is as a neighbor that man is accessible: as a face" (20/9).

The capacity to hear is central to Lévinas's analysis—"How is the vision of the face no longer vision, but hearing and speech?" (22/11)—and this centrality is deepened in *Otherwise Than Being*. In *Otherwise Than Being* Lévinas notes that apophantic speech, in propositions which attach a predicate to a subject, which state that "A" is "B," presume a relation to the "accusative" and "vocative." "In the verb of apophansis, which is the verb properly so called, the verb *to be*, essence resounds and is heard. A is A but also A is B are understood in such a manner that A's essence resounds, vibrates, or is temporalized."[99] In ontology the resounding of the verb "to be" is comprehended in a substantialization of the sonorous, and of what Lévinas terms "the saying": "Behind every statement of being as being, the saying overflows the very being it thematizes in stating it to the other [*le Dire déborde l'être même qu'il thématise pour l'énoncer à* Autrui]; it is being which is understood in the—first or last—word, but the last saying goes *beyond* the being thematized or totalized" (35/18). If this overflow is given in language it is immediately recalled there, and Lévinas points to this recalling of "the saying," *le Dire*, to the ontologization or nominalization of language, where the accusative or vocative are gathered in "the said," *le Dit*: "But in the said, the essence that resounds is on the verge of becoming a noun" (72/41), and, further, "The verb *to be* in predication (which is its 'natural place') makes essence resound, but this resonance is collected into an entity by the noun. To be thenceforth *designates* instead of *resounding*" (73/42). What occurs in "resounding" is immediately exposed to and is in excess of "the said": "Every nameable identity can turn into a verb" (74/43). "Fundamental ontology itself," Lévinas writes, as he explicates the privilege of Heidegger's formulations, "which denounces the confusion between being and beings, speaks of being as an identified being" (74/42–43).

Lévinas explicates subjectivity in relation to "the saying," and I wish to underline this explication here: "Subjectivity is vulnerability, is sensibility. Sensibility, all the passivity of saying, cannot be reduced to an experience that a subject would have of it, even if it makes possible such an experience. An exposure to the other, it is signification, is signification itself, the one-for-the-other to the point of substitution, but a substitution in separation, that is, responsibility" (92/54). In Lévinas's thinking of substitution the reduction of subjectivity to consciousness is displaced. "The reduction of subjectivity to consciousness dominates philosophical thought" (163/103), but the subject is inidentical in relation to itself: "The oneself cannot form *itself*; it is already formed with absolute passivity" (165/104). One is under accusation and responsible for all of the others, "accused of what the others do or suffer, or responsible for what they do or suffer" (177/112). "Everything from the start," Lévinas writes, "is in the accusative" (177/112). Lévinas underlines this non-nominative dimension of subjectivity, where the subject, in its relation to "responsibility for another," is "a hostage": "Responsibility for another is not an accident that happens to a subject, but precedes essence in it, has not awaited freedom, in which a commitment to another would have been made. I have not done anything and I have always been under accusation—persecuted. The ipseity, in the passivity without *arche* characteristic of identity, is a hostage. The word *I* means *here I am*, answering for everything and everyone" (180–181/114). Lévinas writes, translating *Genesis* 22:1 and 22:11, where, in response to God's address, "And he said to him," ויאמר אליו, *ve yomer eilav*, Abraham replies, "Here I am," הנני, *hineini* : "The self is a *sub-jectum*: it is under the weight of the universe, responsible for everything" (183/116). Here Lévinas recalls and interprets the reading of the Greek term ὑποκείμενον, *hupokeimenon*, in its rendering as "subjectum" in Boethius's sixth-Christian-century, Latin translation of the Aristotelian logical books, as explicated in Heidegger's 1928 lecture course on *The Metaphysical Foundations of Logic*.[100] "The self, a hostage, is already substituted for the others [*déjá substitué aux autres*]," and this is what "I," in Lévinas, is, its exposure to and responsibility for all of the others—for "everything."[101]

Lévinas underlines the "neighbor" and "brother" in relation to the "other," in what he calls "fraternity": "The subjectivity of the approaching subject is then preliminary, anarchic, prior to consciousness, an implication, a being caught up in fraternity" (132/82–83). Lévinas understands these terms based on the analysis of substitution he provides: "It is not because the neighbor would be recognized as belonging to the same genus as me that he concerns me. He is precisely *other*. The community with him begins in my obligation to him. The neighbor is a brother" (138/87). In this "community" with the other, the social is to be thought from out of the ethical, and this thinking turns on the form of a listening subject: "In proximity is heard a command [*s'entend un commandement*] come as though from an immemorial past, which was never present, which began in no freedom. The *way* of the neighbor is a face" (141/88). I notice, reading these statements, that Lévinas's exposition, if it points to "an immemorial past, which was never present, which began in no freedom," reiterates, in its privilege of a listening subject, and however "passive" the formulation is, the "reduction of subjectivity to consciousness," of which he also wrote. I wish to ask: Does Lévinas not, then, translate the explication of the "self" as "sub-jectum"—"The self is a *sub-jectum*: it is under the weight of the universe, responsible for everything"—into the terms he wishes to have placed in question?[102] Does he not affirm a distinction between those capable and incapable of language, greeting, accusation, substitution, and face? Does Lévinas, finally, not reiterate his belonging to a tradition—what I've called, in chapter 1, the tradition of "settler life"—where the reflection on the social becomes a domestication or regulating pacification of it, as in Paul's first letter to the Corinthians?

The attention to listening in Lévinas communicates with a privilege of vocality in the "accusative," the "vocative," the "greeting," as well as in "the original dative of the *for the other*," as Lévinas wrote elsewhere, where what language gives is "an I that one does not designate but which says 'here I am.'"[103] "The I is a passivity more passive than any passivity, because it is from the outset in the accusative," and, further, "A hostage for another, it obeys a commandment before having heard it; it is faithful to an engagement that it never made, and to a past that was never present' (113/68). "I respond from the first," Lévinas writes, "to a summons" (117/71). And yet "I," in its capacity to "obey," and to "respond from the first," presumes a linguistic pose in controlled temporal performance, a form that does not "babble" and that is neither "primitive" nor "childish": "Substitution," Lévinas writes in *Otherwise Than Being*, "at the limit of being, ends up in saying—in the giving of signs, a giving of signs of this giving of signs, in expressing. An expression antecedent to all thematization in the said, but which, even so, is not a babbling or still primitive or childish form of saying [*n'est pas balbutiement, ou dire encore primitif ou enfantillage du dire*]."[104] "It is," Lévinas further writes of "responsibility" and "signification," "the subjectivity of the subject that makes itself a sign, but which one would be wrong to take as a babbling utterance of a word [*mais que l'on prendrait à tort un énonce balbutiant d'un mot*], for it bears witness to the glory of the Infinite" (236/151). Lévinas's explication of what is "otherwise than being" is written through a social and ontological containment of the "primitive" and the "child," where, if "the responsibility for everyone goes to the point of substitution," (177/112), Lévinas's subject-centric pose, and its other-obliterating manner, is reformulated in his response to a question regarding the 1982 massacres of Palestinians at the Sabra and Shatila refugee camps at the outskirts of Beirut—an event that transpired six years following the massacre at Tel al-Zaʿatar, in relation to which *The Arab Apocalypse* was written.

When asked, "Emmanuel Lévinas, you are the philosopher of the 'other.' Isn't history, isn't politics the very site of the encounter with the 'other,' and for the Israeli, isn't the 'other' above all the Palestinian?," he replies: "My definition of the other is completely different. The other is the neighbor, who is not necessarily kin, but who can be. And in that sense, if you're for the other, you're for the neighbor. But if your neighbor attacks another neighbor or treats him unjustly, what can you do? Then alterity takes on another character, in alterity we can find an enemy, or at least then we are faced with the problem of knowing who is right and who is wrong, who is just and who is unjust. There are people who are wrong."[105] Lévinas frames his response in the language of *Otherwise Than Being*—"Prior to any act, I am concerned with the Other, and I can never be absolved from this responsibility" (290)—and in this he displaces the ethical with the political, where "alterity takes on another character" and where "in alterity we can find an enemy." It is as if, where there is an "enemy" there is "alterity" but not "the Other," neither a "neighbor" nor a "brother," neither "fraternity" nor "proximity," no "substitution" or "face" but only "politics," a formulation that affirms the sensorium of European-derivative terms, as, in Lévinas's words, "ethically necessary" (292).

If, in Heidegger, being is thought in relation to temporality; if, in Lévinas, sociality is thought in relation to greeting, accusation, and substitution; and if, in Marx, there is an affirmation and disaffirmation of an anontological manner of doing or being; I notice in Adnan's poetry and painting a practice that does not privilege a distinction drawn between beings in relation to a capacity to properly do language but that instead indistinguishes being from life, language from the social, and, in the terms of Aristotle's *Politics*, which I discussed in chapter 1, "life" from "the good life" and "doing" from "making"—*praxis* from *poiēsis*. The fourth chapter of *Otherwise Than Being*, titled "Substitution," takes as an epigraph a passage in Celan, which I've cited above, "Ich bin du, wenn ich ich bin," and of which I've considered Khālid al-Maʿālī's Arabic-language translation. If al-Maʿālī gives us to read, in this translation, another Celan—a Celan of sociality rather than ethicality—this would be to observe a global practice of anontological, anaccumulative form, of social insurgence in excess of any recognizable language or tradition, to which Lévinas, and not only him, capturingly responds.[106] I ask, returning to Adnan, whether there is, in her labor with materials, a form wholly other than that of the logic of property, a submersion in the stuff of matter, an indistinction of language from the social, the social from the ontological, and language from the sea? "An ocean resides between my eye and its eyelid," Adnan writes in a volume titled *Surge*.[107] And I ask whether what transpires in Adnan's poetry and painting does not give a non-masculinist, non-human-centric sense of being, form, language, and life, where the being of the plant intersects that of the person or stone, where a subject in language is the sea in its relation to salt, color, sweat, and rain, and where being is an overflow of matter or things: "It rains," Adnan also notes, "It rains."[108]

The pouring of rain points to the proliferation of algae with number—"One. One plus one. The many added to the many. Proliferation: of the algae at patience's edge"—in their intersection with form and life.[109] The time of matter, like algae, gives a sense of being, of which Adnan writes: "Are you, am I, is anyone *is-ing*, is anyone *be-ing*, is matter real, as real as we are, but aren't we real because we are dying and that matter is infinite and therefore not real?" (34). *There* was translated into Arabic by the Iraqi poet Sargon Būloṣ, and published with Manshūrāt al-Jamal—the publishing house founded by Khālid al-Maʿālī. The first sentences in the passage I've just cited are rendered: هل أنت، هل أنا، هل أيّ أحد هـو—يٌّ، هل أيّ أحد ين—وجد، هل المادة حقيقية، كما أننا حقيقيّون. They may be transliterated in this manner: *hal anti, hal ana, hal ayy aḥad huww-īyyūn, hal ayy aḥad yan-wajid, hal al-māda ḥaqiqiyya, kamā annā ḥaqīqīyyūn*.[110] The language mirrors the italicized phrasings of Adnan's English in relation to the verb "to be" and the noun "being." The former, in

Būloṣ's translation, is generated from the third person singular masculine pronoun, هـو, *huwwa*, which can also serve as a copula, and which Būloṣ transforms, in its verbal function, into a noun: *huww-īyyūn*; the latter, formed from the verb وجد, *wajada*—which, in modern Arabic, renders "to find," and, as a verbal noun, "existence" or "being," وجود, *wujūd*, and which can also, in the idiom of the Arabic philosophical tradition, in the term موجود, *mawjūd*, function as a copula and can mean, as well, "a being" or "an entity"—is reformulated in Būloṣ's translation through a passive voice verb construction which is not used in normative Arabic, as if there were a verb *inwajada*, "to be found," or "to be there," even as this sense is given in a normative passive voice formulation: *yūjad*. It is as if Būloṣ's use of a non-normative verbal form reiterates Adnan's pressing or bending of the English language, "is-ing," "being," while still phrasing a recognizable grammar. Būloṣ's rendering retains the sense of the verb "to be" Adnan's language gives, and it reformulates it through a manipulation of morphological forms in Arabic. Būloṣ's translation becomes a reading of Adnan where the verb "to be," and its indistinction from a nominal form, "being," in Adnan's English sentences, and as Būloṣ renders these in Arabic, gives the anontological sense of being and form, which Adnan's writing and painting transmute. In this, being is a temporal formulation with matter, a doing or making with materials, a sociality in acts, where the distinctions drawn between being and language, and the ontological and the social, remain illegible. And this is what Adnan's language shares and is, what it does in the poetic and with color: "It's good," Adnan notes, "to paint in Marin County."[111] We might also say that in its Arabic-language formulations Būloṣ's translation teaches us the manner in which Adnan's English-language writing shares in the tradition of form, in Arabic, I've studied. And there is, then, a further indistinction of English from Arabic, and of grammatical from ontological sense, a giving in form in which we are schooled in the sort of doing that occurs in the poetry and painting of Etel Adnan.

Insurgent Life

In an essay and collection of drawings titled *Journey to Mount Tamalpais*, published in 1986, Adnan writes: "I make paintings and watercolors of Tamalpais. Again and again. Why do I insist? Am I trying to hold some image, to capture some meaning, to assert its presence, to measure myself to its timelessness, to fight, or to accept?"[112] There is, grammatically, a subject, "I," and yet it is only given through an "insistence," and so there is a practice in "making," "I make paintings and watercolors," that does not devolve upon an intention, which the poet or painter, who "makes" with materials, will have made manifest through their acts, or which will have become localizable in a pronoun—for example, the pronoun "I." It is as if, through this insistence, Adnan gives us to reread this pronoun in its relation to painting, salt, the sea, and "Lucretius," who, she writes, "makes us breathe again" (30).

It is not that in painting Adnan creates a representation of Mount Tamalpais, because in Adnan the distinctions between subject and object, and matter and formal articulation, are blurred, and this blurring gives a wholly other sense of what "making" is: "I am 'making' the mountain as people make a painting" (10), Adnan explains. This "making" is not an appropriating act of possession but instead a being or doing with materials and things. Against the terms of settler life Adnan asserts a poetics of non-possession, a non-propertied mode in the weight of life and form in the American settler state. Color is a locus for this mode: "But there is no possession of color, only the acceptance of its reality. And if there is no possibility for the possession of color, there is no possession at all. Of whatever it is" (51). It is as if the practice of color and its insurgence against a regulating control of line become the form of Adnan's writing about and painting of Mount Tamalpais, to which she returns "as usual": "I am sitting as usual in the front of Tamalpais. I can't get over its deep greens" (51). Adnan's manner of painting occasions a mode of being that is, inidentically, a doing or making, a sociality in form, in what I termed in the introduction to this book a "poetics of things," where "my" being may be, merely, this doing or making, a practice with materials, in the "insistence" of which Adnan has written, and which is indistinguishable from being and life: "I exist," Adnan writes, "because I see colors" (51).

Adnan returns to the practice of painting, and as she does this, she turns to a figure she terms "the Indian," and I wish to linger, now, with this practice of return. Adnan provides an etymology of the mountain's name: "The Indian called the mountain Tamal-Pa, 'The One Close to the Sea.' The Spaniard called it Mal-Pais, 'Bad Country'! The difference between the native and the conqueror is readable in these two different perceptions of the same reality" (15). There is, in this passage, a practice of nomination: "The Indian called the mountain Tamal-Pa." "The Indian" has named the mountain, and if this name is contrasted to the one bestowed by the settler, and what Adnan calls the "conqueror," it is the one with which Adnan affiliates: "Let us be the Indian and let be! What is close to the sea shall remain close to the sea" (15–16). On the one hand, Adnan affirms an affiliation with "the Indian," in a social and lingual assertion of an expansive and definite solidarity with those subjected to "Indigenous elimination," "nonconsensual occupation," and ongoing practices of expropriation, collective decimation, and "colonial management," as Nick Estes has written.[113] In this sense, "Let us be the Indian and let be!" becomes a translation of lingual form, a disaffiliation of poetic utterance and painting practice from the terms of the settler state and white social existence, a formulation for the affirmation of Indigenous sovereignty in Turtle Island—in the expansive topography Adnan sketches in *Journey to Mount Tamalpais* in its Western-hemispheric contexts. It is a phrase which, in its imperative form, is an affirmation. It redefines the terms for being and the social by refusing settler existence, language, and life, and by doing so not through a substantialist understanding of self or world but in a linguistic formulation: an imperative.[114] It is not that the "us," in "Let us be the Indian and let be!", precedes this affirmation but that it is instead called into being through it; "us" is not an already existing social or linguistic collective, a substance, but a gathering in insubstantial form whose existence—whose social being—is given through that affirmation.[115]

And yet Adnan's turn to "the Indian" is also jarring. It is as if Adnan's poetic practice draws on "the Indian" or the "Hopi" (in *The Arab Apocalypse*) as a lexical term in the poetic formulation of "us," a linguistic and social subject that speaks in the first person plural. And it is as if the poem is able to conjure "us," a plural subject in the poetic, only through an appeal to "the Indian," in a gesture that can mirror the extractive logic of capital. It is as if "the Indian" becomes, in these passages, a material through which painting and poetry are formulated, in what Audra Simpson has termed "the demands of a settler landscape."[116] Adnan relates "drawing" to "the South Sea Islanders" in *Journey to Mount Tamalpais*, where "we," a collective subject in painting, are enabled to gain a "new start": "Each time I draw a circle I draw the earth, the moon, or the sun. We see simple things. But the South Sea Islanders see in the very circle a mythological crab which has just emerged into the visible part of the globe. We have sterilized our visions. We need a new start."[117] The word "but" creates a punctuation; it states a contrast between what "we" see and the manner of seeing of "the South Sea Islanders." In this phrasing, "the South Sea Islanders" become a resource for painting—and, further, for "drawing"—and in this sense Adnan's terms rephrase the social logic of settler form, with which she disaffiliates herself and her work, and which she also refuses.[118]

I wish to linger further with this refusal. "I am water and I move," Adnan writes in *Journey to Mount Tamalpais*, "I need to circle the mountain, because I am water."[119] The being that circles, "I," intersects the thinking of matter and form with Adnan's relating of "the Indian," whose being punctuates a harsh division between the living and the dead: "Snow is cold, as cold as the Indian buried underground. And still the Indian was everywhere in the fog, totally a spirit" (43). On the one hand, the juridical and social closure of the settler state, its sovereignty, are refused. And this refusal, in its declining to affirm settler temporality, is topographically expansive, it extends all the way down "the convulsive spine of the American continent": "This is, then, the place where the line is drawn. Tamalpais is the first of the mountains that constitute the convulsive spine of the American continent, all the way to Tierra del Fuego" (17). There is an address to a geography in excess of settler-cadastrality, a refusal of the settler state's form and its self-allocated topographical lexicon, a wholly other sense of being, but Adnan's affirmation of an affiliation with "the Indian" through a contrastive orientation—"We see simple things. But the South Sea Islanders see"—is also a practice in language given through a material formulation with the terms for settler existence.

We may consider Adnan's painting, and her returns to Mount Tamalpais, in this frame. While the paintings give an anontological sense of being and form, I notice that Adnan's materials in painting are formulated in relation to the land, a sort of matter that has been translated—in settler usurpation and capitalist, settler expropriation in the American settler state—as an object of property. If Adnan's painting presses against this becoming-property of earth, and if Adnan is explicit in this—by which I mean that Adnan is explicit in her opposition to the social and epistemic forms of settler life, as I've outlined in a number of passages in her work—her practice in painting is made possible through it. Sketches, such as those in plate 1, and paintings, such as plates 3, 13, and 14, may be re-read in this frame, as occasions wherein a practice of non-propertied, anaccumlative form is formulated through the material or historical violences of settler existence, in relation to which Adnan's practice also generates alternatives, and in relation to which it alternates and becomes—as Adnan's work does—something other than what it is. Adnan's writing and painting refuse the domestication or translation of the mountain into the field of propertied terms to which it has been subjected in "the demands of a settler landscape," and the sense of the social—in the mutation of earth into property—constitutive for settler life, even as this subjection and its ongoing permutations are a condition of her painting and drawing the mountain—as they are, at the same time, and inidentically, a condition for the readings I offer of Adnan in this book. To think this intercorrelation of language and form, and material and composition, is not to reduce one to the other but to suggest shared conditions in social formation and lingual or material practice as terms for collective struggle, to return to a term of Walter Benjamin's I noted in this book's preface—in refusal of settler life.

There is, in a volume of Adnan's titled *The Indian Never Had a Horse and Other Poems*, published in 1985—during the period that intervened between the publication of *L'Apocalypse arabe* and Adnan's English-language translation of it as *The Arab Apocalypse*—an address to the terms of settler life.

Adnan writes:

> The certitude of space is brought
> to me by a flight of birds. It
> is grey outside and there is a trembling:
> fog is too heavy a word.
>
> The zookeeper sends his love
> letters to the female mayor of
> San Diego
> The lioness in her den fainted
> on April fool's day
> the man hanged himself in
> her cage.
>
> A bee fell in love with a peach
> blossom. Shakespeare wrote a story about it.
>
> Sweat runs over my body.
> The river beds are dry.
> We forgot to brush the
> Indians' teeth before the
> final slaughter.
> Oh how perfect the afternoon!
>
> Why is heaven the color of bleach?
> Out of their blood grew green
> grass and picnic tables were used
> for their morbid orations.[120]

Adnan's formulations refuse the aesthetic appropriation of Indigenous life in the settler state: "We forgot to brush the / Indians' teeth before the / final slaughter." The finality of the "final slaughter" is rejected, and the slaughter is, then, ongoing, an unstable object of historical understanding. There are bodies that cut into the landscape, refusing the settler state's curation of death and its plantational and cadastral logic—"You know that your conscience / left you long ago: it got / washed away by summer floods. / A human body is lying on rocks / no vulture can stand in its stink / no cowboy is asking for pardon" (13)—as the terms for white, settler social understanding labor to appropriate Indigenous life and being in aesthetic formalization: "Few flowers survive / a gun fight / and large streams / descend steadily from the / Rockies to the Amazon Basin / The coffeepot is dancing over a fire: 'Oh!' says the cowboy, / 'What a lovely horse'" (15). It is as if Adnan's writing, elsewhere, that "Every avenue of thought leads to some disaster," points to these references to "the Indian," "the South Sea islanders," and the ongoing permutations of "Columbus"—"I can see the new world order becoming a new Columbus expedition. We already know the results"—as Adnan's poetry writes such disasters and their refusal.[121] "We continually miss the mark of the present, the weather's edge" (24), Adnan notes, as "weather" points to "dead bodies" as well as "ocean" and "breeze": "Memory is like this river, full of dead bodies," Adnan writes of the Seine, "but nonetheless flowing to where the ocean lies, the breeze" (36). In Adnan there is no redemption but only a return to disaster and the obliterating violences of settler existence: "Tell Zaatar was the signal for further disaster" (63), Adnan writes in the 1993 volume, *Paris, When It's Naked*, I'm citing here, as she recalls the 1976 massacre of Palestinians in relation to which she wrote *The Arab Apocalypse*. It is a manner and material practice we may translate in relation to what al-Maʿālī termed "despair's precision," where the temporal doing of language refuses the world-evacuating forms or events to which it is nonetheless related and through which it is, in part, formed.[122] It is a non-redemptive manner, a negativity without the absorption of settler obliterations and containments in linguistic mastery or world-reflective appropriation, without their being raised up and conserved, as in Hegel, and without language's being grounded in a subject of proper expression, as in Lévinas, and which, in Adnan's poetry, has everything to do with color and being, as color is a name for the irresolvable weight of loss in the matter of things, the excess of matter over the time of a subject.[123] Language, in Adnan, one might also say, insurges, it is all surge and swell, the bringing up and tossing forward of the detritus and remains carried in the sea and the irrecoverability of matter in formal appropriation. To think this insurgence, to insurge with it—to allow being to insurge, and to be nothing but this—has meant to write of salt, sweat, stickiness, the sea—and, "I told them: come with me to the sea"—and Damascus, the city of Adnan's father's birth:

I would like to tell you two
things:
that I am going to die
and that you are going to
drive a car

that I will live for ever
and that you will plant roses
on the terrace of Damascus.
Syria has two rivers:
the Euphrates

and a
River of Blood.[124]

Adnan's language gives, through its non-redemptive negativity, a practice for doing or thinking, for writing or making, wholly other than what is privileged in settler life: "Billy the Kid has a / bullet in the head, / like the Iraqi boy / that he shot, / willfully," Adnan wrote in *Night*; "Gaza Street is flooded with blood," Adnan wrote in 2008, in *Seasons*; she shares news of George Jackson, in *Journey to Mount Tamalpais*—"On KPFA George Jackson is speaking. We hear a tape made while he was still alive and in prison. He has many voices blended in one, many accents. He cuts his sentences short, sounding like an Englishman. Then his voice slides between his lips, and his longest word, his most important one, the one pronounced with a long, burning, agonizing, pleading and ever sure voice, is the word love"—as the terms for state-formation, the juridicalization of the social, and the ongoing wars against Black and Indigenous peoples are reiterated in settler existence and genocidal life: "We are occupied by winter and the affairs of the Hemisphere, while, among many catastrophes, the Kurdish woman in Beirut carries her headless son through the streets."[125] The terms of the political accelerate the ongoing destructions forwarded and asymmetrically pressed across topographical, hemispheric, and linguistic frames—"Blood on the leaves and blood at the root, / Black bodies swinging in the Southern breeze," Adnan cites Lewis Allan in *Sea and Fog*—as language speaks to us of the transmutations of settler life in globality, in its ongoing exteriorizations and mutations of itself and the losses it continues, still now, to exact: "There have been yellow shells over the mourning of disembowled houses," Adnan also wrote in *The Arab Apocalypse*, "Tons of despair and gigantic rivers filled   with our collective tears."[126] The space Adnan provides, between "filled" and "with," disjoins the semantic resolutions coerced in settler institutions for reading and sense, as it speaks to us of a "collective" practice and form. Rather than a resolution of settler and colonial violence in the institution of the state, its legality, or its pacifications, there is an indetermined doing with matter: "Poetry starts where meaning ceases," Adnan offers.[127] If, as Adnan writes, "Everything is apocalyptic," and if, in apocalypse, "I am seized / eaten / drowned / disappeared / without resurrection," we may read this sense of apocalypse in relation to each and every being or thing, where the coming of the end already occasions a refusal of closural form.[128] In this refusal language insurges as it speaks to us of poetic and sonic gatherings in excess of the time and sense of the settler—and in excess of the temporality of state-determined life. It is not that in this there is a being—a subject—that refuses, but instead that refusal is a sort of act that overflows the form of a subject, rendering indistinct language and world, the ontological and poetic, and the material and formal. Refusal, as we are given to read it in Adnan—and in al-Maʿālī and Celan—is a non-self-determined practice, a doing or making, a using-again, in an indetermination of forms not reducible to subjectively founded social existence.

The articulation of the social, in the tradition of settler life, is nothing but the setting of limits—it is all walls and borders, a never-ceasing delineation of insides and outsides, a "settler ontology," as Estes, Yazzie, Denetdale, and Correia noted, in a passage I cited in the introduction to this book. In the poetry, painting, and translation I've studied in this chapter, such a setting of limits—as in the predominant tradition for critique since Kant, in all of its racialization of world, in all of its containment and obliteration of those beings it understands to be riotous and uncivil, and in all of its propertied determination of form—is displaced with acts of inidentical social being, an indetermined struggle in collectivity. It is not that the social consists in substances—"I" or "we"—that precede such struggle but instead that it is occasioned in acts called into being in refusal, in the sense in which the texts I've studied in this book give us to think this term. Adnan gives this to us, as language becomes a kind of re-use, a material act in *re*fusal, a word I underline listening to the Latin etymology of the verb "refundere," which I noted in this book's preface. It is a sort of act done "again and again," Adnan wrote: "Words are cracked open, reused in bits and pieces," she writes in *Seasons*, and this "reuse" recalls Adnan's rereading Charles Olson with Ammiel Alcalay's *A Little History*, and the ocean: "Rereading *The Maximus Poems*, I read them differently. I saw Melville all over the book. The ocean, the waters, fishermen and their tools, the pleasure to use this parallel language world that any trade uses, and create the proximity of harbors and sails . . . so clearly stated."[129] "Everything is apocalyptic" (*Sea and Fog*), "without resurrection" (*The Indian Never Had a Horse*), Adnan wrote in passages I've cited, and this affirmation asserts a materiality, which holds for Adnan's writing and painting, a practice in what she follows Jalal Toufic to call "a disaster surpassing disasters."[130] It is as if what is given in Adnan is a refusal, as well, to disavow complicities with the terms against which she labors, where language, as Fawwaz Traboulsi wrote of Adnan's, "is vaporized like a blown door or volatilized like body parts," and where form in poetry and painting mirrors a name Adnan gave to the substance and mode of her work: "The Arab Apocalypse."[131]

What I intend in noticing such refusal is this: that since there is no exteriority to settler life and its manner of sending itself, asymmetrically, at the many targets of its death-exacting pose, collective struggle does not address settler life but instead socially refutes it; it is given in acts—and yet in a non-self-identical sense of what an "act" is—in refusal of settler life. And it is a refusal, a sort of doing, I've noticed, that is already underway, in a giving of forms and a doing with materials; it is also, as Adnan teaches us, a manner of reading—and inheriting—in catastrophe.[132] These are acts, which pass on an understanding of being and life in excess of the state-juridical terms for thinking language, the social, and collective existence in post-Ottoman frames, and in refusal of the normalizing and eviscerating violences of our time: "To do as if things mattered," Adnan wrote in 2005. "To look calm, polite, when Gaza is under siege and when a blackish tide slowly engulfs Palestinians. How not to die of rage?"[133] To think this ongoing siege and to decline its terms is, further, "To pray to the ancient gods. To not despair about the past. To not forget," as it is "To live with the knowledge that the Americans, the English, their allies, want the people of Iraq, the children, the men of Iraq, to be destroyed" (105). In this, Adnan's poetry gives "lyric postures" in aphoristic sentences, a kind of parataxis, an adjacency, which, unlike accumulation, makes a "fragility of form in the midst of calamity," to draw upon Anahid Nersessian's reflection.[134] And to think the ongoing siege—in Gaza and elsewhere—is to remain with the sensual or material fact that "I have the firm belief—and that contributes to my chronic insomnia—that it's already late if we want to avoid the disasters that we are preparing for ourselves," as it is to refuse to separate the form of the subject, "I," from the "firmness" of its belief and the chronic dimensions of its corporeal content—"One's unavoidable house is the body"—and its belatedness in relation to disaster.[135] It is to render, again, in poetic or painterly form, another writing, one that has already begun—"The first act of writing was a mutation" (34)—and it is to give another manner of doing or thinking or being or making with matter, a wholly other sense of language and world: "This is how I discovered writing with no alphabet," Adnan also writes. "One sign after another. One wave length after another. The tall eucalyptus trees were the measure" (14).

In the preface to this book I underlined Walter Benjamin's understanding of critique as a "task," *Aufgabe*, and it would perhaps be more accurate to say that through his reflection on tradition and law Benjamin displaces "critique" with "task"—a practice given in what he termed "the tradition of the oppressed," *die Tradition der Unterdrückten*, the tradition of those "pressed under," as we might also hear this term. It is a pressing under or down, a drowning or submersion, in relation to which Benjamin refuses to call upon the law but instead appeals to a "de-posing" of it, where legality is disinstalled as a social form for collective existence.[136] To think "Benjamin in Palestine," I also noticed in this book's preface, has been to think this legality and the modes of unsurvival—the thanatosocial practices and linguistic forms, the obliterations and eviscerations—it foments and sustains. And it has been to observe, as Lenora Hanson has underlined, that primitive accumulation, and settler form, forward modes of life and manners of being, which they have been unable, finally, to destroy or contain.[137] The effort of this book has been, in chapter 1, to textually demonstrate the social form fostered in modern legality and self-reflexive philosophical exposition—what I've termed "settler life." And it has been to understand settler life as the advance of a manner of being, a property-centric form, a generalization of whiteness in the social, and a particular sort of reading in counterinsurgent pose, where language is to the social as matter is to its domestication in the temporally controlling terms of hermeneutic interpretation. Rather than such interpretation, I've lingered with language and materials—in poetry, philosophy, painting, and translation—in a yielding or sharing. Language, as I've studied it in the introduction and chapters 2 and 3, is a non-selfsame lingual doing, a materiality in excess of the subject of property and law, carried in Khālid al-Maʿālī's poetry and translation, in Paul Celan's manner of utterance, and in Etel Adnan's poetic writing and painting. In this book I've turned to a number of words—"poeticality," "anontological form," "insurgence"—and I haven't done so in order to install new terminological forms, but instead to press against the normative vocabularies of collective existence in the settler colony. In this, and thinking and reading with Layli Long Soldier's love—"Instead, I push my love into this world and mail you a summer letter," she wrote—and Mahmoud Darwish's sense of the poetic—"To poetry: place your siege under siege," Darwish offered—I wish to do nothing but give language, something that will never have been "mine," away. This giving-away is, also, a sort of refusal, a declining to coerce language to assume the position of an object in relation to the institutions—and they are settler and plantational institutions—of literary pedagogy; it is, at the same time, a refusal of method as a means to resolve difficulties of syntax, address, form, and line. In this, I wish to affirm only a dependency, a non-self-sufficiency, an inessential leaning or indebtedness, what Fred Moten and Stefano Harney have called "incompletion."[138] It is an affirmation that is hardly "mine," as well, but is instead shared-out in a giving in collectivity, a sonority in form, what settler life can not but set itself against, and one name of which, I've suggested, is "poeticality."

Notes

Acknowledgments

1. Etel Adnan, *Seasons*, 14, 26.

2. Aimé Césaire, *Discourse on Colonialism*, 41. The colonizer, Césaire writes, "in order to ease his conscience gets into the habit of seeing the other man as *an animal* [*s'habitue à voir dans l'autre* la bête], accustoms himself to treating him like an animal, and tends objectively to transform *himself* into an animal." I notice, only, the verbal dimension of this "habit," a "habituation of oneself," a formulation which allows us to hear the social practice occasioned in being-a-colonizer, its manner and pose, its form of life; and see *Discours sur le colonialism*, 21.

3. On "abolition," please see Ruth Wilson Gilmore, "Race, Prisons, and War: Scenes from the History of US Violence," where she underlines the relations among the state, capital, race, accumulation, and the institution of the modern prison, at once "individualized sites of large-scale social control" (188), and, taken in aggregate, "a machine for producing and exploiting group-differentiated vulnerability to premature death" (190). The social logic of the prison, Wilson also explains, advances older, European, Christian practices, mutated in modern and global frames, where the colonized and enslaved are to be "saved" through the wars for white settler existence: "War and incarceration are supposed to bring good things to the places destroyed in the name of being saved; the devastation wrought overseas in Iraq and Afghanistan is both prefigured and shadowed by the history and current experience of life in the United States itself" (190). It is this existence, sustaining as it is for the asymmetric and eviscerating violences of our time, which, Wilson suggests, practices of abolition can—and already do—contribute to bringing to an end.

Preface

1. Lucie Kim-Chi Mercier, "Conference Report," 64.

2. Walter Benjamin, "Über den Begriff der Geschichte," 254–255. Please also see the English translation provided in "Theses on the Philosophy of History," 257, which I have modified. The German reads: "Die Tradition der Unterdrückten belehrt uns darüber, daß der 'Ausnahmezustand,' in dem wir leben, die Regel ist. Wir müssen zu einem Begriff der Geschichte kommen, der dem entspricht. Dann wird uns als unsere Aufgabe die Herbeiführung des wirklichen Ausnahmezustands vor Augen stehen; und dadurch wird unsere Position im Kampf gegen den Faschismus sich verbessern."

3. Carl Schmitt, *Politische Theologie*, 13/*Political Theology*, 5; the published translation is: "Sovereign is he who decides on the state of exception." I thank Sarita See and David Lloyd for their conversation around this sentence.

4. I've tried to think about reading as a settler practice, and as a practice that invests normative institutions and modes of understanding language and the social, in "The Resistance to Boycott."

5. Edward W. Said, *Orientalism*; Werner Hamacher, *Minima Philologica*, 121 ("Je näher die Philologie ihrer Sache rückt, desto ferner tritt sie zurück" [Werner Hamacher, Für—Die Philologie, 29]); Talal Asad, *Secular Translations*, 61. On the philological invention of "religion" see Tomoko Masuzawa, *Invention*; on "semites" see Gil Anidjar, *Semites*; on "language" see Michel Foucault, *The Order of Things*. I study the generalizing advance of "politics" in the coercive privilege of a certain sort of subject—a subject capable of language, neither a "primitive" (as in Emmanuel Lévinas) nor a "slave" (as in Karl Marx)—in chapters 1 and 3. I've tried to contribute to the study of philology, in relation to its racialization of Palestinians, in a reading of Said, in "Palestine and Sovereign Violence."

6. Cedric J. Robinson, *Black Marxism*, 26, passim. And see, as well: "Indeed, capitalism was less a catastrophic revolution (negation) of feudalist social orders than the extension of these social relations into the larger tapestry of the modern world's political and economic relations" (10). And please consider Robin D. G. Kelley, "The Rest of Us," where Kelley asks whether, in relation to Robinson, we might "think about the legacies of settler colonialism in Europe itself?" (272). "In *Black Marxism*," he continues, "Robinson argues that racialization within Europe was very much a colonial process—one involving invasion, settlement, expropriation, and racial hierarchy" (272). I wish here, in affirmation of Kelley's observation—offered in reading Patrick Wolfe's *Traces of History*—to think the manner in which a particular sense of form, initiated in the European, Christian practice of Crusade, beginning in the twelfth century, mutates and is retained in "later" normative terms for linguistic and juridical life in global frames.

7. Scholarship on the *Nakba* is vast; please see, for an incisive collection of essays, *Nakba*, edited by Ahmad H. Sa'di and Lila Abu-Lughod. On the genocidal sanctions regime in Iraq, see Joy Gordon, *Invisible War*.

8. Ibn Khaldūn, *al-Muqaddima*, 1.633: إعلم أنّ اللغة في المتعارف هي عبارة المتكلم عن مقصوده. وتلك العبارة فعل لسانيّ ناشئ عن القصد بإفادة الكلام، فلا بدّ أنْ تصير ملكة متقررة في العضو الفاعل لها، وهو اللسان.

9. On the radical privilege of "I" as a social form and locus for self-representation see Denise Ferreira da Silva, *Toward a Global Idea of Race*; and, in relation to the aesthetic and race, David Lloyd, *Under Representation*. I underline Ferreira Da Silva's and Lloyd's readings of Kant below, in the introduction.

10. Ferreira da Silva, *Toward a Global Idea of Race*, xxxix. I offer a reading of several passages in Frantz Fanon's *The Wretched of the Earth* below, in chapter 1.

11. Here I am thinking with and learning from J. Kameron Carter, in *Race: A Theological Account*, where he studies "the theological constitution of whiteness" and "the problematic of whiteness as a theological phenomenon" (6). In this frame, whiteness is "understood not merely and banally as a pigment but as a structural-aesthetic order and as a socio-political arrangement" (89), and, as Carter shows through a riveting reading of Kant, it is what gives itself access to the "universal," one might also say that it *is* that access, as it institutes the racializing terms Carter outlines, where "the other races have become races in such a way as to be held hostage to their own particularity" (89). "All of this," Carter explains, "bespeaks their improper relation to law, which itself is indicative of their inability to make progress in education" (92). And, further, "Although each race suffers from a different kind of imbalance, the core problem for all of them is their inability to be self-governing or autonomous" (93). In this "structure of white racial perfection" (93) certain beings are able to "express the autonomy and freedom of the subject in itself and for itself" (100), while others "cannot abstract themselves from their own bodies and enter the autonomous way of existence" (104). Through a reference to Paul, Carter notes that law, conceived in a Kantian-Pauline fashion, "grounds the 'religiosity' of whiteness or the 'spirituality' of the species as such" (113), and that in this, "there is also the racial advent of whiteness as a form of governance, as a sociopolitical arrangement, and as a regime of power and knowledge" (118). I wish to suggest, in the preface and chapter 1, that one name for the form of life that generates this "form" and "arrangement," and its manner of knowing and being in asymmetric globality, is "settler life."

12. I learn here from Ella Shohat, "Rethinking Jews and Muslims": "The campaigns against Muslims and Jews, as well as against heretics and witches," she writes of the Crusades, the *Reconquista*, and the Inquisition, in relation to fifteenth- and sixteenth-century "New World" conquest, "made available an entire apparatus of racism and sexism for 'recycling' in the newly raided continents" (332). See, in relation to these terms and their textual and citational histories, John Block Friedman, *The Monstrous Races*; Silvia Federici, *Caliban and the Witch*; Tomaž Mastnak, *Crusading Peace*; Dominique Iogna-Prat, *Order and Exclusion*; Kathleen Biddick, *The Typological Imaginary*; J. Kameron Carter, *Race: A Theological Account*; Gil Anidjar, *Blood: A Critique of Christianity*; and Sylvia Wynter, "1492: A New World View." I offer a reading of "1492," and several other essays of Wynter's, in chapter 1.

13. On the terms for this refusal—a refusal of the modern terms for legality, the social, language, and form—see Samera Esmeir, whose probing reading of the modern institution of juridical life, and what she terms "juridical humanity," points to the death-imparting sociality of legality and "the rule of law," within and in excess of the post-Ottoman contexts I study: "The rule of law," she writes, "resembles aerial technologies of warfare—planes operating from the skies, viewing their targets through the mediation of abstraction" (*Juridical Humanity*, 199).

14. And please also consider Cedric Robinson's discussion of marronage, a certain manner of disengagement, in *Black Marxism*, a practice I wish to understand in its collective and linguistic resonances with the sense of refusal the texts I study here give: "This is perhaps part of the explanation of why, so often, Black slave resistance naturally evolved to marronage as the manifestation of the African's determination to disengage, retreat from contact" (310). I notice that the term "marronage," in the Arabic translation of *Black Marxism*, is rendered as "flight and isolation or withdrawal," الهروب والعزلة, *al-hurūb wa al-ʿuzla* (*al-Marksiyya al-sawdāʾ*, 668), and I observe that we may hear, through this Arabic-language rendering, a practice of isolation from, a refusal of, the destructions of social form, language, being, and life, imparted through transatlantic chattel slavery, colonization, and settler colonization, as well as a relationality of these to the state legality and propertied form privileged in post-Ottoman social formations.

15. Oxford Latin Dictionary, 1598.

16. See Lucretius, *De Rerum Natura*, 1.346–357, where he points to "permeations" and "oozings," as the translator writes, across forms and materials: "Besides, however solid [*quamvis solidae*] things may be thought to be, here is proof that you may discern them to be of less solid consistency. In rocks and caves the liquid moisture of waters oozes through [*permanat aquarum liquidus umor*], and the whole place weeps with plenteous drops. Food is dispersed through all the body in living creatures. Trees grow and at their time put forth their fruits, because their food is distributed all over them from the lowest roots through trunks and through branches. Sounds pass through walls and fly through closed houses, stiffening cold permeates [*rigidum permanat frigus*] to the bones. But, if there were no void there which bodies might pass through in each case, you could not see this happen in any way."

17. Audra Simpson, *Mohawk Interruptus*, 106. And please see Simpson's exhilarating discussion of "ethnographic refusal" in relation to "methods and modalities of knowing—in particular, categorization, ethnological comparison, linguistic translation, and ethnography" (95), which Simpson reads in relation to Indigenous sovereignty, which "interrupts anthropological portraits of timelessness, procedure, and function" (97), and which is practiced in a certain refusal to write or speak in a quite particular manner. "Rather, the deep context of dispossession, of containment, of a skewed authoritative axis and the ongoing structure of both settler colonialism and its disavowal make writing and analysis a careful, complex instantiation of jurisdiction and authority" (105), and suggest a reflection, further, on what it means to write "in the conditions of settlement—this structural condition of

ongoing Indigenous dispossession and disavowal of that dispossession and structure" (105). I wish to cite several passages in full, and suggest, only, that Simpson's framing gives a manner of thinking in refusal, and of thinking refusal in relation to language, ways of knowing, and settler existence and epistemic exertion: "How does one, on the one hand, write about this or analyze what is so clearly offensive to the anthropological sensibilities of access, replicable results, and liberal norms of 'fairness,' and reconcile it, on the other hand, with the plight of those who are struggling every day to maintain what little they have left? And, how does one do this when they are struggling so clearly with the languages and analytics of a foreign culture that occupies their semantic and material space, and naturalizes this occupation through history writing and the very analytics that are used to know them?" (109).

18. Theodor Adorno, *Minima Moralia*, 7/15.

19. Jean-Jacques Rousseau, "Essay on the Origin of Languages," 248.

20. Theodor Adorno, *Minima Moralia*, 7/15.

21. Sinan Antoon (Sinān Anṭūn), *Fihris*, 48/*The Book of Collateral Damage*, 46: "الخسائر اللي ما تنذكر وما تنشاف/*al-khasāʾir illī mā tandhakir wa mā tanshāf.*"

22. Adorno, *Minima Moralia*, 99/80: "Denn der Wert eines Gedankens mißt sich an seiner Distanz von der Kontinuität des Bekannten."

23. In thinking this sociality I learn from and am thinking with Judith Butler, where they address "a collective acting without a preestablished collective subject," a sense of gathering, which "implicates social relationality in the first-person pronoun," where "I am related to others in ways that are essential to any invocation of this 'I'" (*Notes Toward a Performative Theory of Assembly*, 59, 68). In this invocation, "The enactment is part of its very ontology" (61), and, in the reformulation and passing-on of more than one tradition, the doing occasioned in such enactments exceeds and encompasses lingual acts: "Even the speech act," Butler compelling writes, "is implicated in the embodied conditions of life" (9). To think this implication is to think, as well, of "the body" in relation to its conditions of being, language, and life, where "it is not altogether right to conceive of individual bodies as completely distinct from one another" (130). I wish to underline this indistinction, this de-individualized form of social existence, where a gathering or being-in-collectivity "is not reducible to a collection of individuals," and where, as Butler elaborates, "it is, strictly speaking, not individuals who act" (84). In this, where "acts" may be understood in the sense in which Butler invites us to think of this term, there is a "sociality," an "interdependency," and, finally, a "nonfoundation" (119)—a sense of form I study, in its non-identical permutations, in chapters 2 and 3.

24. Nadera Shalhoub-Kevorkian, *Incarcerated Childhood*, 33. In such "dismemberment," as Shalhoub-Kevorkian shows, the genocidal practice of the Zionist settler state renders Palestinians, as a collective, as, at once "captive nonhumans" and an "uncivil noncommunity" (69), in a "racialized logic" (85) and "regime of dispossession" (84).

25. Mahmoud Darwish (Maḥmūd Darwīsh), *Ḥālat ḥiṣār*, 57.
26. Fady Joudah, [. . .], 12, 47.

Introduction: Poeticality

1. Mahmoud Darwish (Maḥmūd Darwīsh), *Aḥad ʿashar kawkaban*, 46. While I offer my own translations of passages contained in this poem here and in what follows, I have learned from the English-language translation of Fady Joudah. I wish to underline, in particular, that although my rendering of this sentence is somewhat more literal, Joudah importantly speaks of what is to be "memorized" as a "bit" of poetry, a translation that captures the bereaved dimensions of poetic utterance in Darwish, and the relation of poetic utterance to a larger corpus of poetry in Arabic, which, if it imparts a tradition, this tradition may not be separated from the many losses, in Palestine and elsewhere, to which poetry is, now, and has been exposed; one may notice, as well, that Joudah's rendering underlines that the colonizer has not been willing, even, to memorize a "little" poetry, not even a "bit," and so Darwish's address also suggests an ongoing Zionist settler manner of obliterating address toward Palestinian persons, individually and in collectivity. Please see Mahmoud Darwish, "The 'Red Indian's' Penultimate Speech to the White Man," translated by Fady Joudah, 157: "Will you not memorize a bit of poetry to halt the slaughter?"
2. Steven Salaita, *Inter/Nationalism*, 128.
3. Darwish, *Aḥad ʿashar kawkaban*, 48.
4. The formulations I offer here learn from Katherine McKittrick's discussion of "long-standing plantocratic and colonial logics" (*Dear Science*, 67) in relation to a collective listening, writing, and struggle in epistemic practice: "The struggles against plantation and postplantation violences foster a range of interlocking perspectives that continually question and disobey geographic and intellectual practices that sequester, watch over, harm, and manage black diasporic peoples" (72); and please see, as well, reading and thinking with McKittrick, Clyde Woods, *Development Arrested*. On the "cadastral" in relation to "histories of spatial and legal containment of Indians" and the dimensions of non-consent occasioned in white settler politicality, social form, and legality, I learn from Audra Simpson, *Mohawk Interruptus*, 143, 142, and, especially, 115–145. I learn as well from Tiffany Lethabo King, who underlines, in relation to eighteenth-century settler mapping practices, "the cartographic disavowal of genocide and slavery" (*The Black Shoals*, 90) in relation to "White logocentric futurity" (91), settler-plantational carcerality—"Imprisonment as an early U.S. spatial formation was a constituent feature of eighteenth-century modes of conquest in what would become North America" (96)—and slavery and Indigenous genocide. "All forms of European settlement in North America occurred within the context of Western expansion and Indigenous genocide" (98), a manner of life exerted through "the extermination of Indigenous peoples and the transformation of Black people into fungible forms of exchange"

(84), and extended in "humanist narratives of labor and development that privilege settlement, productivity, and human domination of the land" (116).

5. Darwish, *Aḥad ʿashar kawkaban*, 38.

6. Glen Sean Coulthard, *Red Skin, White Masks*, 151–152. On the sense of property I underline here and in what follows, in relation to language and primitive accumulation, I also learn from Robert Nichols, *Theft Is Property!*; Mark Rifkin, *Settler Common Sense*; and Alyosha Goldstein, "'In the Constant Flux of Its Incessant Renewal.'" The formulations I offer learn as well from Aileen Moreton Robinson, *The White Possessive*, where she underlines, in settler colonization, a "structure of subjective possession" (50, 114), which functions as a "discursive presupposition" (xxiv) or "organizing principle" (66) for "the social reproduction of whiteness" (30) in relation to "the logic of capital" (117), as she notes, "from the sixteenth century onward" (xxiii), and the ongoing assertions of white settler sovereignty—assertions which, in their panicked and aggressive social obliterations, demonstrate their asovereign form.

7. Sarita Echavez See, *The Filipino Primitive*, 28, 136.

8. For an acute reading of settler colonization in relation to race, the law, and property, as well as language and literacy, see Brenna Bhandar, *Colonial Lives of Property*: "If literacy is the precondition for the interior life of the civilized subject, it also occasions affective, spatial, and material enclosures characteristic of modernity and modern law" (140). Here I also learn from, and am thinking with, Michael Allan's compelling discussion, in *In The Shadow of World Literature*, of a new institution of "literature," of أدب, *adab*, in Arabic, in nineteenth-century Egypt, where this new understanding "implies a command about how to read" (77) in relation to a particular sense of—and relation to—sound and political form: "In a most explicit sense, we are dealing here with the social constraints necessary to be *heard* as a modern political subject" (63). And this, in relation as well to "those worlds foreclosed by the disciplines of literary reading" (93) and, as Allan also writes, "the policing function of the public sphere" (135). And see as well Allan's attention to sonority, to matters of sound and the acoustic, in his underlining of "reverberation" in "Old Media/New Futures," and "resonance," in "Dying to Read," 293.

9. Darwish, *Aḥad ʿashar kawkaban*, 39. In thinking about the sense of the juridical I point to here I learn from Samera Esmeir, *Juridical Humanity*. In relation to Iraq, and the genocidal wars against Iraq conducted in the name of the law and its rule, see Ayça Çubukçu, *For the Love of Humanity*; and, in relation to the Zionist colonization of Palestine, Saree Makdisi's acute discussion of Zionism as a settler practice that imposes itself in the name of "tolerance" and "ethical liberal subjectivity" (*Tolerance Is a Wasteland*, 47). I study the relation of law to settler life, in relation to the work of Robert Cover, Brenna Bhandar, Sora Han, Nasser Hussain, Peter Fitzpatrick, and Samera Esmeir, in chapter 1.

10. In thinking about Darwish in relation to temporality, and in relation to Palestine and Indigenous Studies, I learn from Rana Barakat, in her underlining the manner in which a presumption of settler forms, and a particular understanding of

settler colonialism and its critique, "privileges the history and historical narratives of the settlers" ("Writing/Righting Palestine Studies," 356). Barakat notes the manner in which both settler colonial studies as well as Zionism privilege a rhetoric of endings—"Written outside the framework of Indigenous resistance, the story of the *Nakba* is one of endings: the story of the making of a refugee population and the memory of what Palestine once was—as opposed to being the story framed around the return of refugees and Palestinian resistance" (361)—and I notice, in relation to the reading I'm offering here, and learning from and thinking with Barakat, that this is a "story" in relation to which Darwish offers poetic statement in refusal of such endings. In the formulations I offer I am also thinking with and learning from Lara Sheehi and Stephen Sheehi, in their study of psychoanalysis in Palestine, in particular where they note the reiteration of "the logic and authority of the checkpoint" within and in excess of institutional psychoanalysis in the settler colony: "While Palestinians devise many ways to survive under what is intended to be a crushing and eviscerating system of occupation," they write, "we also identify how systems such as education, medicine, social work, and therapy also reproduce the logic and authority of the checkpoint" (*Psychoanalysis under Occupation*, 65). What Lara Sheehi and Stephen Sheehi outline as the Zionist demand addressed to the Palestinian person that they "transcend" and "elevate" themself "into the shared humanity of the settler and the Euro-American savior-mediators," where the Palestinian is to become a "rational and moral individual" who has left behind what the Zionist settler understands to be the "inherently backward, misogynistic, and patriarchical culture" (139) of Palestinian individual and collective life, points, as well, to a history of reading and form, a coercive delimitation and ongoing obliteration of language and life, which the poetry of Mahmoud Darwish also teaches us to think.

11. Darwish, *Aḥad ʿashar kawkaban*, 92.

12. Nick Estes, Melanie K. Yazzie, Jennifer Nez Denetdale, and David Correia, *Red Nation Rising*, 6; and, on "logistics," Stefano Harney and Fred Moten, "Fantasy in the Hold," in *The Undercommons*, 85–99.

13. In my use of the term "evisceration," here and elsewhere in this book, I learn from and am thinking with Dylan Rodríguez, where he notes that this term has "etymological roots in the Latin word for disembowelment or the removal of the viscera," and which may be understood in relation to "violence exerted on the complex totality of physiology across the individual and collective scales" (*White Reconstruction*, 170).

14. Please see the discussion in Walter Benjamin, "Zur Kritik der Gewalt" ("Toward the Critique of Violence"), where, after observing that "A gaze directed only at what is closest at hand can at most become aware of a dialectical back-and-forth in the formations of violence into its law-positing and law-preserving kinds," Benjamin notes that "A new historical era is founded on breaking through this cycle that spins under the spell of mythical forms of law, and on de-posing law [*auf der Entsetzung des Rechts*] together with all the forms of violence on which it depends,

just as they depend on it, and finally, therefore, on de-posing state violence [*Staatsgewalt*]" (63–64/60), and, therefore, on de-posing—disinstalling, dissolving, and, in a different idiom, abolishing—the state and the terms for social and linguistic understanding it generates and which generate it is a locus for the social. I notice that in its German formulation this passage begins with the "breaking through" of the "cycle" of law-positing and law-preserving violence—it opens, "Auf der Durchbrechnung dieses Umlaufs," and closes, "begründet sich ein neues geschichtliches Zeitalter"—and that this "breaking through" is followed, in Benjamin's formulation, by the "de-posing" of law, and only then by the "founding" of a "new historical era." We might say that the explication of the de-posing of law mirrors the decomposing, dissolving terms of its analysis, and that the reading Benjamin poses, therefore, does not affirm a wholly new "ground" but instead one that is founded through practices of "breaking though" and "de-posing," a "ground" that is afounded, or, better, de-founded, one that is, therefore, "de-posed."

15. In thinking this sense of "insurgence" I learn from and am thinking with a number of interventions, in relation to the study of the "resonant possibilities of collective thought and action," which "must be understood beyond the questions of resistance and of opposition to hegemonic structures or the authoritarianism of the state," and which "do not readily translate into the modes of knowledge production in discourses of power and their conceptual languages," in Ayman El-Desouky, *The Intellectual and the People*, 93, 104, 12; of "Arabophone solidarities," across Indonesian, Egyptian, and West African contexts, in their relation to "the common act of listening" at odds with what Annette Damayanti Lienau has called "segregated literacies" (*Sacred Language, Vernacular Difference*, 113, 174, 220); of philological "solidarity" in "Arab Indology" in Esmat Elhalaby, "Empire and Arab Indology" (25); of the "resonance" of "internationalisms," both pre- and post-Bandung, in Hala Halim, "'A Theatre—or, More Aptly, a Laboratory'" (50, 70); of the forms of "discord, disagreement, and mistranslation" which such resonances and solidarities can occasion, as Sophia Azeb has underlined ("Crossing the Saharan Boundary," 93), and where language, or collective practice, as Azeb importantly notes, can be thought as "invocation" and "medium" rather than an instrument for "linear" (111) coherency; of what Alex Lubin has termed, "the Afro-Arab international" and the "grammar" of its poetics (*Geographies of Liberation*, 144, 170); and, more broadly, and across and between languages, of "the brief period of unprecedented translation of communism across West Asia" in Soviet and Turkish linguistic, theoretical, and revolutionary "entanglements" from the 1920s to the 1960s (Nergis Ertürk, *Writing in Red*, 6), in relation to a manner of thinking language, which does not privilege "a uniform and homogenous continuum" (195)—neither "stagist models of development" nor "absolute rupture" (74)—in an "irregular communist seriality without transcendence" (214), and where a particular, indetermined sense of language, like the "communist," in the textual field Ertürk studies, has "not yet been exhausted" (208). In a different frame, I've tried to offer a discussion of "insurgence" elsewhere, in "Fanon's Insurgence."

16. See Ghassan Kanafani (Ghassān Kanafānī), *Adab al-muwqāwama fī Filastīn al-muḥtalla: 1948–1966* (published in 1966); and *al-Adab al-Filastīnī al-muqāwim taḥt al-iḥtilal: 1948–1968* (published in 1968). In thinking about refusal in Darwish and Kanafani I learn from Kamran Rastegar's discussion of the Palestinian filmmaker Elia Suleiman's "refusal" of "the narrative closures that characterize normative cinematic techniques" (*Surviving Images*, 7), where, as Rastegar observes, there are patterns of "incompletion, question, and irresolution" (107) rather than "objective" distance—"Suleiman's camera infrequently adopts what is most common in normative cinematic language, that is, an objective or disinterested position" (115)—and where cinematic practice generates "exegetical aporias" (115) rather than formally articulated sense. For a reading of Kanafani, with an attention to form, see Bashir Abu-Manneh, "Ghassan Kanafani's Revolutionary Ethics," in *The Palestinian Novel*; I've tried to offer a reading of Kanafani, in relation to form and temporality, in "The Politics of Death and the Question of Palestine."

17. Nouri Gana, *Melancholy Acts*, 9, 27.

18. Martin Heidegger, *Der Satz vom Grund*, 89/*The Principle of Reason*, 48.

19. In Heidegger's discussion of language in "Das Wesen der Sprache" ("The Nature of Language"), he outlines an understanding of language in relation to "what something is, τὸ τί ἐστιν, whatness," which "comprises since Plato what one commonly calls the 'nature,' the *essentia* of a thing [*was man gewohnterweise 'das Wesen,' die essentia einer Sache nennt*]," where "Essence [*Wesen*] so understood becomes restricted to what is later called the concept [*Begriff*], the representation [*die Vorstellung*] by means of which we propose to ourselves and grasp what a thing is" (201/94). "And that is the language of being," Heidegger observes, as he underlines that "in this phrase, 'essence' assumes the role of the subject that possesses language [*hat 'das Wesen' die Rolle des Subjekts, dem die Sprache eignet*]" (201/95). At the same time Heidegger notes a sense of being, distinct from this, in relation to language and a certain "hearing," to which he wishes to appeal: "However, the word 'essence' now no longer means what something is. We hear 'essence' as a verb, as in 'being present' and 'being absent.' 'Essence' means to perdure and persist" (201/95). But the sonority Heidegger underlines, and to which he appeals with the term "saying"—"The guide-word beckons us away from the current notions about language, to the experience of language as saying [*in die Erfahrung der Sprache als Sage*]" (202/96)—is drawn down to the subject of "experience." "If we take language directly in the sense of something that is present, we encounter it as the act of speaking, the activation of the organs of speech, mouth, lips, tongue. Language manifests itself in speaking, as a phenomena that occurs in man" (203/96), Heidegger writes, but if language is reduced in this manner, and if Heidegger wishes to underline this and displace it, he affirms the subjective being of "man" and its "experience": "But the question remains whether what is most proper [*das Eigene*] of the sounds and tones of speech is thus ever experienced or kept before our eyes [*erfahren und im Blick behalten wird*]" (205/98), as if "what is most proper" were a possible object for "us." He continues, subjugating "sound," "ring,"

and "vibration" to a subject's proper "experience" of "spoken words," and this subjugation asserts the pose, as well as the mode of being, of what I'm terming "settler life": "It is just as much a property of language to sound and ring and vibrate, to hover and to tremble, as it is for the spoken words of language to carry a meaning. But our experience of this property is still exceedingly clumsy, because the metaphysical-technological explanation gets everywhere in the way, and presses us away from its proper sense" (205/98).

20. I've tried to offer a reading of Adorno, drawing on a number of passages in *Minima Moralia*, in terms that mirror these, where Adorno's language can presuppose a property-centric sense of form and the social, which Adorno also gives us to read, in "'The Visual Poetry of the Work.'" In this, Adorno, and however much he will have detested such a statement, is quite a bit closer to Heidegger than he may ever have wished to acknowledge.

21. See Eric Williams, *Capitalism and Slavery*; and Cedric J. Robinson, *Black Marxism*. And see, in relation to capital in its relation to race, slavery, colonization, and settler-colonization: Rosa Luxemburg, *The Accumulation of Capital*; Andre Gunder Frank, *Capitalism and Underdevelopment*; Walter Rodney, *How Europe Underdeveloped Africa*; Immanuel Wallerstein, *The Modern World System*; and the foundational work of W. E. B. Du Bois, in *Black Reconstruction in America*.

22. See Jacques Derrida, "*Ousia* and *Grammē*"; and please see as well: "It is therefore in proximity to the proper meaning of being or the light of being that every other being is clarified," including, as Derrida underlines, the "absolute proximity" implied in "The *I am* or the I am here or the now or the *present*, the presence of the present" (Jacques Derrida, *Heidegger*, 55).

23. Heidegger, *Der Satz vom Grund*, 47/23–24, 45/22.

24. Cheryl I. Harris, "Whiteness as Property"; J. Kēhaulani Kauanui, *Hawaiian Blood*, 21–25.

25. Please see, on the mutations of the terms I'm outlining here in relation to Zionist settler colonization in Palestine, Nadera Shalhoub-Kevorkian, *Incarcerated Childhood*; and Noura Erakat, "Whiteness as Property in Israel" and *Justice for Some*. And see also, and earlier, the foundational essays of Edward W. Said, "Zionism from the Standpoint of Its Victims"; and Ella Shohat, "Sephardim in Israel: Zionism from the Standpoint of Its Jewish Victims"; as well as, earlier still, Fayez A. Sayegh, *Zionist Colonialism in Palestine*. I also learn from and am thinking with Amanda Batarseh, "Love, Countryside, and the Fellah," in her discussion of the formulation of the Palestinian as a "primitive remnant" (292), in a "negative ontology" (287) Batarseh outlines in relation to "European knowledge production and its institutions," which "regulated colonized existence itself" (290), in contrast to which Batarseh brings out "the continuous deep time of Palestinian inhabitation into the present" (290); and Samiha Khalil, who explicates the manner in which the "Philistine" is drawn upon to authorize "the Zionist portrayal of the Palestinian as a backward subject who lacks the capacity to cultivate the land, nationality, culture, sovereignty, and self-determination" ("Philistine Imaginings," 14), as the Philistine

becomes a "transatlantic matter" (2), a figure in universality, if in its "negative constitution, signifying human, or more accurately, European bourgeois incapacity for culture, beauty, and intelligence" (2), in relation to the Atlantic's becoming "the site of European aspirations and promises of new openings, development, and freedom" (3) and in "the construction of the Philistine as an important vehicle of othering the human, in general, and the Palestinian person, in specific" (4).

26. See, on Kant and the racialization of form: Denise Ferreira da Silva, *Toward a Global Idea of Race*, 57–62; J. Kameron Carter, *Race: A Theological Account*, 79–121; David Lloyd, *Under Representation*, 19–68; R. A. Judy, "Kant and the Negro"; Robert Bernasconi, "Will the Real Kant Please Stand Up"; Huaping Lu-Adler, "Kant on Lazy Savagery, Racialized."

27. Ferreira da Silva, *Toward a Global Idea of Race*, xiii, xxxix.

28. See Immanuel Kant, *Kritik der reinen Vernunft / Critique of Pure Reason*, 215/158-159; A107: "Now there can take place in us no cognitions, and no connection and unity of cognitions among one another, without that unity of consciousness which precedes all data of intuitions, and by reference to which all presentation of objects is alone possible. Now this pure, original, and immutable consciousness I shall call *transcendental apperception*."

29. Kant, *Kritik der reinen Vernunft*, 178/177; B132. And consider the observation of Rei Terada, who notes, reading Kant and Hegel, that "the conflict between transcendental and historical reason includes their common assumption of another scene of mayhem in the world" (*Metaracial*, 146), against which, in their social panic, they set themselves.

30. Heidegger, *Der Satz vom Grund*, 89–90/49.

31. The formulations I offer here I learn from Nahum D. Chandler, *X: The Problem of the Negro as a Problem for Thought*, in particular where Chandler addresses "the very historicity of modern thought" (43) in relation to "a logic of racial distinction pertinent to our entire historical modernity" (108), which is also, he underlines, "an ontological question" (57) and a question of reading, and "traditional interpretation"—"Hence," Chandler writes of Du Bois, "his thought proposes the possibility and necessity of a desedimentation of the root presuppositions of canonical philosophical conceptions of identity or a traditional interpretation of them" (108)—a manner of reading and mode of thinking about being installed "since the sixteenth century" (12, 130), as Chandler notes; as well as R. A. Judy, *Sentient Flesh: Thinking in Disorder,* Poiēsis *in Black*. I learn, in particular, from Judy's intervention, in relation to a sense of reading where language or being "cannot be properly possessed, allegorized, or sacrificed" (456), and as he thinks a "para-semiosis" that is also a certain "being-in-common" (448), even as I wish to ask, thinking with and learning from Judy, about the "living flesh" "as such"—"It is at the point of untranslatability that the irreducible living flesh is traced as such" (384)—as well as, and in a consonant manner, Judy's thinking of "poiēsis," in relation to the ninth-century Arabic-language writer al-Jāḥiẓ, of whom I offer a reading in chapter 3, where Judy underlines, in al-Jāḥiẓ, a sense of language,

or the poetic, in relation to what is "fundamental," in particular, where "poiēsis" is a "fundamental transformative activity, the activity of giving coherent expression in transmutational forms" (445).

32. See Martin Heidegger, *Sein und Zeit (Being and Time)*, §6–7; and, in particular, in Heidegger's discussion of Kant, in *Critique of Pure Reason*, who, "in spite of the fact that he was bringing the phenomenon of time back into the subject again, his analysis of it remained oriented toward the traditional way in which time had been ordinarily understood," and where, further, "Because of this double effect of tradition the decisive connection between time and the 'I think' was shrouded in utter darkness; it did not even become a problem" (§6). And yet, with this attention to temporality, Heidegger nonetheless recalls being, in passages that are too numerous to cite, to what is its "own," for example, "the ownmost meaning of the question of Being": "Here what is asked about has an essential pertinence to the inquiry itself, and this belongs to the ownmost meaning of the question of Being [*gehört zum eigensten Sinn der seinsfrage*]" (§2).

33. Judith Butler, *Giving an Account of Oneself*, 136.

34. Heidegger, *Der Satz vom Grund*, 147/87. I wish to notice, as well, that if what I'm calling "settler life" is a mutation in forms, and if it extends from the twelfth European, Latin, Christian century until today, it is also a practice of translation, in excess of this temporal frame, reaching back, at least, to the translation of Greek philosophical terms into Latin: "The process begins with the appropriation of the Greek words by Roman-Latin thought; ὑποχείμενον becomes *subjectum*; ὑπόστασις becomes *substantia*; συμβεβηκός becomes *accidens*. This translation of Greek names into the Latin language is by no means without consequences—as, even now, it is still held to be" (Martin Heidegger, "The Origin of the Work of Art," 6). I do not wish to affirm Heidegger's thinking of this translation, or others, where translation displaces an "equiprimordial experience" (6), but instead to observe the manner in which the Latin translation of Greek terms—for example, the translation of "zōon" as "animal," and "logichon" and "rationalis," in Boethius's sixth-century Latin rendering of Porphyry's *Isagoge*—is sent at us, still, today, asymmetrically, and with unequal consequence, routed through a non-stable, ever-mutating, catachrestic lexicon. I study these terms, below, in the introduction, as well as in chapter 1; I note Boethius's translation of Porphyry's *Isagoge*, in relation to the Arabic reading and translation of this text, in chapter 2.

35. Layli Long Soldier, *WHEREAS*, 51.

36. Ludwig Wittgenstein, *Philosophical Investigations*, §23; I discuss Arendt, Foucault, and Agamben below, in chapter 1. In thinking about language and life I learn from the discussion of "the philology of life" as Kevin McLaughlin studies it in the work of Walter Benjamin. McLaughlin underlines Benjamin's discussion of "living on," "Fortleben," where "life" is "not reducible to the lives of individual living and dying beings" (*The Philology of Life*, 4), where "language" is not subordinated to the life of an individual being or a history of languages, but instead is thought in relation to a "layering," "das Geschichte" (8), in a "suspension" (12, 16)

of progressive temporal development and a practice of reading, which "is focused on language rather than value" (24) and which gives "a sense of being alive that does not definitively exclude death" (27). In this sense, life "goes beyond itself" (67), in what McLaughlin terms "the language-character of experience" (126), where experience is not the experience of a subject, since "the conventional concepts of space and time as independent, self-consistent elements of experience" (122) are "deactivated" (81, 103), and philology, as Benjamin and McLaughlin give us to read it, becomes a practice of reading which, as Benjamin suggests in a passage I underlined in the preface to this book, is also a "task," "Aufgabe." We might say, then, that philology is an occasion for the liberation of language, and reading, from the subject, as a well as a practice for the disintallation or abolition of the subject of experience as a determining social form.

37. Up until the twelfth century, Bernard G. Dod explains, knowledge of Aristotle in Latin, Christian Europe was limited for the most part to Boethius's translations of Aristotle's *Categories* and *On Interpretation*, and Porphyry's *Isagoge*. By the middle of the twelfth century more translations had been produced, including *Physics*, *On the Soul*, and parts of *Metaphysics* (translated by James of Venice), and others, some based on Arabic translations of Aristotle or translations of passages of Aristotle's works contained in lemmata of Arabic-language commentaries. However, by the middle of the thirteenth century William of Moerbeke, translating from Greek into Latin, had "translated anew or revised virtually the whole Aristotelian corpus, including two works, the *Politics* and *Poetics*, that had not been translated before," as Dod writes of this translation history ("Aristoteles latinus," 49, passim). It was these thirteenth-century translations—with the exception of Boethius's translations of most of the *Organon* and *Isagoge*, and James of Venice's translation of *Posterior Analytics*—which became, Dod further underlines, the predominantly studied texts of Aristotle in European Latinity during this period.

38. Please see, on the anti-Islamic dimensions of this passage in Aquinas, and its reference to the figure of the "Saracen," a catachrestic term into which non-Christian forms of alterity in Christian Europe were subsumed following the twelfth century, where, as in this passage, the Jew, Muslim, Saracen, heretic, apostate, and schismatic become indistinct: James V. Tolan, *Saracens*; Debra Higgs Strickland, *Saracens, Demons, and Jews*; M. Lindsay Kaplan, *Figuring Racism in Medieval Christianity* (the canonist Hostiensis, Kaplan explains, "conflates Muslims and Jews as the children of the slave woman, Hagar, in contrast to Christians, the children of the free woman, Sarah who symbolizes the Church" [142]); and, earlier, Norman Daniel, *Islam and the West*, who explains that, while "Islam was reckoned the greatest enemy of the Christian Church" (211) it was also understood to be a "heresy" even as "in spite of this widespread image of Islam as the culmination or summit of all heresy it was not at all certain that technically it was a heresy at all" (212). Daniel continues to note that, in the medieval, Christian polemical works he studies, "Islam often made a third with heresy and Judaism, and the word *perfidiae*

covered them all" (214), and, in particular works of Raymond of Lull, "he classed all who broke the unity of mankind, Muslims, Jews, schismatics, heretics, Tartars, together" (217), while, simultaneously, in this discursive field, "The distinction was also blurred in some cases by the opinion that Islam itself was primarily a schism, rather than a heresy" (217). The illegibility of these forms, mediating the interiority and exteriority of the corporate body of the Church, in a policing operation that does not cease to blur the terms it propels outward, is further noted in Daniels: "All schism is error," he writes of this textual corpus, "and all error was thought of as in some sense schismatic" (218). On the Saracen in relation to the Crusades see Tomaž Mastnak, *Crusading Peace*, and the pages of his study I cite in chapter 1; and Jonathan Riley-Smith, who underlines the "difficulty the crusaders had in making any distinction between Jews and Muslims as enemies of the faith" (*The First Crusade*, 54). On the Jew in medieval Christian law, theology, and polemic, see Jeremy Cohen, *Living Letters of the Law* ("Gratian's *Decretum* and most subsequent compilations of medieval canon law typically legislated concerning Jews and pagans/Muslims under the same rubric," he explains, and, further, "Against the backdrop of the changing map of twelfth-century Christendom, they [spokesmen for Christianity] directed their polemic at Jews and at other infidels, grouping the Jews together with Muslims, other pagans, and heterodox Christians" [162, 217]); and Amos Funkenstein, "Changes in Christian Anti-Jewish Polemics." On the modern reformulations of this terminology, in relation to "liberalism," see Joseph Massad, *Islam in Liberalism*, where Massad underlines "the modern Euro-American and European liberal political vocabulary of 'democracy' and 'despotism'" (97) and its division of "citizen" from "subject" (53), which is constitutively founded, he compelling argues, through a division of the white, liberal, rights-bearing individual from "Islam," understood as lacking "civil society" (138), and which is therefore in need of white, secular "salvation and rescue" (138) routed through "Christian generosity" (212) and its modern interpretive forms, all of which constitutes, he writes, "the very figuration of Orientalism" (54) and its ongoing mutations, "not only in the eighteenth, nineteenth, and twentieth centuries, but as we shall see, all the way to the present" (54).

39. Hosam Aboul-Ela, *Domestications*, 111.

40. My use of the term "peripatetic" follows al-Fārābī, who writes, "As for that group, which is named for the sort of acts made apparent among its adherents, they are the peripatetics [المشاؤن/*al-mashā'ūn*], who are the followers of Plato and Aristotle [أصحاب أرسطو وأفلاطون/*aṣḥāb Arisṭū wa Aflāṭūn*], and that is because these two used to teach people while they were walking, in order to exercise the body while training the soul [كيما يرتاض البدن مع رياضة النفس/*kaymā yartāḍ al-badan ma' riyāḍat al-nafs*]" (al-Fārābī, "Mā yanbaghī ta'alummuhu qabla al-falsafa," 274). I discuss, further, the sense of "training" in al-Fārābī, in relation to the practice of *askēsis*, below, chapter 2, note 10.

41. Omnia El Shakry, *The Arabic Freud*, 60. El Shakry's study addresses translations of psychoanalysis, focusing on twentieth-century Egypt, and observes

the manner in which translation draws upon older idioms—in relation to *tahdhīb al-nafs*, the "attunement or training of the soul," *riyaḍat al-nafs*, the "disciplining of the soul," and *siyāsat al-badan*, the "governance of the body" (70)—as well as routes translational practice through a number of twentieth-century transformations. El Shakry notes the "production of normalized psychosexual subjects" and "the inculcation of heterosexual desire and companionate marriage" (78); a privilege of "a variety of technologies of the self, most notably introspection, self analysis, and confessional modes of self narration" (79); and "the emergence of the juridical individual" (88) and the invention of "the criminal as an enemy of the common good," all in relation to "a fundamental transformation in legal regimes from Ottoman to colonial Egypt" (89), where "modern legal personhood in Egypt increasingly came to signify the self-governing autonomous subject" (89) and its experience. The texts El Shakry studies affirm an opposition between the "social animal" and the "criminal" (100), in sync with efforts "to stave off social anomie and political upheaval" (101) and develop "a political psychology that secured the consent of the governed" (104). In this, "Ultimately, theorists and practitioners opted for a view of the transparency of the human subject, one in which criminal intent could be rendered visible, and the criminal could be further subject to the technocratic gaze of the postcolonial state" (109). If psychoanalysis mediates this transparency, El Shakry also observes an "excess" (81) over these terms, what she also calls an "opacity": "Such an opacity at the heart of the human subject oftentimes subverted the terms of psychological discourse and demonstrated its inability to fully incarcerate the subject as the homogenous product of its disciplinary practices and epistemic categories" (81). I learn from and am thinking with El Shakry's compelling study, as I consider, in chapters 2 and 3, the manner in which an Arabic-language, anontological tradition for a reflection on being and form is carried in Adnan and al-Maʿālī, in excess of both historical narrativization and linguistic belonging.

42. In the formulations I offer here I learn from a number of interventions in Arabic studies, which have destabilized the reduction of language to subjectivity. In particular, I learn from Anna Ziajka Stanton's discussion, in *The Worlding of Arabic Literature*, of "material formations" (141) in language and translation, where the body of the translator, in their corporeal acts, is not rendered legible "as a singular or stable object of inquiry" (111), and where, in translation, there is a "radical corporeal porosity" (85), in which the "self" of the translator "emerges in relation to other things, beings, and forms" (84) in "nonhermeneutic modes of textual engagement" (78); and Hoda El Shakry, *The Literary Qurʾān*, where El Shakry observes reverberations of the "sonic texture" (23, 53) of the Qurʾān in twentieth-century, Arabic- and French-language, North African literary, critical, and theoretical writing, in relation to the "embodied act of reading" (74) and "the physical nature of Qurʾānic methods of study" (114), in a manner that displaces the sort of reading, which is presumed in modern literary disciplinarity and "the *nahḍa* and the Arab modernist movement" (159), in the desire to "tame" (24) the Qurʾān—and language—which such reading can exert.

43. In relation to the Arabic nineteenth century, I learn from the ongoing work of a collective of scholars, in the study of the reconfigurations or reformulations in the sense of "language," اللغة, *al-lugha*, in Shaden Tageldin, *Disarming Words*; of "knowledge," العلم, *al-ʿilm*, in Marwa Elshakry, *Reading Darwin in Arabic*; of "literature," الأدب, *al-adab*, in Michael Allan, *In the Shadow of World Literature*; of "education," التربية, *al-tarbiyya*, in its relation to *adab* and a "civilizing project" "meant to forge the civilized—and civil—subject of the modern nation state," in Tarek El-Ariss, *Leaks, Hacks, and Scandals*, 62; of the "law," الشرع, *al-sharʿ*, and its world, in Samera Esmeir, *Juridical Humanity*; of "society," المجتمعة, *mujtamaʿ*, as "an object of scientific study, social control, and management," in Omnia El Shakry, *The Great Social Laboratory*, 8; of "perspective," المنظر, *al-manẓar*, in Stephen Sheehi, *The Arab Imago*, xviii, 3, in relation to "the reproduction of social relations" (6); of "the collective," الناس, *al-nās*, understood, as Maha AbdelMegeed writes in *Literary Optics*, as "the collective that arises from the act of coming together itself" (164); of the study of "heterolingualism" and the "uncontrollability" of language, and languages, in excess of "practices of proper reading" in nineteenth-century frames, in Rebecca C. Johnson, *Stranger Fictions*, 58, 112, 106; the new privilege of the monolingual state in Kamran Rastegar, *Literary Modernity*; the speculative promise of futurity, in Elizabeth Holt, *Fictitious Capital*; as well as, in Rana Issa, *The Modern Arabic Bible*, the outlining of a new institution of "common solitary reading practices" (70) in relation to a subordination of language to "ownership" (103), generated through translation activities overseen by Protestant missionaries, aimed at "all speakers of the [Arabic] language, regardless of their religious belonging" (163). In contribution to this work, I've tried to study the privilege of historicity, and the formation of a disciplinary object for Arabic literature studies, in *Iterations of Loss*, 77–145.

44. Aristotle, *Metaphysics*, 1022b24–36. Here I follow the translation of Hugh Tredennick in the Loeb edition. In the sentence that follows I transcribe the rendering of *Metaphysics* 1022b32–36 offered by Harry A. Wolfson in "Infinite and Privative Judgments," 174ff.

45. Hortense Spillers, "Mama's Baby, Papa's Maybe," 213; Colin Dayan, *The Law Is a White Dog*; David Lloyd, "The Racial Thing." And see, as well, for a reflection on "the thing" in relation to "the abolition of the subject of expression," David Lloyd, *Beckett's Thing*, 86, passim.

46. Lloyd, "The Racial Thing," 70.

47. See David Lloyd, "The Social Life of Black Things," 85, passim; and Fred Moten, *The Universal Machine*, 207.

48. Denise Ferreira da Silva, *Unpayable Debt*, 161, 273, 119. And see, as well, Ferreira da Silva's discussion of an "indeterminability" in relation to matter ("Hacking the Subject," 38), as well as her thinking of "the thing" as an "excess" that "threatens the accomplishment of colonial and national juridicoeconomic goals and has no place in the ontoepistemological grammar that governs post-Enlightenment accounts of existence" ("To Be Announced," 50).

49. Shaden Tageldin, "Hugo, Translated," 634. I learn from Tageldin's intervention, where she shows, through a reading of Rūḥī al-Khālidī's study of Victor Hugo, published between 1902 and 1904, that al-Khālidī aligns the Arabic language with a practice for representational thought, where "eloquence," بلاغة, *balāgha*, is to inhere "in a modern potential, common to all languages, to make words mirror worlds," in a "redefinition" (617) of what "eloquence" is, where the Qur'ān is "relocated" in "the philological folds of literary history and criticism" (618), and where language is to be understood as a practice for semiotic transparency: "Staging semiotic transparency as that which underwrites the equality of signs, their utterers, and their receivers, al-Khālidī affirms Hugo's conviction that poetry lies in ideas, not forms" (618). This semiocentrism affirms, Tageldin underlines, a particular sense of reading, where the sort of doing occasioned in literary writing is to privilege "making meaning transparent to common readers" (618) in a "leveling" (624) that generalizes a particular practice and pose: "Simplicity, not difficulty," Tageldin writes, "becomes the measure of literary virtuosity, as well as of comparability" (629). If, in this, language is conscripted to the modern terms for politicality, where, as Tageldin cites al-Khālidī, "all words are equal," جميع الالفاظ سواء, *jamīʿ al-alfāẓ sawāʾ* (618), there are ongoing destructions in the transformations Tageldin describes, if ones that are not final, even as the material form of linguistic utterance is given through them. I learn here, as well, from the work of Michael Allan, Kamran Rastegar, and Samera Esmeir, which I underline elsewhere in this book.

50. Fred Moten, *The Universal Machine*, 96.

51. Long Soldier, *WHEREAS*, 43.

1. Settler Life

1. Frantz Fanon, *Les damnés de la terre*, 44/*The Wretched of the Earth*, 41.

2. I modify the translation of Constance Farrington: "For it is the settler who has brought the native into existence and who perpetuates his existence" (*The Wretched of the Earth*, 36).

3. What I term "settler life" is in excess of settler colonial practices; it is not reducible to them, even as it generates collective social destruction, within and outside of the settler colony. The reading I offer, then, differs from the understanding of settler colonialism in Patrick Wolfe's "Settler Colonialism" where "elimination" is "an organizing principle of settler-colonial society rather than a one-off (and superseded) occurrence" (388). I do not wish to place in question the constitutive and structural dimension of "elimination"; instead I take literally the notion that "settler colonialism was foundational to modernity" (394), as I underline its present tense—"is" rather than Wolfe's "was"—and its absolutely generalizing and eviscerating formulation through the normative terms for linguistic, social, and philosophical self-understanding in post-twelfth-Christian-century, post-Latinate frames. I do not understand settler life as a "foundation," nor elimination as a

"principle," but instead I suggest it is a multiplying and divided exteriorization of terms, a coercive institution of world-evacuating forms. If we are to consider this a "Lockean" moment, as in *Traces of History*, where Wolfe points, reading settler colonization in the Americas, to "the Indians' incurable savagery"—"In keeping with the Lockean narrative informing the wider discourse of discovery, a stubborn incapacity for agriculture was central to this savagery" (166)—in relation to "the colonial rule of private property" (199), I study these formulations as terminological exertions through which a particular sense of being, language, and the social is aggressively advanced in a counterinsurgent, non-principled, afoundational attack.

4. Frantz Fanon, *Les damnés de la terre*, 240/250.

5. In citing *Politics* I follow Aristotle, *Politics*, translated by H. Rackham in the Loeb edition; I learn as well from the translation of Hippocrates G. Apostle and Lloyd P. Gerson. I occasionally modify the Loeb translation following Apostle and Gerson, and I at times modify it otherwise.

6. In citing *On the Soul* I follow Aristotle, *On the Soul*, translated by W. S. Hett in the Loeb edition; I learn as well from the translation of Hippocrates G. Apostle. I occasionally modify the Loeb translation following Apostle, and I at times modify it otherwise.

7. See Daniel Heller-Roazen, *The Inner Touch*, where he underlines, reading these pages in Aristotle, an "equivocation in the basic expression of life," an "ambiguity" in formulation (25), and, through this, an intersection or indistinction of tactility, being, and life: "It senses," he writes of "the animal," "and therefore it is: a touching thing whose powers never cease to skim, however lightly, the fragile surface of its being" (63). In this, Heller-Roazen also explicates an indistinction of "life" from "sense," and "touch" from "thought," as he notes in reading Aristotle: "Like touch," he writes, "thought has no proper object, no clear organ of operation, and no medium to call its own, if not one that vanishes from perception in the act of thinking" (295).

8. Aristotle, *On the Soul*, 435a12–13, 435a17.

9. Aristotle, *On Interpretation*, 16b26; Aristotle, *Nicomachean Ethics*, 1170a16–18. In both of these passages, I follow and slightly modify the Loeb translations.

10. And please see the illuminating discussion of these passages, with a particular attention to *On the Soul* and *Nicomachean Ethics*, in Claudia Baracchi, *Aristotle's Ethics as First Philosophy*, 105–109, passim.

11. Hannah Arendt, *The Human Condition*, 36–37; and consider also Arendt, "The Decline of the Nation-State and the End of the Rights of Man," where the loss of "right," and "a right to have rights," entails "the loss of the relevance of speech (and man, since Aristotle, had been defined as a being commanding the power of speech and thought), and the loss of all human relationship (and man, again since Aristotle, has been thought of as the 'political animal,' that is one who by definition lives in a community), the loss, in other words, of some of the most essential characteristics of human life" (296, 297). And see as well the compelling reading offered by Judith Butler, in relation to these Arendtian distinctions: "Arendt's view

clearly meets its limit here, for the body is itself divided into the one that appears publicly to speak and act and another one, sexual, laboring, feminine, foreign, and mute, that generally is relegated to the private and prepolitical sphere" (*Notes Toward a Performative Theory of Assembly*, 86).

12. Michel Foucault, *The Order of Things*, 160; Michel Foucault, *The History of Sexuality*, 139–140.

13. Giorgio Agamben, *Homo Sacer*, 107.

14. Here I learn from and am thinking with Anthony C. Alessandrini's discussion of "reduction" in reading, his relating twentieth-century debates about "multiculturalism" to Robinson's *Black Marxism*, and his discussion of twelfth-century Europe, the role of the Latin translations of Aristotle, and the relations among capitalism and race (*Decolonize Multiculturalism*, 85, 61, 62–72), all of which remains piercingly legible in the reflection on life in Arendt, Foucault, and Agamben. I learn, as well, from the discussion of C. Heike Schotten, in *Queer Terror*, where they notice that "settler sovereignty cannot, in other words, do without the death-native it brings into being" (55), even as I wish to underline, in affirmation of Schotten's terms, that this "inability" refers also to the normative forms of linguistic and social existence in post-twelfth-Christian-century, post-Latinate philosophy and critique, which assume a pose in reiterated aggression directed against all non-white, non-Christian, non-hetero-normative beings.

15. See Alexander G. Weheliye, *Habeas Viscus*, 6–7, 33–45; Aileen Moreton-Robinson, *The White Possessive*, 129; and Ann Laura Stoler, *Race and the Education of Desire*, 29.

16. Dylan Rodríguez, *White Reconstruction*, 130.

17. Foucault, *The History of Sexuality*, Volume 1, 143.

18. I learn here from Page Dubois, *Slaves and Other Objects*.

19. Hortense Spillers, "Mama's Baby, Papa's Maybe," 212, 206.

20. See Glen Sean Coulthard, *Red Skin, White Masks*, 151–152; Cedric J. Robinson, *Black Marxism*.

21. Denise Ferreira da Silva, *Unpayable Debt*, 180.

22. Karl Marx, *Ökonomische-philosophische Manuskripte*, 391/*Economic and Philosophic Manuscripts*, 350.

23. Marx, *Ökonomische-philosophische Manuskripte*, 363/322.

24. Karl Marx, *Grundrisse der Kritik der politischen Ökonomie*, 404/*Grundrisse: Foundations of the Critique of Political Economy*, 496.

25. Marx, *Ökonomische-philosophische Manuskripte*, 364/323–324.

26. And please consider, in the first volume of *Capital*, Marx's reiteration of the privilege of "man" as a sort of being that "labors" in relation to "nature": "The labor process, as we have just presented it in its simple and abstract elements, is purposeful activity [*zweckmäßige Tätigkeit*] aimed at the production of use-values. It is an appropriation of what exists in nature for the requirements of man, the universal condition for the metabolic interaction between man and nature [*zwischen Mensch und Natur*], the everlasting nature-imposed condition of human

life [*des menschlichen Lebens*], and it is therefore independent of every form of that life, or rather it is equally common to all of the social forms that sustain human life" (Karl Marx, *Das Kapital*, 198 / *Capital*, 290).

27. Marx, *Ökonomische-philosophische Manuskripte*, 369/328.

28. And consider that Hegel, in *Philosophy of Right*, a text of which Marx was a reader, underlined that "the ways and means by which the *animal* can satisfy its needs are limited in scope, and its needs are likewise limited. Though sharing this dependence [*Abhängigkeit*], the *human being* is at the same time able to transcend it and to show his universality, first by *multiplying* his needs and means, and secondly by *dividing* and *differentiating* the concrete need into individual parts and aspects which then become different needs, *particularized* and hence *more abstract*" (§190). There is a differentiation and linking of "the animal" to and from "the human being" in relation to the latter's capacity for universality in transcending the former, and "the human being" therefore only becomes itself through this universalization, as "man" secures its "freedom" in its relation to law and the state (in the movement from "abstract right" to "morality" to what Hegel terms *Sittlichkeit*, a term rendered by H. B. Nisbet as "Ethical Life," but which we might think of as "ethicality," a certain pose and mode). And yet to present this self-transcendence and freedom Hegel must introduce "the savage," a sort of being incapable of freedom and universality: "For a condition in which natural needs as such were immediately satisfied would merely be one in which spirituality was immersed in nature, and hence a condition of savagery [*Rohheit*] and unfreedom; whereas freedom consists solely in the reflection of the spiritual into itself, its distinction from the natural, and its reflection upon the latter" (§194). "The savage" is exterior to "freedom," and the "human being" can become a subject of property, a "person"—"A person has the right to place his will in any thing. The thing thereby is *mine* and acquires my will as its substantial end (since it has no such end within itself), its determination, and its soul—the absolute right of appropriation which human beings have over all things" (§44)—and the "human being" is, further, capable of movement through the negations of speculative thought, from "the family" to "civil society" to "the state" in "self-formation" or "education." "Education [*Die Bildung*], in its absolute determination, is therefore liberation and work towards a higher liberation; it is the absolute transition to the infinitely subjective substantiality of ethical life, which is no longer immediate and natural, but spiritual and at the same time raised to the shape of universality" (§187), but "the slave" is exteriorized from this movement. If "the activity of thought" is "this process whereby the particular is superseded and raised to the universal," "the slave," Hegel explains, "does not know his essence, his infinity and freedom; he does not know himself as an essence—and he does not know himself in this way, for he does not *think* himself [*er* denkt *sich nicht*]. This self-consciousness which comprehends itself as essence through thought and thereby divests itself of the contingent and the untrue constitutes the principle of right, of morality, and of all ethics" (§21). The temporal formulation of capital in Marx mirrors Hegel's terms as Hegel repeats the exteriorization of "the savage" and

"slave" from property, universality, and a capacity for self-reflective thought—"er *denkt* sich nicht," Hegel wrote—even as Hegel is all excess, an unending exertion in speculative thought.

29. Marx, *Ökonomische-philosophische Manuskripte*, 369/329.

30. In thinking about "the animal" in Marx I learn from Jacques Derrida's *The Animal That Therefore I Am*, where the distinction drawn between "man" and "animal" is a "plural and repeatedly folded frontier" (30): "Whenever 'one' says 'The Animal,' each time a philosopher, or anyone else, says 'The Animal' in the singular and without further ado, claiming this to designate every living thing that is held not to be human (man as *rational animal*, man as political animal, speaking animal, *zōon logon echon*, man who says 'I' and takes himself to be the subject of a statement that he proffers on the subject of the said animal, etc.), well, each time the subject of the statement, this 'one,' this 'I,' does that he utters an *asininity*" (31). I wish, in reading Marx, to notice a history of reading and a stabilization of terms, where excessively illegible divisions, such as the division between the "herd animal" and "ζῷον πολιτικόν in the political sense," are coerced, in particular acts of reading, to appear as if they were stable, clear, and, finally, legible.

31. Marx, *Ökonomische-philosophische Manuskripte*, 426/366. On Marx's bees, in the first volume of *Capital*, please see: "A spider conducts operations which resemble those of the weaver, and a bee would put many a human architect to shame by the construction of its honeycomb cells. But what distinguishes the worst architect from the best of bees is that the architect builds the cell in his mind, before he constructs it in wax. At the end of every labor process, a result emerges which had already been conceived by the worker at the beginning, hence already existed ideally. Man not only effects a change of form in the materials of nature; he also realizes his own purpose [*seinen Zweck*] in those materials" (*Das Kapital*, 193/284).

32. Jodi A. Byrd, "Loving Unbecoming," 225; I learn in the formulations I offer here, as well, from Byrd's *The Transit of Empire*; on "man's" "realization" of its "purpose" in labor see that pages in *Capital* cited above, note 31.

33. Marx, *Grundrisse*, 372/460. And please see Cedric J. Robinson, *An Anthropology of Marxism*, where Robinson underlines, in relation to Marx and Engels, a certain "propulsion" in their writing, a non-resolvability of Marx's language in relation to itself: "Inevitably, the several contours of meaning in their work, representing compelling and perhaps antonymous desires, propelled discrete and sometimes competing systems of signification" (110). If Robinson underlines this irresolution, a surging of more than one Marx "within" Marx, he also notices a history of rebellion, insurgence, and communal and communist thought and practice, against which Marx, in particular instances, sets his theorization of capital. In addressing, in particular, what he terms "histories" of "socialism" and "non-capitalism," Robinson points to an "encasing" operation in Marx, a practice of subjecting various sorts of communal life and thought to an "evolutionary history": "These histories, however, are encased by Marxism and political economy [as well as Marx—JS] in the evolutionary history of capitalism" (118). "Thus slaves and

peasants are conceptualized as pre-capitalist forms of labor or as 'primitive accumulation' for capitalism" (118), he also observes, and I wish here—reading and thinking with Robinson, Ferreira da Silva, and Coulthard—to draw out the form of life, which Marx's language, in particular terminological formulations, advances in the social, as his language simultaneously carries forward other manners of thinking, being, and doing: a tradition of anontological form.

34. And consider Marx's discussion, in *Capital*, of "free workers," "slaves," "serfs," and "capitalist production" and its "own feet": "In themselves, money and commodities are no more capital than the means of production and subsistence are. They need to be transformed into capital. But this transformation can itself only take place under particular circumstances [*unter bestimmten Umständen*], which meet together at this point [*die sich dahin zusammenspitzen*]: the confrontation of, and the contact between, two very different kinds of commodity owners [in a more literal, and less substantial translation, which decomposes the temporal coordination Marx's language also promises, "Two very different kinds of commodity owners must stand opposite the other and come into contact," "Zweierlei sehr verschiedne Sorten von Warenbesitzern müssen sich gegenüber und in Kontakt treten"—JS]; on the one hand, the owners of money, means of production, means of subsistence, who are eager to valorize the sum of values they have appropriated by buying the labor-power of others; on the other hand, free workers, the sellers of their own labor-power, and therefore the sellers of labor. Free workers, in the double sense that they neither form part of the means of production themselves, as would be the case with slaves, serfs, etc. [*wie Sklaven, Leibeigne, usw.*], nor do they own the means of production, as would be the case with self-employed peasant proprietors." Marx continues, as he installs "the mode of production corresponding to capital" through the exteriorization of "slaves" and "serfs" from the "two very different kinds of commodity owners"; he outlines: "With the polarization of the commodity-market into these two classes, the fundamental conditions of capitalist production are present. The capital-relation presupposes a complete separation between the workers and the ownership of the conditions for the realization of their labor. As soon as capitalist production stands on its own feet [*auf eignen Füßen steht*], it not only maintains this separation, but reproduces it on a constantly [*stets*] extending scale. The process, therefore, which creates the capital-relation can be nothing other than the process which divorces the worker from the ownership of the conditions of his own labor; it is a process which operates two transformations, whereby the social means of subsistence and production are turned into capital, and the immediate producers are turned into wage-labourers. So-called primitive accumulation, therefore, is nothing else than the historical process of divorcing the producer from the means of production. It appears as 'primitive' because it forms the pre-history of capital [*Vorgeschichte des Kapitals*], and of the mode of production [*Produktionsweise*] corresponding to it" (*Das Kapital*, 742/874–875).

35. Marx, *Grundrisse*, 377/464–465.

36. Karl Marx, *Das Kapital*, 381/377.

37. Marx, *Grundrisse*, 377/465.

38. Lisa Lowe, *The Intimacies of Four Continents*, 50.

39. And please see Louis Althusser, "The Object of Capital," where he affirms Marx's imperative to study "the capitalist mode of production" in relation to its "specific difference" in relation to others, and in relation to an explication of "transition": "For Marx could only study the specific difference of the capitalist mode of production on condition that at the same time he studied *the other modes of production*, not only the other modes of production as types of specific *Verbindung* or unity between the factors of production, but also the *relations between different modes of production* in the process of the constitution of modes of production," and, further, "All Marx's texts on the primitive accumulation of capital constitute the material if not already the outline of this theory, where the constitution process of the capitalist mode of production is concerned—i.e., the transition from the feudal mode of production to the capitalist mode of production" (353). It is not my intention to affirm in Marx an "anthropology of the subject" (327) or "the radical anthropology of the *1844 Manuscripts*" (290), as Althusser wrote. Instead, and in a manner that does not cease to learn from Althusser, who taught us that the languages of Marx consist in nothing but discontinuities, and not solely "between" the "early" and "mature" Marx (*For Marx*, 34–35), I notice that the self-determined, autonomous form of a subject is carried forward in Marx at precisely the moment at which Althusser's desire to secure the temporal coherency of "the capitalist mode of production" is perhaps most acute: "There is a theoretical problem," he writes, "which must be posed and resolved in order to explain the mechanism by which history has produced as its result the contemporary capitalist mode of production" ("The Object of Capital," 67). If "the abstract economic reality" is "the effect of a deeper, more concrete reality: *the mode of production* of a determinate social formation" (*For Marx*, 110), and if this "mode" is to be understood through the temporal designation of its interiority—"What counts *in* [my emphasis—JS] a mode of production, what makes it such and such, is *the mode of domination* of the structure over its elements" ("The Underground Current," 203)—Althusser's affirmation of the "constitution" of "modes of production" and their "determination" preserves a privilege of subject-centric social thought and philosophical practice I wish to make legible in its globality as an extension of or mutation in Europe's ongoing, if still Christian twelfth century.

40. Marx, *Grundrisse*, 393/485.

41. If, in an elucidating intervention in *Reading Capital*, Étienne Balibar reads Marx's formulations as providing for a reflection on "production" outside of a relation to "the acts of any subjects, their practical *cogito*," I notice that the form of a subject understood as a social being that acts upon an object, "nature," is presumed in Marx's explication ("On the Basic Concepts of Historical Materialism," 436), and that this form is affirmed through Marx's discussion of capital, labor, modes of production, and the drawing of a distinction between the "formal" and "real" "subsumption" of labor by capital (463–480). If, in this, primitive accumulation is to

be understood in relation to the "constitution" of modes of production—"The analysis of primitive accumulation is therefore, strictly speaking, merely *the genealogy of the elements which constitute the structure of the capitalist mode of production*" (448)—one may wonder whether the affirmation of the "constitution" of modes of production, if only "structurally," must absorb "primitive accumulation" into a "genealogy" rather than think it as both ongoing and formative.

42. "From this point of view, the most consistent limit of Marxist thought is perhaps of a methodological order" (Antonio Negri, *Marx beyond Marx*, 181).

43. I learn here from Jacques Lezra's reading of Marx in relation to translation, in the affirmation of a certain irreducibility of language to sense, and translation to itself, where "'translation' is not a concept whose object can be strictly or rigidly determined; its borders cannot be fixed; it is not, under any aspect, identical with itself" (*On the Nature of Marx's Things*, 23), where Marx, like "the corpus of Lucretius's poem, the *interpretation* of the poem, will swerve just the slightest bit from what the understanding lays out before us as self-evident and self-understood" (52), and where, in the turbulence of language and "the violence of the sea" (48), there is a non-coincidence of language in its relation to itself, a deformulation of terms, an "ontological uncertainty (105), in what Lezra underlines is "*defective* rather than contradictory" (68), and not reducible to—or liftable into—philosophical sense.

44. Marx, *Grundrisse*, 195/270.

45. And see, as well: "As regards the individual, it is clear e.g. that he relates even to language itself *as his own* only as the natural member of a human community. Language as the product of an individual is an impossibility [literally, it is an "absurdity," a "non-thing," an "Unding"—JS]. But the same holds for property" (*Grundrisse*, 398/490). If these sentences can open a reflection on a sociality of language in excess of what I'm calling "settler life," Marx's formulations delimit this opening as they teach us to read it; this passage thinks about language, first, "as regards the individual," *in bezug auf den einzelnen*, and only then relates language, and one's relating onself to it "as *his own*," *als* seiner eignen, to a speaker's being "a natural member of a human community," *als natürliches Mitglied eines menschlichen Gemeinwesens*. And, I wish to underline, as did Marx: "But the same holds for property." In this: "Language" is subordinated to the "individual," and what is "communal" is related to language in a manner that first delimits it in relation to an "individual's" orientation toward it, a formulation we may read alongside the passages in the 1844 *Manuscripts* and *Capital* I've noted, as well as the following sentence, at the opening of Marx's "Introduction": "The human being [*Der Mensch*] is in the most literal sense a ζῶον πολιτικόν, not merely a gregarious animal [*ein geselliges Tier*], but an animal which can individuate itself only in the midst of society [*sondern ein Tier, das nur in der Gesellschaft sich vereinzeln kann*]" (*Grundrisse*, 20/84). I observe that it is Marx's illegible writing of "the human being" in its relation to "the animal," which generates "society," the form in relation to which "life" is exactingly distributed and withheld in a racialization of terms, which Marx repeats: the "animal," the "slave," the "savage," and their divided mediation in "language."

46. And see, in *Grundrisse*, on "the slave" in relation to "nature" and "cattle," where "one part of society is treated by the other as itself merely an *inorganic and natural* condition of its own reproduction": "The slave stands in no relation whatsoever to the objective conditions of his labor; rather, *labor* itself, both in the form of the slave and in that of the serf, is classified as *an inorganic condition* of production along with other natural beings, such as cattle [*das Vieh*], as an accessory of the earth." "The slave" is related to "labor," and "human beings," as "earth," "cattle," and "other natural beings," forms which only later, with the historical and formal institution of capital "as such," "als solches," come to be "separated," in "a separation [*eine Trennung*] which is completely posited only in the relation of wage labor and capital" (397/489).

47. Talal Asad, "Reflections on Violence, Law, and Humanitarianism," 396.

48. Gil Anidjar, *Blood: A Critique of Christianity*, 124, 133; and Tomaž Mastnak, *Crusading Peace* (and note 56, below), as well as Carl Erdmann, *The Origin of the Idea of Crusade* (and note 51, below).

49. For English translations of Paul I follow *The New Oxford Annotated Bible*; for the Greek of the Pauline letters, I follow *Novum Testamentum Graece*; for the Latin of the Vulgate I follow the edition provided with the Douay-Rheims translation, *The Vulgate Bible*. And see Kathleen Biddick, *The Typological Imaginary*, 1; Tomaž Mastnak, *Crusading Peace*, 106. I underline Mastnak's study, below (at note 56), in relation to the Crusades and the lexical and juridical-theological institution of the "Saracen"; I underline here only that, while I have learned from Biddick's intervention, I wish to think about "Christian temporal practices" not in relation to a "core"—"Instead, I am trying to historicize the Christian cultural imaginary at whose core lies a relation to Judaism" (Biddick, *The Typological Imaginary*, 58–59)—but in relation to Christianity's excessive address toward non-Christian alterities, understood in medieval, Latin, Christian writings as a blurred collective, a "common danger," generated through an illegibility these writings also create, and which gives place, in globality, to a pose reiterated in modern linguistic and philosophical form; see, for example, "The point of all this is that for many western Europeans throughout the Middle Ages, Saracens were pagans, and pagans were Saracens: the two words became interchangeable" (John V. Tolan, *Saracens*, 128), and, in relation to "Jews, heretics, and Saracens," as Tolan explains, "The three groups were increasingly linked in the twelfth and thirteenth centuries and were often seen to represent a common danger" (164), all of whom, following "the widespread failure of the missionary movements" were "all too obsessed with the literal and carnal to understand the intellectual or the spiritual" (277). And see, in relation to the anti-Islamic frame of crusading forms and their morphing in the normative terms for Western-hemispheric life, Talal Asad, *On Suicide Bombing*, 9: "It was only with the Crusades that the papacy promoted the ideology of a unified Christendom at war with a unified Islam." In this, and in part drawing on Mastnak's *Crusading Peace*, Asad notes that the mutating forms of jurisdictional allocation and Christian life are reiterated in the modern state and its management of violence—

"All constitutional states rest on a space of violence that they call legitimate" (29)—in a Christian understanding of sacrifice, and the crucifixion, where "God's only begotten son gave his life willingly and deliberately in order to redeem mankind" (84), which routes a social logic of Crusade and its terminological forms for the appropriation and translation of non-Christian alterities, as it gives the figure of the "citizen," whose life is sacrificed, in "a shifting pattern of convergence and dispersal" (95), in the practices of modern state law and its juridical form.

50. Pope Urban II, "Urban's Letter," 44. Pope Urban II's call for the Crusade is recorded in divergent textual instances, which underline the internal "destruction" of "pagans" (within the topographical space of Latin Christianity) and the "liberation" of "the holy places" through their cleansing from "pollution" and "filth": "Let the deeds of your ancestors move you and incite your minds to manly achievements," Robert of Rheims reports, "the glory and greatness of King Charles the Great, and of his son Louis, and of your other kings, who have destroyed the kingdoms of the pagans, and have extended in these lands the territory of the holy church. Let the holy sepulcher of the Lord our Saviour, which is possessed by unclean nations, especially incite you, and the holy places which are now treated with ignominy and irreverently polluted with their filthiness" ("Speech of Urban: The Version of Robert of Rheims," 27). Crusade is further called for, since "this land which you inhabit" is "too narrow for your large population" and "furnishes scarcely enough food for its cultivators," so in order to reroute violence among Latin Christians Crusade extends itself at "Jerusalem," "the navel of the world": "Hence it is that you murder one another, that you wage war, and that frequently you perish by mutual wounds. Let therefore hatred depart from among you, let your quarrels end, let wars cease, and let all dissensions and controversies slumber. Enter upon the road to the Holy Sepulchre; wrest that land from the wicked race, and subject it to yourselves" (28). The logic is sacrificial, where one is to give one's life "as a living sacrifice" in an extension of Christian social understanding: "Whoever, therefore, shall determine upon this holy pilgrimage and shall make his vow to God to that effect and shall offer himself to Him as a living sacrifice, holy, acceptable to God, shall wear the sign of the cross of the Lord on his forehead or on his breast" (29). And this logic frames itself as defensive—"We wish you to know what a grievous cause has led us to your country, what peril threatening you and all the faithful has brought us" (27)—and enacted out of Christian charity: "You should shudder, brethren, you should shudder at raising a violent hand against Christians; it is less wicked to brandish your sword against Saracens. It is the only warfare that is righteous, for it is charity to risk your life for your brothers" ("The Speech of Urban: The Version of Baldric of Dol," 32). One is to become a "soldier of Christ"—"Now, let those, who until recently existed as plunderers, be soldiers of Christ" (*The Chronicle of Fulcher of Chartres*, Book I, 53) in Pauline form. "When the Roman Church, from which all Christendom must obtain correction, is in disorder, it happens that all the subordinate members, being affected by the diseased fibers of the head, become weakened," Fulcher of Chartres further wrote (56). "But," he

continues, "when all these evils had been renounced because of the warning of Pope Urban, it was necessary to substitute war against the pagans for wars between Christians" (56). No mercy is offered—"With drawn swords, our people ran through the city," Fulcher of Chartres writes of the siege of Jerusalem, "Nor did they spare anyone, not even those pleading for mercy" (91–92)—and this practice of form is reiterated, in its exteriorizing and substituting pose, in the modern terms for social and linguistic existence, philosophical self-reflection, and juridical form. See, on the Crusade as a pacifying form, Tomaž Mastnak, *Crusading Peace*; on the first Crusade, Jonathan Riley-Smith, *The First Crusade and the Idea of Crusading* and "Crusading as an Act of Love"; and, earlier, Carl Erdmann, *The Origin of the Idea of Crusade*. I've learned, as well, from the work of James Muldoon, *Popes, Lawyers, and Infidels*; and Robert A. Williams Jr., "The Medieval Discourse of Crusade," in *The American Indian in Western Legal Thought*, 13–58.

51. Carl Schmitt, *Der Nomos der Erde*, 112/*The Nomos of the Earth*, 140. And see, on Gregory VII, the illuminating discussion of Carl Erdmann, who notes, in Gregory, whose papacy extended from 1073 to 1085, an internal pacification in the "Peace of God" movement. "The true war of the church," Erdmann writes, "was to be directed against heretics and schismatics, excommunicates and rebels within the church" (*The Origin of the Idea of Crusade*, 265). If, as Erdmann outlines, what transpires is a mutation in the sense of the term "militia Christi," where, if it "still retained its old spiritual meaning in the days of Gregory VII" (201), in Gregory's letters, "He [Gregory—JS] applied the traditional term *christiana militia* to the church, or Christendom, and spoke especially of bishops as *milites Christi*" (202), and in this he "drew no hard and fast line of demarcation between pious devotion and an obligation to feudal military service" (209). In this blurring of lines a frame is opened through which Urban II, who served as pope from 1088 to 1099, elaborated crusade as a form: "By the end of the century, the knightly meaning had acquired a general currency. *Miles Christi* or *miles Dei* became the term for a crusader during the First Crusade," and, further, "The expression *athlete Christi* now celebrated the brave crusader, and no longer the confessor or ascetic saint. Accordingly, the crusading army as a whole was called *exercitus Dei*, *militia Christi*, *militia christiana*, or the like" (340–341). At the same time this transformation in the sense of "militia Christi" is invested across a distinction drawn and blurred between inside and outside, and a directing of force at non-Christian, heathen, and infidel alterity. As Erdmann explains, "At the Council of Clermont, Urban II did not confine himself to declaring the crusade: he was also the first pope to announce a general Peace of God, on the grounds that knights should direct their activity outward against the infidels" (116). In this, there is a social practice of "Christian expansion" (316) and "armed pilgrimage": "The idea of armed pilgrimage was proclaimed for the first time at Clermont" (331). Crusade occasioned the formation of "Christendom" as it forwarded "the idea of the community of all Christendom against the heathen" (331). If "Urban II's crusade was not a beginning but the culmination of a long development" (348)—and, as Erdmann underlines in the opening chapter of *Origin*,

"Augustine and Gregory [Pope Gregory I—JS] thus gave holy war a dual intellectual basis: war against heretics within, to preserve the purity of the church; missionary wars without, to extend the faith" (11)—I observe the pacifying pose of the crusading textual corpus and the linguistic formulations that succeed it as they reformulate "the old ecclesiastical concept of *pax*, which expressed not just an actual state of peace but the harmonious world order desired by God" (232).

52. "Then the Franks entered the city [Jerusalem] magnificently at the noonday hour on Friday, the day of the week when Christ redeemed the whole world on the cross" (*The Chronicle of Fulcher of Chartres*, Book I, 90). In *Nomos of the Earth* Schmitt reads such legality in relation to the interpretation he offers of the word "nomos": "In its original sense, however, *nomos* is precisely the full immediacy of a legal power not mediated by laws; it is a constitutive historical event—an act of legitimacy, whereby the legality of a mere law first is made meaningful" (42/73). I do not wish to uphold Schmitt's distinction between "constitutive acts and constituted institutions" (50/82)—a distinction Walter Benjamin had drawn, and which he also blurred, in his 1921 essay "Zur Kritik der Gewalt" ("Toward the Critique of Violence"), in his discussion of "law-making" and "law-preserving" violence—yet I observe reiterations and relocations of these violences in settler life and its juridical forms. For a reading of the illegibility of the distinction between "law-making" and "law-preserving" violence—and what Schmitt termed "constitutive" and "constituted" "acts" and "institutions"—see Jacques Derrida, "Force of Law."

53. Schmitt, *Der Nomos der Erde*, 82/113; 71/102.

54. Please consider the discussion of James Muldoon, who notes that in Vitoria's discussion of "*dominium*," which Muldoon glosses as "primarily the right of men to govern themselves," this is to be understood as "the natural possession of all men" (*Popes, Lawyers, and Infidels*, 146). As is a right to "life": "No group of people could voluntarily renounce their right to live" (149), Muldoon observes, as he glosses Vitoria. And this, in the context of the colonizer's giving to itself a right to extend its sense of "life" to each and every individual or collective to which it addresses itself, in particular in relation to Vitoria's "argument supporting a Christian conquest of an infidel society in which the infidel rulers were tyrannizing their subjects." "Even without papal authorization," Muldoon continues, "a Christian ruler could invade such a land and bring it under his own control for the good of the people who were so abused. Vitoria pointed to human sacrifice and the killing of innocent victims for the purpose of cannibalism as sufficient cause for removing an infidel ruler" (149). It was, thus, that the doctrine of colonization for the sake of the other was recapitulated, mutating the discourse on "Crusade" into a discourse on the "protection" of the colonized, their being saved, through the settler-colonial activities of the white, European, Christian collective: "Under such circumstances, Christians could intervene to protect the people from being killed even if they did not wish to be so protected" (149).

55. Schmitt, *Der Nomos der Erde*, 76/107, 82/113. And consider the Vulgate translation of Galatians 5:14: "Omnis enim lex in uno sermone impletur: Diliges

proximum tuum sicut teipsum"; Paul follows the third-century-before-Christ Septuagint translation of Leviticus 19:18: "Καὶ ἀγαπήσεις τὸν πλησίον σου ὡς σεαυτόν/*kai agapēseis ton plēsion sou hōs seauton*," as does Paul's rendering of the Hebrew "חק," "ḥoq," as "νόμος," "nomos" (i.e., at Leviticus 19:19): "And you shall observe my law [Τὸν νόμον μου φυλάξεσθε/*ton nomon mou phulaxesthe*]."

56. Mastnak, *Crusading Peace*, 124, 166. I learn throughout from Mastnak's study of the Crusades, and his linking of the Crusades to the "Peace of God" movement (following Erdmann) and Christian warfare—"Also specifically Christian, of course, was the demand that soldiers wage war against schismatics and heretics" (32)—within Latin Christendom and, in Pope Urban II's call for Crusade, without. Crusade made socially manifest "the general idea of making war on non-Christians as the alternative to Christians killing each other" (41), and this "general idea" occasioned a mutation of intra-Christian war, where "most of the Carolingians' warlike energies were directed at wars against the Lombards, Saxons, Avars, Normans, Danes, and Slavs" (106), to an exteriorizing violence targeting "pollution"—"The pope [Pope John VIII] considered any contact with the infidel as polluting the body of Christian society and any alliance with the impious as contagious" (110)—and, beginning in the late eleventh century, Muslims, who took on a distinct role as "*the* enemy of Christianity and Christendom" (115). At the same time if, prior to the Crusades, there was an indistinction in internal forms of alterity, the Crusades become a vector through which the term "Saracen" is generalized and blurred: "Whereas from the Carolingian times onward, holy wars had been fought against infidels in general, the crusade was at its inception the war of Christendom against Muslims, animated by a 'generalized hatred of Islam'" (115). In this, "*Saracen* gradually became the generic term for Christians' enemies altogether" (116); it is "the fundamental enemy of Christendom" (117), and, further, it is the enemy through which "Christendom" established itself. In some English sources, Mastnak explains, "The Danes (together with Scots and Irishmen) and Saxons are named *Sarazins* or *Saracens*," and "In the *chansons de geste*, Vandals, Vikings, Arabs, and other 'unbelievers' appear under the generic heading of *Saracens*" (116–117), a heading that points to the expansive, warlike social form that came, in this eighth-through twelfth-century documentary field, to morph into "Europe." If, in this, "Christendom was actually frontierless. It was a mobile, moving space" (123), the Crusades occasioned "the transportation of violence from Latin Christendom to the Holy Land" (162) as they also became a locus for the articulation of the social. The "Saracen," an illegible form of non-Christian alterity, became a site of disorder against which the modern, European territorial state—the form which succeeded "the idea of political society as *corpus Christi*" (255), Mastnak's writes—does not cease to direct itself: "Since order meant understanding and loving God," Mastnak writes of Ramon Lull, "the Saracens were an element of disorder" (226). If the modern forms of conceptualization for language, being, and life are given through this designation and its mutations, the fundamental principle of Christian life is rephrased in them yet again—"Peace among Christians and war against the

infidels!" (341)—as Crusade "survives," as I try to show in this chapter, through the hegemonic terms of social existence in Western hemispheric frames—in what I term "settler life": "The crusade idea survived the decline of Christendom," Mastnak also observes, "which the crusade had helped to create" (279).

57. Schmitt, *Der Nomos der Erde*, 78/109; 81/112.

58. Frederick H. Russell, *The Just War in the Middle Ages*, 55.

59. And please consider the notes offered in Talal Asad, "Medieval Heresy," where Asad underlines, in relation to "heresy," that "it is in its attempt to *extend* and secure its authority that the Church comes to define and deal with heresy as a danger to the Truth" (355). If, as Asad underlines, "the Church regards differences as potential negations" (359), we may understand this manner of "regarding" differences as manifesting itself in the law, the state, and its practices, and by transmuting a particular manner of dealing with, and policing, both Christian and non-Christian life. "It was not enough for the religious to learn to recognize and avoid dangers; it now appeared increasingly necessary for 'true Christians' to discover, locate, and attack them" (359).

60. Russell, *The Just War in the Middle Ages*, 175, 178.

61. St. Thomas Aquinas, *Summa theologiae*, 3.Q8.A1; 3.Q8.A3. In citing *Summa theologiae* I cite each passage by Part, Question, and Article. This citation indexes the third part, the eighth question, and first and third articles. On the term "corpus mysticum" see Henri de Lubac, *Corpus Mysticum* ("In the second half of the twelfth century, the Church therefore began to be called a '*mystical body*,' and it would appear that from then on this expression spread rapidly" [106]); on the mutations in the sense of this term in twelfth-century Christian Europe, see Ernst Kantorowicz, *The King's Two Bodies*, 195–197, where Kantorowicz underlines a "transference" (115) of terms from the theological to the juridical, as well as a persistence in form; and, for a most illuminating reading of these texts in relation to modern racial terms, see Gil Anidjar's discussion of blood, of "the novel community that emerged through the Eucharist" (*Blood*, 67) and its relation to the "theologico-bio-juridical form" of "the modern state" (122). In this, "It was now becoming possible to enact, practice and enforce, for the love of God, a newfound distinction *between bloods*" (133), a possibility Anidjar links to "the Statutes of the Purity of Blood," which "were first proclaimed in 1449 in Toledo, Spain" (61), and the modern institution of race and "a recognition that the blood of race is derivative of a larger preoccupation with blood" (98), in an "asymmetric" (56) and "generalized hematology" (97), which points to a history of Christianity, which I underline, learning from and thinking with Anidjar, to consider settler life's ongoing self-exteriorization and mutation in its dividing—and divided—pose.

62. Aquinas, *Summa theologiae*, 2.2.Q10.A8.

63. And consider, in relation to thinking these Pauline formulations, the discussion of resurrection in medieval Christian theology, where, as Caroline Walker Bynum explains, resurrection "unites us to Christ's body, which is integer in heaven, however much we masticate it here on earth" (*The Resurrection of the Body*,

149). And yet if there is a "uniting" in resurrection, its theorization presumes that in it "the material and particular body we possess on earth" (154) is "reassembled" or "re-collected." For Peter Lombard, for example, "his basic image of the resurrected body is of particles or bits re-collected into a whole" (123), and this image points to what Bynum calls "the oxymoron of incorruptible matter" (112), an oxymoron carried in Christian debates and passed on in medieval, Latin Christian thought of the twelfth and thirteenth centuries. If this points to "the triumph of integrity over partition, of stasis and incorruption over decay" (108), and if in this there is an emphasis on "the beauty of wholeness" (104), where "we can rise to incorruption" (97), I wish to observe that the "oxymoron" Bynum underlines presses itself out as a social form in the consolidation or coercion of a Christian collective in the pronoun "we." By this I mean: If, as Bynum notes, "The Fourth Lateran Council in 1215 required Cathers and other heretics to assent to the proposition that 'all rise with their own individual bodies, that is, the bodies which they now wear'" (154–155), this formulation articulates a demand that the flesh be "reassembled," or "reconstituted," in the sort of event that resurrection is. The sense of resurrection attributed to "heretics"—"By the early decades of the thirteenth century, only heretics thought the elect would leave body behind in the ascent to salvation" (225)—may therefore be understood as a refusal of this oxymoronic demand. In this frame, we may understand the Fourth Lateran Council as advancing a domestication of non-Christian, heretical, and schismatic forms, and the interpretive locus for this domestication is a demand that matter be raised up to "life," and flesh be lifted from "death" and "dissolution and deformity" (124) to "peace." "Salvation is the triumph of whole over part" (190), but the demand for "peace" is a social exertion leveled at all beings, which is transmuted and rephrased in the modern terms for philosophical sense and the redemptive form of what Bynum called, elsewhere, the "Christian God": "For matter is by definition locatable, divisible, temporal, changeable; the Christian God is by definition whole, immutable, and transcendent; yet that Christian God is understood to redeem, not merely transcend, the material" (*Christian Materiality*, 175).

64. Please see Mastnak, *Crusading Peace*, 115–117, and note 56, above.

65. Kantorowicz, *The King's Two Bodies*, 249, 308. And please also see John of Salisbury, *Policraticus*, where Salisbury underlines "law" in relation to "the prince": "There is wholly or mainly this difference between the tyrant and the prince: That the latter is obedient to law, and rules his people by a will that places itself at their service, and administers rewards and burdens within the republic under the guidance of law," and this in a manner wherein, if "individuals merely look after individual affairs, princes are concerned with the burden of the entire community" (28). The form of the body mediates law as a social practice: "In this, nature, that best guide to living, is to be followed, since it is nature which has lodged all of the senses in the head as a microcosm, that is, a little world, of man, and has subjected to it the totality of the members in order that all of them may move correctly provided that the will of a sound head is followed" (28). Law, at the same time,

identifies "transgressors": "For since law will prosecute the blameworthy without personal animosity, the prince most properly punishes transgressors not according to some wrathful motive, but by the peaceful will of law" (31). Such transgressors are on the side of carnality, those "who open their hands and keep occupied with all manner of sensual activity" (18), and if these are innumerable—"it is easier to encounter these than it is to enumerate them, since they are present everywhere on the earth" (18)—they are subjected to law's violence: "All law is opposed to such persons, all legal rights stand jointly against them, and all creatures will someday take up arms against these enemies of public welfare" (18). The Pauline reference to the "letter" of the law and its "spirit" is routed through these meditations on legality, jurisdiction, administration, and peace; for those who properly interpret the law, "the letter of the law is followed in such a fashion that there is no divergence at all from the purity of its spirit. For in fact the letter destroys, while the spirit confers life" (41), as Salisbury writes. Salisbury is speaking here of "the law of Deuteronomy," so the reading of law, in relation to these Pauline statements, is figural, where "the law of Deuteronomy" is fulfilled in the law of the territorial state: "This refers not to the letter of the law, which mortifies, but to its spirit, which stimulates the qualities of sanctity of mind, cleanliness of body, sincerity of faith, and charitableness of works" (41–42). Christian charity organizes this reflection on law—"For the good and dignified governor agrees to take care that his province is peaceful and quiet; this will be easily preserved if, moved by solicitude, he searches the province for bad men and removes them. For he ought to round up the sacrilegious, the bandits, the thieves, the plunderers, and, just as he clears away all these offenders, so he ought to turn his attention to those who shelter them and without whom the bandit cannot long escape detention" (95)—just as it does the reading of philosophical texts such as the logical books of Aristotle, cited in *Policraticus*: "He who acquires and enlarges charity on the basis of philosophy itself is pursuing the ends of the philosopher himself. And so it is the true and immutable rule of philosophers that one engages in all sorts of reading and studying, acting and refraining from acting, to the end that charity may be advanced" (161). We may understand the twelfth-century institution of law in this frame, in relation to a generalized attack against those engaged in "sensual activity," those improperly comported, non-Christian, heretical, schismatic, apostate, or other beings, "the sacrilegious, the bandits, the thieves, the plunderers," as well as those who house and protect them, in the interest of Christian charity—and the Crusades, contemporaneous with this text, were carried out in the interest of such "charity" as well, as Urban II stated—and a "secure life" in Christian, if however "secular," terms: "The public welfare is therefore that which fosters a secure life both universally and in each person" (14).

66. Isidore of Seville, *Etymologies*, VII.i.1.

67. Russell, *The Just War in the Middle Ages*, 263, 297; Kantorowicz, *The King's Two Bodies*, 19.

68. Kantorowicz, *The King's Two Bodies*, 115.

69. Vitoria, *Relectio de Indis*, 82, 87/"On the American Indians," 280, 284.

70. Antony Anghie, "Francisco de Vitoria," 23. And please consider the illuminating discussion of María Josefina Saldaña-Portillo, in relation to Vitoria, Sepúlveda, and Las Casas, where she underlines a "recalibration" and "transposition" of European, Christian categories (*Indian Given*, 266n8, 49). "Indeed, Christian community is transposed onto American geography through the reasoned sociality of indigenous peoples" (49), and this, in an effort of translation that is, Saldaña-Portillo shows, a regulating containment, an institution of the social through its pacifying domestication in "love": "When Vitoria theorizes the law of nations, he argues that the Indians were compelled to 'love' the Spaniards (his words) as they would love any other neighbor, revealing once more the Christian trace within secular reasoning" (51). This transposition of "Christian community" generates, as well, a "colonial model of domination through Christian unity" (138), which imparts an "ontological bifurcation" (178), a racializing transmutation of the "brutal logic of abstract liberal equality" (132), as this logic reduplicates itself, within the settler colony and without, and, in its global extensions, in the US wars in Iraq, Afghanistan, and, Saldaña-Portillo writes, "the US genocidal present in the Middle East" (258).

71. Thomas Aquinas, *Sententia libri politicorum*, A77–78/*Commentary on Aristotle's Politics*, 15. And please also consider that "in relation to the question, in which sense Thomas used the term *civitas*, it must next be brought out that Moerbeke [the translator of the Latin version of Aristotle's *Politics*, which Aquinas read—JS] translated *polis* with *civitas*, and that Thomas adopted this word. This fact, together with the guideline that a commentary should remain close to the author, suggests that *civitas*, in *Sententia libri politicorum*, is a technical term for the Aristotelian *polis*" (Bernhard Stengel, *Der Kommentar des Thomas von Aquin zur* Politik *des Aristoteles*, 115). Commenting on William of Moerbeke's Latin translation of Aristotle's *Politics*, Eckart Schütrumpf points, as well, to Moerbeke's translation of "polis" as "civitas" (*The Earliest Translations of Aristotle's* Politics, 19), and he further underlines that Nicole Oresme's fourteenth-century translation of *Politics* into French, based on Moerbeke, occasioned the coinage of the French word "politique," and, through that French term, Schütrumpf also explains, with reference to the Grimm brothers *Deutsches Wörterbuch*, the German "Politik": "Ultimately the German term owes its existence to Nicole Oresme's translation of Aristotle's *Politics*" (27n88).

72. Vitoria, *Relectio de Indis*, 98/291.

73. Sylvia Wynter, "New Seville: Part Two," 52, 50, 52.

74. Sylvia Wynter, "New Seville: Part One," 25.

75. And consider as well Lewis Hanke, who underlines that Las Casas, as he argued against "Sepúlveda's contention that the Indians had no real capacity for political life," noted that "the American Indians compared very favorably with the peoples of ancient times, were eminently rational beings, and in fact fulfilled every one of Aristotle's requirements for the good life" (*Aristotle and the American Indians*, 54). And yet if Las Casas intended on "establishing the Indians in the eyes of the Spanish community as human beings with a culture it must respect" (55), one may

think Las Casas's language, as Hanke explicates it, as a generalization of a particular sense of what it means to be a being, if also an "eminently rational" one. If in this terminological practice a distinction is drawn between "rational" and "non-rational" beings, we may think this distinction, and others—for example a distinction between those educable and those not, and Las Casas, as Hanke also writes, "believed passionately that all people could be civilized through education and Christianization" (*All Mankind Is One*, 154)—as a pressing out and carrying on of a tradition for social and linguistic form, which Wynter gives us to think.

76. Sylvia Wynter, "The Ceremony Must Be Found," 25, 32, 53.

77. Sylvia Wynter, "1492: A New World View," 9.

78. See Hans Blumenberg, *The Legitimacy of the Modern Age*.

79. Wynter, "1492: A New World View," 36, 38.

80. Aquinas, *Sententia libri politicorum*, A84/*Commentary on Aristotle's Politics*, 24.

81. Aquinas, *Sententia libri politicorum*, A93/*Commentary on Aristotle's Politics*, 38.

82. See Spillers, "Mama's Baby, Papa's Maybe," 206. And please consider, as well, Spillers's discussion of Gomes Eannes de Azurara's *Chronicle of the Discovery and Conquest of Guinea, 1441–1448*, where a burst of European, Christian terms, in "the peculiar myopia of the medieval Christian mind" (211), is set out in naming its objects of "discovery" and "conquest," and where "Azurara records encounters with 'Moors,' 'Mooresses,' 'Mulattoes,' and people 'black as Ethiops'" (211), as Spillers cites Azurara. "The intimate choreography that the Portuguese narrator sets going between the 'faithless' and the 'ugly' transforms a partnership of dancers into a single figure" (212), Spillers writes, and this "transformation," she suggests, reformulates the "pagan" within the frames of capitalism, the transatlantic slave trade, and settler colonization, in the capture of a certain motion, a "partnership of dancers," and its coercive translation. The "captives" (212), of whom Azurara wrote, are, in the passages of the *Chronicle* Spillers cites, "yet pagans, without the clearness and the light of the Holy Faith," "they lived like beasts, without any custom of reasonable beings," and "they had no understanding of good, but only knew how to live in bestial sloth" (212). I notice, through Spillers's discussion, that the "grammar of description" (211) she outlines retains a field of terms—"'Moors,' 'Mooresses,' 'Mulattoes,' and people 'black as Ethiops'"—which Azurara's *Chronicle* relocates, repeating a lexicon while redistributing it into a new "grammar," and this language use points to the catachrestic form of the terms Wynter outlines, a manner of "*naming*" (216), which, Spillers also writes, belongs to "the *ideological* and hegemonic cadences of dominance" (219).

83. Wynter, "1492: A New World View," 39.

84. And please see, regarding Las Casas's terminology, his discussion of "barbarians in the absolute and strict sense of the word" and "unbelievers" (*In Defense of the Indians*, 33, 55). On the one hand, Las Casas outlines the many faults of such "barbarians": They lack "reason," "natural government," "political institutions," and "laws"; and, "Finally, caring nothing for life in a society, they lead a life very much like that of brute animals" (33). And yet, Las Casas explains, "our

Indians" do not fall under this category: "They are not ignorant, inhuman, or bestial. Rather, long before they had heard the word 'Spaniard' they had properly organized states, wisely ordered by excellent laws, religion, and custom" (42). Under what category do "our Indians" fall? "Now the fourth kind of barbarian refers to those who are outside the faith of Christ, and this includes all unbelievers" (53). Las Casas outlines that "unbelievers who have never accepted the faith of Christ are not actually subject to Christ and therefore not to the Church or its authority" (55), and yet the task of spreading the word of Christ is mandated in, and routed through, conquest and mission: "Indeed, this is the truly Christian reason why God should first give us the land as our possession, that is, in order that the idolaters who own the idols be converted and then, as a result, that they destroy their idols and abolish idolatry—in order that we should teach idolaters the truth of the gospel and lead them to the net of the Church by persuasion" (68). If Las Casas underlines that it is not the role of the Church to "punish" idolaters, since they are not under the "jurisdiction" (84) of the Church, he presents a comparative analysis of non-Christian beings. Since the Church "does not punish the blindness of the Jews or those who practice the Mohammedan superstition," and given that "the Jews and Saracens have heard the words of Christ," and yet have not accepted them, it should not punish, or find cause to incite war against, "the Indians," who "have never heard the teaching of Christian truth even through hearsay" (78), as Las Casas explains. But what about the jurisdiction of the Church? Unlike a territorial state, the Church is non-territorial, "In fact, the Church is nothing other than the whole Christian people strengthened in faith and united in the society and communion of the sacraments. And these sacraments are the borders or walls by which the Church is surrounded" (80). And, further, "The gate to this city (that is, the Church) is baptism" (80). He clarifies the Church's jurisdiction, underlining that "there is a place to which the Church does not extend, specifically, the place where the truth of faith is not known and the true sacrifice is not offered, which is not to be shared with dogs (that is, heretics, schismatics, Jews, idolaters, and pagans)" (81). One might say that, recirculating a post-twelfth-Christian-century language, Las Casas, in these formulations, blurs the terms he seems to uphold, where "idolaters" are similar to and distinct from "Jews," "Saracens," and "dogs," where "heretics" and "schismatics" are not wholly distinguishable from "our Indians," from whom they are, at the same time separated. In this, the jurisdiction of the Church is, quite literally, baptized, as the distinctions between "barbarians in the absolute and strict sense" and "barbarians" who are "unbelievers" collapses—they both, at this precise moment, lack a capacity for "self-government" (42)—as the baptismal form of the Church becomes a locus through which its terms are excessively exteriorized: "Now to be inside or outside the Church is the same as to lack baptism or regeneration by baptism, for those who have been baptized and have that faith that is the door of the Church are in the Church, whereas those who lack the faith are outside the Church, where no salvation can be expected for anyone (81–82).

85. Wynter, "1492: A New World View," 13, 30. On the term "Judaeo-Christian" see Tomoko Masuzawa, *The Invention of World Religions*, where she explains that

this term points to the incorporation of "Judaism" into the discourse on "world religions" and its appropriation into "a dominant universalist scheme of Christianity, particularly of Protestant Christianity" (301), and where she notes that this took place, "in the far western satellite region of Euro-Christendom, namely, in the United States, beginning in the late 1920s and early 1930s" (301). She outlines: "This was the period in which an alliance of Judaism and Christianity became a matter of great political exigency for the mixed population of that country, when the surging tide of fascism threatened Europe, and when the Americans were about to enter the fray. In this moment of crisis—and no doubt also in reaction to the new domestic situation where they began to see a swelling number of immigrants from Asia and other non-Christian territories—certain liberal Protestants, Jews, and some Catholics in tow attempted to form a united spiritual front of 'Judeo-Christian' tradition" (301). This tradition, newly invented, was to include writers such as Moses, Spinoza, and Marx, as well as "Theodor Herzl" (302). Masuzawa continues, detailing the manner in which this terminological formulation "displaced" and "occluded" others, obscuring, in part, its Christian and settler history: "Today, the idea of the Judeo-Christian West seems to have displaced and occluded the notion of Christian Europe and usurped the subject position of the world historical unfolding" (302–303), a displacement and occlusion which, Masuzawa suggests, "amounted to further obscuring, and at the same time sheltering and preserving, the hegemonic logic of the epistemic regime formerly instituted on the authority of Euro-Christendom" (303).

86. Wynter, "1492: A New World View," 31. Wynter's use of the term "Judaeo-Christian" occurs when her remarks are summative or interpretive. For example: "If the symbolic representational system of Judaeo-Christianity has continued to provide the 'ultimate reference point' for Western societies, whatever the transformations of their modes of production and therefore of their historical 'system-ensembles,' the political historian J. G. A. Pocock provides us with the key to the process by which Western Europe was to effect its shift from the founding religious form of the 'ultimate reference point' of the Judaeo-Christian symbolic representational or cultural system to its later secular variants" (13), where this term mediates Wynter's explanation of a shift from "religion" ("the founding religious form") to the "secular" ("its later secular variants"). This pattern repeats in a second citational moment, in relation to Columbus: "In other words, Columbus would behave prescriptively within the limits of a *propter nos* whose primary reference was that of securing the well-being of himself and his fellow Christians. At the same time, as the represented universality of his Christian apocalyptic millenarianism, as well as of the new *statal*, yet still Judaeo-Christian concept of *Man*, also enabled him to perceive the well-being of himself and of his fellow Judaeo-Christian statal subjects, as if this well-being were isomorphic with that of mankind, including the Tainos/Arawaks (who would pay the price of extinction for this belief), in general" (30). I wish, in this context, only to note that the notion of a "Judaeo-Christian statal subject," to which Columbus and his "fellows" belonged, in Wynter's argument—and this is not a

notion that existed in vocabularies of Christian theological or juridical practice in medieval or early modern Europe—enables Wynter's explanation of the "isomorphism" she outlines, where a particular social form and lexicon presents itself as if it were universal, "isomorphic with that of mankind." And yet this particularity is not "Judaeo-Christian," but merely *Christian*, not so much "*theocentric*" (26) but instead Christo-centric, an effect and ongoing practice of what Wynter also calls "Latin-Christian Europe" (24), a formulation which does not obscure—as Wynter's analyses sometimes can—the manner in which post-twelfth-Christian-century Latin formulations relate themselves to non-Christian alterities, as well as the persistence of this in the globality of settler life, as Wynter also helps us to understand.

87. Sylvia Wynter, "Columbus, the Ocean Blue, and Fables That Stir the Mind," 157; Wynter, "New Seville: Part One," 26.

88. And please also consider the formulations in Wynter's "Unsettling the Coloniality of Being/Power/Truth/Freedom," where she emphasizes a "shift" "from being a primarily religious subject, for whom the 'name of what is evil' was/is that of a common enslavement by all mankind to Original Sin, to that of being a political subject of a state" (308), where this shift is interpreted in relation to "the West's degodding of its religious Judeo-Christian descriptive statement" (299) and, at the same time, in the broader terms Wynter outlines, what she calls "an a-Christian premise": "For the indigenous peoples of the New World, together with the mass-enslaved peoples of Africa, were now to be reclassified as 'irrational' because 'savage' Indians, and as 'subrational' Negroes, in the terms of a formula based on an a-Christian premise of a by-nature difference between Spaniards and Indians, and, by extrapolation, between Christian Europeans and Negroes" (296). And yet, as Wynter also teaches us, this "premise" is not so much "a-Christian" as it is a mutation within Christianity as it extends and reorganizes itself in globality.

89. Russell, *The Just War in the Middle Ages*, 61.

90. Alexis de Tocqueville, "Lettre sur l'Algérie," 45/"Second Letter on Algeria," 15.

91. Alexis de Tocqueville, "Travail sur l'Algérie," 103/"Essay on Algeria," 63.

92. Alexis de Tocqueville, "Notes du voyage en Algérie de 1841," 62/"Notes on the Voyage to Algeria in 1841," 36.

93. Tocqueville, "Travail sur l'Algérie," 126/81.

94. Tocqueville, "Notes du voyage en Algérie de 1841," 80/48–49.

95. Tocqueville, "Lettre sur l'Algérie," 56/23.

96. Tocqueville, "Notes du voyage en Algérie de 1841," 63/37.

97. John Locke, *An Essay Concerning Human Understanding*, II.ix.9.

98. On "stasis" please see Liddell and Scott, *A Greek-English Lexicon*, 1634; as well as "akatastasis," which is, Liddell and Scott write, "instability," "anarchy," "confusion" (48).

99. In thinking about the institution of the social in the frame I'm considering here, and throughout this chapter, I learn from and am thinking with the discussion, in Saidiya V. Hartman's *Scenes of Subjection*, of "norms of liberal

equality" (118), as well as her reflection on "the normative category 'person'" (56) and what she terms "traditional notions of the political": "In considering the determinations and limits of practice it becomes evident that resistances are engendered in everyday forms of practice and that these resistances are excluded from the locus of the 'political proper.' Both aspects of this assessment are significant because too often the interventions and challenges of the dominated have been obscured when measured against traditional notions of the political and its central features: the unencumbered self, the citizen, the self-possessed individual, and the volitional and autonomous subject" (61). If these terms coerce a particular institution of the social in its relation to slavery—"The slave is the object or the ground that makes possible the existence of the bourgeois subject and, by negation or contradistinction, defines liberty, citizenship, and the enclosure of the social body" (62)—I wish to ask whether we might think of these "traditional notions" as moments in the ongoing wars against Black, Indigenous, colonized, and enslaved collectives, where the practice of "definition" may be understood as a response to the unregulated social and linguistic life of those collectives, in what Hartman also calls "black excess" (88) and its sociality. Hartman has taught us that "black subordination and white dominance" is "the very foundation of the social order" (148), an extension of "plantation management" (138), and I wish to ask, as well, how we might think such notions in their globality, outside of the frames of Western hemispheric life, and in relation—as I try to suggest in chapters 2 and 3—to their material or lingual forms in Arabic-language frames.

100. Locke, *An Essay Concerning Human Understanding*, II.i.8.

101. Etienne Balibar, "'My Self,' 'My Own': Variations on Locke," 79, 83, 80, 91; and, on "invention," and, further, "the European invention of consciousness," Etienne Balibar, *Identity and Difference*.

102. Brenna Bhandar, *Colonial Lives of Property*, 167; and see C. B. Macpherson, *The Political Theory of Possessive Individualism*.

103. Locke, *An Essay Concerning Human Understanding*, II.i.19.

104. And consider the reading of H. L. A Hart's *The Concept of Law* offered in Nasser Hussain, *The Jurisprudence of Emergency*, where Hussain underlines the normativity of a "mental attitude" in the form of a subject that is, in Locke's words, "capable of a law": "For Hart, the crucial source of law is that there is a mental attitude toward rules, an internal aspect that differentiates them from mere habits and provides them with their normative force and sanction" (37). Law, Hussain underlines, "regulates" violence in a manner that is "located not so much in the substantive aspects of the law as in legal procedure" (69), and in this manner law is generative of "the construction of legal subjects and their normative conduct" (84). Such a construction is constitutive for law and articulated through it. "All law, after all," Hussain compellingly writes, "has to be enforced on bodies—protocols of interpretation, procedures of institutions, require the body, require its constraint and movement, signature, and utterance" (121). And see Peter Fitzpatrick's discussion of the law's creation of "legal subjects" through its institution of a field of oppositions

between the white, European, and rational, over and against the non-white, "savage," and "native," a "racial division creating law's identity" where "the subject stands in constant and essential difference to the 'native' and various other equivalents of the savage state," in *Mythology of Modern Law*, 166, 202–23, 118, 130, and, especially, in relation to Hart, the chapter of *Mythology of Modern Law* titled "Law as Myth," 183–210; and, as well, Hart, *The Concept of Law*: "Reflection on this aspect of things reveals a sobering truth: the step from the simple form of society, where primary rules of obligations are the only means of social control, into the legal world with its centrally organized legislature, courts, officials, and sanctions brings it solid gains at a certain cost" (202). I do not wish to affirm Hart's parsing of "cost" and "gains," but to observe the developmental frame of his reflection, attended to by Hussain and Fitzpatrick.

105. Locke, *An Essay Concerning Human Understanding*, II.xxviii.10, II.xxviii.9. And see the discussion in James Tully, *A Discourse on Property*, where he underlines that "Man," in Locke, "has a property in, or is the proprietor of his person and, he is also the proprietor of the actions of his person" (105). Here, there is a subordination of "act" to "person," of "person" to "consciousness," and of "consciousness" to "property"—a collocation of arguments congealed in the term "Forensick" subject. If "Locke's point is that the person is necessarily aware of performing his actions through the consciousness accompanying his thinking" (107), and if this "point" labors to subject "act" to "person," in relation to its "awareness," this sense of what a "person" is, in relation to its "acts," is based upon a concept of property: "To own one's actions is equivalent to being the proprietor of them" (108). I observe that this field of argumentation, as it redefines what an "act" is, by subordinating it to the "person," presses itself at all beings—as in the pages in Locke I'm reading here—in a delimitation, an extension and withdrawal, of survival and life. For example, in the generalizing force of the word "always": "The criterion of personhood is the consciousness which always accompanies thought and action" (109).

106. Robert Cover, "Violence and the Word," 1601, 1628.

107. Robert Cover, "The Supreme Court, 1982 Term—Foreword: Nomos and Narrative," 31, 9.

108. Zakiyyah Iman Jackson, *Becoming Human*, 184.

109. I learn here from Sora Han's acute discussion of the "formal act" occasioned in legal interpretation (*Letters of the Law*, 53), where acts of reading in law presume and reformulate a privilege of "the abstract legal subject" (49) as well as, in relation to legal interpretation, "the catachrestic recording of slavery across its archive, and the haunting of the slave's fugitivity in the law's various protections of personal sovereignty" (19). "Every writing and reading of law is a materialization of burial and demarcation" (104), and so, too, may we think of every writing of the philosophical form of the "subject," each textual formulation of the legal "person," as such "materialization," as Han gives us to read it, within and in excess of the archive she studies.

110. John Locke, *The Second Treatise of Government*, chap. VIII, para. 95.

111. Locke, *An Essay Concerning Human Understanding*, II.x.9
112. Stefano Harney and Fred Moten, *The Undercommons*, 17.
113. Ferreira da Silva, *Unpayable Debt*, 174.

2. Anontological Form

1. Al-Kindī, "Risāla fī kammiyyat kutub Arisṭūṭālīs," 364/"Letter on the Quantity of Aristotle's Books," 282. I have learned from the published English-language translations of the Arabic texts I study in this chapter, and I occasionally modify these translations in order to attend to or emphasize particular uses of language, vocabulary, and sentence structure; in all instances in which I cite an English translation, I provide the Arabic pagination followed by that of the English. When an English translation is not cited, I have provided my own.
2. Ibn Abī Uṣaybiʿa, *ʿUyūn al-anbāʾ fī ṭabaqāt al-aṭibbāʾ*, 1.207.
3. Abū Qāsim ibn Ṣāʿīd al-Andalusī, *Kitāb ṭabaqāt al-umam*, 52.
4. Ibn Abī Uṣaybiʿa, *ʿUyūn al-anbāʾ fī ṭabaqāt al-aṭibbāʾ*, 1.207.
5. Richard Walzer, *Greek into Arabic*, 60; Gerhard Endress, "Mathematics and Philosophy in Medieval Islam," 144. And see also, on the Arabic translation and commentary traditions, Gerhard Endress, "The Circle of al-Kindī"; Cristina D'Ancona Costa, "Commenting on Aristotle: From Late Antiquity to the Arab Aristotelianism"; Dimitri Gutas, *Greek Thought, Arabic Culture*; and Peter Adamson, *The Arabic Plotinus*. For a discussion of the Syriac translations of Aristotle, a crucial background to the notes I offer here, see John W. Watt, "The Syriac Aristotle."
6. al-Kindī, "Risāla fī kammiyyat kutub Arisṭūṭālīs," 363.
7. al-Kindī, "Letter on the Quantity of Aristotle's Books," 281.
8. Ibn Manẓūr, *Lisān al-ʿArab*, قنا, *qanā*; ثبت, *thabata*.
9. al-Kindī, "Risāla fī kammiyyat kutub Arisṭūṭālīs," 363/281.
10. In the reading I offer of al-Kindī here, and al-Fārābī and Ibn Sīnā in the following sections of this chapter, I learn from Pierre Hadot's discussion of *askēsis*, "the practice of spiritual exercises" ("Spiritual Exercises," 82), which he studies in relation to the Stoa, and, in particular, Seneca and Epictetus: "The Stoics, for instance, declared explicitly that philosophy, for them, was an 'exercise.' In their view, philosophy did not consist in teaching an abstract theory—much less in the exegesis of texts—but rather in the art of living. It is a concrete attitude and determinate lifestyle, which engages the whole of existence" (83). "Philosophy teaches us how to act," Hadot cites Seneca, "not how to talk" (111n9), and, further, as he cites Epictetus in his *Discourses*: "The subject-matter of the art of living (i.e., philosophy) is the life of every individual" (110n11). I've learned, as well, from Hadot, *Plotinus or the Simplicity of Vision*: "Yet philosophy near the end of antiquity was, more than anything else, a way of life" (75); and Hadot, *What Is Ancient Philosophy?*, a text one may read with Peter Brown, *The Making of Late Antiquity*. And see also Claudia Baracchi's most illuminating reading, where, in a discussion of Aristotle's *Metaphysics* 995a12–14: "Therefore, one should already be trained in how to accept

statements, for it is absurd to be seeking science and at the same time the way of acquiring science; and neither of them can be acquired easily"; she notes that "what is thus intimated is a certain impossibility of metaphysics understood as emancipation from *phusis* and, *mutatis mutandis*, of *theōria* understood as transcendence of *praxis*" (*Aristotle's Ethics as First Philosophy*, 9). The Arabic inheritance of late antique practice may be considered in al-Fārābī's discussion of Plato, where, in asking in what "the human being's perfection" consists, and in asking whether "in order to attain the happiness that gives them their ultimate perfection, is it sufficient for the human being to have some or all of these?," and in noting that there is "something else" without which one may not attain perfection, he writes: "Then he [Plato—JS] investigated what this other thing must be. It became evident to him that this other thing, whose attainment is the attainment of happiness, is a certain knowledge and a certain way of life [علم ما وسيرة ما / *ʿilmun mā wa sīratun ma*]" (al-Fārābī, *Falsafat Aflāṭūn* 5–7/*Philosophy of Plato*, 53–54).

11. Ibn Manẓūr, *Lisān al-ʿarab*, ذلك, *dhalika*.

12. Ibn Manẓūr, *Lisān al-ʿarab*, روى, *rawā*.

13. In relation to the poetic and juridical traditions I point to here, see Suzanne Stetkevych, *Abū Tammām and the Poetics of the ʿAbbāsid Age*; Samer Ali, *Arabic Literary Salons*; Lara Harb, *Arabic Poetics*; and Ahmed El Shamsy, *The Canonization of Islamic Law*. I learn, as well, in relation to orality, transmission, language, and practices of knowing in Arabic, from Abdelfattah Kilito, *Les Séances*; Gregor Schoeler, *The Genesis of Literature in Islam*; Shawkat Toorawa, *Ibn Abi Tahir Tayfur and Arabic Writerly Culture*; Houari Touati, *Islam and Travel in the Middle Ages*; Muhsin al-Musawi, *The Medieval Islamic Republic of Letters*; Elias Muhanna, *The World in a Book*; Alexander Key, *Language between God and the Poets*; and Beatrice Gruendler, *The Rise of the Arabic Book*. And please consider, in this frame, Gruendler's discussion of the codex's "gaining acceptance" from the "outgoing eighth and the beginning of the ninth century" (5, 3), in relation to an intercorrelation of writing with orality: "Writing, however, did not do away with orality, not even gradually; instead, the two modes merged with each other in a variety of ways. One might say that Arab book culture embraced and celebrated oral practices" (7), she writes. She continues, outlining the role of transmitters in relation to poetic practice: "Poetry, for instance, the first major form of Arabic literature, relied on human memory as its medium: poets composed it orally and transmitters (*ruwāt*), often apprentice poets themselves, performed it, preserved it, and handed it down" (7). In what follows in this chapter, in relation to the reading I offer of al-Kindī here, of al-Fārābī in relation to pedagogy in logic, and of Ibn Sīnā in relation to his emphasis on modal logic, in particular, I learn from and am thinking with Gruendler's placing an emphasis on "book writing" and what she terms "oral situations" (166), where I try to underline a relation between language and form in philosophical practice.

14. Plotinus, *Uthūlūjīyyā Arisṭūṭālīs*, 134.

15. Plotinus, *Theologia*, 2.291.

16. Plotinus, *Risāla fī al-ʿilm al-ilāhī*, 178/*Epistola de Scientia Divina*, 2.333.

17. I follow the Greek in *Plotini Opera*, 2.332; and the English translation in Plotinus, *The Enneads*, 577.

18. Plotinus, *Risāla fī al-ʿilm al-ilāhī*, 178/*Epistola de Scientia Divina*, 2.333.

19. Plotinus, *Nuṣūṣ mutafarriqa lī Aflūṭīn*, 184/*Dicta Sapientis Graeci*, 2.275.

20. Plotinus, *Uthūlūjīyyā Arisṭūṭālīs*, 112–113.

21. Plotinus, *Theologia*, 2.271.

22. al-Kindī, *Kitāb al-Kindī ilā al-Muʿtaṣim bi-allāh fī al-falsafa al-ūlā*, 1.97/*Al-Kindī's Metaphysics*, 55.

23. Plotinus, *Risāla fī al-ʿilm al-ilāhī*, 178/*Epistola de Scientia Divina*, 2.333.

24. al-Kindī, *Fī al-falsafa al-ūlā*, 113.

25. al-Kindī, *Al-Kindī's Metaphysics*, 67.

26. Proclus, *Proclus Arabus*, 9; and see Proclus, *The Elements of Theology*, 5, prop. 5.

27. al-Kindī, "Risālat al-Kindī fī ḥudūd al-ashyāʾ wa rusūmihā," 169/"Al-Kindī's Letter on the Definitions and Descriptions of Things," 302; al-Kindi, *Fī al-falsafa al-ūlā*, 162/113.

28. al-Kindi, *Fī al-falsafa al-ūlā*, 162/113.

29. al-Kindī, "Risālat al-Kindī fī ḥudūd al-ashyāʾ wa rusūmihā," 169/302.

30. al-Fārābī, *Falsafat Arisṭūṭālīs*, 75–76.

31. al-Fārābī, *Philosophy of Aristotle*, 85.

32. On the privilege of "certainty," in its relation to "demonstration," البرهان, *al-burhān*, in the Arabic philosophical tradition please see the discussion of Dimitri Gutas in "Paul the Persian," where Gutas underlines the transmission of the Alexandrian late antique Aristotelian commentary tradition from Elias to Paul the Persian—whose text is preserved in an Arabic-language translation, which itself was preserved through its transcription in texts of al-Fārābī and the tenth-eleventh-century philosopher Miskawayh—to the Arabic translation of Paul's text, most likely, Gutas underlines, by Abū Bishr Mattā ibn Yūnus, the teacher of al-Fārābī, and then to Miskawayh. In this, Gutas notes that, if in Elias, a sixth-century Greek language commentator, logic is described as "divided" into "what precedes demonstration" (*Categories*, *On Interpretation*, and *Prior Analytics*), "what teaches the very method of demonstration" (*Posterior Analytics*), and what follows this teaching (*Topics*, *Rhetoric*, *Sophistical Refutations*, and *Poetics*), Miskawayh states that "the noblest [*ashraf*—JS] of these books is *Posterior Analytics* [*Kitāb al-burhān*], because it is the primary purpose [of logic]" (242). As Miskawayh also writes, emphasizing the centrality of *Posterior Analytics*, and likely citing Paul: "The first three books [of the *Organon*—JS] introduce it; the last four protect it" (234). For more on the study of logic in Arabic, in its relation to the late antique, Greek-language commentary tradition, see Dimitri Gutas, "The Starting Point of Philosophical Studies," "Aspects of Literary Form and Genre in Arabic Logical Works," as well as Gutas's discussion of "the Neoplatonic school of Alexandria" in *Avicenna and the Aristotelian Tradition*, 228–232; Deborah L. Black, *Logic and Aristotle's* Rhetoric *and* Poetics *in Medieval*

Arabic Philosophy; Ibrahim Madkour, *L'Organon d'Aristote dans le monde arabe*; and, in relation to post-sixteenth-century texts in the practice and study of logic in Arabic, Khaled El-Rouayheb, *Islamic Intellectual History in the Seventeenth Century*.

33. al-Fārābī, *Kitāb al-alfāẓ al-musta'mala fī al-manṭiq*, 111.

34. In this frame, please see the engrossing discussion of pedagogy, in relation to the study of logic, in El-Rouayheb's *Islamic Intellectual History in the Seventeenth Century*, and, in particular, the chapter titled "The Rise of Deep Reading." There, El-Rouayheb offers a contrastive reading of two sets of texts in relation to a transformation from a privilege of "listening" and the "oral," where, "In this pedagogical model listening, discussing, repeating, memorizing, and reciting were of paramount importance" (97) to a "supplementation" of this model and its terms by another, "deep reading," مطالعة عميقة, *muṭāla'a 'amīqa* (121), which was, El-Rouayheb writes, "more impersonal and textual": "In what follows, I present evidence for the emergence of a more impersonal and textual model of the transmission of knowledge in the central Ottoman lands in the seventeenth and eighteenth centuries" (98). In explicating this El-Rouayheb studies an earlier tradition of works on pedagogy, which, since the ninth century, had focused on "the proprieties of student-teacher interaction" as well as "the proper demeanor and conduct expected of student and teacher" (100), and he underlines the twelfth-thirteenth-century jurist Burhān al-Dīn al-Zarnūjī and the thirteenth-fourteenth-century scholar Badr al-Dīn Ibn Jamā'a. "Like Zarnūjī," El-Rouayheb writes of Ibn Jamā'a, "he stressed that knowledge should be taken from scholars, not from books" (105). He contrasts this manner of thinking about "learning," تعلّم, *ta'allum*, and "knowledge," علم, *'ilm*, which "were paradigmatic for a number of later treatments of education" (105), with two later works, of the seventeenth-century scholar Aḥmed ibn Lütfallāh Mevlevī, who is known as Müneccimbāsī, and the seventeenth-eighteenth-century scholar Meḥmed Sāçaklīzāde. In these, the practice of "listening," سمع, *sam'*, becomes a particular moment in a more general practice of pedagogical formation; in Müneccimbāsī's treatise on آداب المطالعة, *ādāb muṭāla'a*, "the proper manner of perusing books," a student, El-Rouayheb explains, "in the earliest stages of seeking knowledge is not in a position to engage in *muṭāla'a* and derive meanings from written expressions; rather his concern is to take what he seeks from the mouths of men" (109). In this, and as a preparation provided through the "instrumental disciplines," of which El-Rouayheb outlines "syntax, logic, dialectic, and semantics-rhetoric" (109), a new sense of reading is also given. Referring to the works of Müneccimbāsī and Sāçaklīzāde, El-Rouayheb writes, "They both evince a distinct shift of emphasis away from the student-teacher relationship and the oral-aural model for the transmission of knowledge, and focus instead on the proper reading of texts" (125). If this shift temporally correlates with the institution of capitalism in the Ottoman empire, "after the sixteenth century" (128), I notice as well that, through the transformations El-Rouayheb so meticulously describes, a sense of language, a practice of being and life, which I've

outlined in al-Fārābī's treatises, is carried forward, where a shift can also suggest a persistence, a certain carrying on.

35. al-Fārābī, *Kitāb al-alfāẓ*, 96.

36. Aristotle, *Posterior Analytics*, trans. Hugh Tredennick and E. S. Forster; and see also the English-language translation offered by Jonathan Barnes.

37. Aristotle, *Kitāb 'Anūlūṭīqā al-awākhir,'* 71b17–19.

38. The biographical notice on Aristotle in the historian al-Qifṭī remains instructive. If at the opening of his notice al-Qifṭī underlines that Aristotle was "the first to arrive at the art of demonstration [البرهان/*al-burhān*], among all of the arts of logic," and that he "made these arts a tool for the theoretical sciences, to the extent that he named them 'the art of logic' [وجعلها آلة للعلوم النظرية حتى لقب بصناعة المنطق/*wa ja'alahā āla lil-'ulūm al-niẓariyya ḥattā laqaba bi-ṣinā'at al-manṭiq*]," and if he only then notes of Aristotle that "he has, in all of the philosophical sciences, distinguished books" (al-Qifṭī, *Ikhbār al-'ulamā'*, 22), this points not only to the priority of demonstration in relation to logic, but also to the manner of comportment and the sort of doing, the form of life, which the practice of demonstration occasions, where this manner, acquired through the discipline and practice of logic, is presumed in and for philosophy. And so if there is a priority of demonstration, as al-Qifṭī presumes, the listing of the books of the *Organon*, later in the same notice, preserves their standard order in the tradition of the late antique study of logic.

39. The reading I offer of the term *ḥikma*, in its relation to *manṭiq*, "logic," learns from the discussion of Frank Griffel, who underlines, in relation to Ibn Sīnā, that "whereas Avicenna's philosophy is an expression of the process of appropriation in which the Greek origins of many of his teachings are clearly visible and even stressed, al-Ghazālī, who adopted and adapted many of Avicenna's teachings, obscured their origins and thus contributed to—and maybe even initiated—the process of naturalization" (*The Formation of Post-Classical Philosophy in Islam*, 7). If, in this, "The movement of *falsafa* can thus be regarded as the continuation of Greek philosophy in Arabic" (7), "subsequently, the appropriated Greek science of philosophy becomes naturalized as *ḥikma*" (7–8). Griffel goes on to underline that "in his *Tahāfut al-falāsifa* [*The Precipitance of the Philosophers*], al-Ghazālī uses the word *falsafa* to describe the kind of Aristotelianism that is taught in the books of Avicenna" (9), and, further, that "starting with al-Ghazālī's *Tahāfut*, the Arabic (and Persian) word *falsafa* meant Avicennism" (10). Griffel explains, as well, that if "in earlier works of philosophy the word *ḥikma* had always existed as an alternative name for philosophy" (101), and that if, in the post-Ghazālīan context the understanding of "philosophy" as "a distinct set of teachings" (106) persisted in the understanding of what *falsafa* was, in two other senses—as "a universal science," in its relation to logic, and "as a scholarly tradition among many" (106)—"philosophy" was referred to by the name *ḥikma*. The understanding of philosophy as a practice, carried through its sense as "a universal science defined by the method of *burhān* (*apodeixis*)" (97), persists in the "post-Classical" texts Griffel studies, where the sense of philosophy as a particular manner, and as a form or way of life, made manifest in

al-Fārābī's pedagogical manuals on logic, and in relation to the term *ḥikma*, is presumed. And please consider also, in this frame, Richard M. Frank's discussion of al-Ghazālī in relation to Ibn Sīnā, where Frank outlines that if, on one hand, al-Ghazālī's language is "quasi-Avicennan" (*Creation and the Cosmic System*, 37), and if "with the phrase 'necessarily existent in all its aspects,'" as he writes, "al-Ghazālī would seem intentionally to mimic the language of Avicenna" (72), at the same time, "'*Wājibah*,' moreover, is hardly to be taken as a mere synonym for '*qadīmah*'" (76), as it would be if al-Ghazālī were presuming the "traditional Ash'arite doctrine" (37), to which Frank also refers. Frank underlines, as well, a certain generalization of Ibn Sīnā's language, his terminological formulations, in al-Ghazālī's exposition of the relations among God, creation, and world: "The finality of the created universe, sc., the optimum good of created beings," he further explains, glossing al-Ghazālī, "is grounded not in God's goodness and wisdom but in the natures of the contingent essences that are given for Him as possible objects of His action. God chooses but has no choice. On the contrary, because of His liberality and justice He wills necessarily to create what has to be (*mā yanbaghī*) 'as it has to be and in the measure that has to be'" (85).

40. Ibn Rushd, *Tafsīr mā ba'd al-ṭabī'a*, 2.699; 2.697.

41. Aristotle, *Kitāb 'Anūlūṭīqā al-awākhir*,' 71b19–22.

42. Aristotle, *Kitāb 'Anūlūṭīqā al-awākhir*,' 71b23–24.

43. And please consider the gloss Ibn Rushd provides on these passages in *Posterior Analytics*: "Whoever admits the existence of demonstration must, of necessity, acknowledge that there are principles that are known in themselves. This is to say: If it is necessary to know the premises of a demonstration, we must know them through an intermediary or without an intermediary. If they are known through an intermediary, the question returns, also, to that intermediary—is it known in itself or through an intermediary? The matter will either continue without end, in all soundness, and there will not be demonstration at all, or there will be principles that are known in themselves, or there will be a vicious circle. We do not wish to yield to the Sophists, who hold that the principles of demonstration are not known through something other than themselves. Instead, we say that they are known through reason, which is what comprehends the parts of a proposition, which are known in themselves" (Ibn Rushd, *Talkhīṣ kitāb al-burhān*, 44, para. 13). I notice only that, if Ibn Rushd argues, in this passage, against "the Sophists," and if they are those who argue that "the principles of demonstration are not known through something other than themselves," he does not wish to suggest that these are known through themselves, or through another principle, but instead through "reason," العقل, *al-'aql*, which is, he explains, what comprehends the structure and content of a "proposition." It is as if "reason," in this frame, is substituted for what Aristotle, and al-Fārābī, called a premise which may not be demonstrated, and so one might say that the structure of the argument is preserved, as Ibn Rushd displaces "principle" with "reason," and as "reason" becomes a discursive form, a practice subsumed within the more general sociality of philosophical argument I've outlined.

44. al-Fārābī, *Falsafat Arisṭūṭālīs*, 75 / *Philosophy of Aristotle*, 85.

45. Please see, for al-Fārābī's discussion of سيرة ما, *sīratun mā*, al-Fārābī, *Falsafat Aflāṭūn* 5–7 / *Philosophy of Plato*, 53–54; and note 10, above.

46. al-Shahrastānī, *al-Milal wa al-niḥal*, 498. In this sense, al-Fārābī's writings may be considered to be a kind of translation, in the sense in which Ḥunayn Ibn Isḥāq, the father of Isḥāq ibn Ḥunayn, the translator of *Posterior Analytics* into Syriac, spoke of the sort of language practice, which translation is. "He said," al-Bayhaqī writes of Ḥunayn, "Whoever lays down a science or an art [من وضع علماً وصناعةً / *man waḍʿa ʿilman wa ṣināʿatan*], it is as if they were like one who builds a house. And whoever explains or interprets that foundation [ومن شرح وفسّر ذلك الأصل / *wa man sharaḥa wa fassara dhālik al-aṣl*], it is as if they were like one who coats its surface with clay and whitewashes it. For the one who whitewashes a house and sweeps it out is not like the one who builds it [وليس من جصّص داراً وكنسها كمن بناها / *wa laysa man jaṣṣaṣa dāran wa kanasahā ka man banāhā*] (*Tārīkh ḥukamāʾ al-Islām*, 18). If this passage suggests an unlikeness of the one who coats with clay and whitewashes, on the one hand, and the one who builds, on the other, and if the latter may seem primary and the former secondary, a working with the materials made available by the first, there is, at the same time, a doing with matter, which destabilizes a distinction between what is more originary and what less, between "laying down" a "science or an art," on one hand, and "explaining" or "interpreting" it: a destabilization which imparts an indetermined understanding of the relation between "original" and "derivative" in "translation," نقل, *naql*, as well: "He was," al-Bayhaqī notes, "the first who interpreted the Greek language, and carried it over to Syriac and Arabic [كان أوّل من فسّر اللغة اليونانية، ونقلها إلى السريانية والعربية / *kān awwal man fassara al-lugha al-yunāniyya, wa naqalahā ilā al-surīyāniyya wa al-ʿarabiyya*]. There was not at this time, after Alexander, a person more knowledgeable than him in Arabic or in Greek" (16).

47. al-Fārābī, *Kitāb al-alfāẓ al-mustaʿmala fī al-manṭiq*, 46.

48. al-Fārābī, *Kitāb al-ḥurūf*, 165.

49. Aristotle, *Kitāb Arisṭūṭālīs al-musammā 'Qāṭīghūrīyā,' ayy 'al-Maqūlāt,'* 5.2a11–18. Please note that it was Ḥunayn ibn Isḥāq, as al-Sijistānī records it, who recommended to his son Isḥāq ibn Ḥunayn that he study *Categories*. After asking his father, in relation to the "formation" or "training," تهيّؤ, *tahayyuʾ*, required of one who would wish to be prepared to "receive knowledge," لقبول العلم, *li-qubūl al-ʿilm*, Ḥunayn notes that one ought study: "The matter which, as you know, the Greek terms 'lūgus,' and which the Arab terms, in some places, 'speech' [نطق / *nuṭq*], and he therefore names the human being from this term, calling it 'a speaking being,' and which the Arab calls in other places 'statement' [قولاً / *qawlan*], yet it is not their custom to derive the name of the human being from the term 'statement' as it is the custom of the Greek to do so: from 'lūgus' he derives 'lūghutis.' And the Greek terms the study of this part of the human being, which is the most noble of its parts, 'the study of lūghus' [نظراً لوغسياً / *naẓran lūghusīyyan*], derived from 'lūghus,' or 'statement,' and this is what the Arab terms 'the study of speech' [نظراً منطقياً / *naẓran manṭiqiyyan*]" (*Ṣiwan al-ḥikma*, 280–281). Al-Sijistānī continues to report that Isḥāq

then asks: "If the books contained within this art and those that describe it are many, direct me to a book and the places within it with which I must first begin." Ḥunayn replies: "You should begin with the book *Qāṭīghūrīyās* of the Philosopher." "Why," Isḥāq asks, "have you chosen for me the book *Qāṭīghūrīyās*, firstly, and why a book of the Philosopher?" Ḥunayn explains: "As for the book *Qāṭīghūrīyās*, it is the beginning of this science. And as for the Philosopher, there is no one other than him present at this time who comprehends this science's intended meaning" (281). "Logic," منطق, *manṭiq*, a manner of knowing given through a practice of asking, is rendered, by al-Sijistānī, as a manner of "study" that addresses and is formulated in language. We might say that logic is an occasion for the formation of a sort of being which, in "training"—as al-Kindī's letter underlined—occasions a sociality in language through which beings come to be what they are.

50. al-Fārābī, *Kitāb al-ḥurūf*, 166–167.

51. Porphyry, *Iysāghūjī Furfūrīūs*, 1026–1027. And please see: "For to the question, 'What sort of thing is man?' we reply, 'Rational' [ἐν γὰρ τῷ ἐρωτᾶν ποῖόν τί ἐστιν ὁ ἄνθρωπὸσ φαμεν ὅτι λογιχόν/*en gar tō erōtan poion ti estin ho anthrōpos phamen hoti logichon*]"; and to the question 'What sort of thing is a crow?' we reply, 'Black.' Rational is a difference, black is an accident. When, however, we are asked what man is, we answer, 'Animal' [ζῷον/*zōon*]. Animal is the genus of man" (Porphyry, *Isagoge*, trans. Edward W. Warren, 32/*Porphuriou Eisagōge*, 3; and compare the English rendering in Porphyry, *Introduction*, trans. Jonathan Barnes, 4-5). Boethius's sixth-century Latin translation of Porphyry's *Isagoge* privileges the terms reproduced in Warren and Barnes, in the rendering of *logichon* as "rational" and *zōon* as "animal," a translation which sets in motion the manner of understanding what "language" and a "living being" are, which is carried and reproduced, at once preserved and transmuted, in the tradition I called, in chapter 1, "settler life": "Interroganti enim, qualis est homo, dicimus rationalis, et in eo quod qualis est corvus dicimus quoniam niger; est autem rationale quidem differentia, nigrum ver accidens. Quando autem quid est homo interrogamur, animal respondemus; erat autem hominis genus animal" (*Porphyrii Introductio in Aristotelis Categorias a Boethio Translata*, 28).

52. And please also consider the sixth-century Greek-language commentator Ammonius, who explains of Aristotle, in relation to the term "substance," οὐσία, *ousia*, that "he says of this substance that some is primary and some secondary, calling the particular primary and the universal secondary" (*On Aristotle Categories*, 46), as he points, as well, to a "commonality" generated through the reflection on "substance," where "secondary substance," "universals," occasion a shared aspect—"genus" and "species"—among things: "But with primary and secondary substance there is a commonality not only of name but also of definition. For Socrates, who is a primary substance, is called by the name of the secondary, that is, by the name 'human being'; moreover, Socrates and the universal *human being* also have the same definition" (49). One might say that, in this, language occasions a manner of relationality—in the tradition of thinking what is "common" in relation to universals, where "Socrates, who is a primary substance, is called by the name of the

secondary"—which, if it is, in part, reiterated through al-Fārābī, as I underline in the next section of this chapter, where al-Fārābī speaks of what is "common," عام, *ʿām*, it also points to a sense of lingual formulation, in the late antique commentary tradition, which persists across languages.

53. al-Fārābī, *Kitāb al-ḥurūf*, 100–101.

54. al-Fārābī, *Risāla fī aghrāḍ mā baʿd al-ṭabīʿa*, 35.

55. al-Fārābī, "Letter on the Aims of Aristotle's *Metaphysics*," 79; I occasionally modify this translation following Amos Bertolacci in *The Reception of Aristotle's* Metaphysics *in Avicenna's* Kitāb al-Shifāʾ, 68.

56. al-Fārābī, *Risāla fī aghrāḍ mā baʿd al-ṭabīʿa*, 35/"Letter on the Aims of Aristotle's *Metaphysics*," 79; and Bertolacci, *The Reception of Aristotle's* Metaphysics, 68.

57. And please see Bertolacci's translation of the passage in al-Fārābī I'm considering here, where he renders داخلا في, *dākhilan fī*, which I've translated as "contained within," as "belongs to": "The divine science ought to belong to this [universal] science because God is a principle of the absolute existent, not of one existent to the exclusion of another" (*The Reception of Aristotle's* Metaphysics, 68).

58. al-Fārābī, *Risāla fī aghrāḍ mā baʿd al-ṭabīʿa*, 37/81.

59. al-Fārābī, *Iḥṣāʾ al-ʿulūm*, 61.

60. And please also consider the sentences, which immediately follow the passage I've translated above, in *Iḥṣāʾ al-ʿulūm*: "And then it makes known how the beings were originated from him, and how they acquired their being from him. And then it investigates the order of beings, and how that order came to be, and through what thing each rank is suited to be at the level at which it is, and it clarifies their arrangement and connection to each other, and through what thing this order and arrangement are formed" (62). If one may read these passages in relation to the pages on "emanation" in al-Fārābī's *Mabādiʾ ārāʾ ahl al-madīna al-fāḍila*, where al-Fārābī underlines that "the first being is the cause of the being of all of the other beings," and where he also states that "the substance of the first being is a substance from which every being emanates [يفيض عنه كل وجود/*yafīḍ ʿanhu kull wujūd*], however it may be, whether perfect or deficient" (57, 95), I notice that this explication can, even as al-Fārābī notes that the first "is different in its substance from everything else" (59), decompose the distinctions it seems also to affirm, as it carries the tradition of indistinction or inidenticality, it seems to guard against.

61. Ibn Sīnā, *al-Ishārāt wa-al-tanbīhāt, al-Ilāhiyyāt*, 3.4.9.19. I follow and occasionally modify the translation in *Ibn Sīnā's Remarks and Admonitions: Physics and Metaphysics*, translated by Shams C. Inati. I cite this text by part, class (each part is divided into "classes," *anmāṭ* [sing., *namaṭ*]), chapter, and by the page number of the Arabic edition.

62. al-Ṭūsī, *Sharḥ al-ishārāt wa-al-tanbīhāt, al-Ilāhiyyāt*, 19.

63. Ibn Sīnā, *al-Ishārāt wa-al-tanbīhāt, al-Ilāhiyyāt*, 3.4.10.20.

64. And please consider that, in response to a question regarding the proper title of *Categories*, Porphyry, the third-century Greek-language editor and commentator, born in Tyre, explained that it "definitely ought not to be given the titles *On the*

Genera of Being or *On the Ten Genera*," since "beings and their genera and species, and differentiae are things, not words" (*On Aristotle Categories*, 32). He clarifies, explaining in relation to Aristotle's ten categories that "if the combination of these is what produces an affirmation, and an affirmation is something that has its existence as significant speech and as a declarative sentence, then the treatise cannot be about the genera of being nor about things *qua* things, but instead is about words that are used to signify things" (32–33). Such a manner of using words is, in *Categories*, termed "predication," the title of the work. As Porphyry further explains, "He [Aristotle] adopted the word, and chose to call those utterances in which significant expressions are applied to things, 'predications'" (30–31), "katēgoriai," as the translator of the English edition of Porphyry's commentary notes. I underline only, that if Porphyry affirms a distinction between statements about language and statements about being—or statements about "words" and "things"—his description of what predication is convolutes that distinction, suggesting an implication of language in the reflection on being, and of logic with ontology, which the tradition in which Ibn Sīnā writes may be said to inherit.

65. Ibn Sīnā, *Kitāb al-Shifā', al-Ilāhiyyāt* (Cairo, 1960) and Avicenna (Ibn Sīnā), *The Metaphysics of The Healing*, translated by Michael Marmura, 1.1.8.5. I follow and occasionally modify Marmura's translation. I cite this text by book, chapter, paragraph number (as the paragraphs have been numbered in Marmura's English-Arabic facing-page edition) and by the pagination of the 1960 Arabic edition.

66. And please consider the discussion of necessity, possibility, and impossibility in the *Logic* of *Remarks and Admonitions*. Ibn Sīnā outlines two senses of the term "possibility," the first of which is "that which accompanies the negation of the necessity of non-existence," where "the negation of the necessity of non-existence" is "the impossibility attributed to a subject," and according to which "that which is not possible is, then, impossible," while the second of which is "that which accompanies the negation of both the necessity of non-existence and the necessity of existence, attributed to a subject, in accordance with the proper sense that has been handed down to us" (1.4.3.272). The second sense "is applicable to a thing," he goes on, "in both its affirmation and its denial, so that it is possible for the thing to be, and possible for the thing to not be, or, that it is not impossible for it to be and not impossible for it not to be" (1.4.3.272). In this, as Ibn Sīnā continues, he observes that, unlike in the first understanding of possibility, where a thing is either "possible" or "impossible," according to the second meaning, there are three modes: "possible," "impossible," and "necessary": "Since possibility in the second sense is applicable to both aspects of a thing," which is to say, "the negation of both the necessity of non-existence and the necessity of existence" of a thing, "this sense is properly designated by the name 'possibility,' and what is necessary is not comprehended by this designation [فصار الواجب لا يدخل فيه/*fa ṣāra al-wājib lā yadkhul fīhi*]. According to this, things are either possible, necessary, or impossible" (1.4.3.273). I follow and occasionally modify the translation in *Ibn Sīnā's Remarks and Admonitions, Part One: Logic*, translated by Shams C. Inati. I cite this text by

part, method (each part is divided into "methods," *nuhūj* [sing., *nahj*]), chapter, and the page number of the Arabic edition.

67. Ibn Sīnā, *Kitāb al-Shifā', al-Manṭiq, al-Burhān*, 3.1.194. I cite this text by book, chapter, and page. The citation I offer here indexes book 3, chapter 1, page 194.

68. And please see the related passages in the *Logic* of *Remarks and Admonitions*, where Ibn Sīnā, in discussing "the sciences" explains that "for every one of the sciences, there is one or more things appropriate to it and whose state or states we study," and where he notes that "for every science there are principles and questions," that "principles," المبادئ, *al-mabādi'*, are "the definitions and premises of which the syllogisms of the science are composed," that "premises," المقدّمات, *al-muqaddimāt*, are either "propositions that must be accepted [واجبة القبول/*wājiba al-qubūl*]," "propositions that are admitted by virtue of confidence in the teacher [على سبيل حسن الظنّ بالمعلّم/*'alā sabīl ḥusn al-ẓann bi al-mu'allim*]," or "propositions that are admitted for the time being [في الوقت/*fī al-waqt*], until they are made evident," and, finally, where he observes that since the determination of the validity of a principle in relation to a science cannot be determined within that science, "the demonstration for any posited principle in a science is drawn from another science [فكل أصل موضوع في علم فإنّ البرهان عليه من علم آخر/*fa kull aṣl mawḍū' fī 'ilmin fa inna al-burhān 'alayhi min 'ilm ākhar*]" (Ibn Sīnā, *al-Ishārāt wa al-tanbīhāt, al-Manṭiq*, 1.9.3.474–477). And consider also Aileen R. Das, *Galen and the Arabic Reception of Plato's* Timaeus, where Das notes Ibn Sīnā's delimitation of "medicine," الطبّ, al-*ṭibb*, in a study of Ibn Sīnā's *al-Qānūn fī al-ṭibb*, in relation to "the science of metaphysics," علم ما بعد الطبيعة, *'ilm mā ba'd al-ṭabī'a*, in which the demonstration of the principles of any particular science is grounded, as Ibn Sīna teaches (145ff.).

69. Ibn Sīnā, *Kitāb al-Shifā', al-Manṭiq, al-Burhān*, 2.10.184.

70. Ibn Sīnā, *Kitāb al-Shifā', al-Ilāhiyyāt*, 1.1.7.4.

71. "There is a science which studies being insofar as it is being [ἔστιν ἐπιστήμη τις ἣ θεορεῖ τὸ ὂν ᾗ ὂν/*estin episteme tis hē theorei to on hē on*], and the properties inherent in it in virtue of its own nature. This science is not the same as any of the so-called particular sciences, for none of the others contemplates being generally insofar as it is being [καθόλου περὶ τοῦ ὄντος ᾗ ὂν/*katholou peri tou ontos hē on*]; they divide off some portion of it and study the attribute of this portion, as do for example the mathematical sciences" (Aristotle, *Metaphysics* 10003a20–27).

72. Aristotle, *Metaphysics* 10028b3–5. And consider the observation of Ibrahim Madkour, that "Ibn Sina fully adopted the Aristotelian theory of demonstration. His interpretation of *Posterior Analytics* is perhaps the most literal and servile of his commentaries on the *Organon*" (*L'Organon d'Aristote dans le monde arabe*, 222). And yet one might note that Ibn Sīnā's emphasis on necessity in relation to possibility, and the crossing-over of these terms with those through which he explicates demonstration, suggest, as I'll underline below, an interpenetration of logic with ontology, and an illegibility between them, which we may also think of as a certain manner of reading the Aristotelian logical books, in particular. And see

also Madkour's note, in relation to "the most important of the Arab philosophers," that "instead of separate logic from the other branches of philosophy, as was done in late antiquity and Western scholasticism, they related it, on the contrary, to properly physical and metaphysical questions, such as the theory of causality and the problem of the necessary and the contingent" (52). In a different frame, please consider the observation of Damien Janos, who underlines, compellingly, that if there is, in Ibn Sīna, an "ontologization of a matrix of logical distinctions," this suggests an "interface" between "the epistemological and ontological planes," "planes" which are, Janos writes, "inextricably meshed in Avicenna's writings" (*Avicenna on the Ontology of Pure Quiddity*, 7, 67, 69).

73. Ibn Sīnā, *Kitāb al-Shifā', al-Ilāhiyyāt*, 1.6.3.38.

74. See the autobiographical text of Ibn Sīnā's, *Sīrat al-shaykh al-ra'īs*, which was completed by his student al-Juzjānī, where Ibn Sīna underlines that he was not able to understand the "aim,"غرض, *gharaḍ*, of Aristotle's *Metaphysics*—"I read the *Metaphysics* but did not understand its content and the aim of its author was obscure to me even as I reread it forty times and memorized it"—until reading al-Fārābī's "Letter on the Aims of Aristotle's *Metaphysics*." After having been offered it by a bookseller, Ibn Sīnā explains, "I returned to my home and hastened to read it, and all at once the aims of that book were disclosed to me [فانفتح عليّ في الوقت أغراض ذلك الكتاب/*fa infataḥa ʿalayya fī al-waqt aghraḍ dhālik al-kitāb*] because I had memorized it by heart" (*Sīrat al-shaykh al-ra'īs*, 34). I follow and slightly modify the translation in Gutas, *Avicenna and the Aristotelian Tradition*, 17–18; and see the discussion at 285, and 270–288.

75. Ibn Sīnā, *Sharḥ kitāb ḥarf al-lām*, 23.

76. Themistius, *Min Sharḥ Thāmisṭūs li-ḥarf al-lām*, 13.

77. Aristotle, *Faṣl fī ḥarf al-lām min kitāb mā baʿd al-ṭabīʿa' li-Arisṭūṭālīs*, 1071b5. On the Arabic translation of *Book Lambda* see Ibn al-Nadīm, *al-Fihrist*, 352.

78. Themistius, *Min Sharḥ Thāmisṭūs li-ḥarf al-lām*, 18–19.

79. Ibn Sīnā, *Sharḥ kitāb ḥarf al-lām*, 23.

80. Ibn Sīnā, *Kitāb al-Shifā', al-Ilāhiyyāt*, 8.7.1.363.

81. Please see the discussion of Ibn Sīnā, in relation to necessity, causality, emanation, and being in Peter Adamson, "From the Necessary Existent to God," where Adamson observes, in relation to these, that Avicenna "has shown that there is a necessary existent that is the cause for the existence of contingent things" (172), and further that, at the same time, the necessary being has a ماهية, *māhiyya*, "whatness" or "quiddity," and yet only insofar as this "whatness" or "quiddity" is its "sheer existence" (175); and Stephen Menn, "Avicenna's Metaphysics," where he underlines, in contrast to *Book Lambda* of *Metaphysics*, in which, as Menn summarizes, "Aristotle argues for God primarily as a first cause of motion," that "it is very important for Avicenna to argue for God instead as a first cause of *being*" (146), and where, as well, in relation to *wujūd*, "being," Menn observes that "God does not *have* this *wujūd*, but *is* this *wujūd*" (157).

82. Ibn Sīnā, *Kitāb al-Shifā', al-Ilāhiyyāt*, 9.4.3.402.

83. And consider, as well, that in his discussion of "the recent philosophers," אלמתאכרין מנ אלפלאספה, *al-muta'akhirīn min al-falāsifa*, a terminological formulation

that refers to the philosophical language of Ibn Sīnā as it became a locus for the reading of Aristotle, Ibn Maymūn (Maimonides) explains that "Aristotle says, concerning that which exists in general [פי אלוגוד בגמלתה / *fī al-wujūd bi jumlatihi*], that this particular thing necessarily proceeds from that and so forth until the series ends with the first cause [אלי אן ינתהי ללעלה אלאולי / *ilā an yantahī lil-ʿilla al-ūlā*], as he himself says, or the first intellect [אלעקל אלאול / al-ʿaql al-awwal] or however you may wish to call it. All of us aim at one and the same principle [מבדא / *mabdaʾ*]. But he holds, as I have recounted to you, the necessity of everything other than it proceeding from it [לזום קל מא סואה ענה / *luzūm kull mā sawāhu ʿanhu*]" (*Dalālat al-ḥāʾirīn*, 2.47–48 / *Guide for the Perplexed*, 2.316).

84. Ibn Sīnā, *Kitāb al-Shifāʾ*, *al-Ilāhiyyāt*, 8.7.5.364.

85. And please consider, on "necessary" and "possible" being, Ibn Sīnā, *al-Najāt*, *al-Ilāhiyyāt*, 262–263: "It has become clear that anything whose being is necessary through another [واجب الوجود بغيره /*wājib al-wujūd bi ghayrihi*], its being is possible in itself [ممكن الوجود بذاته /*mumkin al-wujūd bi-thātihi*]. This can be inverted: Anything whose being is possible in itself, if it comes to be that it is, it is necessary in being through another. For it is necessary that either it possess being in actuality or that it does not. And it is impossible that it does not possess being in actuality, for if it did not possess being in actuality its being would be impossible, and so what remains is that it is the case that it possesses being in actuality, for then either its being is necessary or it is not. And that whose being is not necessary is still possible, and its being is not distinguished, in this perspective, from its non-being. There is no difference between this state [حالة/*ḥāla*] and the first, because it was, before coming to be, possible in being, and now it is in the state it had been in."

86. Ibn Sīnā, *Kitāb al-Shifāʾ*, *al-Ilāhiyyāt*, 9.4.4.403.

87. Please see, for a discussion of causality in Ibn Sīna, in relation to contingent beings and the necessary being, "The Metaphysics of Efficient Causality in Avicenna," where Michael Marmura underlines, in relation to contingent beings, that "the existing contingent, though in itself possible, must become necessary through its cause and 'with respect to it'" (180); and yet the necessary being is not necessary through its relation to the beings of which it is the cause, but is instead the cause of the being of such beings, without its being dependent on them, a relation explicated in Ibn Sīnā, as I've outlined in this chapter, in relation to "emanation": "If, then," Marmura explains, "the world proceeds from God in successive steps, the model for the cause-effect relation must be modified accordingly. From the One, from God, as Avicenna proclaims, only one proceeds. The one direct effect of divine causality is the first celestial intelligence from which the rest of creation successively emanates. This one effect is necessitated by God" (176).

88. Ibn Sīnā, *Kitāb al-Shifāʾ*, *al-Ilāhiyyāt*, 9.4.4.403.

89. Ibn Sīnā, *al-Ishārāt wa-al-tanbīhāt*, *al-Ilāhiyyāt*, 3.6.5.125.

90. Ibn Sīnā, *Kitāb al-Shifāʾ*, *al-Ilāhiyyāt*, 8.7.12.367

91. And please note, as well, that *inna*, as Ibn Jinnī explains in his tenth-century handbook of Arabic grammar, in relation to a discussion of "*inna* and its sisters,"

which are "*inna, anna, ka'anna, lākinna, layta,* and *la'alla,*" that "each of these particles has a subject [مبتدأ/*mubtada'*] and a predicate [خبر/*khabar*], that the subject takes a *naṣab* ending, and becomes its noun-subject [إسمها/*ismahā*], and the predicate takes the *raf'* ending, and becomes its *khabar* [خبرها/*khabarahā*]. Its *ism* resembles that which is acted upon, and its *khabar* resembles the subject of a verb" (*al-Lum' fī al-'arabiyya*, 92); the meaning of both *inna* and *anna*, both of which may be rendered as "that," is "the assertion of a precise relation," تحقيق, *taḥqīq* (93). At the same time, al-Fārābī explains, in *Kitāb al-ḥurūf*, that "the meaning of *inna* is stability, permanence, completeness, and firmness in being and in the knowledge of a thing." He goes on: "The philosophers therefore call complete being the 'thatness' of a thing [إنّية الشيء / *inniyyat al-shay'*]—what is, in its particularity, its whatness [وهو بعينه ماهيته / *wa huwwa bi-'aynihi māhiyyatuhu*]—and they say 'what is the thatness of a thing' meaning what is its most complete being, and this is its whatness, however the particles *inna* and *anna* are only used to state something, not to ask a question" (61). I might only observe that a particle, "inna," in its transformation in the Arabic philosophical tradition, mutates the stating of a relation between subject and predicate in grammar into a manner of philosophical elaboration, where, if "thatness" points to what is stable, permanent, complete, and firm, this can only be stated in a manner that reiterates the linguistic dimension of philosophical assertion.

92. And please see, in *The Metaphysics of The Healing*: "Every being has a species of relation and reference toward other beings, and in particular the being from whom all being emanates. But what we mean by our statement that this being is one in essence and does not become multiple is that it is as such in its essence. If, thereafter, any positive and negative relations become attendant on it, these are necessary concomitants [لوازم / *lawāzim*] of the essence that are caused by the essence. They exist after [بعد / *ba'd*] the being of the essence, do not render the essence subsistent, and are not parts of it" (Ibn Sīnā, *Kitāb al-Shifā', al-Ilāhiyyāt*, 8.4.2.344).

93. Ibn Sīna, *Kitāb al-Shifā', al-Manṭiq, al-Burhān*, 2.1.118.

94. And please see the discussion of Tiana Koutzarova, who underlines, in relation to Ibn Sīnā, that "the absolute simplicity of God, then, in metaphysics, is known, insofar as it is possible for human beings, by means of the most originary of all of God's attributes, namely 'necessity'" (*Das Transzendentale bei Ibn Sīnā*, 394), even as I wish to ask, regarding this "most originary" or "most particular," "eigentümlichsten," attribute, whether Ibn Sīnā's writing of it points to a manner of philosophical formulation where "necessity" is a terminological moment that blurs or indistinguishes the terms on which philosophical explication can also seem to rely, and where, in this, "the necessary being" in its "absolute simplicity," "schlechthinnige Einfachheit," which Koutzarova glosses as "basāta," becomes an inessential linguistic form.

95. Ibn Sīnā, *Kitāb al-Shifā', al-Ilāhiyyāt*, 9.1.1.373.

96. Aristotle, *Metaphysics* 996b27–31: "Again, with respect to the demonstrative principles as well, it may be disputed whether they too are the objects of one science or of several. By demonstrative I mean the common notions [τὰς κοινὰς δόξας/*tas*

koinas doxas] from which all demonstration proceeds, e.g. 'everything must be either affirmed or denied' [πᾶν ἀναγκαῖον ἢ φάναι ἢ ἀποφάναι/*pan anagkaion ē phanai ē apophanai*], and 'it is impossible at once to be and to not be' [ἀδύνατον ἅμα εἶναι καὶ μὴ εἶναι/*adunaton hama einai kai mē einai*], and all other such premises"; and see as well *Metaphysics* 1005b19–20, where Aristotle states what he calls "the most certain of all principles": "It is impossible for the same attribute at once to belong and not to belong to the same thing and the same relation." I wish to underline: If these "common notions" have been taken to affirm a particular sense of being, they partake in a manner of thought that is, Claudia Baracchi has noticed, a kind of "habit" (*Aristotle's Ethics as First Philosophy*, 171, 187), both a manner of comportment and a form of life, which gives us, as I've suggested reading al-Kindī, al-Fārābī, and Ibn Sīnā, to think these notions otherwise, where they decompose the privilege they can seem to advance.

97. Please see the discussion of Robert Wisnovsky, in *Avicenna's Metaphysics in Context*, where he underlines, in relation to the "perfection" of the necessary being, where this being is at once "perfect," تامّ, *tāmm*, and, borrowing the language of the Arabic Plotinus, فوق التمام, *fawq al-tamām*, "above perfection," a "tension" (188) in Ibn Sīnā. If "Avicenna starts by saying that God is perfect (*tāmm*), in the sense that He does not lack anything and is by implication causally self-sufficient," as Wisnovsky explains, "he then adds that God is in fact 'above perfection' (*fawq al-tamām*), by which Avicenna seems to mean that God is not simply full of existence and hence causally self-sufficient, but is also overflowing with existence, and hence a cause of others" (188); and 186–196, where Wisnovsky discusses several related passages in *Theology of Aristotle*; as well as the discussion of *fawq al-tamām* in *Theology of Aristotle* in Adamson, *The Arabic Plotinus*, 121–22, and Adamson's discussion of "emanation" in Ibn Sīnā, 141, and 137–142. These passages, in relation to *Theology of Aristotle*, are briefly discussed in Amos Bertolacci, *The Reception of Aristotle's* Metaphysics *in Avicenna's* Kitāb al-Shifāʾ, 455–457, as well as "the doctrine according to which God knows the things of the world by knowing Himself as their principle" (456), in relation to which I try to draw out, in conversation with Wisnovsky's analysis, as well as Adamson's and Menn's notes, the aporetic form of the sense of relation, as well as the insubstantial sense of the necessary being, in the passages in Ibn Sīnā I've outlined.

3. Insurgence: A Poetics of Things

1. Etel Adnan, *The Arab Apocalypse*, 7.

2. On "propositional" or "apophantic" statements, please see the notes provided in Aristotle, *On Interpretation*: "A simple proposition [ἡ ἁπλῆ ἀπόφανσις/*hē haplē apophansis*], more fully, is a statement possessing a meaning [φωνὴ σημαντικὴ/*phonē sēmantikē*], affirming or denying the presence of some thing [περὶ τοῦ ὑπάρχειν τι ἢ μὴ ὑπάρχειν/*peri tou huparchein ti ē mē huparchein*] in a subject in time past or present or future" (17a23–24).

3. On al-Maʿālī see Khālid al-Maʿālī, Arno Böhler, and Suzanne Granzer, "Nietzsche and the Literature of Defiance"; and on "the start of absolute dictatorship" in 1979 in Iraq see Muhsin J. al-Musawi, *Reading Iraq*, 69ff., 82–84. On Adnan see Etel Adnan, "To Write in a Foreign Language"; Sonja Mejcher-Atassi, "Etel Adnan," 110–117; and Ammiel Alcalay, "'A Dance of Freedom.'"

4. In thinking about property-centric form in post-Ottoman frames I learn from Malissa Taylor's study of the 1858 Ottoman Land Code, where, she underlines, the Code reformulates transformations in law since the sixteenth century and installs a field for the interpellation of subjects in language and law. In the Land Code, rather than multiple subjects of use there is to be "a singular mold for the generic Ottoman subject," where the law is extended to "all who were subject to the sultan's legal jurisdiction in the nineteenth century" (*Land and Legal Texts*, 126, 123). This delimitation presses into the social a "responsibility for obeying laws and paying taxes" as well as a privilege of "individuation" and "productivity" (121), modes of comportment for a particular sense of the subject. The Land Code, further, reorganized prior legal statements in relation to itself, subordinating them to the terms it generated as it "presented all of its content as equally authoritative" (115), and in this the law took on the form of a self-determined or autonomous subject, which it called into being through the generalization of rights in property, even as these were articulated through the terminological languages of Ottoman administrative practice and law. "Generally, the Code preserved the cultivator's bundle that most muftis of the empire's eastern Mediterranean provinces had come to know and affirm by the eighteenth century, including its terminology; the Code defined this bundle of rights as *tasarruf* ["use"—JS] and the person possessing these rights as a *mutasarrif* [a "user" or "disposer"—JS]" (108). Taylor underlines the *Kanun-i Cedid-i Osmani*, a late-seventeenth to early eighteenth-century compilation of Ottoman land law, which recorded the sixteenth-century juridical and administrative statements of the jurist Ebu's Su'ud (Abū al-Suʿud), which defined "most of the lands of Ottoman Europe and Anatolia as treasury-owned, or *miri* land, with a special regime of law governing it" (18), and which, through this, enacted a juridical and spatial "conquest" (33), a practice of "redefinition" (33, 46), where *miri* land, if it remained the property of the Ottoman treasury, was understood as an abstraction extended cartographically, a feature of early modern capitalist sense. This mutation, Taylor notes, was to become "ubiquitous," where "land" appeared as an object in relation to which individuals could affirm a right to "use"—"From the late seventeenth century, the law governing *miri* land had achieved a new uniformity and a new ubiquity: a standard definition and treatment of it could be found across every genre of legal text circulating in the Ottoman Empire" (85)—and these terms are intensified in the 1858 Land Code. Law, in the Land Code, mirrors the form of the subject, and in this it generalizes a propertied sense of social and lingual existence, with which the texts I study, in chapters 2 and 3, are not reconcilable. For further discussion of law in relation to language, property, and capital, see notes 8-9, below.

5. Khālid al-Maʿālī, *ʿUyūn fakkarat bi-nā*, 51.

6. On the Arabic nineteenth century and its fallout please see the work of Shaden Tageldin, Marwa El Shakry, Michael Allan, Rebecca Johnson, Omnia El Shakry, Sherene Seikaly, Stephen Sheehi, Maha AbdelMegeed, Rana Issa, and Kamran Rastegar.

7. Khālid al-Maʿālī, *ʿUyūn fakkarat bi-nā*, 51; Sara Pursley, *Familiar Futures*, 23, 125, 133, 177, 219, 101. In relation to a sense of the poetic in excess of the interiorizing terms to which it is conscripted in twentieth- and twenty-first-century frames, please see the discussion of Khaled Furani, *Silencing the Sea*, where Furani points to a subordination of "the acoustic" and "sonic repetition" to a "modern conception of reading the poem" and its privilege of ocularity, where sonority appears as "noise": "The ear, which brings noise, becomes inferior to the eye, which takes you to depth. The deferral that comes with sound loses out to the immediacy of vision" (139, passim).

8. See, on *siyāsa*, "governance," in relation to "the state," *al-dawla*, and "the law," *qānūn*, Hüseyin Yilmaz, *Caliphate Redifined*; Heather L. Ferguson, *The Proper Order of Things*; Baki Tezcan, *The Second Ottoman Empire* and "Law in China or Conquest in the Americas"; and Halil Inalcik, "Suleiman the Lawgiver and Ottoman Law." See also, in a comparative frame, Aziz al-Azmeh, *Muslim Kingship*; and in relation to the social institution of Islamic law as a corporate practice, Khaled Abou El Fadl, *Rebellion and Violence in Islamic Law*. On modern law in the Egyptian context, see Samera Esmeir, *Juridical Humanity* and "On the Coloniality of Modern Law"; and in relation to *siyāsa* and its relation to *sharīʿ*, Khaled Fahmy, *In Quest of Justice*. In relation to the differentiating terms for the social the law installs, see Talal Asad, "Reconfigurations of Law and Ethics in Colonial Egypt"; Saba Mahmood, *Religious Difference in a Secular Age*; Asli Igsiz, *Humanism in Ruins*; as well as Maya Mikdashi, *Sextarianism*.

9. On capitalism in a world frame see Samir Amin, *Accumulation on a World Scale*; Immanuel Wallerstein, *The Modern World System*; and Andre Gunder Frank, *Capitalism and Underdevelopment*. On older social and economic formations, see Janet Abu Lughod, *Before European Hegemony*. In relation to the capitalist institution of property regionally, and the 1858 Ottoman Land Code, see, in addition to Taylor, Huri Islamoglu, "Property as a Contested Doman"; Martha Mundy and Richard Saumarez Smith, *Governing Property*; Hanna Batatu, who underlines that while in "Ottoman-Mamluk Baghdad," "'Property' was not, therefore, at that time, the dominant basis of [class] stratification" (*The Old Social Classes*, 8), in relation to mid- and late-nineteenth-century Iraq, there is a "stabilization, expansion, and, eventually, extreme concentration of private property" (11) through the "expropriation" of "communal tribal land," "the greater role of money," "the rise of speculation in real estate," and "the simultaneous placing of property on firmer juridical foundations," as well as "the increasing consolidation and centralization of state power" (11) and the "deepening of English economic penetration and tying of Iraq to the world of capitalism" (22); Jens Hanssen, who underlines, in relation to nineteenth-century Beirut, "individual taxation" in relation to land, as well as "security and transferability of title" (*Fin de Siècle Beirut*, 142–143); the studies of

Halil Inalcik, "The Ottoman State, Society, and Economy, 1300–1600," and "Capital Formation in the Ottoman Empire," and Inalcik's discussion, in the latter, of "the development of the Ottoman Economy into a money economy" (139n94); and Baki Tezcan, who notes "the monetization of the Ottoman economy" in the sixteenth century (*The Second Ottoman Empire*, 50). Please see as well Timothy Mitchell's' discussion of cadastral, surveying, taxation, and irrigation practices in nineteenth-century Egypt, where the land "appeared as a system of objects to be possessed and exchanged" (*Rule of Experts*, 91); and, in the Iraqi context, alongside Batatu's foundational study, Samira Haj, *The Making of Iraq*; and Dina Rizk Khoury, *State and Provincial Society*; and, in several proximate frames, Raouf Abbas and Assem El-Dessouky, *The Large Landowning Class*; Nada Moumtaz, *God's Property*; Muriam Haleh Davis, *Markets of Civilization*; and Sherene Seikaly, *Men of Capital*.

10. al-Maʿālī, *ʿUyūn fakkarat bi-nā*, 51.

11. Khālid al-Maʿālī, *al-Hubūt ʿalā al-yābisa*, 22.

12. Kamran Rastegar, "*Gulistan*," 303.

13. Khālid al-Maʿālī, *Ḥidāʾ*, 12.

14. Khālid al-Maʿālī, *Aṭyāf Hūldirlīn*, 40.

15. al-Maʿālī, *Aṭyāf Hūldirlīn*, 97.

16. Etel Adnan, *Seasons*, 42.

17. al-Maʿālī, *Aṭyāf Hūldirlīn*, 124.

18. al-Maʿālī, *Ḥidāʾ*, 61.

19. Khālid al-Maʿālī, *al-ʿAwda ilā al-ṣaḥrāʾ*, 46.

20. al-Maʿālī, *ʿUyūn fakkarat bi-nā*, 117.

21. al-Maʿālī, *Ḥidāʾ*, 47–48.

22. al-Maʿālī, *Aṭyāf Hūldirlīn*, 115.

23. al-Maʿālī, *ʿUyūn fakkarat bi-nā*, 117.

24. al-Jāḥiẓ, *al-Bayān wa-al-tibyīn*, 1.58.

25. al-Jāḥiẓ, *al-Bayān wa-al-tibyīn*, 1.79.

26. Ibn Rashīq, *al-ʿUmda*, 1.241. And consider the discussion of the "training" or "habituation," تعويد, *taʿwīd*, of the tongue in al-Rāghib al-Iṣfahānī's *Muḥāḍarāt al-udabāʾ*, 31: "Al-ʿItābī said: Those who have mastered speech are those who have trained their run-away tongues in the field of words [من عوّد لسانه الراكض في ميادين الألفاظ / *man ʿawwada lisānahu al-rākiḍ fī mayādīn al-alfāẓ*]."

27. al-Qāḍī al-Quḍāʿī, *Light in the Heavens*, 1.180.

28. al-Jāḥiẓ, *al-Bayān wa-al-tibyīn*, 1.79. And see also the discussion of poetic meter in the grammarian al-Akhfash's *Kitāb al-ʿarūḍ*, where he explains, "As for the laying down of poetic meter, they gathered all of the forms of the Arabs that had been passed down to them and specified the number of the phonemic utterances which are followed by a vowel and those which are not. And such a form, which is composed of speech, is what the Arabs call poetry." He continues, and I wish to place an emphasis on the verb "to hear" in the following passage, "If it were said, Have you set down all of the forms? Do you not know that there may be many forms of which you have not heard? I would say: I don't know. But I only confirm what I

have heard [ما سمعت/*mā sami'tu*]" (56). In relation to the ear and *ṣawt* see as well al-Sharīf al-Jurjānī, *Kitāb al-ta'rīfāt*, 210, where *al-ṣawt*, is defined as "a quality carried by the air, which it bears into the inner ear [كيفية قائمة بالهواء يحملها إلى الصماخ/*kayfiyya qā'ima bi al-hawā' yaḥmiluhā 'ilā al-ṣimākh*]."

29. Ibn Rashīq, *al-'Umda*, 1.134, 1.151.

30. Abū Hilāl al-'Askarī, *Kitāb al-ṣinā'atayn*, 74, 194.

31. Ibn Rashīq, *al-'Umda*, 1.187. And see also the discussion of listening in relation to eloquence in al-'Askarī: "And perhaps eloquence resides in listening, for the addressee, if they do not listen well [إذا لم يحسن الإستماع/*idhā lam yuḥsin al-istimā'*], will not understand the meaning conveyed to them in the speech" (*Kitāb al-ṣinā'atayn*, 25). And please consider the discussion of form in Lara Harb's *Arabic Poetics*, where Harb notes, in relation to 'Abd al-Qahir al-Jurjānī's *Asrār al-balāgha* and the notion of *bayān*, "eloquence": "Poetic beauty for him lies in the way speech conveys meaning and elucidates it" (140). There is, further, a privilege of "condensation," *talkhīṣ*, in relation to "convolution," *ta'qīd*, where the latter "hinders your thinking and obstructs your search for meaning" (144), and where this privilege articulates an economy in form. There is a privilege of a particular manner of working with detail in the formation of an image, where, al-Jurjānī explains, as Harb translates him, "The more deeply [an image] goes into details, the more one needs to stop, remember, contemplate, and slow down" (148). In this, the explication of *bayān* in relation to the poetic is also the explication of a certain sort of reading, a "stopping" and a coming to a "pause" (150), and a temporality in lingual apprehension: "The rarer the comparison," Harb underlines, "the stranger it is, and hence the more time and effort it takes to grasp it" (150). In the later formulations of the tradition Harb studies, this sense of form is formalized. "The more details are incorporated in a simile and the more aspects are added, the stranger and (hence) more eloquent it is" (160), Harb notes, paraphrasing al-Sakkākī and al-Khaṭīb al-Qazwīnī. This sense of form gives what Harb terms "poeticity" (88), a reflection on language and the poetic where what is privileged is "what makes language poetic in general" (28), and where "the value of poetic speech is located in aspects intrinsic to the poetic utterance" (261). Learning from and thinking with Harb, I notice a practice of form in relation to utterance, and in relation to its material sonority, which I study here with a particular attention to al-Jāḥiẓ.

32. Ibn Manẓūr, *Lisān al-'Arab*, نوى, *nawā*.

33. And please consider, as well, the discussion of Alexander Key, where, through a reading of 'Abd al-Qahir al-Jurjānī, he underlines a formalism in Arabic writing: "Al-Jurjānī did not write hermeneutics. He was concerned with how poetry worked" (*Language between God and the Poets*, 196). In this, he continues, "he wrote what we may call a linguistic, stylistic, and formalist criticism, in which he used the Arabic conceptual vocabulary of mental content to explain the processes at work" (196). "Vocal forms," Key also explains, "no longer simply refer to mental contents; they are rather threaded into patterns of vocal form that generate patterns of mental content" (197). In this, al-Jurjānī was concerned with "combinations of words" and

the manner of their combination—what al-Jurjānī termed النظم, *al-naẓm*—"Individual words can have grammatical and syntactical functions (the mental contents of grammar), but only combinations of words constitute syntax or produce images" (197)—and this attention to "combination" did not privilege "the subjectivity of personal experience" (201), but was instead "discursive and formalist" (205), and, through this, it articulated a particular "account of beauty in language," which addressed "everything about words and how they relate to each other" (228), Key compellingly observes. "He knew," as Key further writes of al-Jurjānī, "that when people spoke they could do more than just refer to mental content; they could choose to create beauty" (199).

34. al-Jāḥiẓ, *Kitāb al-ḥayawān*, 7.35.

35. I learn here from Jeannie Miller's "Man Is Not the Only Speaking Animal," where she underlines that although "al-Jāḥiẓ argues strenuously that animal vocalization communicates meaning, and thus satisfies the criterion for communication," "at the same time al-Jāḥiẓ suggests that the use of *bayān* to describe the communication of animals and inanimate objects is in fact not literally correct but rather idiomatic" (98), a manner of argument Miller outlines in detail. And yet if there is a distinction drawn, in al-Jāḥiẓ, between "animal vocalization" and "human speech" (101), as al-Jāḥiẓ writes of these, one may ask whether the sense of language presumed in both does not extend across these fields. Al-Jāḥiẓ draws out a distinction between "animal" and "human" speech, but these are, in another sense, as Miller elucidates, of the same "kind": "In other words, animal vocalizations constitute communication of the same kind as human speech," Miller writes, "but animals have less to communicate and so their communication tools are simpler" (101). Miller observes that "the originary moment when God gave humanity language would appear to distinguish humans from animals" (105), and she notes that al-Jāḥiẓ wishes his readers "not to confuse animal status with human status" (106)—"This is an absolute boundary" (107), Miller also writes of al-Jāḥiẓ's reflection on "responsibility" in relation to "actions." Yet al-Jāḥiẓ's discussion also points to an intercontamination, an illegibility, across what Miller calls a "threshold" (108), and across the distinction between "absolute" and "general," which also undermines the "sharp distinction" (109) he both affirms and collapses. Al-Jāḥiẓ "sees all things as speaking, more or less, while only humans speak absolutely" (119), yet I wish to notice, through al-Jāḥiẓ's formulations, and Miller's acute reading, an anterior indistinction, a belonging of the "human" to the world of "animals" and "things," which al-Jāḥiẓ's language also carries.

36. Ibn Qutayba, *Adab al-kātib*, 304.

37. Ibn Manẓūr, *Lisān al-ʿarab*, فصح, *faṣaḥa*. And consider also the notes related to "the tongue," اللسان, *al-lisān*, in al-Nuwayrī, *Nihāyat al-arab fī funūn al-adab*, where he explains in relation to the "beautiful qualities," محاسن, *maḥāsin*, of the tongue that: "If a man is well-bounded in his language [حاد اللسان/*ḥād al-lisān*], and capable of speech, his tongue is sharp and precise [فهو ذرب اللسان، وفتيق اللسان/*fa huwwa dharib al-lisān, wa fatīq al-lisān*]. And if his speech is well-formed, he is eloquent

[فإذا كان جَيِّدَه، فهو لَسِن/*fa idhā kāna jayyidahu, fa huwwa lasina*]. And if he places it where he intends, his speech is fluent [ذليق/*dhalīq*]. And if he speaks properly, and his pronunciation is clear, he is skilled [فإذا كان فصيحا بَيِّن اللهجة، فهو حُذاقِيّ/*fa idhā kāna faṣīḥan bayyin al-lahja, fa huwwa hudhāqī*]" (2.64); and please consider also al-Tha'ālabī, *Fiqh al-lugha*, where, three centuries earlier, in a chapter titled "Fī ḥiddat al-lisān wa al-faṣāha," "On the Well-Bounded and Proper Tongue," a nearly identical phrasing is provided (*Fiqh al-lugha*, 101). I wish to underline, through these passages, that we may consider the "beauty" of language in its relation to a well-formed practice, a well-bounded, and if also "sharp" or "cutting," manner, where one "tongues," or, even—and these may, finally, be indistinguishable, one "languages": *lasina*.

38. in these formulations I learn from and am thinking with the discussion of language as "medium," in Shaden Tageldin, "Beyond Latinity," 117, 130; of "collectivizing movement," in Ayman El-Desouky, *The Intellectual and the People*, 75; of "a general collective that does not refer to an original specific quality other than collectivity itself," in Maha AbdelMegeed, *Literary Optics*, 164–165; and of forms of life "outside of the grammar of the modern state," in "the possibility of another collectivity or being-in-common," and in "bringing back forms of life that were once possible"—in a manner of thinking and "inhabiting the world and moving across its different surfaces, horizontally and vertically, *without staging and capturing it*," in Samera Esmeir, "Bandung," 93, 89.

39. Ibn Manẓūr, *Lisān al-'arab*, نطق, *naṭaqa*.

40. Khālid al-Ma'ālī, *Anā min arḍ Kilkāmish*, 59.

41. Khālid al-Ma'ālī, *Khayāl min qaṣab*, 96.

42. Paul Celan, *Der Meridian*, 11/*The Meridian*, 11, translated by Pierre Joris; I learn as well from "The Meridian," translated by Rosemarie Waldrop, 53. Throughout, I follow the German edition, edited by Bernhard Böschenstein and Heino Schmull, as well as Joris's translation. I also occasional modify Joris's translation, at times in relation to Waldrop's, in order to underline a particular lexical, grammatical, or formal moment. And see Paul Celan, *Die Gedichte*, 643–644, where the editor, Barbara Wiedemann, explains that time of the "genesis," *Entstehung*, of the lines I'm reading here was July 1956, whereas the volume in which they were published, *Sprachgitter*, appeared in 1959.

43. Paul Celan, *Lichtzwang*, in *Die Gedichte*, 301/*Lightduress*, in *Breathturn into Timestead*, 307, translated by Pierre Joris. Throughout, in citing Celan's poetry, I follow the *Kommentierte Gesamtausgabe* and Joris's translations, which I occasionally modify to underline a particular argument, or to follow a particular lexical, grammatical, or formal moment.

44. Paul Celan, *Sprachgitter*, in *Die Gedichte*, 111 / *Speechgrille*, in *Memory Rose into Threshold Speech*, 223.

45. Celan, *Der Meridian*, 98/*The Meridian*, 98. Since the pagination in these two volumes is identical, I cite them, parenthetically, with a single page number.

46. Paul Celan, *Mikrolithen sinds, Steinchen*, 20, paragraph 10.1; 108, paragraph 180.

47. Marc Redfield, *Shibboleth*, 76–77.

48. Celan, *Der Meridian*, 97/*The Meridian*, 97.

49. Yvonne Al-Taie, *Poetik der Unverständlichkeit*, 370, 371.

50. Celan, *Sprachgitter*, 96/*Speechgrille*, 181. As Werner Hamacher has underlined, in Celan "linguistic signs are not referential indicators coordinated by autonomous subjects with their representations, nor are they the self-presentation of their objectivity" ("The Second of Inversion," 225). In Celan, Hamacher continues, language "can no longer be conceived as an exchange between two or more already constituted subjects of a linguistic community" (237), and the poem, therefore, "speaks as the movement of alteration and thereby stops being merely *this* poem and merely a *poem*" (248). This "speaking" gives a sense of "language held in common," where "this commonality is articulated in the suspension of commonality" (245), a sense of the social not derived from preexisting forms. Al-Maʿālī, through his translations of Celan, gives us to read such a sense of form by rendering "the rigorous connection between linguisticity and temporality" (236), in a manner where form is, further, without form, and without a determining temporal locus, where the poem, in each and every instance, "becomes other than it is" (236).

51. Paul Celan, *Fadensonnen*, in *Die Gedichte*, 258/*Threadsuns*, in *Breathturn into Timestead*, 211.

52. Samera Esmeir, "On the Coloniality of Modern Law"; and see, as well, "1927: How Seismology Received Islamic Theology," 340–341; and, more generally, *Juridical Humanity*.

53. Samera Esmeir, "On Becoming Less of the World," 95, 98, 102.

54. Celan, *Der Meridian*, 9–10/*The Meridian*, 10; and see as well "The Meridian," 50.

55. Celan, *Der Meridian*, 9/"The Meridian," 49. Here I follow Waldrop's translation closely; please see as well Joris's rendering in *The Meridian*, 9.

56. Paul Tsīlān, "Khaṭṭ al-ẓahīra," in *Samaʿtu man yaqūl*, 297–298.

57. Celan, *Der Meridian*, 8/*The Meridian*, 8; and see as well "The Meridian," 48.

58. Tsīlān, "Khaṭṭ al-ẓahīra," 295.

59. Celan, *Der Meridian*, 7/*The Meridian*, 8; and see as well "The Meridian," 48. The Arabic appears in Tsīlān, "Khaṭṭ al-ẓahīra," 294.

60. Tsīlān, "Khaṭṭ al-ẓahīra," 295.

61. Paul Celan, *Mohn und Gedächtnis*, in *Die Gedichte*, 37/*Poppy and Memory*, in *Memory Rose into Threshold Speech*, 33. The Arabic appears in Paul Tsīlān, *Samaʿtu man yaqūl*, 38.

62. Paul Celan, *Zeitgehöft*, in *Die Gedichte*, 357/*Timestead*, in *Breathturn into Timestead*, 423.

63. Erin Graff Zivin, *Figurative Inquisitions*, 76.

64. Khālid al-Maʿālī, *al-Iqāma fī al-ʿarāʾ*, 102.

65. Ammiel Alcalay has pointed to the importance of Adnan's practice as a painter, and I learn, throughout, from his observation; see *Memories of Our Future*, 141. I also learn from a number of interventions in relation to Adnan's painting, in

particular: Sonja Mejcher-Attasi, "The Forbidden Paradise"; Silvia Naef, "Painting in Arabic"; and, in relation to painting and its relation to the Arabic language, Wen-Chin Ouyang, "From Beirut to Beirut," 75.

66. Etel Adnan, *Sea and Fog*, 74.

67. Laleh Khalili, *Sinews of War and Trade*, 83, 101, 192.

68. Etel Adnan, *There*, 58.

69. Adnan, *Sea and Fog*, 6.

70. The reading I offer here learns from the exhilarating study of Nada Moumtaz, where she underlines, in the Lebanese context, a "new property regime" through which "in the course of the nineteenth century, individual and absolute property ownership replaced the much more layered understanding of property" (*God's Property*, 5), in relation to the formation of "a new sense of interiority" and "new conceptions of self" (6) called into being through nineteenth-century Ottoman legal acts. Moumtaz focuses on "the deep structural changes that these reforms have initiated, independent of their origins or agents" (13), as she outlines this "reform" moment, from the 1839 imperial edict, *Gülhane Hatt-i Serif*, which initiated the "Tanzimat," to "a penal code in 1840, a commercial code in 1850, a land code in 1858 [which I discussed above, through the work of Malissa Taylor, in note 4—JS], and a maritime code in 1863" (15), among others. Moumtaz focuses on transformations in the institution of the *waqf*, the pious endowment, and considers its mutations in relation to legal reform, capital, and French colonial legality. In this, a shift occurs, which "participated in the introduction of a new kind of subject whose intentions are disembodied from actions" (26), and which is also linked to "capital accumulation": "The requirements of capital accumulation not only contributed to reshuffling control of the means of production and of social relations but also left a mark on the conception of the person and the grammar of intent in the Islamic tradition" (140). There is a "modern grammar of interiority" (114), which intersects with "an abstract logic of merit" (192), a new "debt regime," installed through the 1850 Code of Commerce, "which was based on the 1807 French commerce code" (127), as well as, in relation to Beirut, "a new land registry" (56) enacted by the French mandatory powers, in sync with a 1930 Real Estate Code, which redefined "land" as "real estate," a lexical maneuver which signaled "the rise of a private property regime where land is mostly a financial asset" (54). In this, as Moumtaz studies the *waqf* in particular, she observes that "rather than being a kind of ownership, divine ownership, that differs from state ownership or private ownership, *waqf* became a right that one can have in private property" (54). I notice, only, that this "property regime" extends itself to the field of language, an extension which, as Moumtaz underlines, contributes to the "reproduction" (230) of a particular sense of legibility in the social.

71. Adnan, *The Arab Apocalypse*, 11.

72. See Fawwaz Trabulsi, *A History of Modern Lebanon*, 201; and, generally, 187–204.

73. Adnan, *The Arab Apocalypse*, 64.

74. Etel Adnan, *L'Apocalypse arabe*, 58.

75. Adnan, *The Arab Apocalypse*, 64; Adnan, *L'Apocalypse arabe*, 58.

76. See Etel Adnan, *Sitt Marie Rose*; Edward W. Said, *The Question of Palestine*; Ussama Makdisi, *The Culture of Sectariansim*; and Maya Mikdashi, *Sextarianism*. I've tried to offer a reading of *Sitt Marie Rose* in these terms in "Against Simplicity." I learn, in the formulations I offer here, from Mikdashi's discussion of what she terms "sextarianism," in Lebanon, a technology for the stabilization of the social pressed through a juridical and bureaucratic institution and perforation of categories. "But sectarian citizens do not sprout, like mushrooms, from the ground. Instead they are structurally produced through laws and bureaucracies that regulate sexuality and gender" (*Sextarianism*, 28). It is a production that points to "the sextarian nature of the legal system as a whole" (41), and which, in a practice of social differentiation and an allocation of violences, transmutes "liberal" forms. "Citizenship, secularism, and religion are not only ethical, authorizing, affective, and embodied practices or epistemes. They are also biopolitical modes of governance" (115), and I notice, thinking with Mikdashi's reading, and her linking of such "modes of governance" to "classical political theory" (46) and "liberal abstraction and universalization" (3), that we may consider this "abstraction" and "universalization" as reformulating themselves, differentially reiterating themselves, in a history Mikdashi draws out (in relation to the 1932 census, for example) and in relation to a longer history to which "classical political theory" also belongs, from the Crusades until today, and which is materially transmuted in the juridical fields she studies and the "bureaucratic praxis" (40) through which "sexual difference" is constituted in its relation to "global whiteness and white supremacy" (125) in its intersection with the state, sovereignty, law, secularism, and the stabilization—the domesticating regulation—of the social. In this frame, we may consider Adnan's language, her practice in the poetic and painting, and the dense locus of forms in her work as material refusals of these terms.

77. Adnan, *There*, 5.

78. Adnan, *Sea and Fog*, 57.

79. And see Lucretius, *De rerum natura*, 5.416–431, where there is not a single "first beginning" but "many first beginnings of things in many ways," which are, themselves, already underway, "struck with blows and carried along by their own weight from infinite time": "But next in order I will describe in what ways that assemblage of matter established earth and sky and the ocean deeps, and the courses of sun and moon. For certainly it was no design of the first beginnings that led them to place themselves each in its own order with keen intelligence, nor assuredly did they make any bargain what motions each should produce; but because many first beginnings of things in many ways [*sed quia multa modis multis primordia rerum*], struck with blows and carried along by their own weight from infinite time up to the present, have been accustomed to move and to meet in all manner of ways [*omnimodisque*], and to try all combinations, whatsoever they could produce by coming together, for this reason it comes to pass that being spread abroad through a

vast time, by attempting every sort of combination and motion, at length those come together which, being suddenly brought together, often become the beginnings of great things, of earth and sea and sky and the generation of living creatures."

80. Etel Adnan, *Night*, 21.

81. Etel Adnan, "La Mer," 15.

82. Adnan, *Sea and Fog*, 31.

83. Etel Adnan, *Shifting the Silence*, 2, 7–8.

84. J. Kameron Carter, *The Anarchy of Black Religion*, 113. And consider, in relation to a thinking of the sea, property, capital, and debt, the discussion of law and economy in the Indian Ocean, and in relation to Oman, East Africa, Zanzibar, and the Western coast of India (Gujarat, Bombay, Calicut) in Fahad Ahmad Bishara, *A Sea of Debt*, where, in the nineteenth century, practices of legality and personhood are reformulated in relation to "an ontology of debt and credit" (68), a transformation in an understanding of "terrestrial space" (87), a becoming-commodity of the "landscape" (89), "the changing forms of contracting that modern capitalism demanded" (91), "an agricultural frontier that seemed to continually unfold" (105), as well as, in relation to the dimensions of abstraction generated in capitalist life, an expansion of law's "jurisdiction" (156) and a new "legibility in the eyes of the law" in relation to a "property regime that would preserve the positions of inidivudal landowners" (170). And all of this, in relation to regional slavery—"The work of slaves permeated almost every dimension of economic life in the Western Indian Ocean" (46)—and racialized social determinations in law and legal personhood.

85. Etel Adnan, *Of Cities and Women*, 40.

86. Adnan, *Sea and Fog*, 43, 58.

87. Simone Fattal, "On Perception," 93.

88. Kaelen Wilson-Goldie, *Etel Adnan*, 99.

89. Mahmoud Darwish, *Athar al-farāsha*, 222.

90. Etel Adnan, *Surge*, 17.

91. On the Suez canal, see Samera Esmeir, *Juridical Humanity*, 89, 209.

92. Fattal, "On Perception," 90.

93. Etel Adnan, with Laurie Adler, *The Beauty of Light*, 21.

94. Etel Adnan, "Growing Up," 11.

95. Adnan, *Seasons*, 10.

96. Adnan, *Night*, 13.

97. Etel Adnan, *Journey to Mount Tamalpais*, 31.

98. Emmanuel Lévinas, "L'Ontologie est-elle fondamentale?", 16/ "Is Ontology Fundamental?" 5.

99. Lévinas, *Autrement qu'être*, 72/*Otherwise Than Being*, 41.

100. See Martin Heidegger, *The Metaphysical Foundations of Logic*, 30: "The relation of subject and predicate is a λέγειν τι κατά τινός," Heidegger wrote, citing and glossing Aristotle in *On Interpretation*, "a stating something about something (*de aliquo*). That 'about which' is what underlies, the ὑποκείμενον, the *subjectum*. The predicate is that which is said about something." In placing an emphasis on the sort

of statement a proposition is, and in noting its lingual dimensions—"The expression 'logic' is an abbreviation of the Greek λογική. To complete it ἐπιστήμη must be added: the science that deals with λόγος. Here logos means as much as 'speech,' specifically in the sense of *statement*, predication" (1)—Heidegger underlines the relation of "logic," and propositional statements about what "is," to "the question of being as such," which he traces in the lecture course. "I will anticipate only with a suggestion to make clear how with this theory of λόγος, with these logical problems, we find ourselves immediately in the most central metaphysical questions, in the ontological problematic, the question about being as such" (39). I wish to share only that we may read Lévinas, and his situating of *Otherwise Than Being* in its relation to "ontology," in relation to these pages in Heidegger's lecture course.

101. Lévinas, *Autrement qu'être*, 187/118.

102. I learn here from the reading of Lévinas in Jacques Derrida, "Violence and Metaphysics," an essay published in 1964. Derrida underlines that there is, in Lévinas, a privilege of self-identicality and an internal non-differentiation: "Without using these terms themselves, Lévinas often warned us against confusing *identity* and *ipseity*, Same and Ego: *idem* and *ipse*." As Derrida further observes: "We have seen this: according to Lévinas there would be no interior difference, no fundamental and autochthonous alterity within the ego" (109).

103. Emmanuel Lévinas, "Dieu et la philosophie," 120, 119/ "God and Philosophy," 73, 72.

104. Lévinas, *Autrement qu'être*, 31/15.

105. Emmanuel Lévinas, "Ethics and Politics," 294.

106. I notice, reading Lévinas reading Celan, that Lévinas observes, in relation to Celan's formulations in "The Meridian," "A language of and for proximity, more ancient than that of the 'truth of being'—which it probably bears and supports—the first of languages, a response prior to the question, a responsibility for the neighbor, making possible, through its 'for the other,' the whole miracle of giving," as he asks, "Does he not suggest poetry itself [*la poésie elle-même*] as an unheard [*inouïe*] modality of the 'otherwise than being'?" (Lévinas, *Paul Celan*, 18, 35).

107. Adnan, *Surge*, 43.

108. Adnan, *Sea and Fog*, 95.

109. Adnan, *There*, 47.

110. Etel Adnan, *Hunāka*, 58.

111. Etel Adnan, *Paris*, 16.

112. Adnan, *Journey to Mount Tamalpais*, 55.

113. Nick Estes, *Our History Is the Future*, 89, 98, 138.

114. What is refused in these passages in Adnan, in relation to landscape, is the white, settler, social and epistemic form, made manifest, as Iyko Day has written, through "the contradictory logics of settler colonialism, which engage in the violent elimination and dispossession of Indigenous peoples and simultaneously express a desire to become Indigenous to the landscape, to naturalize settler colonialism through symbolic projection" (*Alien Capital*, 102).

115. I thank David Lloyd, Sarita See, and Heidi Brevik-Zender for their conversations around this sentence—"Let us be the Indian and let be!"—in *Journey to Mount Tamalpais.*

116. Audra Simpson, *Mohawk Interruptus*, 91. I learn as well from the observation of Christopher Pexa that in the juridical life of the American settler state, "the translational process of settler-colonial law converts Indigenous place into space and homelands into property" in relation to "a Lockean liberalism and a capitalist temporality" where Indigenous and Native peoples appear as "a detribalized object," "the generic Indian who, in a settler-colonial logic of replacement, could be imitated, absorbed, and co-opted" (*Translated Nation*, 133, 153, 93). And please see Beth H. Piatote, *Domestic Subjects*, where, in an incisive sentence, which follows a discussion of "the Marshall Trilogy," the "Doctrine of Discovery," and the 1887 General Allotment Act, which "divided communally held reservation lands into sections, then assigned as individual title to Indian men, women, and children," Piatote observes that "in other words, private property could do the work of domestication that military conquest alone could not" (101, 102). I also learn, here and throughout, in relation to "property," from Robert Nichols, who underlines that property is "a mode of social organization," where "property does not refer to a set of things but a species of relations" (*Theft Is Property!*, 130). "Land," he writes, is "not a material object but a mediating device," with a particular relation to capital and settler colonization: "This is why dispossession can be said to create its own object of appropriation: dispossession generates and then monopolizes a distinct medium of human activity in the world via the legal and conceptual construct of 'land'" (83). I also learn, in relation to the terms Simpson, Pexa, Piatote, and Nichols study, from J. Kēhaulani Kauanui, *Hawaiian Blood*; Kevin Bruyneel, *Settler Memory*; Joanne Barker, *Native Acts*; and Jodi A. Byrd, *The Transit of Empire.*

117. Adnan, *Journey to Mount Tamalpais*, 34.

118. I learn here from Maile Arvin's discussion of the articulation of race with settler colonization, Indigenous dispossession, and anti-Blackness in what she terms "a logic of possession through whiteness" (*Possessing Polynesians* 3), where Polynesians are included into whiteness through their rhetorical proximity to it, a gesture that affirms, Arvin shows, white settler expropriation and Indigenous dispossession. In this logic, Arvin explains through close readings of philological, sociological, and biological discourses, "the Polynesian race is repeatedly positioned as almost white (even literally as descendants of the Aryan race), in a way that allows white settlers to claim indigeneity in Polynesia, since, according to this logic, whiteness itself is indigenous to Polynesia" (3). It is a social logic that is in sync with the decimation of subsistence, a principal locus of attack in settler life—"Planting taro, fishing, and weaving, of course, were all forms of work and sustainable living that were being eradicated by the imposition of capitalism and the plantation economy" (108), Arvin writes of 1920s and 1930s Hawaiʻi—and an assertion in appropriating determination: "Far from simply dehumanizing the subjects of their studies, social scientific knowledge production allowed white settlers to (selectively)

identify with and as Polynesians" (208). It is not my argument that Adnan reiterates this social logic; it is my argument that Adnan's poetry and painting are generated in part through a relation to the form of life that sustains such logics, and that this being-generated points to the materiality of Adnan's work in the dense catastrophe, the ongoing apocalypse, of settler life.

119. Adnan, *Journey to Mount Tamalpais*, 18.

120. Etel Adnan, *The Indian Never Had a Horse*, 3–5.

121. Adnan, *Paris*, 32, 34.

122. Khalid al-Maʿālī, *Aʿīsh khārij sāʿatī*, 79.

123. This even as, in Hegel, there is a consumption or interiorization that does not cease, as well as a non-homogeneity, an improper rupture, stance, and salutation: "But nothing," Jacques Derrida has written, "is ever homogeneous in the different ruptures, stances or salutations of speculative dialectics" (*Glas*, 198).

124. Adnan, *The Indian Never Had a Horse*, 90, 31; "I told them: come with me to the sea," appears at p. 90.

125. Adnan, *Night*, 47; *Seasons*, 23–24; *Journey to Mount Tamalpais*, 14, 23. Adnan's statement, "The Kurdish woman in Beirut carries her headless son through the streets," points to the formation of the modern Turkish state, in its relation to the Armenian genocide and the Turkish state's genocidal destruction of Kurdish life, as well as to the formation of the Israeli state in Palestine and the ongoing, genocidal *Nakba*. As Nazan Üstündağ explains, in relation to "the [Turkish—JS] project of nationalist homogenization and centralization," "early military and administrative authorities adopted violent strategies to intervene in Kurdish regions and destroyed existing ways of life, balances of power, ecologies, and communities," and "In response, religious and community leaders, elite families, and kinship-based tribes of Kurdistan have started numerous insurgencies against the Turkish state and faced extreme forms of state terror in return" (*The Mother, the Politician, and the Guerrilla*, 8). Among such forms of "state terror" Üstündağ outlines "linguicide" and "matricide," what she explicates as "the denial and destruction of the Kurdish language and the symbolic killing of Kurdish mothers," which "constitute," she writes, "the kernel of the Turkish state's genocidal law against Kurds" (30). "The linguicide of Kurdish," she explains, "has taken many different forms in Turkey: bans on speaking Kurdish in public spaces, prisons, and schools; denial of the existence of Kurdish as a distinct language with its own grammar, vocabulary, and history; naming it as an 'unidentified utterance' in court and Parliament; changing place names from Kurdish to Turkish; preventing families from giving their children Kurdish names; and punishing those who speak Kurdish and/or listen to Kurdish music" (33–34). The Turkish state's address to the Kurdish people, individually and collectively, is therefore a kind of "strangulation" (107), where, in relation to the Turkish state and its "ear" (41), in its "unleashing a constant and wild suspicion over accents, words, songs, and sounds" (41), the Kurdish language appears as a kind of "noise" (38), an "ontological threat" (38) to the social, a logic gestured in Adnan's statement, and which belongs to the genocidal forms her work refuses.

126. Adnan, *Sea and Fog*, 49; *The Arab Apocalypse*, 69. Adnan's reference, in *Sea and Fog*, is to the murder of Stanley Williams by the state of California in 2005: "Stanley 'Tookie' Williams requests us, before his death by lethal injection, to remember 'Strange Fruit,' Lewis Allan's song of 1940: Southern trees bear strange fruit/Blood on the leaves and blood at the root,/Black bodies swinging in the Southern breeze . . ." (*Sea and Fog*, 49; Adnan's ellipses). Through Adnan's formulation, we are given to read this distribution of death and unsurvival in the genocidal violences against Palestinians, Kurds, and Armenians, and against Indigenous and Black peoples in Turtle Island, and in these violences' permeations through, and their institution of, the social; as João H. Costa Vargas writes, in relation to the 1992 rebellions in Los Angeles, and, by extension, the social, epistemic, and linguistic spaces to which Adnan's citation refers: "[T]he killing of the body, mind, and soul of Black people is intrinsic to this society's boundaries of valuable humanity," a genocide which "is not conditioned on Black people's greater or lesser acceptance of this society's norms; rather, genocide is the very condition of this polity" (*Never Meant to Survive*, 77). And please consider, as well, Marc Nichanian's underlining the genocidal operation of historiography, what he also terms a "historiographical stranglehold" (*The Historiographic Perversion*, 8), where, he shows, historical understanding relies on a genocidal logic, which this understanding also reformulates. Thinking with and learning from Costa Vargas and Nichanian, as well as the passages in Dylan Rodríguez's *White Reconstruction* I've underlined above, in chapter 1, I wish to suggest that we may understand "settler life" as a genocidal formation in globality, which reformulates itself as "polity" (in Costa Vargas), "white statecraft and civil life" (in Rodríguez's *White Reconstruction*, 93), the "historical" (in Nichanian), and, I wish to underline, as a social form regenerated through the subject of legality and its capacity for proper listening and temporally stabilizing reading.

127. Etel Adnan, *The Spring Flowers Own*, 49.

128. Adnan, *Sea and Fog*, 58; *The Indian Never Had a Horse*, 96.

129. Adnan, *Seasons*, 10; Etel Adnan, "Letter," 10. "I am so happy you gave me a chance to speak of Olson, as it made me reread, this time carefully, *The Maximus Poems*. Some many months ago that interest was awakened by Ammiel's book around and about Olson: 'A Little History.' A long history in fact. It came as an illumination. A book of passion carefully advancing like a tide" (9), Adnan also writes. And see, as well, and in relation to the sea, Charles Olson, *The Maximus Poems*: "It is undone business, I speak of, this morning,/with the sea/stretching out/from my feet" (I.53), a passage through which one might read, following Adnan, who notes that Olson is an "Atlantic man" ("Letter," 10), the unfinishedness of the "situation" of *The Maximus Poems*, its relation to "islands," "shores," and "stones"—"Portuguese/are part Phoenician (?/Canary Islanders/Cro-Magnon/Islands,/to islands,/headlands/and shores,/Megalithic/stones/Stations/on shores/And Sable/Then England/an Augustine/land" (II.81)—and a "poetics": "The poetics of such a situation," Olson further writes, "are yet to be found out" (II.79). I learn here, as well, from Ammiel Alcalay, who notes that after returning to Gloucester in the

1940s "Olson is rethinking the nature of political life" (A *Little History*, 102), and, further, as Alcalay writes, in a manner that is in sync with Adnan's sense of form, materials, temporality, and "concerns and experiences of daily life": "To acknowledge the cosmic, cataclysmic nature of such possibilities is not at all to give up on politics. On the contrary, it is to return politics to the concerns and experiences of the cosmos through concerns and experiences of daily life, wherever and however it is lived," and this, in relation to "Olson's grasp of this relationship between forms of writing, living, and larger social, spatial, and cosmic structures such forms parallel and enact" (146).

130. Adnan, "Letter," 15; and see Jalal Toufic, *What Was I Thinking?* 188–189, passim.

131. Fawwaz Traboulsi, "Untitled," 90.

132. "If *to inherit* means *to read*—to read the cracks and fissures in what we inherit, the fugitive shards and fragments of historical ruination—this inheritance not only transmits catastrophe but also passes its legacy forward in modes of transmission that are themselves catastrophic," Eduardo Cadava and Sara Nadal-Melsió write, in a manner that illumines the poetic practice of Adnan—and al-Maʿālī and Celan—in its relation to temporality and language. "A militant understanding of the inevitable negativity of transmission," they continue, "sets the catastrophic character of transmission against the catastrophe that capital is and, embracing this negativity, remains faithful to what is most enigmatic in what we inherit, resists fixed determinations of what is transmitted to us" (*Politically Red*, 286–287).

133. Etel Adnan, *In the Heart of the Heart of Another Country*, 106.

134. Anahid Nersessian, *The Calamity Form*, 52, 54.

135. Adnan, *In the Heart of the Heart of Another Country*, 51, 84.

136. Walter Benjamin, "Zur Kritik der Gewalt," 64/"Toward the Critique of Violence," 60. I learn from the reading of this passage, and of the word *Entsetzung*, in Werner Hamacher's "Afformative, Strike," and his discussion of Benjamin's reading of the general strike and its de-posing, "afformative" form, as "political *a-thesis*" (1138), which, as Hamacher writes, "suspends its previous forms, and inaugurates another history no longer dominated by forms of positing and work, by forms of presentation and production, and no longer by forms" (1155).

137. Please see Lenora Hanson's reflection on "subsistence," from which I learn in the formulations I offer here: "These chapters seek to hold open subsistence ways of meaning and ways of living in order to track a different understanding of the relationship between capital accumulation and the everyday from the narratives that industrial capitalism gives us. Instead, these texts provide a collection of transient ways of life and translational ways of meaning as the combined effect of enclosure and survival through it" (*The Romantic Rhetoric of Accumulation*, 26), where subsistence, if it is "recorded in the historical record as riots, theft, executions, and labor disciplining" (63), it is, as well, a "wayness" (19), "both a form of life and a form of language" (15), not wholly superseded, overcome, or absorbed in capital or its abstractions.

138. "There is a settler rhythm, this one-two of capitalist production, a rhythm of citizen and subject, of dividuation and individuation, of genocide and law," Stefano Harney and Fred Moten write, and this rhythm responds to our "inclining" toward one another and places it under attack—"It is our incompletion that inclines us toward one another"—as our inclining is also a certain love, a leaning, an inessential dependency, "fucking up the production line that's supposed to improve us all," as well as a "being-incomplete": "Is it too much to put this the other way around? To say," Harney and Moten also write, "that love is the undercommon self-defense of being-incomplete?" (*All Incomplete*, 55, 41).

Works Cited

Abbas, Raouf, and Assem El-Dessouky. *The Large Landowning Class and the Peasantry in Egypt, 1837–1952*. Translated by Amer Mohsen with Mona Zirri. Syracuse, NY: Syracuse University Press, 2011.

AbdelMegeed, Maha. *Literary Optics: Staging the Collective in the Nahda*. Syracuse, NY: Syracuse University Press, 2024.

Abou El Fadl, Khaled. *Rebellion and Violence in Islamic Law*. New York: Cambridge University Press, 2001.

Aboul-Ela, Hosam. *Domestications: American Empire, Literary Culture, and the Postcolonial Lens*. Evanston, IL: Northwestern University Press, 2018.

Abu Lughod, Janet. *Before European Hegemony: The World System A.D. 1250–1350*. New York: Oxford University Press, 1991.

Abu-Manneh, Bashir. *The Palestinian Novel: From 1948 to the Present*. New York: Cambridge University Press, 2016.

Abū Qāsim ibn Ṣāʿīd al-Andalusī. *Kitāb ṭabaqāt al-umam*. Edited by Luis Cheikho. Beirut: al-Matbaʿa al-Katāthūlīkiyya, 1912.

Adamson, Peter. *The Arabic Plotinus: A Philosophical Study of the "Theology of Aristotle."* 2002. Piscataway, NJ: Gorgias Press, 2019.

———. "From the Necessary Existent to God." In *Interpreting Avicenna: Critical Essays*, edited by Peter Adamson, 170–189. Cambridge: Cambridge University Press, 2013.

Adnan, Etel. *L'Apocalypse arabe*. 1980. Paris: L'Harmattan, 2006.

———. *The Arab Apocalypse*. Sausalito, CA: Post-Apollo Press, 1989.

———. "Growing Up to Be a Woman Writer in Lebanon." In *Opening the Gates: An Anthology of Arab Feminist Writing*, 2nd ed., edited by Margot Badran and miriam cooke, 5–20. 1990. Bloomington: University of Indiana Press, 2004.

———. *Hunāka: Fī ḍiyāʾ wa ẓulma al-nafs wa al-ākhar*. Translated by Sargon Būloṣ. Köln: Manshurat al-Jamal, 2000.

——. *In the Heart of the Heart of Another Country*. San Francisco: City Lights, 2005.

——. *The Indian Never Had a Horse and Other Poems*. Sausalito, CA: Post-Apollo Press, 1985.

——. *Journey to Mount Tamalpais: An Essay*. Sausalito, CA: Post-Apollo Press, 1986.

——. "La Mer." In *Je suis un volcan criblé de météores: Poésies 1947–1997*, edited by Yves Michaud, 15–24. Paris: Gallimard, 2023.

——. "Letter." In *Letters for Olson*, gathered and edited by Benjamin Hollander, 9–15. New York City: Spuyten Duyvil, 2016.

——. *Night*. Callicoon, NY: Nightboat Books, 2016.

——. *Of Cities and Women: Letters to Fawwaz*. Sausalito, CA: Post-Apollo Press, 1993.

——. *Paris, When It's Naked*. Sausalito, CA: Post-Apollo Press, 1993.

——. *Sea and Fog*. Callicoon, NY: Nightboat Books, 2012.

——. *Seasons*. Sausalito, CA: Post-Apollo Press, 2008.

——. *Shifting the Silence*. New York: Nightboat Books, 2020.

——. *Sitt Marie Rose*. Translated by Georgina Kleege. Sausalito: Post-Apollo Press, 1982.

——. *The Spring Flowers Own and Manifestations of the Voyage*. Sausalito, CA: Post-Apollo Press, 1990.

——. *Surge*. New York: Nightboat, 2018.

——. *There: In the Light and the Darkness of the Self and of the Other*. Sausalito, CA: Post-Apollo Press, 1997.

——. "To Write in a Foreign Language." In *To Look at the Sea Is to Become What One Is: An Etel Adnan Reader*, vol. 1, edited by Thom Donovan and Brandon Shimoda, 245–257. Brooklyn, NY: Nightboat Books, 2014.

Adnan, Etel, with Laurie Adler. *The Beauty of Light: Interviews*. Translated by Ethan Mitchell. New York: Nightboat Books, 2023.

Adorno, Theodor. *Minima Moralia: Reflections from Damaged Life*. Translated by E. F. N. Jephcott. London: Verso, 1974.

——. *Minima Moralia: Reflexionen aus dem beschädigten Leben*. 1951. Suhrkamp: Frankfurt am Main, 1969.

Agamben, Giorgio. *Homo Sacer: Sovereign Power and Bare Life*. Translated by Daniel Heller-Roazen. Stanford, CA: Stanford University Press, 1998.

al-Akhfash. *Kitāb al-ʿarūḍ*. Edited by Sayyed al-Baḥrāwī. Cairo: Dār al-Sharqiyyāt, 1998.

Aland, Barbara, and Kurt Aland, Johannes Karavidopoulos, Carlo M. Martini, and Bruce M. Metzger, eds., based on the edition of Eberhard and Nestle. *Novum Testamentum Graece*. Stuttgart: Deutsche Bibelgesellschaft, 2016.

Alcalay, Ammiel. "'A Dance of Freedom': In the Worlds of Etel Adnan." In *To Look at the Sea Is to Become What One Is: An Etel Adnan Reader*, vol. 1, edited by Thom Donovan and Brandon Shimoda, iii–xv. Brooklyn, NY: Nightboat Books, 2014.

———. *A Little History*. Edited by Fred Dewey. Los Angeles: UpSet Press, 2013.
———. *Memories of Our Future: Selected Essays, 1982–1999*. San Francisco: City Lights Books, 2001.
Alessandrini, Anthony C. *Decolonize Multiculturalism*. New York: OR Books, 2023.
Ali, Samer M. *Arabic Literary Salons in the Islamic Middle Ages: Poetry, Public Performance, and the Presentation of the Past*. Notre Dame, IN: University of Notre Dame Press, 2010.
Allan, Michael. "Dying to Read: Reflections on the Ends of Literacy." *New Literary History* 51, no. 2 (Spring 2020): 281–298.
———. *In the Shadow of World Literature: Sites of Reading in Colonial Egypt*. Princeton, NJ: Princeton University Press, 2016.
———. "Old Media/New Futures: Revolutionary Reverberations of Fanon's Radio." *PMLA* 134, no. 1 (2019): 188–193.
Al-Taie, Yvonne. *Poetik der Unverständlichkeit: Schreibweisen der obscuritas als problematisiertes Weltverhältnis bei Johann Fischart, Johann Georg Hamann, Franz Kafka, und Paul Celan*. Paderborn: Brill Fink, 2022.
Althusser, Louis. *For Marx*. Translated by Ben Brewster. 1965. London: Verso, 1996
———. "From Capital to Marx's Philosophy." In *Reading Capital: The Complete Edition*, edited by Louis Althusser, Étienne Balibar, Roger Establet, Pierre Machery, and Jacques Rancière, and translated by Ben Brewster and David Fernbach, 9–72. 1965. London: Verso, 2015.
———. "The Object of Capital." In *Reading Capital: The Complete Edition*, edited by Louis Althusser, Étienne Balibar, Roger Establet, Pierre Machery, and Jacques Rancière, and translated by Ben Brewster and David Fernbach, 215–355. 1965. London: Verso, 2015.
———. "The Underground Current of the Materialism of the Encounter." In *Philosophy of the Encounter: Later Writings, 1978–1987*, translated by G. M. Goshgarian, 163–207. London: Verso, 2006.
Amin, Samir. *Accumulation on a World Scale: A Critique of the Theory of Underdevelopment*. Vols., 1–2. Translated by Brian Pearce. New York: Monthly Review Press 1974.
Ammonius. *On Aristotle Categories*. Translated by S. Marc Cohen and Gareth B. Matthews. London: Bloomsbury, 1991.
Anghie, Antony. "Francisco de Vitoria and the Colonial Origins of International Law." In *Imperialism, Sovereignty, and the Making of International Law*, 13–31. New York: Cambridge University Press, 2004.
Anidjar, Gil. *Blood: A Critique of Christianity*. New York: Columbia University Press, 2014.
———. *Semites: Race, Religion, Literature*. Stanford, CA: Stanford University Press, 2007.
Antoon, Sinan (Sinān Anṭūn). *The Book of Collateral Damage*. Translated by Jonathan Wright. New Haven, CT: Yale University Press, 2019.
———. *Fihris*. Beirut: Manshūrāt al-Jamal, 2016.

Aquinas, St. Thomas. *Commentary on Aristotle's Politics*. Translated by Richard J. Regan. Indianapolis: Hackett Publishing, 2007.

———. *Sententia libri politicorum*. In *Opera omnia*, vol. 48. Rome: Dominican Friars of Santa Sabina, 1971.

———. *Summa theologiae*. In *Opera omnia*, vols. 4–12. Rome: Polyglotta, 1888–1906.

———. *The "Summa theologica" of St. Thomas Aquinas*. Translated by the Fathers of the English Dominican Province. London: Washbourne, 1915.

Arendt, Hannah. "The Decline of the Nation-State and the End of the Rights of Man." In *The Origins of Totalitarianism*, 267–302. 1948. New York: Harvest, 1973.

———. *The Human Condition*. 1958. Chicago: University of Chicago Press, 1998.

Aristotle. *Aristotle's On the Soul*. Translated by Hippocrates G. Apostle. 1981. Merrimack, NH: Thomas Moore College Press, 2021.

———. *Categories*. Translated by H. P. Cooke and Hugh Tredennick. Cambridge, MA: Harvard University Press, Loeb Classical library, 1938.

———. *Faṣl fī ḥarf al-lām min kitāb mā baʿd al-ṭabīʿa li-Arisṭūṭālīs*. In *Arisṭū ʿind al-ʿArab*, edited by ʿAbd al-Raḥmān Badawī, 1–11. Kuwait: Wikālat al-Maṭbūʿāt, 1978.

———. *Kitāb ʻanūlūṭīqā al-awākhir,' wa huwwa al-maʿrūf bi-kitāb ʻal-burhān' li-Arisṭūṭālīs*. In *Manṭiq Arisṭū*, vol. 2, edited by ʿAbd al-Raḥmān Badawī. Cairo: Maṭbaʿat Dār al-Kutub al-Miṣriyya, 1949.

———. *Kitāb Arisṭūṭālīs al-musammā ʻqāṭīghūrīā,' ʾayy ʻal-maqūlāt.'* In *Manṭiq Arisṭū*, vol. 1, edited by ʿAbd al-Raḥmān Badawī, translated by Isḥāq ibn Ḥunayn. Cairo: Maṭbaʿat Dār al-Kutub al-Miṣriyya, 1948.

———. *Metaphysics*, Books 1–9. Translated by Hugh Tredennick. Cambridge, MA.: Harvard University Press, Loeb Classical Library, 1933.

———. *Nicomachean Ethics*. Translated by H. Rackham. Cambridge, MA: Harvard University Press, Loeb Classical library, 1934.

———. *On Interpretation*. Translated by H. P. Cooke and Hugh Tredennick. Cambridge, MA: Harvard University Press, Loeb Classical Library, 1938.

———. *On the Soul*. Translated by W. S. Hett. Cambridge, MA: Harvard University Press, Loeb Classical Library, 1957.

———. *Aristotle's Politics*. Translated by Hippocrates G. Apostle and Lloyd P. Gerson. Grinnell, IA: Peripatetic Press, 1986.

———. *Politics*. Translated by H. Rackham. Cambridge, MA: Harvard University Press, Loeb Classical Library, 1944.

———. *Posterior Analytics*. Translated by Hugh Tredennick and E. S. Forster. Cambridge, MA: Harvard University Press, Loeb Classical Library, 1960.

———. *Posterior Analytics*. Translated by Jonathan Barnes. Oxford: Clarendon, 1993.

Arvin, Maile. *Possessing Polynesians: The Science of Settler Colonial Whiteness in Hawaiʻi and Oceania*. Durham, NC: Duke University Press, 2019.

Asad, Talal. "Medieval Heresy: An Anthropological View." *Social History* 11, no. 3 (October 1986): 345–362.

———. *On Suicide Bombing*. New York: Columbia University Press, 2007.

———. "Reconfigurations of Law and Ethics in Colonial Egypt." In *Formations of the Secular: Christianity, Islam, Modernity*, 205–256. Stanford, CA: Stanford University Press, 2003.
———. "Reflections on Violence, Law, and Humanitarianism." *Critical Inquiry* 41, no. 2 (Winter 2015): 390–427.
———. *Secular Translations: Nation-State, Modern Self, and Calculative Reason.* New York: Columbia University Press, 2018.
al-ʿAskarī, Abū Hilāl. *Kitāb al-ṣināʿatayn al-kitāba wa-al-shiʿr.* Edited by Mufīd Qumīḥa. Beirut: Dār al-Kutub al-ʿIlmiyya, 1984.
St. Augustine. *The City of God against the Pagans.* Edited and translated by R. W. Dyson. Cambridge: Cambridge University Press, 1998.
Azeb, Sophia. "Crossing the Saharan Boundary: Lotus and the Legibility of Africanness." *Research in African Literatures* 50, no. 3 (Fall 2019): 91–117.
al-Azmeh, Aziz. *Muslim Kingship: Power and the Sacred in Muslim, Christian, and Pagan Polities.* London: I. B. Tauris, 2001.
Balibar, Étienne. *Identity and Difference: John Locke and the Invention of Consciousness.* Translated by Warren Montag. London: Verso, 2013.
———. "'My Self,' 'My Own': Variations on Locke." In *Citizen Subject: Foundations for Philosophical Anthropology*, translated by Steven Miller, 74–91. New York: Fordham University Press, 2017.
———. "On the Basic Concepts of Historical Materialism." In *Reading Capital: The Complete Edition*, edited by Louis Althusser, Étienne Balibar, Roger Establet, Pierre Machery, Jacques Rancière, and translated by Ben Brewster and David Fernbach, 357–480. 1965. London: Verso, 2015.
Baracchi, Claudia. *Aristotle's Ethics as First Philosophy.* New York: Cambridge University Press, 2008.
Barakat, Rana. "Writing/Righting Palestine Studies: Settler Colonialism, Indigenous Sovereignty, and Resisting the Ghost(s) of History." *Settler Colonial Studies* 8, no. 3 (2018): 349–363.
Barker, Joanne. *Native Acts: Law, Recognition, and Cultural Authenticity.* Durham, NC: Duke University Press, 2011.
Batarseh, Amanda. "Love, Countryside, and the Fellah: Tawfiq Canaan's Romantic Translation." *Studies in Romanticism* 62, no. 2 (Summer 2023): 283–295.
Batatu, Hanna. *The Old Social Classes and the Revolutionary Movements of Iraq: A Study of Iraq's Old Landed and Commercial Classes and of Its Communists, Baʿathists, and Free Officers.* 1978. London: Saqi, 2004.
al-Bayhaqī. *Tārīkh ḥukamāʾ al-Islām.* Edited by Muḥammad Kurd ʿAlī. Damascus: al-Majmaʿ al-ʿIlmī al-ʿArabī, 1946.
Benjamin, Walter. "Theses on the Philosophy of History." In *Illuminations*, translated by Harry Zohn, 253–264. New York: Schocken, 1968.
———. "Toward the Critique of Violence." In *Toward the Critique of Violence: A Critical Edition*, edited by Peter Fenves and Julia Ng, 39–61. Stanford, CA: Stanford University Press, 2021.

———. "Über den Begriff der Geschichte." In *Illuminationen*, 251–261. Frankfurt am Main: Suhrkamp, 1974.
———. "Zur Kritik der Gewalt." In *Zur Kritik der Gewalt und andere Aufsätze*, 29–65. Frankfurt am Main: Suhrkamp, 1965.
Bernasconi, Robert. "Will the Real Kant Please Stand Up: The Challenge of Enlightenment Racism to the Study of the History of Philosophy." *Radical Philosophy* 117 (2003): 13–22.
Bertolacci, Amos. *The Reception of Aristotle's* Metaphysics *in Avicenna's* Kitāb al-Shifāʾ*: A Milestone in Western Metaphysical Thought*. Leiden: Brill, 2006.
Bhandar, Brenna. *Colonial Lives of Property: Law, Land, and Racial Regimes of Ownership*. Durham, NC: Duke University Press, 2018.
Biddick, Kathleen. *The Typological Imaginary: Circumcision, Technology, History*. Philadelphia: University of Pennsylvania Press, 2003.
Bishara, Fahad Ahmad. *A Sea of Debt: Law and Economic Life in the Western Indian Ocean*. New York: Cambridge University Press, 2017.
Black, Deborah L. *Logic and Aristotle's* Rhetoric *and* Poetics *in Medieval Arabic Philosophy*. Leiden: Brill, 1990.
Blumenberg, Hans. *The Legitimacy of the Modern Age*. Translated by Robert M. Wallace. Cambridge, MA: MIT Press, 1985.
Branton, Lancelot C . L., trans. *The Septuagint with Apocrypha*. 1851. Peabody, MA: Hendrickson, 1986.
Brown, Peter. *The Making of Late Antiquity*. Cambridge, MA: Harvard University Press, 1978.
Bruyneel, Kevin. *Settler Memory: The Disavowal of Indigeneity and the Politics of Race in the United States*. Chapel Hill: University of North Carolina Press, 2021.
Butler, Judith. *Giving an Account of Oneself*. New York: Fordham University Press, 2005.
———. *Notes Toward a Performative Theory of Assembly*. Cambridge, MA: Harvard University Press, 2015.
Bynum, Caroline Walker. *Christian Materiality: An Essay on Religion in Late Medieval Europe*. New York: Zone Books, 2011.
———. *The Resurrection of the Body in Western Christianity, 200–1336*. New York: Columbia University Press, 1996.
Byrd, Jodi A. "Loving Unbecoming: The Queer Politics of the Transitive Native." In *Critically Sovereign: Indigenous Gender, Sexuality, and Feminist Studies*, edited by Joanne Barker, 207–227. Durham, NC: Duke University Press, 2017.
———. *The Transit of Empire: Indigenous Critiques of Colonialism*. Minneapolis: University of Minnesota Press, 2011.
Cadava, Eduardo, and Sara Nadal-Melsió. *Politically Red*. Cambridge, MA: The Massachusetts Institute of Technology Press, 2023.
Carter, J. Kameron. *The Anarchy of Black Religion: A Mystic Song*. Durham, NC: Duke University Press, 2023.

———. *Race: A Theological Account.* Oxford: Oxford University Press, 2008.

Celan, Paul. *Breathturn into Timestead: The Collected Later Poetry.* Translated by Pierre Joris. New York: Farrar, Straus and Giroux, 2014.

———. *Der Meridian: Endfassung—Vorstuffen—Materialen.* Edited by Bernhard Böschenstein and Heino Schmull, with Michael Schwarzkopf and Christiane Wittkop. Frankfurt am Main: Suhrkamp, 1999.

———. *Die Gedichte: Kommentierte Gesamtausgabe.* Edited by Barbara Wiedemann. Frankfurt am Main: Suhrkamp, 2003.

———. *Memory Rose into Threshold Speech: The Collected Earlier Poetry.* Translated by Pierre Joris. New York: Farrar, Straus and Giroux, 2014.

———. "The Meridian." In *Collected Prose,* translated by Rosemarie Waldrop, 37–55. Riverdale-on-Hudson, NY: Sheep Meadow Press, 1986.

———. *The Meridian: Final Version—Drafts—Materials.* Translated by Pierre Joris. Stanford, CA: Stanford University Press, 2011.

———. *Mikrolithen sinds, Steinchen: Die Prosa aus dem Nachlaß.* Edited by Barbara Wiedmann and Bertrand Badiou. Frankfurt am Main: Suhrkamp, 2005.

Césaire, Aimé. *Discourse on Colonialism.* Translated by Joan Pinkham. Introduction by Robin D. G. Kelly. 1972. New York: Monthly Review Press, 2000.

———. *Discours sur le colonialisme.* 1955. *Paris*: Présence Africaine, 2004.

Chandler, Nahum D. X: *The Problem of the Negro as a Problem for Thought.* New York: Fordham University Press, 2014.

Cohen, Jeremy. *Living Letters of the Law: Ideas of the Jew in Medieval Christianity.* Berkeley: University of California Press, 1999.

Costa Vargas, João H. *Never Meant to Survive: Genocide and Utopias in Black Diasporic Communities.* Lanham, MD: Rowman and Littlefield, 2008.

Coulthard, Glen Sean. *Red Skin, White Masks: Rejecting the Colonial Politics of Recognition.* Minneapolis: University of Minnesota Press, 2014.

Cover, Robert. "The Supreme Court, 1982 Term—Foreword: Nomos and Narrative." *Harvard Law Review* 97, no. 1 (November 1983): 4–68.

———. "Violence and the Word." *Yale Law Journal* 95, no. 8 (July 1986): 1601–1629.

Çubukçu, Ayça. *For the Love of Humanity: The World Tribunal on Iraq.* Philadelphia: University of Pennsylvania Press, 2018.

D'Ancona Costa, Cristina. "Commenting on Aristotle: From Late Antiquity to the Arab Aristotelianism." In *Der Kommentar in Antike und Mittelalter,* edited by Wilhelm Geerlings and Christian Schulze, 201–251. Leiden: Brill, 2002.

Daniel, Norman. *Islam and the West: The Making of an Image.* 1960. Oxford: Oneworld, 2009.

Darwish, Mahmoud (Maḥmūd Darwīsh). *Aḥad ʿashar kawkaban.* 1992. Beirut: Dār al-Jadīd, 1999.

———. *Athar al-farāsha: Yawmiyyāt.* Beirut: Riyāḍ al-Rayyis, 2008.

———. *Ḥālat ḥiṣār.* Beirut: Riyāḍ al-Rayyis, 2002.

———. "The 'Red Indian's' Penultimate Speech to the White Man." Translated by Fady Joudah. *Harvard Review* 36 (2009): 152–159.

Das, Aileen R. *Galen and the Arabic Reception of Plato's* Timaeus. Cambridge: Cambridge University Press, 2020.

Davis, Muriam Haleh. *Markets of Civilization: Islam and Racial Capitalism in Algeria.* Durham, NC: Duke University Press, 2022.

Day, Iyko. *Alien Capital: Asian Racialization and the Logic of Settler Colonial Capitalism.* Durham, NC: Duke University Press, 2016.

Dayan, Colin. *The Law Is a White Dog: How Legal Rituals Make and Unmake Persons.* Princeton, NJ: Princeton University Press, 2011.

De Lubac, Henri. *Corpus Mysticum: The Eucharist and the Church in the Middle Ages.* 1949. Translated by Gemma Simmonds, with Richard Price and Christopher Stephens. Notre Dame, IN: University of Notre Dame Press, 2007.

Derrida, Jacques. *The Animal That Therefore I Am.* Edited by Marie-Louise Mallet. Translated by David Wills. New York: Fordham University Press, 2008.

———. "The Force of Law: The 'Mystical Foundation of Authority.'" Translated by Mary Quaintance. *Cardozo Law Review* 11, no. 5–6 (July/August 1990): 920–1045.

———. *Glas.* Translated by John P. Leavey Jr. and Richard Rand. Lincoln: University of Nebraska Press, 1986.

———. *Heidegger: The Question of Being and History.* Translated by Geoffrey Bennington. Chicago: University of Chicago Press, 2016.

———. "*Ousia* and *Grammē*: Note on a Note from *Being and Time.*" In *Margins of Philosophy,* translated by Alan Bass, 29–67. Chicago: University of Chicago Press, 1982.

———. "Violence and Metaphysics: An Essay on the Thought of Emmanuel Lévinas." In *Writing and Difference,* translated by Alan Bass, 79–153. Chicago: University of Chicago Press, 1978.

Dod, Bernard G. "Aristoteles latinus." In *The Cambridge History of Later Medieval Philosophy,* edited by Norman Kretzman, Anthony Kenny, and Jan Pinborg, 45–79. 1982. New York: Cambridge University Press, 1997.

Du Bois, W. E. B. *Black Reconstruction in America: 1860–1880.* 1935. Introduction by David Levering Lewis. New York: Free Press, 1998.

Dubois, Page. *Slaves and Other Objects.* Chicago: University of Chicago Press, 2008.

El-Ariss, Tarek. *Leaks, Hacks, and Scandals: Arab Culture in the Digital Age.* Princeton, NJ: Princeton University Press, 2019.

El-Desouky, Ayman A. *The Intellectual and the People in Egyptian Literature and Culture: Amāra and the 2011 Revolution.* London: Palgrave, 2014.

Elhalaby, Esmat. "Empire and Arab Indology." *Modern Intellectual History* 19, no. 4 (2022): 1–25.

El-Rouayheb, Khaled. *Islamic Intellectual History in the Seventeenth Century: Scholarly Currents in the Ottoman Empire and the Maghreb.* New York: Cambridge University Press, 2015.

El Shakry, Hoda. *The Literary Qur'ān: Narrative Ethics in the Maghreb*. New York: Fordham University Press, 2020.
Elshakry, Marwa. *Reading Darwin in Arabic*. Chicago: University of Chicago Press, 2014.
El Shakry, Omnia. *The Arabic Freud: Psychoanalysis and Islam in Modern Egypt*. Princeton, NJ: Princeton University Press, 2017.
———. *The Great Social Laboratory: Subjects of Knowledge in Colonial and Postcolonial Egypt*. Stanford, CA: Stanford University Press, 2007.
El Shamsy, Ahmed. *The Canonization of Islamic Law: A Social and Intellectual History*. Cambridge: Cambridge University Press, 2015.
Endress, Gerhard. "The Circle of al-Kindī: Early Arabic Translations from the Greek and the Rise of Arabic Philosophy." In *The Ancient Tradition in Christian and Islamic Hellenism*, edited by Gerhard Endres and Remke Kruk, 43–76. Leiden: CNWS Publications, 1997.
———. "Mathematics and Philosophy in Medieval Islam." In *The Enterprise of Science in Islam: New Perspectives*, edited by Jan P. Hogendijk and Abdelhamid I. Sabra, 121–176. Cambridge, MA: MIT Press, 2003.
Erakat, Noura. *Justice for Some: Law and the Question of Palestine*. Stanford, CA: Stanford University Press, 2019.
———. "Whiteness as Property in Israel: Revival, Rehabilitation, and Removal." *Harvard Journal on Racial and Ethnic Justice* 31 (2015): 1–31.
Erdmann, Carl. *The Origin of the Idea of Crusade*. Translated by Marshall W. Baldwin and Walter Goffart. 1935. Princeton: Princeton University Press, 1977.
Ertürk, Nergis. *Writing in Red: Literature and Revolution across Turkey and the Soviet Union*. New York: Columbia University Press, 2024.
Esmeir, Samera. "1927: How Seismology Received Islamic Theology." *Comparative Studies of South Asia, Africa, and the Middle East* 40, no. 2 (August 2020): 329–344.
———. "Bandung: Reflections on the Sea, the World, and Colonialism." In *Bandung, Global History, and International Law: Critical Pasts and Pending Futures*, edited by Luis Eslava, Michael Fakhri, and Vasuki Nesiah, 81–94. New York: Cambridge University Press, 2018.
———. *Juridical Humanity: A Colonial History*. Stanford, CA: Stanford University Press, 2011.
———. "On Becoming Less of the World." *History of the Present* 8, no. 1 (Spring 2018): 88–116.
———. "On the Coloniality of Modern Law." *Critical Analysis of Law* 2, no. 1 (2015): 19–41.
Estes, Nick. *Our History is the Future: Standing Rock versus the Dakota Access Pipeline and the Long Tradition of Indigenous Resistance*. London: Verso, 2019.
Estes, Nick, Melanie K. Yazzie, Jennifer Nez Denetdale, and David Correia. *Red Nation Rising: From Bordertown Violence to Native Liberation*. Foreword by Radmilla Cody and Brandon Benallie. Oakland, CA: PM Press, 2021.

Fahmy, Khaled. *In Quest of Justice: Islamic Law and Forensic Medicine in Modern Egypt*. Oakland: University of California Press, 2020.

Fanon, Frantz. *Les damnés de la terre*. 1961. Paris: Découverte, 2002.

———. *The Wretched of the Earth*. Translated by Constance Farrington. New York: Grove Press, 1963.

al-Fārābī, Abū Naṣr. *Falsafat Aflāṭūn wa ajzāʾuhā wa marātib ajzāʾihā min awwalihā ilā ākhirihā*. In *Aflāṭūn fī al-Islām*, edited by ʿAbd al-Raḥmān Badawī, 5–27. Tehran: Muʾassasat Muṭāliʿāt Islāmī Danishgah Makgīl, 1974.

———. *Falsafat Aristūṭālīs wa ajzaʾ falsafatihi wa marātib ajzāʾihā wa al-mawḍiʿ alladhī minhu ibtadāʾ wa ilayhi intahā*. Edited by Muḥsin Mahdī. Beirut: Dār Majallat Shiʿr, 1961.

———. *Iḥṣāʾ al-ʿulūm*. Edited by ʿUthmān Amīn. Cairo: Maktabat al-Khānjā, 1931.

———. *Kitāb al-alfāẓ al-mustaʿmala fī al-manṭiq*. Edited by Muḥsin Mahdī. Beirut: Dār al-Mashriq, 1968.

———. *Kitāb al-burhān*. In *al-Manṭiq ʿind al-Fārābī*, vol. 4, edited by Mājid Fakhry, 17–96. Beirut: Dār al-Mashriq, 2012.

———. *Kitāb al-ḥurūf*. 1969. Edited by Muḥsin Mahdī. Beirut: Dār al-Mashriq, 2004.

———. "Letter on the Aims of Aristotle's Metaphysics." In *Classical Arabic Philosophy: An Anthology of Sources*, translated by Jon McGinnis and David C. Reisman, 78–81. Indianapolis: Hackett, 2007.

———. *Mabādiʾ ārāʾ ahl al-madīna al-fāḍila*. Arabic and English facing pages. Revised and translated by Richard Walzer. 1985. Chicago: Kazi Publications, 1998.

———. "Mā yanbaghī taʿalummuhu qabla al-falsafa." In *al-Rasāʾil al-falsafiyya al-ṣughrā*, edited by ʿAbd al-Amīr al-Aʿsam, 269–282. Damascus: Dār al-Takwīn, 2012.

———. *The Philosophy of Aristotle: The Parts of His Philosophy, the Ranks of Order of its Parts, the Position from Which He Started and the One He Reached*. In *The Philosophy of Plato and Aristotle*, edited and translated by Muḥsin Mahdī, 69–130. 1962. Ithaca, NY: Cornell University Press, 2001.

———. *The Philosophy of Plato: Its Parts, the Ranks of Order of Its Parts, From the Beginning to the End*. In *The Philosophy of Plato and Aristotle*, edited and translated by Muḥsin Mahdī, 51–67. 1962. Ithaca, NY: Cornell University Press, 2001.

———. *al-Rasāʾil al-falsafiyya al-ṣughrā*. Edited by ʿAbd al-Amīr al-Aʿsam. Damascus: Dār al-Takwīn, 2012.

———. *Risāla fī aghrāḍ mā baʿd al-ṭabīʿa*. In *Alfārābī's Philosophische Abhandlungen*, edited by Friedrich Dieterici, 34–38. Leiden: Brill, 1890.

Fattal, Simone. "On Perception: Etel Adnan's Visual Art." In *Etel Adnan: Critical Essays on the Arab-American Writer and Artist*, edited by Lisa Suhair Majaj and Amal Amireh, 89–102. Jefferson, NC: McFarland, 2001.

Federici, Silvia. *Caliban and the Witch: Women, the Body, and Primitive Accumulation*. Brooklyn, NY: Autonomedia, 2004.

Ferguson, Heather L. *The Proper Order of Things: Language, Power, and Law in Ottoman Administrative Discourses*. Stanford, CA: Stanford University Press, 2018.

Ferreira da Silva, Denise. "Hacking the Subject: Black Feminism and Refusal beyond the Limits of Critique." *philoSOPHIA* 8, no. 1 (Winter 2018): 19–41.
———. "To Be Announced: Radical Praxis or Knowing (at) the Limits of Justice." *Social Text* 114 31, no. 1 (Spring 2013): 43–62.
———. *Toward a Global Idea of Race*. Minneapolis: University of Minnesota Press, 2008.
———. *Unpayable Debt*. London: Sternberg, 2022.
Fitzpatrick, Peter. *Mythology of Modern Law*. London: Routledge, 1992.
Foucault, Michel. *The History of Sexuality*. Vol. 1. 1976. Translated by Robert Hurley. New York: Random House, 1990.
———. *The Order of Things*. 1966. New York: Vintage 1994.
Frank, Andre Gunder. *Capitalism and Underdevelopment in Latin America: Historical Studies of Chile and Brazil*. 1967. New York: Monthly Review Press, 2009.
Frank, Richard M. *Creation and the Cosmic System: Al-Ghazālī and Avicenna*. Heidelberg: Carl Winter Universitätsverlag, 1992.
Friedman, John Block. *The Monstrous Races in Medieval Art and Thought*. 1981. Syracuse, NY: Syracuse University Press, 2000.
Fulcher of Chartres. *The Chronicle of Fulcher of Chartres*, Book I. In *The First Crusade: The Chronicle of Fulcher of Chartres and Other Source Materials*. 2nd ed. Edited by Edward Peters, 47–101. Philadelphia: University of Pennsylvania Press, 1998.
Funkenstein, Amos. "Changes in Christian Anti-Jewish Polemics in the Twelfth Century." In *Perceptions of Jewish History*, 172–201. Los Angeles: University of California Press, 1993.
Furani, Khaled. *Silencing the Sea: Secular Rhythms in Palestinian Poetry*. Stanford, CA: Stanford University Press, 2012.
Gana, Nouri. *Melancholy Acts: Defeat and Cultural Critique in the Arab World*. New York: Fordham University Press, 2023.
Gilmore, Ruth Wilson. "Race, Prisons, and War: Scenes from the History of US Violence." In *Abolition Geography: Essays toward Liberation*, edited by Brenna Bhandar and Alberto Toscano, 176–195. London: Verso, 2022.
Goldstein, Alyosha. "'In the Constant Flux of Its Incessant Renewal': The Social Reproduction of Racial Capitalism and Settler Colonial Entitlement." In *Colonial Racial Capitalism*, edited by Susan Koshy, Lisa Marie Cacho, Jodi A. Byrd, and Brian Jordan Jefferson, 60–87. Durham, NC: Duke University Press, 2023.
Gordon, Joy. *Invisible War: The United States and the Iraq Sanctions*. Cambridge, MA: Harvard University Press, 2010.
Graff Zivin, Erin. *Figurative Inquisitions: Conversion, Torture, and Truth in the Luso-Hispanic Atlantic*. Evanston, IL: Northwestern University Press, 2014.
Griffel Frank. *The Formation of Post-Classical Philosophy in Islam*. New York: Oxford University Press, 2021.

Gruendler, Beatrice. *The Rise of the Arabic Book*. Cambridge, MA: Harvard University Press, 2020.

Gutas, Dimitri. "Aspects of Literary Form and Genre in Arabic Logical Works." In *Glosses and Commentaries on Aristotelian Logical Texts: The Syriac, Arabic, and Medieval Latin Traditions*, edited by Charles S.F. Burnett, 29–76. London: Warburg Institute, 1993.

———. *Avicenna and the Aristotelian Tradition: Introduction to Reading Avicenna's Philosophical Works*. 2nd rev. and enl. ed. Leiden, Brill 2014.

———. *Greek Thought, Arabic Culture: The Graeco-Arabic Translation Movement in Baghdad and Early ʿAbbasid Society*. New York: Routledge, 1998.

———. "Paul the Persian on the Classification of the Parts of Aristotle's Philosophy: A Milestone between Alexandria and Baghdad." In *Greek Philosophers in the Arabic Tradition*, 231–267. 1983. Burlington, VT: Ashgate Varorium, 2000.

———. "The Starting Point of Philosophical Studies in Alexandrian and Arabic Aristotelianism." *Greek Philosophers in the Arabic Tradition*, 115–123. 1985. Burlington, VT: Ashgate Varorium, 2000.

Hadot, Pierre. *Plotinus or the Simplicity of Vision*. Translated by Michael Chase. Chicago: University of Chicago Press, 1998.

———. "Spiritual Exercises." In *Philosophy as a Way of Life*, edited with an introduction by Arnold Davidson, translated by Michael Chase, 81–125. Malden, MA: Blackwell, 1995.

———. *What Is Ancient Philosophy?* Translated by Michael Chase. Cambridge, MA: Harvard University Press, 2022.

Haj, Samira. *The Making of Iraq, 1900–1963: Capital, Power, Ideology*. Albany: State University of New York Press, 1997.

Halim, Hala. "'A Theatre—or, More Aptly, A Laboratory': India in the 1940s Egyptian Left as an Antecedent of Bandung." *Comparative Literature Studies* 59, no. 1 (2022): 49–76.

Hamacher, Werner. "Afformative, Strike." Translated by Dana Hollander. *Cardozo Law Review* 13 (1991): 1133–1157.

———. *Für—Die Philologie*. Frankfurt am Main: Roughbooks, 2009.

———. *Minima Philologica*. Translated by Catharine Diehl and Jason Groves. New York: Fordham University Press, 2015.

———. "The Second of Inversion: Movements of a Figure through Celan's Poetry." In *Word Traces: Readings of Paul Celan*, edited by Aris Fioretos, translated by Peter Fenves, 219–263. Baltimore: Johns Hopkins University Press, 1994.

Han, Sora. *Letters of the Law: Race and the Fantasy of Colorblindness in American Law*. Stanford, CA: Stanford University Press, 2015.

Hanke, Lewis. *All Mankind Is One: A Study of the Disputation between Bartolomé de Las Casas and Juan Ginés de Sepúlveda*. De Kalb: Northern Illinois University Press, 1974.

———. *Aristotle and the American Indians: A Study in Race Prejudice in the Modern World*. Chicago: Henry Regnery, 1959.

Hanson, Lenora. *The Romantic Rhetoric of Accumulation*. Stanford, CA: Stanford University Press, 2023.
Hanssen, Jens. *Fin de Siècle Beirut: The Making of an Ottoman Provincial Capital*. Oxford: Oxford University Press, 2005.
Harb, Lara. *Arabic Poetics: Aesthetic Experience in Classical Arabic Literature*. New York: Cambridge University Press, 2020.
Harney, Stefano, and Fred Moten. *All Incomplete*. New York: Minor Compositions, 2021.
———. *The Undercommons: Fugitive Planning and Black Study*. New York: Minor Compositions, 2013.
Harris, Cheryl I. "Whiteness as Property." *Harvard Law Review* 106, no. 8 (June 1993): 1707–1791.
Hart, H. L. A. *The Concept of Law*. 3rd ed. 1961. Oxford: Oxford University Press, 2012.
Hartman, Saidiya V. *Scenes of Subjection: Terror, Slavery, and Self-Making in Nineteenth-Century America*. New York: Oxford University Press, 1998.
Hegel, G. W. F. *Elements of the Philosophy of Right*. Edited by Allan Wood. Translated by H. B. Nisbet. Cambridge: Cambridge University Press, 1991.
———. *Grundlinien der Philosophie des Rechts*. Edited by Klaus Grotsch. Hamburg: Felix Meiner, 2009.
Heidegger, Martin. *Being and Time*. Translated by John MacQuarrie and Edward Robinson. New York: Harper, 1962.
———. *The Metaphysical Foundations of Logic*. Translated by Michael Heim. Bloomington: University of Indiana Press, 1984.
———. "The Nature of Language." In *On the Way to Language*, translated by Peter D. Hertz, 57–108. New York: Harper and Row, 1971.
———. "The Origin of the Work of Art." In *Off the Beaten Track*, edited and translated by Julian Young and Kenneth Haynes, 1–56. Cambridge: Cambridge University Press, 2002.
———. *The Principle of Reason*. Translated by Reginald Lilly. Bloomington: University of Indiana Press, 1991.
———. *Der Satz vom Grund*. Pfullingen: Neske, 1965.
———. *Sein und Zeit*. 1926. Tübingen: Max Niemeyer, 1993.
———. *Das Wesen der Sprache*. In *Unterwegs zur Sprache*, 157–216. Stuttgart: Neske, 1959.
Heller-Roazen, Daniel. *The Inner Touch: Archaeology of a Sensation*. New York: Zone Books, 2007.
Holt, Elizabeth M. *Fictitious Capital: Silk, Cotton, and the Rise of the Arabic Novel*. New York: Fordham University Press, 2017.
Hussain, Nasser. *The Jurisprudence of Emergency: Colonialism and the Rule of Law*. 2003. Ann Arbor: University of Michigan Press, 2019.
Ibn Abī Uṣaybiʿa. *ʿUyūn al-anbāʾ fī ṭabaqāt al-aṭibbāʾ*. Edited by August Müller. Cairo: al-Matbʿa al-Wahbiyya, 1882.

Ibn Jinnī. *al-Lumʿ fī al-ʿarabiyya*. Edited by Ḥāmid al-Muʾmin. Beirut: Maktabat al-Nahḍa al-ʿArabiyya, 1985.
Ibn Khaldūn. *al-Muqaddima*. Beirut: Dār al-Kutub al-ʿIlmiyya, 1992.
Ibn Maymūn. *Dalālat al-ḥāʾirīn*. Vols. 1–3. 1856–1866. Edited by Salomon Munk. Piskataway: Gorgias Press, 2010.
——. *The Guide of the Perplexed*. Vols. 1–2. Translated by Shlomo Pines. Chicago: University of Chicago Press, 1963.
Ibn Manẓūr. *Lisān al-ʿarab*. 12 Volumes. Beirut: Dār al-Kutub al-ʿIlmiyya, 2003.
Ibn al-Nadīm. *al-Fihrist*. Edited by Musṭafā Muḥammad. Cairo: al-Maktaba al-Tijāriyya al-Kubrā, 1929.
Ibn Qutayba. *Adab al-kātib*. Edited by Darwīsh Juwaydī. Beirut: al-Maktaba al-ʿAsriyya, 2019.
Ibn Rashīq. *al-ʿUmda fī maḥāsin al-shiʿr wa ādābihi wa naqdihi*. Beirut: Dār al-Jīl, 1981.
Ibn Rushd. *Tafsīr mā baʿd al-ṭabīʿa*. Edited by Maurice Bouyges. Beirut: al-Maṭbaʿa al-Kāthūlīqiyya, 1942.
——. *Talkhīṣ kitāb al-burhān*. Edited by Muḥammad Qāsim. Revised, completed, and annotated by Charles Butterworth and Aḥmad ʿAbd al-Majīd Harīdī. Cairo: al-Hayʾa al-Miṣriyya al-ʿĀma lil-Kitāb, 1982.
Ibn Sīnā. *Ibn Sīnā's Remarks and Admonitions: Physics and Metaphysics*. Translated by Shams C. Inati. New York: Columbia University Press, 2014.
——. *al-Ishārāt wa-al-tanbīhāt: al-Ilāhiyyāt*. Vol. 3. Edited by Sulaymān Dunyā. Cairo: Dār al-Maʿārif, n.d.
——. *al-Ishārāt wa-al-tanbīhāt: al-Manṭiq*. Vol. 1. Edited by Sulaymān Dunyā. Cairo: Dār al-Maʿārif, 1960.
——. *Kitāb al-taʿlīqāt*. Edited by Ḥasan Majīd al-ʿUbaydī. Damascus: Dār al-Farqad, 2011.
——. *Kitāb al-Shifāʾ, al-Ilāhiyyāt*. Vol. 1. Edited by Georges C. Qanawātī and Saʿīd Zāyid. Vol. 2. Edited by Muḥammad Yūsuf Mūsā, Sulaymān Dunyā, Saʿīd Zāyid. Cairo: al-Hayʾa al-ʿĀma li-Shuʾūn al-Maṭābiʿ al-Amīrīyya, 1960.
——. *Kitāb al-Shifāʾ, al-Manṭiq, al-Burhān*. Vol. 5. Edited by Abū al-ʿAlā ʿAfīfī. Revised by Ibrāhīm Madkūr. Cairo: al-Maṭbaʿa al-Amīriyya, 1956.
——. *The Metaphysics of the Healing*. Arabic and English facing pages. Translated by Michael Marmura. Provo, Utah: Brigham Young University Press, 2005.
——. *Al-Najāt: al-Ilāhiyyāt*. Edited by Majid Fakhry. Beirut: Dār al-Āfāq al-Jadīda, 1982.
——. *Remarks and Admonitions, Part One: Logic*. Translated by Shams C. Inati. Toronto: Pontifical Institute of Medieval Studies, 1984.
——. *Sharḥ kitāb ḥarf al-lām*. In *Arisṭū ʿind al-ʿArab*, edited by ʿAbd al-Raḥmān Badawī, 22–33. Kuwait: Wikālat al-Maṭbūʿāt, 1978.
——. *Sīrat al-shaykh al-raʾīs*. In *The Life of Ibn Sīnā: A Critical Edition and Annotated Translation*, translated by William E. Gohlman, 16–113. Albany: State University of New York Press, 1974.

Iğsiz, Aslı. *Humanism in Ruins: Entangled Legacies of the Greek-Turkish Population Exchange*. Stanford, CA: Stanford University Press, 2018.

Inalcik, Halil. "Capital Formation in the Ottoman Empire." *Journal of Economic History* 29, no. 1 (March 1969): 97–140.

———. "The Ottoman State, Society, and Economy, 1300–1600." In *An Economic and Social History of the Ottoman Empire*, vol. 1, edited by Halil Inalcik with Donald Quataert, 9–409. Cambridge: Cambridge University Press, 1994.

———. "Suleiman the Lawgiver and Ottoman Law." In *The Ottoman Empire: Conquest, Organization, and Economy*, 105–138. 1969. London: Varorium, 1978.

Iogna-Prat, Dominique. *Order and Exclusion: Cluny and Christendom Face Heresy, Judaism, and Islam (1000–1150)*. Translated by Graham Robert Edwards. Ithaca, NY: Cornell University Press, 2002.

Isidore of Seville. *Etymologies*. Translated by Stephen A. Barney, W. J. Lewis, J. A. Beach, and Oliver Berghof. New York: Cambridge University Press, 2006.

al-Iṣfahānī, al-Rāghib. *Muḥāḍarāt al-udabāʾ wa muḥāwarāt al-shuʿarāʾ wa al-bulaghāʾ*. Edited by Ibrahīm Zaydān. Cairo: Maṭbaʿat al-Hilāl, 1902.

Islamoglu, Huri. "Property as a Contested Domain: A Reevaluation of the Ottoman Land Code of 1858." In *New Perspectives on Property and Land in the Middle East*, edited by Roger Owen, 1–61. Cambridge, MA: Harvard Middle East Monographs, 2000.

Issa, Rana. *The Modern Arabic Bible: Translation, Dissemination, and Literary Impact*. Edinburgh: Edinburgh University Press, 2023.

Jackson, Zakiyyah Iman. *Becoming Human: Matter and Meaning in an Antiblack World*. New York: New York University Press, 2020.

al-Jāḥiẓ. *al-Bayān wa-al-tibyīn*. Edited by Darwīsh Juwaydī. Beirut: al-Maktaba al- ʿAsriyya, 2003.

———. *Kitāb al-ḥayawān*. Edited by ʿAbd al-Salām Muḥammad Hārūn. Beirut: al-Maktaba al-ʿAsriyya, 2015.

Janos, Damien. *Avicenna on the Ontology of Pure Quiddity*. Berlin: De Gruyter, 2020.

John of Salisbury. *Policraticus*. Edited and translated by Cary J. Nederman. Cambridge: Cambridge University Press, 1990.

Johnson, Rebecca C. *Stranger Fictions: A History of the Novel in Arabic Translation*. Ithaca, NY: Cornell University Press, 2020.

Joudah, Fady. *[. . .]*. Minneapolis: Milkweed Editions, 2024.

Judy, R. A. "Kant and the Negro." *Surfaces* 1, no. 8 (1991): 1–81.

———. *Sentient Flesh: Thinking in Disorder, Poiēsis in Black*. Durham, NC: Duke University Press 2020.

al-Jurjānī, al-Sharīf. *Kitāb al-taʿrīfāt*. Edited by Muḥammad ʿAbd al-Raḥmān al-Marʿashlī. Beirut: Dār al-Nafāʾis, 2018.

Kanafani, Ghassan (Ghassān Kanafānī). *al-Adab al-Filastīnī al-muqāwim taḥt al-iḥtilāl: 1948–1968*. 1968. Beirut: Muʾassasat al-Abḥāth al-ʿArabiyya, 1987.

———. *Adab al-muqāwama fī Filastīn al-muḥtalla: 1948–1966*. 1966. Beirut: Muʾassasat al-Abḥāth al-ʿArabiyya, 1987.

Kant, Immanuel. *Critique of Pure Reason*. Translated by Werner S. Pluhar. Indianapolis: Hackett, 1996.

——. *Kritik der reinen Vernunft*. Edited by Jens Timmerman. Hamburg: Felix Meiner, 1998.

Kantorowicz, Ernst. *The King's Two Bodies: A Study in Medieval Political Theology*. 1957. Princeton, NJ: Princeton University Press, 1997.

Kaplan, M. Lindsay. *Figuring Racism in Medieval Christianity*. New York: Oxford University Press, 2019.

Kauanui, J. Kēhaulani. *Hawaiian Blood: Colonialism and the Politics of Sovereignty and Indigeneity*. Durham, NC: Duke University Press, 2008.

Kelley, Robin D. G. "The Rest of Us: Rethinking Settler and Native." *American Quarterly* 69, no. 2 (June 2017): 267–276.

Key, Alexander. *Language between God and the Poets:* Maʿnā *in the Eleventh Century*. Oakland: University of California Press, 2018.

Khalil, Samiha. "Philistine Imaginings and the Naissance of a World Other." *Atlantic Studies* (2023): 1–20. https://doi.org/10.1080/14788810.2023.2250964.

Khalili, Laleh. *Sinews of War and Trade: Shipping and Capitalism in the Arabian Peninsula*. London: Verso, 2021.

Khoury, Dina Rizk. *State and Provincial Society in the Ottoman Empire: Mosul, 1540–1834*. New York: Cambridge University Press, 1997.

Kilito, Abdelfattah. *Les Séances: Récits et codes culturels chez Hamadhanī et Harīrī*. Paris: Sindabad, 1983.

al-Kindī. "Al-Kindī's Letter on the Definitions and Descriptions of Things." In *The Philosophical Works of al-Kindī*, edited and translated by Peter Adamson and Peter E. Pormann, 300–311. Karachi: Oxford University Press, 2012.

——. *Al-Kindī's Metaphysics: A Translation of Yaʿqūb ibn Isḥāq al-Kindī's Treatise "On First Philosophy."* Translated by Alfred L. Ivry. Albany: State University of New York Press, 1974.

——. *Kitāb al-Kindī ilā al-Muʿta ṣim bi-allāh fī al-falsafa al-ūlā*. In *Rasāʾil al-Kindī al-falsafiyya*, vol. 1, edited by Muḥammad ʿAbd al-Hadī Abū Rida, 97–162. Cairo: Dār al-Fikr al-ʿArabī, 1950–1953.

——. "Letter on the Quantity of Aristotle's Books and what Is Required for the Attainment of Philosophy." In *The Philosophical Works of al-Kindī*, edited and translated by Peter Adamson and Peter E. Pormann, 281–296. Karachi: Oxford University Press, 2012.

——. "Risāla fī kammiyyat kutub Arisṭūṭālīs wa ma yuhtāj ilayhi fī taḥṣīl al-falsafa." In *Rasāʾil al-Kindī al-falsafiyya*, vol. 1, edited by Muḥammad ʿAbd al-Hadī Abū Rida, 363–384. Cairo: Dār al-Fikr al-ʿArabī, 1950–1953.

——. "Risālat al-Kindī fī ḥudūd al-ashyāʾ wa rusūmihā." *Rasāʾil al-Kindī al-falsafiyya*, vol. 1, edited by Muḥammad ʿAbd al-Hadī Abū Rida, 165–180. Cairo: Dār al-Fikr al-ʿArabī, 1950–1953.

King, Tiffany Lethabo. *The Black Shoals: Offshore Formations of Black and Native Studies*. Durham, NC: Duke University Press, 2019.

Kinney, Angela M., ed. *The Vulgate Bible*. Vol. 6. *The New Testament. Douay-Rheims Translation*. Latin and English facing pages. Cambridge, MA: Harvard University Press, Dumbarton Oaks Medieval Library, 2013.

Koutzarova, Tiana. *Das Transzendentale bei Ibn Sīnā: Zur Metaphysik als Wissenschaft erster Begriffs- und Urteilsprinzipien*. Leiden: Brill, 2009.

Las Casas, Bartolomé de. *In Defense of the Indians*. Translated by Stafford Poole. DeKalb: Northern Illinois University Press, 1992.

Lévinas, Emmanuel. *Autrement qu'être ou au-dela de l'essence*. Leiden: Martinus Nijhoff, 1974.

———. "Dieu et la philosophie." In *De Dieu qui vient à l'idée*, 93–127. 1982. Paris: Vrin, 1986.

———. "Ethics and Politics." In *The Lévinas Reader*, edited by Seán Hand, translated by Jonathan Romney, 289–297. Oxford: Blackwell, 1989.

———. "God and Philosophy." In *Of God Who Comes to Mind*, translated by Bettina Bergo, 55–78. Stanford, CA: Stanford University Press, 1998.

———. "Is Ontology Fundamental?" In *Entre Nous: Thinking-of-the-Other*, translated by Michael B. Smith and Barbara Harshav, 1–11. New York: Columbia University Press, 1998.

———. "L'Ontologie est-elle fondamentale?" In *Entre nous: Essais sur le penser-à-l'autre*, 12–22. Paris: Grasset, 1991.

———. *Otherwise Than Being, or Beyond Essence*. Translated by Alphonso Lingis. Pittsburgh: Duquesne University Press, 1981.

———. *Paul Celan: De l'être à l'autre*. 1976. Fontfroide le haut: Fata Morgana, 2002.

Lezra, Jacques. *On the Nature of Marx's Things: Translation as Necrophilology*. New York: Fordham University Press, 2018.

Liddell, Henry George, and Robert Scott. *A Greek-English Lexicon*. Revised and augmented by Sir Henry Stuart Jones, with the assistance of Roderick McKenzie. Oxford: Clarendon, 1996.

Lienau, Annette Damayanti. *Sacred Language, Vernacular Difference: Global Arabic and Counterimperial Literatures*. Princeton, NJ: Princeton University Press, 2023.

Lloyd, David. *Beckett's Thing: Painting and Theater*. Edinburgh: Edinburgh University Press, 2016.

———. "The Racial Thing." *Text zur Kunst* 117 (March 2020): 68–89.

———. "The Social Life of Black Things: Fred Moten's *consent not to be a single being*." *Radical Philosophy* 2, no. 7 (Spring 2020): 79–92.

———. *Under Representation: The Racial Regime of Aesthetics*. New York: Fordham University Press, 2019.

Locke. John. *An Essay Concerning Human Understanding*. Edited by Peter H. Nidditch. Oxford: Clarendon, 1975.

———. *The Second Treatise of Government*. In *Two Treatises of Government*, edited by Peter Laslett, 265-428. 1960. New York: Cambridge University Press, 2013.

Long Soldier, Layli. *WHEREAS*. Minneapolis: Graywolf Press, 2017.

Lowe, Lisa. *The Intimacies of Four Continents*. Durham, NC: Duke University Press, 2015.

Lu-Adler, Huaping. "Kant on Lazy Savagery, Racialized." *Journal of the History of Philosophy* 60, no. 2 (April 2022): 253–275.

Lubin, Alex. *Geographies of Liberation: The Making of an Afro-Arab Political Imaginary*. Chapel Hill: University of North Carolina Press, 2014.

Lucretius. *De rerum natura*. Edited by Jeffrey Henderson. Translated by W. H. D. Rouse. Revised by Martin Ferguson Smith. 1924. Cambridge, MA: Harvard University Press, Loeb Classical library, 1992.

Luxemburg, Rosa. *The Accumulation of Capital*. Translated by Agnes Schwarzschild. London: Routledge, 2003.

al-Maʿālī, Khālid. *Aʿīsh khārij sāʿatī*. Baghdad: Manshūrāt al-Jamal, 2017.

———. *Anā min Arḍ Kilkāmish*. Cologne: Manshūrāt al-Jamal, 2013.

———. *Aṭyāf Hūldirlīn*. Cologne: Manshūrāt al-Jamal, 2011.

———. *al-ʿAwda ilā al-ṣaḥrāʾ*. Beirut: Dār al-Nahar, 1999.

———. *Ḥidāʾ*. Cologne: Manshūrāt al-Jamal, 2002.

———. *al-Hubūt ʿalā al-yābisa*. Cologne: Manshūrāt al-Jamal, 1997.

———. *al-Iqāma fī al-ʿarāʾ*. Cologne: Manshūrāt al-Jamal, 2006.

———. *Khayāl min qaṣab*. Cologne: Manshūrāt al-Jamal, 1994.

———. *ʿUyūn fakkarat bi-nā*. London: Riyāḍ al-Rayyis, 1990.

al-Maʿālī, Khālid, Arno Böhler, and Suzanne Granzer. "Nietzsche and the Literature of Defiance: An Interview with Khalid al-Maaly." Translated by Yunus Tuncel. http://www.nietzschecircle.com/Al-Maaly_English.pdf. Accessed September 4, 2023.

Macpherson, C. B. *The Political Theory of Possessive Individualism*. 1962. New York: Oxford, 2011.

Madkour, Ibrahim. *L'Organon d'Aristote dans le monde arabe*. 2nd ed. 1934. Paris: Vrin, 1969.

Mahmood, Saba. *Religious Difference in a Secular Age: A Minority Report*. Princeton, NJ: Princeton University Press, 2016.

Makdisi, Saree. *Tolerance Is a Wasteland: Palestine and the Culture of Denial*. Oakland: University of California Press, 2022.

Makdisi, Ussama. *The Culture of Sectarianism: Community, History, and Violence in Nineteenth-Century Ottoman Lebanon*. Berkeley: University of California Press, 2000.

Marmura, Michael E. "The Metaphysics of Efficient Causality in Avicenna (Ibn Sīnā)." In *Islamic Theology and Philosophy: Studies in Honor of George F. Hourani*, edited by Michael E. Marmura, 172–187. Albany: State University of New York Press, 1984.

Marx, Karl. *Capital: A Critique of Political Economy*. Vol. 1. Translated by Ben Fowkes. New York: Vintage, 1977.

———. *Economic and Philosophic Manuscripts*. In *Early Writings*, translated by Rodney Livingstone and Gregor Benton, 279–400. London: Penguin, 1992.

———. *Grundrisse: Foundations of the Critique of Political Economy*. Translated by Martin Nicolaus. London: Penguin, 1993.

——. *Grundrisse der Kritik der politischen Ökonomie*. In Karl Marx and Friedrich Engels, *Werke*, Band 42. Berlin: Dietz Verlag, 1983.
——. *Das Kapital: Kritik der politischen Ökonomie*. Erster Band. In Karl Marx and Friedrich Engels, *Werke*, Band 23. Berlin: Dietz Verlag, 1962.
——. *Ökonomische-philosophische Manuskripte*. In Karl Marx and Friedrich Engels, *Gesamtausgabe*, Band 2. Berlin: Dietz Verlag, 1982.
Massad, Joseph A. *Islam in Liberalism*. Chicago: University of Chicago Press, 2015.
Mastnak, Tomaž. *Crusading Peace: Christendom, the Muslim World, and Western Political Order*. Los Angeles: University of California Press, 2002.
Masuzawa, Tomoko. *The Invention of World Religions: Or, How European Universalism Was Preserved in the Language of Pluralism*. Chicago: University of Chicago Press, 2005.
May, Herbert G., and Bruce M. Metzger, eds. *The New Oxford Annotated Bible*. New York: Oxford University Preess, 1973.
McKittrick, Katherine. *Dear Science and Other Stories*. Durham, NC: Duke University Press, 2021.
McLaughlin, Kevin. *The Philology of Life: Walter Benjamin's Critical Program*. New York: Fordham University Press, 2023.
Mejcher-Atassi, Sonja. "Etel Adnan." In *Reading across Modern Arabic Literature and Art*, 109–138. Wiesbaden: Reichert, 2012.
——. "The Forbidden Paradise: How Etel Adnan Learnt to Paint in Arabic." In *Arabic Literature: Postmodern Perspectvies*, edited by Angelika Neuwirth, Andreas Pflitsch, and Barbara Winckler, 311–320. London: Saqi, 2010.
Menn, Stephen. "Avicenna's Metaphysics." In *Interpreting Avicenna: Critical Essays*, edited by Peter Adamson, 143–169. Cambridge: Cambridge University Press, 2013.
Mercier, Lucie Kim-Chi. "Conference Report: Benjamin in Ramallah." *Radical Philosophy* 196 (March/April 2016): 60–64.
Mikdashi, Maya. *Sextarianism: Sovereignty, Secularism, and the State in Lebanon*. Stanford, CA: Stanford University Press, 2022.
Miller, Jeannie. "Man Is Not the Only Speaking Animal: Thresholds and Idiom in al-Jāḥiẓ." In *Arabic Humanities, Islamic Thought*, edited by Joseph E. Lowry and Shawkat M. Toorawa, 94–121. Leiden: Brill, 2017.
Mitchell, Timothy. *Rule of Experts: Egypt, Techno-Politics, Modernity*. Berkeley: University of California Press, 2002.
Moore, R. I. *The Formation of a Persecuting Society*. 2nd ed. Malden, MA: Blackwell, 2007.
Moten, Fred. *The Universal Machine*. Durham, NC: Duke University Press, 2018.
Moumtaz, Nada. *God's Property: Islam, Charity, and the Modern State*. Los Angeles: University of California Press, 2021.
Muhanna, Elias. *The World in a Book: Al-Nuwayri and the Islamic Encyclopaedic Tradition*. Princeton, NJ: Princeton University Press, 2018.
Muldoon, James. *Popes, Lawyers, and Infidels*. Philadelphia: University of Pennsylvania Press, 1979.

Mundy, Martha, and Richard Saumarez Smith. *Governing Property, Making the Modern State: Law, Administration, and Production in Ottoman Syria*. London: I. B. Tauris, 2007.

al-Musawi, Muhsin J. *The Medieval Islamic Republic of Letters: Arabic Knowledge Construction*. Notre Dame, IN: University of Notre Dame Press, 2015.

———. *Reading Iraq: Culture and Power in Conflict*. London: I. B. Tauris, 2006.

Naef, Silvia. "'Painting in Arabic': Etel Adnan and the Invention of a New Language." *Manazir* 1 (2019): 14–22.

Negri, Antonio. *Marx beyond Marx: Lessons on the Grundrisse*. Translated by Harry Cleaver, Michael Ryan, and Maurizio Viano. Brooklyn, NY: Autonomedia, 1991.

Nersessian, Anahid. *The Calamity Form: On Poetry and Social Life*. Chicago: University of Chicago Press, 2020.

Nichanian, Marc. *The Historiographic Perversion*. Translated by Gil Anidjar. New York: Columbia University Press, 2009.

Nichols, Robert. *Theft Is Property! Dispossession and Critical Theory*. Durham, NC: Duke University Press, 2020.

al-Nuwayrī. *Nihāyat al-arab fī funūn al-adab*. Vol. 2. Cairo: Dar al-Kutub al-Misriyya, 1928.

Olson, Charles. *The Maximus Poems*. Edited by George F. Butterick. Los Angeles: University of California Press, 1983.

Ouyang, Wen-Chin. "From Beirut to Beirut: Exile, Wandering, and Homecoming in the Narratives of Etel Adnan." In *Etel Adnan: Critical Essays on the Arab-American Writer and Artist*, edited by Lisa Suhair Majaj and Amal Amireh, 67–88. Jefferson, NC: McFarland, 2001.

Pexa, Christopher. *Translated Nation: Rewriting The Dakhóta Oyáte*. Minneapolis: University of Minnesota Press, 2019.

Piatote, Beth H. *Domestic Subjects: Gender, Citizenship, and Law in Native American Literature*. New Haven, CT: Yale University Press, 2013.

Plato. *The Republic*. Vols. 1–2. Translated by Paul Shorey. Cambridge, MA: Harvard University Press, Loeb Classical Library, 1935.

Plotinus. *Dicta Sapientis Graeci*. In *Plotini Opera*, edited by Paul Henry and Hans-Rudolph Schwyzer, translated by Geoffrey Lewis. Paris: Desclée de Brouwer, 1959.

———. *The Enneads*. Edited by Lloyd P. Gerson. Translated by George Boys-Stones et al. New York: Cambridge University Press, 2018.

———. *Epistola de Scientia Divina*. In *Plotini Opera*, edited by Paul Henry and Hans-Rudolph Schwyzer, translated by Geoffrey Lewis. Paris: Desclée de Brouwer, 1959.

———. *Nuṣūṣ mutafarriqa lī Aflūṭīn*. In *Aflūṭīn ʿind al-ʿArab*, edited by ʿAbd al-Raḥmān Badawī, 184–194. Cairo: Maktabat al-Nahḍa al-Miṣriyya, 1955.

———. *Plotini Opera*. Vols. 1–2. Edited by Paul Henry and Hans-Rudolph Schwyzer. Translated Geoffrey Lewis. Paris: Desclée de Brouwer, 1959.

———. *Risāla fī al-ʿilm al-ilāhī*. In *Aflūṭīn ʿind al-ʿArab*, edited by ʿAbd al-Raḥmān Badawī, 165–183. Cairo: Maktabat al-Nahḍa al-Miṣriyya, 1955.

———. *Theologia*. In *Plotini Opera*, edited Paul Henry and Hans-Rudolph Schwyzer, translated by Geoffrey Lewis. Paris: Desclée de Brouwer, 1959.

———. *Uthūlūjīyyā Arisṭūṭālīs*. In *Aflūṭīn ʿind al-ʿArab*, edited by ʿAbd al-Raḥmān Badawī, 8–164. Cairo: Maktabat al-Nahḍa al-Miṣriyya, 1955.

Pope Urban II. "The Speech of Urban: The Version of Baldric of Dol." In *The First Crusade: The Chronicle of Fulcher of Chartres and Other Source Materials*, 2nd ed., edited by Edward Peters, 29–33. Philadelphia: University of Pennsylvania Press, 1998.

———. "The Speech of Urban: The Version of Robert of Rheims." In *The First Crusade: The Chronicle of Fulcher of Chartres and Other Source Materials*, 2nd ed., edited by Edward Peters, 26–29. Philadelphia: University of Pennsylvania Press, 1998.

———. "Urban's Letter to His Supporters in Bologna, September 1096." In *The First Crusade: The Chronicle of Fulcher of Chartres and Other Source Materials*, 2nd ed., edited by Edward Peters, 44. Philadelphia: University of Pennsylvania Press, 1998.

Porphyry. *Introduction*. Translated, with a commentary by Jonathan Barnes. Oxford: Clarendon, 2003.

———. *Isagoge*. Translated by Edward W. Warren. Toronto: Pontifical Institute of Medieval Studies, 1975.

———. *Iysāghūjī Furfūrīūs*. In *Manṭiq Arisṭū*, vol. 3, edited by ʿAbd al-Raḥmān Badawī, translated by Abī ʿUthmān Dimashqī, 1019–1068. Cairo: Maṭbaʿat Dār al-Kutub al-Misriyya, 1952.

———. *On Aristotle Categories*. Translated by Steven K. Strange. London: Bloomsbury, 1992.

———. *Porphuriou Eisagōge*. In *Porphyrii Isagoge et in Aristotelis Categorias Commentarium*. Commentario in Aristotelem Graeca, vol. 4, edited by Adolfus Busse, 1–22. Berlin: Georgh Reimer, 1887.

———. *Porphyrii Introductio in Aristotelis Categorias a Boethio Translata*. In *Porphyrii Isagoge et in Aristotelis Categorias Commentarium*. Commentario in Aristotelem Graeca, vol. 4, edited by Adolfus Busse, 23–51. Berlin: Georgh Reimer, 1887.

Proclus. *The Elements of Theology*. Edited and translated by E. R. Dodds. Oxford: Clarendon, 1963.

———. *Proclus Arabus: Zwanzig Abschnitte aus der Institutio Theologica in Arabischer Übersetzung*. Edited by Gerhard Endress. Beirut: Orient Institute/ Imprimerie Catholique, 1973.

Pursley, Sara. *Familiar Futures: Time, Selfhood, and Sovereignty in Iraq*. Stanford, CA: Stanford University Press, 2019.

al-Qāḍī al-Quḍāʿī. *Light in the Heavens: Sayings of the Prophet Muḥammad*. Arabic and English facing pages. Edited and translated by Tahera Qutbuddin. New York: New York University Press, 2016.

al-Qifṭī. *Ikhbār al-ʿulamāʾ bi-akhbār al-ḥukamāʾ*. Edited by al-Sayyed Muḥammad Amīn. Cairo: Maṭbaʿat al-Saʿāda, 1908.

Rastegar, Kamran. "*Gulistan*: Sublimity and the Colonial Credo of Translatability." In *Migrating Texts: Circulating Translations around the Ottoman Mediterranean*, edited by Marilyn Booth, 300–317. Edinburgh: Edinburgh University Press, 2019.
———. *Literary Modernity between the Middle East and Europe: Textual Transactions in Nineteenth-Century Arabic, English, and Persian Literatures*. New York: Routledge, 2007.
———. *Surviving Images: Cinema, War, and Cultural Memory in the Middle East*. New York: Oxford University Press, 2015.
Redfield, Marc. *Shibboleth: Judges, Derrida, Celan*. New York: Fordham University Press, 2021.
Rifkin, Mark. *Settler Common Sense: Queerness and Everyday Colonialism in the American Renaissance*. Minneapolis: University of Minnesota Press, 2014.
Riley-Smith, Jonathan. "Crusading as an Act of Love." *History* 65, no. 214 (1980): 177–192.
———. *The First Crusade and the Idea of Crusading*. 2nd ed. Philadelphia: University of Pennsylvania Press, 2009.
Robinson, Aileen Moreton. *The White Possessive: Property, Power, and Indigenous Sovereignty*. Minneapolis: University of Minnesota Press, 2015.
Robinson, Cedric J. *An Anthropology of Marxism*. 2001. Preface by Avery F. Gordon. Foreword by H. L. T. Quan. Chapel Hill: University of North Carolina Press, 2019.
———. *Black Marxism: The Making of the Black Radical Tradition*. 1983. Foreword by Robin D. G. Kelly. Chapel Hill: University of North Carolina Press, 2000.
———. *al-Marksiyya al-sawdāʾ: Takwīn ḥarrāk thawrī lil-shuʿūb al-sawdāʾ*. Translated by ʿĀtif Muʿtamid and ʿAzzat Zayyān. Cairo: al-Markaz al-Qawmī lil-Tarjama, 2015.
Rodney, Walter. *How Europe Underdeveloped Africa*. 1972. London: Verso, 2018.
Rodríguez, Dylan. *White Reconstruction: Domestic Warfare and the Logics of Genocide*. New York: Fordham University Press, 2021.
Rousseau, Jean-Jacques. "Essay on the Origin of Languages." In *The Discourses and Other Early Political Writings*, edited by Victor Gourevitch, 247–299. New York: Cambridge University Press, 1997.
Russell, Frederick H. *The Just War in the Middle Ages*. Cambridge: Cambridge University Press, 1975.
Sacks, Jeffrey. "Against Simplicity: The Languages of Pain in Talal Asad and Etel Adnan." *Modern Language Notes* 133, no. 5 (2018): 1304–1336.
———. "Fanon's Insurgence." *Postcolonial Studies* 24, no. 2 (2021): 234–250.
———. *Iterations of Loss: Mutilation and Aesthetic Form, al-Shidyaq to Darwish*. New York: Fordham University Press, 2015.
———. "Palestine and Sovereign Violence." *Comparative Studies of South Asia, Africa, and the Middle East* 43, no. 2 (2014): 368–388.
———. "The Philological Thesis: Language without Ends." *boundary 2* 48, no. 1 (2021): 65–107.
———. "The Politics of Death and the Question of Palestine." *Comparative Literature* 71, no. 4 (2019): 357–380.

———. "The Resistance to Boycott: Palestine, BDS, and the Modern Language Association." *Radical History Review* 134 (May 2019): 233–244.

———. "'The Visual Poetry of the Work': Critique, Form, and Life in the Art of Mona Hatoum and the Language of Theodor Adorno." *Critical Times* 6, no. 1 (2023): 114–142.

Sa'di, Ahmad H., and Lila Abu-Lughod, eds. *Nakba: Palestine, 1948, and the Claims of Memory*. New York: Columbia University Press, 2007.

Said, Edward W. *Orientalism*. New York: Vintage, 1978.

———. *The Question of Palestine*. New York: Vintage 1979.

———. "Zionism from the Standpoint of Its Victims." *Social Text* 1 (Winter 1979): 7–58.

Salaita, Steven. *Inter/Nationalism: Decolonizing Native America and Palestine*. Minneapolis: University of Minnesota Press, 2016.

Saldaña-Portillo, María Josefina. *Indian Given: Racial Geographies across Mexico and the United States*. Durham, NC: Duke University Press, 2016.

Sayegh, Fayez A. *Zionist Colonialism in Palestine*. Beirut: Palestine Liberation Organization Research Center, 1965.

Schmitt, Carl. *The Nomos of the Earth in the International Law of the* Jus Publicum Europaeum. Translated by G. L. Ulman. New York: Telos Press, 2003.

———. *Der Nomos der Erde im Völkerrecht des Jus Publicum Europaeum*. 1950. Berlin: Duncker & Humblot, 1997.

———. *Political Theology: Four Chapters on the Concept of Sovereignty*. Translated by George Schwab. Chicago: University of Chicago Press, 1985.

———. *Politische Theologie: Vier Kapitel zur Lehre von der Souveränität*. 1922. Berlin: Duncker and Humblot, 2004.

Schoeler, Gregor. *The Genesis of Literature in Islam: From the Aural to the Read*. Rev. ed. In Collaboration with and translated by Shawkat M. Toorawa. Edinburgh: Edinburgh University Press, 2009.

Schotten, C. Heike. *Queer Terror: Life, Death, and Desire in the Settler Colony*. New York: Columbia University Press, 2018.

Schütrumpf, Eckart. *The Earliest Translations of Aristotle's* Politics *and the Creation of Political Terminology*. Paderborn: Wilhelm Fink, 2014.

See, Sarita Echavez. *The Filipino Primitive: Accumulation and Resistance in the American Museum*. New York: New York University Press, 2017.

Seikaly, Sherene. *Men of Capital: Scarcity and Economy in Mandate Palestine*. Stanford, CA: Stanford University Press, 2015.

al-Shahrastānī. *al-Milal wa al-niḥal*. Edited by Sa'īd al-Ghānimī. Beirut: Manshūrāt al-Jamal, 2013.

Shalhoub-Kevorkian, Nadera. *Incarcerated Childhood and the Politics of Unchilding*. New York: Cambridge University Press, 2022.

Sheehi, Lara, and Stephen Sheehi. *Psychoanalysis under Occupation: Practicing Resistance in Palestine*. New York: Routledge, 2022.

Sheehi, Stephen. *The Arab Imago: A Social History of Portrait Photography*. Princeton, NJ: Princeton University Press, 2016.

Shohat, Ella. "Rethinking Jews and Muslims: Quincentennial Reflections." In *On the Arab-Jew, Palestine, and Other Displacements: Selected Writings*, 331–338. London: Pluto, 2017.

———. "Sephardim in Israel: Zionism from the Standpoint of Its Jewish Victims." *Social Text* 19/20 (Autumn 1988): 1–35.

al-Sijistānī. *Ṣiwān al-ḥikma wa thalāth rasāʾil ukhrā*. Edited by ʿAbd al-Raḥmān Badawī. Tehran: Bunyād-i Farhang-i Īrān, 1974.

Simpson, Audra. *Mohawk Interruptus: Political Life across the Borders of Settler States*. Durham, NC: Duke University Press, 2014.

Spillers, Hortense. "Mama's Baby, Papa's Maybe: An American Grammar Book." In *Black, White, and in Color: Essays on American Literature and Culture*, 203–229. Chicago: University of Chicago Press, 2003.

Stanton, Anna Ziajka. *The Worlding of Arabic Literature: Language, Affect, and the Ethics of Translatability*. New York: Fordham University Press, 2023.

Stengel, Bernard. *Der Kommentar des Thomas von Aquin zur* Politik *des Aristoteles*. Marburg: Tectum Verlag, 2011.

Stetkevych, Suzanne Pinckney. *Abū Tammām and the Poetics of the ʿAbbāsid Age*. 1991. Leiden, Brill 2020.

Stoler, Ann Laura. *Race and the Education of Desire: Foucault's* History of Sexuality *and the Colonial Order of Things*. Durham, NC: Duke University Press, 1995.

Stouter, A., J. M. Wyllie, and Cyril Bailey, et al., eds. *Oxford Latin Dictionary*. Oxford: Oxford University Press, 1968.

Strickland, Debra Higgs. *Saracens, Demons, and Jews: Making Monsters in Medieval Art*. Princeton, NJ: Princeton University Press, 2003.

Tageldin, Shaden M. "Beyond Latinity, Can the Vernacular Speak?" *Comparative Literature* 70, no. 2 (2018): 114–131.

———. *Disarming Words: Empire and the Seductions of Translation in Colonial Egypt*. Los Angeles: University of California Press, 2011.

———. "Hugo, Translated: The Measures of Modernity in Muḥammad Rūḥī al-Khālidī's Poetics of Comparative literature." *PMLA* 138, no. 3 (2023): 616–639.

Taylor, Malissa. *Land and Legal Texts in the Early Modern Ottoman Empire*. London: I. B. Tauris, 2023.

Terada, Rei. *Metaracial: Hegel, Antiblackness, and Political Identity*. Chicago: University of Chicago Press, 2023.

Tezcan, Baki. "Law in China or Conquest in the Americas: Competing Constructions of Political Space in the Early Modern Ottoman Empire." *Journal of World History* 24, no. 1 (March 2013): 107–134.

———. *The Second Ottoman Empire: Political and Social Transformation in the Early Modern World*. New York: Cambridge, 2010.

al-Thaʿālabī. *Fiqh al-lugha wa sirr al-ʿarabiyya*. Edited by Fāʾiz Muḥammad. Beirut: Dār al-Kitāb al-ʿArabī, 2006.

Themistius. *Min sharḥ Thāmistūs li-ḥarf al-lām*. In *Arisṭū ʿind al-ʿArab*, edited by ʿAbd al-Raḥmān Badawī, 12–21. Kuwait: Wikālat al-Maṭbūʿāt, 1978.

Tocqueville, Alexis de. "Essay on Algeria (October 1841)." In *Writings on Empire and Slavery*, edited and translated by Jennifer Pitts, 59–117. Baltimore: Johns Hopkins University Press, 2001.
——. "Lettre sur l'Algérie." In *Sur l'Algérie*, edited by Seloua Luste Boulbina, 43–60. Paris: Flammarion, 2003.
——. "Notes du voyage en Algérie de 1841." In *Sur l'Algérie*, edited by Seloua Luste Boulbina, 61–96. Paris: Flammarion, 2003.
——. "Notes on the Voyage to Algeria in 1841." In *Writings on Empire and Slavery*, edited and translated by Jennifer Pitts, 36–58. Baltimore: Johns Hopkins University Press, 2001.
——. "Second Letter on Algeria (22 August 1837)." In *Writings on Empire and Slavery*, edited and translated by Jennifer Pitts, 14–26. Baltimore: Johns Hopkins University Press, 2001.
——. "Travail sur l'Algérie." In *Sur l'Algérie*, edited by Seloua Luste Boulbina, 97–177. Paris: Flammarion, 2003.
Tolan, John V. *Saracens: Islam in the Medieval European Imagination*. New York: Columbia University Press, 2002.
Toorawa, Shawkat M. *Ibn Abi Tahir Tayfur and Arabic Writerly Culture: A Ninth Century Arabic Bookman in Baghdad*. London: Routledge, 2004.
Touati, Houari. *Islam and Travel in the Middle Ages*. Translated by Lydia G. Cochrane. Chicago: University of Chicago Press, 2010.
Toufic, Jalal. *What Was I Thinking?* Berlin: Sternberg Presss, 2017.
Trabulsi, Fawwaz. *A History of Modern Lebanon*. London: Pluto, 2007.
——. "Untitled." In *Homage to Etel Adnan*, 88–91. Sausalito, CA: Post-Apollo Press, 2012.
Tsīlān, Paul. "Khaṭṭ al-ẓahīra." In *Samaʿtu man yaqūl: mukhtārāt shiʿiriyya wa nathriyya*, translated by Khālid al-Maʿālī, 284–302. Cologne: Manshurāt al-Jamal, 1999.
Tully, James. *A Discourse on Property: John Locke and his Adversaries*. Cambridge: Cambridge University Press, 1980.
al-Ṭūsī, Naṣīr al-Dīn. *Sharḥ al-ishārāt wa-al-tanbīhāt: al-Ilāhiyyāt*. In *al-Ishārāt wa-al-tanbīhāt: al-Ilāhiyyāt*, vol. 3, edited by Suleimān Dunyā. Beirut: Muʾassasat al-Niʿmān, 1993.
Üstündağ, Nazan. *The Mother, the Politician, and the Guerrilla: Women's Political Imagination in the Kurdish Movement*. New York: Fordham University Press, 2023.
Vitoria, Francisco de. "On the American Indians." In *Political Writings*, edited by Anthony Pagden and Jeremy Lawrance, 231–292. Cambridge: Cambridge University Press, 1991.
——. *Relectio De Indis*. Edited by L. Pereña and J.M. Perez Prendes. Madrid: Consejo Superior de Investigaciones Cientificas, 1967.
Wallerstein, Immanuel. *The Modern World System: Capitalist Agriculture and the Origins of the European World-Economy in the Sixteenth Century*. 1974. Los Angeles: University of California Press, 2011.

Walzer, Richard. *Greek into Arabic: Essays on Islamic Philosophy*. Cambridge, MA: Harvard University Press, 1962.
Watt, John W. "The Syriac Aristotle between Alexandria and Baghdad." In *The Aristotelian Tradition in Syriac*, 47–71. London: Routledge, 2019.
Weheliye, Alexander G. *Habeas Viscus: Racializing Assemblages, Biopolitics, and Black Feminist Theories of the Human*. Durham, NC: Duke University Press, 2014.
Williams, Eric. *Capitalism and Slavery*. 1944. Chapel Hill: University of North Carolina Press, 1994.
Williams, Robert A., Jr. *The American Indian in Western Legal Thought: The Discourse of Conquest*. New York: Oxford University Press, 1990.
Wilson-Goldie, Kaelen. *Etel Adnan*. London: Lund Humphries, 2018.
Wisnovsky, Robert. *Avicenna's Metaphysics in Context*. Ithaca, NY: Cornell University Press, 2003.
Wittgenstein, Ludwig. *Philosophical Investigations*, rev. 4th ed., translated by G. E. M. Anscombe, P. M. S. Hacker, and Joachim Schulte. Malden, MA: Wiley-Blackwell, 2009.
Wolfe, Patrick. "Settler Colonialism and the Elimination of the Native." *Journal of Genocide Research* 8, no. 4 (2006): 387–409.
——. *Traces of History: Elementary Structures of Race*. London: Verso, 2016.
Wolfson, Harry A. "Infinite and Privative Judgments in Aristotle, Averroes, and Kant." *Philosophy and Phenomenological Research* 8, no. 2 (December 1947): 173–187.
Woods, Clyde. *Development Arrested: The Blues and Plantation Power in the Mississippi Delta*. Introduced by Ruth Wilson Gilmore. London: Verso, 2017.
Wynter, Sylvia. "1492: A New World View." In *Race, Discourse, and the Origin of the Americas: A New World View*, edited by Vera Lawrence Hyatt and Rex Nettleford, 5–57. Washington, DC: Smithsonian Institution Press, 1995.
——. "The Ceremony Must Be Found: After Humanism." *boundary* 2 12, no. 3–13, no. 1 (1984): 19–70.
——. "Columbus, the Ocean Blue, and Fables That Stir the Mind: To Reinvent the Study of Letters." In *Poetics of the Americas: Race, Founding, and Textuality*, edited by Bainard Cowan and Jefferson Humphries, 141–163. Baton Rouge: Louisiana State University Press, 1997.
——. "New Seville and the Conversion Experience of Bartolomé de Las Casas: Part One." *Jamaica Journal* 17, no. 2 (1984): 25–32.
——. "New Seville and the Conversion Experience of Bartolomé de Las Casas: Part Two." *Jamaica Journal* 17, no. 3 (1984): 46–56.
——. "Unsettling the Coloniality of Being/Power/Truth/Freedom: Towards the Human, After Man, Its Overrepresentation—An Argument." *CR: The New Centennial Review* 3, no. 3 (Fall 2003): 257–337.
Yilmaz, Hüseyin. *Caliphate Redifined: The Mystical Turn in Ottoman Political Thought*. Princeton, NJ: Princeton University Press, 2018.

Index

abstraction, xvii, xxi, 14, 64–65, 238n76, 244n137; asymmetric demand, 39; division between those capable and incapable of abstraction, xx, 4; Hegel, 195–196n28; interiority, 142; Locke, 59–60; modern law, 178n13, 239n84, 208n70, 214n109; 1858 Ottoman Land Code, 121; Paul, 14, 39, 45, 48; property, 230n4; whiteness, 177n11; subordination of sound to sense, xvi–xvii, 64–65, 124, 231n7; Saracen, 48. *See also* Asad, Talal; law; Paul; settler life
Aboul-Ela, Hosam, 14
Abū Bishr Mattā ibn Yūnus, 88, 110, 217n32
Abū Qāsim ibn Ṣā'īd al-Andalusī, 67
Abū 'Uthmān Dimashqī, 95
Adnan, Etel, xviii, xix, 15–16, 118–121, 126–127, 148–174; Ammiel Alcalay, 172, 236–237n65, 243–244n129; anontological form, 118, 120, 137, 147, 149, 150, 157–158, 164, 165, 168; *L'Apocalypse arabe*, 118, 150–152, 159, 168 ; *The Arab Apocalypse*, 118–119, 148–152, 154–156; Sargon Būloṣ, 164–165; color, 118, 148–150, 153, 154–159; Columbus, 152, 170; Mahmoud Darwish, 157; Gaza, 171, 173; gesture, 158; Indian, 152, 166–170; *The Indian Never Had a Horse*, 168–171, 172; indistinction of language from the social, 145, 149, 164, 165; *In the Heart of the Heart of Another Country*, 173; *Hunāka*, 164–165; *Journey to Mount Tamalpais*, 165, 167, 171; Lucretius, xvii, 153, 166; Khālid al-Ma'ālī, 164, 170; matter, 148–149, 153, 156, 157, 159, 164–165, 173; "La Mer," 153; *Night*, 171; non-propertied form of life, 150, 158, 166, 168; *Of Cities and Women*, 154; Charles Olson, 172, 243–244n129; painting, 148–150, 152, 155–159; Palestine, 16, 150, 152, 154, 155, 170, 173; *Paris, When It's Naked*, 170; poetic generosity, 153; poetics of things, 148–149, 153, 156, 158, 164, 166, 170; refusal, 121, 153, 167–168, 170, 171–173; rumor, 153; the sea, 153–154, 155, 164, 166, 170; *Sea and Fog*, 149; *Seasons*, 171, 172; *Shifting the Silence*, 153–154; *Sitt Marie Rose*, 152; slaughter, 148, 169; *The Spring Flowers Own*, 171; *Surge*, 164; *There*, 149, 152. *See also* anontological form; collective; insurgence; refusal; poeticality; poetics of things
Adorno, Theodor, xix–xx, 185n20
Agamben, Giorgio, 14, 25, 26, 187n36, 194n14
al-Akhfash, 232–233n28
āla (tool), 84–85, 219n38. See also *manṭiq*
Alcalay, Ammiel, 172, 230n3, 236n65, 243–244n129
Alessandrini, Anthony, 194n14
Alexander of Aphrodesias, 80, 83
Algeria, 14, 53–58
'Alī ibn Abī Ṭālib, 133
Allan, Michael, 181n8, 191n43, 192n49, 231n6

Althusser, Louis, 198n39
ʿām (common), 15, 97, 120, 223n52
Amin, Samir, 231n9
Ammonius, 222–223n52
Anidjar, Gil, 38, 39, 176n5, 177n12, 200n48, 205n61
inniyya (thatness), 77, 115, 228n91
anontological form, xviii, xix, 12, 14–17, 28, 66–117, 118–121; anaccumulative, xix, xxi, 5–6, 18, 65, 158, 164; aporetic form, 116–117; Arabic peripatetic philosophy, 14–15; collective life, 137; common form, 101; demonstrative knowledge, 91; Etel Adnan, 118, 148–165; excess, 101; al-Fārābī, 96–97, 100–101; *ḥikma*, 92; giving, 83, 101, 111, 112–117; Ibn Sīnā, 110–112, 116–117; inheritance, 15–16, 65; insubstantiality, 92–97; al-Jāḥiẓ, 137; Sargon Būloṣ, 164–165; Paul Celan, 147, 149; al-Kindī, 82–83; language indistinct from ontology, 66, 111–112, 164–165; Marx, 37, 164; matter, 118, 131, 141, 148–149, 164, 170, 173; Khālid al-Maʿālī, 124, 126–127, 137–140, 147–148; nonselfsame manner, 82, 134; modal formalization of being, 111–112; modal ontology, 116–117; non-subjective linguistic and social existence, 118; ontological indetermination, 102, 164–165; overflow, 82, 83, 98, 111, 113, 117, 164; painting, 157–158, 168; sharing, 97, 101, 113, 117. *See also* collective; form; insurgence
Antoon, Sinan (Sinān Anṭūn), xx
Aquinas, St. Thomas, 14, 43–46, 50–51, 58, 60, 61, 64, 188–189n38, 205n61, 208n71; St. Augustine, *City of God*, 46; *Commentary* on Aristotle's *Politics*, 48, 51; *corpus mysticum*, 43; Vitoria, Francisco de, 47–48; Jews, 43–45; living well, 46, 48; Pauline demand, 45; Saracens, 44–45; the temporal tranquility of the state, 46. *See also* counterinsurgent pose; Crusades; settler life
Arabic nineteenth century, 16–17, 122, 123, 191n43, 231n6
Arendt, Hannah, 14, 24–26, 28, 187n36, 193–194n11, 194n14
Aristotle, xviii, 8, 10, 11, 14, 15, 17, 21–26, 28, 29, 32, 47, 50–51, 65, 120, 121, 189n40, 193n7, 193n10, 194n14, 206–207n65, 208n71, 208–209n75, 215n5, 215–216n10; Ammonius, 222–223n52; Aquinas, 43–46; *Categories*, 94, 95; common notions, 228–229n96; demonstration, 88–92; *Ethics*, 24; *eū zēn*, 21–26, 47–48; al-Fārābī, *Book of Expressions used in Logic*, 84–88; al-Fārābī, *Book of Letters*, 93–97; al-Fārābī, "Letter on the Aims of Aristotle's *Metaphysics*," 97–101; al-Fārābī, *Philosophy of Aristotle*, 83–84; Ibn Maymūn, 226–227n83; Ibn al-Nadīm, 226n77; Ibn Rushd, 89–90, 220n43; Ibn Sīnā, *Commentary* on *Book Lambda* of *Metaphysics*, 106–112; illegibility of distinction between "life" and "the good life," 22–24; al-Kindī, "Letter on the Quantity of Aristotle's Books," 67–73; Language, 23–24; Latin Aristotle, 14, 24, 47–48, 188n37; Marx, 27, 29, 37–38; *Metaphysics*, 15, 17, 89, 105, 106–112, 117, 225n71; *On Interpretation*, 24, 229n2; *On the Soul*, 23–24; *Politics*, 11, 14, 21–22, 26, 164; Porphyry, 223–224n64; *Posterior Analytics*, 88–92, 102–103, 116–117; al-Qifṭī, 219n38; al-Sijistānī, 221–222n49; stabilization of Aristotelian aporetic form post-twelfth-Christian century, 14, 24–25; Vitoria, Francisco de, 46–48; slave, 22, 26, 47–48, 51–52; *Zōon politikon*, 22. See also *askēsis*; *burhān*; *eū zēn*; al-Fārābī; Ibn Sīnā; *ʿilla*; *ʿilm*; al-Kindī; *manṭiq*
Asad, Talal, xvi–xvii, 38–39, 200–201n49, 205n59, 231n8
al-ʿAskarī, 133–134, 233n31
askēsis, 189n40, 215–216n10. *See also* Hadot, Pierre
Aufgabe (task), xv–xvi, 173, 176n2, 188n36. *See also* Benjamin, Walter
Augustine, St., 42, 43, 46, 203n51, 243n129

Balibar, Étienne, 61, 62, 198–99n41, 213n101
Baracchi, Claudia, 193n10, 215–216n10, 229n96
Barakat, Rana, 181–182n10
bayān (eloquence), 131–132, 135–137, 137, 233n31, 234n35
al-Bayhaqī, 221n46
Beirut, xii, 121, 154, 155, 163, 171, 231n9, 237n70, 242n125

Benjamin, Walter, xv–xvi, xxi, xiii, 5, 168, 173, 176n2, 182–183n14, 187–188n36, 203n52, 244n136. See also *Aufgabe; Entsetzung*
Bhandar, Brenna, 61, 181n8, 181n9
Black Study, 17–18
Blumenberg, Hans, 50
Boethius, 162, 187n34, 188n3; *Isagoge*, 222n51
Būloṣ, Sargon, 164–165
burhān (demonstration), 15, 88–92, 102, 116, 217n32, 219n38, 219n39, 220n43, 225n68
Butler, Judith, 11, 179n23, 193–194n11
Byrd, Jodi A., 33, 196n32, 197n33

Carter, J. Kameron, 9, 154, 177n12, 186n26, 239n84; whiteness, 177n11
Celan, Paul, xviii, 15, 16, 19, 20, 121, 137, 140–148, 149, 164, 172, 174, 236n50; *Dunkelheit*, darkness, 142; *Fadensonnen*, 142; law, 142–143; *Lichtzwang*, 140; *Der Meridian*, 140–148; *Mikrolithen sinds, Steinchen*, 141; *Mohn und Gedächtnis*, 147; *poröse Gebilde*, porous things, 141; *Sprachgitter*, 141, 142; *Zeitgehöft*, 147. *See also* poeticality; poetics of things
Chandler, Nahum D., 186n31
collective, xi, xv–xvi, xx, xxi–xxii, 5, 12, 66, 68, 85; Aristotle, *Politics*, 21–22; Black Study, 17–18; beauty, 132; gathering, 16, 132–133, 137, 167, 183n15, 235n38; genocide, xi, xx, 166, 179n24, 242n125; "I," 11, 17–18, 179n23; insurgence, xxi–xxii, 5; al-Jāḥiẓ, 16, 132–133, 137; *jamāʿa*, collective, 137; language, 88, 132–133, 137, 167, 171; Locke, 63; Khālid al-Maʿālī, 140, 146; Marx, *Grundrisse*, 36; marronage, in Cedric J. Robinson, *Black Marxism*, 178n14; modern, juridical-centric existence, 41, 125, 173; *al-nās*, 191n43; non-Christian, non-European alterities, 42, 200n49; pedagogy in Arabic logic, 83–92; the poetic, 12–13, 15, 18, 26, 123, 134, 137, 140, 144, 146, 159, 171; race, 4, 59–61, 63; refusal, 149; settler panic, 54–56, 59–61, 45, 212–213n99; Sioux Uprising, 12; sociality, xx, 133, 140, 152; sonority, 126, 171; study, xv, 4, 180n4; struggle, xvi, 54, 168, 172; tears, 171; thought, 150, 152. *See also* Adnan, Etel; Benjamin, Walter; Black Study; Celan, Paul; Darwish, Mahmoud; Kanafani, Ghassan; Long Soldier, Layli; al-Maʿālī, Khālid; *muqāwama*; poeticality; riot
Columbus, 3–4, 5, 8, 49, 152, 170; Sylvia Wynter, 211–212n86
Containment, 12–13, 18, 26, 157, 163, 170–172, 178–179n17, 180–181n4, 208n70. *See also* settler life
Coulthard, Glen Sean, 3, 27, 197n33
counterinsurgent pose, xvii–xviii, 9, 10, 25, 27, 29, 38, 43, 48, 52, 60, 117, 118, 172, 174, 175n2, 192–193n3, 194n14, 200–201n49, 205n61; Aquinas, 45–46; Crusades, 39–41, 201–202n50, 202–203n51; Hegel, 195–196n28; Heidegger, 184–185n19; Emmanuel Lévinas, 163; Locke, 59–62; Tocqueville, Alexis de, 54, 57; Vitoria, Francisco de, 47. *See also* Crusades; law; settler life
Cover, Robert, 63, 181n9
critique, xv, xix, 8–9, 24–25, 172, 173, 194n14; Walter Benjamin, "Toward the Critique of Violence," 182–183n14, 203n52, 244n136; Immanuel Kant, *Critique of the Power of Judgment*, 157; Immanuel Kant, *Critique of Pure Reason*, xvii–xviii, 8–9, 126, 186n28, 187n32; "I think," 9, 11; post-twelfth-Christian century, post-Latinate critical thought, 14, 16, 24–26, 39, 60, 120, 176n6, 187n34, 194n14; racialization of form, 9, 42–43, 49–50, 172, 186n26, 188–189n38; proper setting of limits, 4, 9, 172, 177n11. *See also* Crusades; settler life
Crusades, xvii, 14, 25, 38–39, 42, 177n12, 238n76; abstracting Christian demand, 14; Talal Asad, *On Suicide Bombing*, 200–201n49; Christian charity, 38–39, 201–202n50, 207n65; Carl Erdmann, *The Origin of the Idea of Crusade*, 202–203n51; exteriorization of intra-Latin-Christian violence, 39, 201–202n50, 204–205n56; frontierless, 41, 63; Tomaž Mastnak, *Crusading Peace*, 39, 41, 204–205n56; pacification, 39, 202–203n51; rephrasing in modern subject of proper linguistic form, 25, 176n6, 202n50; reproduction in subject of philosophical representation, xvii, 14; 202n50; Saracens, 188–189n38, 200–201n49, 204–205n56; Pope Urban II, 39. *See also* genocide; Kant, Immanuel; Locke, John,; Paul; riot; settler life; Zionism

Darwish, Mahmoud (Maḥmūd Darwīsh), xxi, 1–6, 8, 12, 19, 157, 174, 180n1, 181–182n10, 184n16; *Aḥad ʿashar kawkaban*, 4; *Athar al-farāsha*, 157; *Ḥālat ḥiṣār*, xxi, 174; "Khuṭbat ʻal-Hindī al-aḥmar'—mā qabla al-akhīra—amām al-rajul al-abyaḍ," 1–6
Dayan, Colin, 17
Derrida, Jacques, 7–8, 185n22, 196n30, 203n52, 240n102, 242n123
dhāt (essence), 80–82, 93, 96, 101, 106, 110, 112, 116
DuBois, W.E.B., 185n21, 186n31

eigentum (property), 7, 28, 35, 38, 144–146, 228n94
El-Desouky, Ayman, 183n15, 235n38
El-Rouayheb, Khaled, 218n32, 218–219n34
Elshakry, Marwa, 191n43, 231n6
El Shakry, Omnia, 16, 189–190n41, 191n43, 231n6
Epictetus, 215–216n10
Ertürk, Nergis, 183n15
Esmeir, Samera, 142–143, 178n13, 181n91
Estes, Nick, 4, 166, 172
Entsetzung (de-posing), xxi–xxii, 5, 182–183n14, 244n136
eū zēn (living well, good life), 21–26, 47, 164, 208–209n75; Theodor Adorno, xix–xx; Aquinas, 45–48, 51–52; Aristotle, *Politics*, 21–23; Latin Christianity, 14, 24, 26, 51–52; Marx, 29, 32; post-Latinate reading in critical social thought, 24–25; settler life, 13–14, 47–48
extraction, 122, 149, 156, 167

Fanon, Frantz, xii, xviii, 8, 19–21, 25, 177n10, 183n15; *The Wretched of the Earth*, 19–21
al-Fārābī, xviii, 15, 83–101, 106, 120, 216n13, 217–218n32, 218–219n34, 219–220n39, 220n43, 222–223n52; *askēsis*, 215–216n10; common, 15, 97, 222–223n52; demonstration, 83–92; *Falsafat Aflāṭūn*, 215–216n10, 221n45; *Falsafat Aristūtālīs*, 83–84; *ḥikma*, 84, 91–92; *Iḥṣāʾ al-ʿulum*, 99–101, 223n60; *Kitāb al-alfāẓ al-mustaʿmala fī al-manṭiq*, 84–88; *Kitāb al-burhān*, 88–91; *Kitab al-ḥurūf*, 93–97; "Mā yanbaghī taʿalummuhu qabla al-falsafa," 189n40; pedagogy in logic, 84–88; *Mabādiʾ ārāʾ ahl al-madīna al-fāḍila*, 223n60; peripatetic, 189n40; *Risāla fī aghrāḍ mā baʿd al-ṭabīʿa*, 97–101; *sīratun mā*, 215–216n10, 221n45
faṣāḥa (proper speech, eloquence), 132, 136, 234–35n37
Fattal, Simone, xii, 155, 157–158
fayḍ (overflow, emanation), 83, 114
Federici, Silvia, 177–178n12
Ferreira da Silva, Denise, xviii, 9, 17, 25, 27, 65, 177n9, 186n26, 186n27, 191n48, 197n33; political subjugation in general, 65; primitive accumulation, 27; temporality of the economic concept of capital, 27; subjects of affectability, xix, 25; subject of transparency, 9; *Toward a Global Idea of Race*, 177n9, 186n26; the *transparent I* in the scene of representation, 17, 27; the thing, 17, 191n48; *Unpayable Debt*, 17–18, 27, 65. *See also* Black Study
fiʿl lisānī (lingual act), xvii, 131, 177n8
al-falsafa al-ūlā (first philosophy), 77, 104–105
Foucault, Michel, 14, 24–25, 26, 176n5, 187n36, 194n14

Gana, Nouri, 5
Gaza, xi, xiii, xx, xxi, 171, 173
genocide, xi, xiii, xx–xxi, 3–5, 11, 16, 25, 26, 50, 120, 180n4, 245n138; anti-Black genocide, 243n126; Armenian genocide, 242n125; genocidal logic, 243n126; Indigenous genocide, 166, 192–193n3, 240n114; genocidal war and sanctions regime in Iraq, xvii; Palestine, 150, 152, 154, 163, 170, 185–186n25; proper listening subject, 3, 14, 19, 21, 41, 58, 201–202n50, 243n126; Zionist genocide in Gaza, xi, xiii, xx–xxi, 173, 179n24. *See also* settler life
al-Ghazālī, 219–22n39
Gilmore, Ruth Wilson, 175n3
Gratian, 41–42, 189n38
Gregory VII, 38, 202–203n51
Gruendler, Beatrice, 216n13

Hadot, Pierre, 215–216n10
Hamacher, Werner, xvi, 176n5; Walter Benjamin, 244n136; Paul Celan, 236n50
Han, Sora, 181n9, 214n109
Harney, Stefano, 4, 64, 174, 182n12, 245n138
Harris, Cheryl I., 8
Hartman, Saidiya, 212–213n99

Hegel, G.W.F., 32, 170, 186n29, 242n123; *Philosophy of Right*, 195–196n28
Heidegger, Martin, xviii, 6–11, 13, 14, 18, 64, 144, 159, 161, 162, 164, 185n20, 185n22; *Being and Time*, 10, 159, 187n32; *Bildung*, 7–8; *The Principle of Reason*, 6–11; "Das Wesen der Sprache," 184–185n19; *Homo ist animal rationale*, 11; proper listening subject, 184–185n19; Roman-Latin thought, 187n34; *The Metaphysical Foundations of Logic*, 239–240n100; subject of self-determined comportment, 9–11. *See also* Lévinas, Emmanuel
ḥikma (philosophy), 84, 89, 91–92, 104–105, 120, 219–220n39, 221–222n49
Ḥunayn ibn Isḥāq, 221an46, 221–222n49
huwiyya (being), 74, 78, 82–83, 89

Ibn Abī Uṣaybiʿa, 67–68
Ibn Khaldūn, xvii, 131, 177n8
Ibn Manẓūr, 69, 71, 134, 136, 137; Khālid al-Maʿālī, 128
Ibn Maymūn, *Dalālat al-ḥaʾirīn*, 226–227n83
Ibn al-Nadīm, *al-Fihrist*, 226n77
Ibn Qutayba, 136–137
Ibn Rashīq, 132–134
Ibn Rushd, 89–90; *Talkhīṣ kitāb al-burhān*, 220n43
Ibn Sīnā, xviii, 15, 101–117, 120, 215–216n10, 216n13, 219–220n39; anontological form, 102, 111–112, 116–117; Aristotle, *Faṣl fī ḥarf al-lām min kitāb mā baʿd al-ṭabīʿa*, 108–109; *fiʿl*, act, 112–115; *ḥaraka*, motion, 106–112; Ibn Maymūn, 226–227n83; *inbijās*, overflow, 111; indistinction of logic from ontology, 111–112, 116–117, 223–224n64; *al-Ishārāt wa-al-tanbīhāt*, 101, 224–225n66, 225n68; *jūd*, generosity, 112–117; *al-Najāt, al-Ilāhiyyāt*, 222n85; *Sharḥ kitāb ḥarf al-lām*, 106–112; *al-Shifāʾ, Kitāb al-burhān*, 101–104; *al-Shifāʾ, Kitāb al-Ilāhiyyāt*, 102–106; *Sīrat al-shaykh al-raʾīs*, 226n74; *al-Taʿlīqāt*, 112; Themistius, *Min sharḥ Thāmisṭūs li-ḥarf al-lām*, 106–109; *wājib al-wujūd*, necessary being, 101–112
ʿilla (cause), 74, 77, 80–82, 89, 102, 106, 109; Arabic Plotinus, "Theology of Aristotle," 73–74; Ibn Maymūn, 226–227n83; Ibn Sīnā, necessary being, 106; Ibn Sīnā, *Sharḥ kitāb ḥarf al-lām*, 106–112; Khālid al-Maʿālī, 121
ʿilm (knowledge, science), demonstrative knowledge in *Posterior Analytics*, 90–91; al-Fārābī, *Iḥṣāʾ al-ʿulūm*, 99–101; al-Fārābī, sciences of language, 85; al-Fārābī, the science of what is after physics, 98–99; al-Kindī, *Fī al-falsafa al-ūlā*, 77, 83; Ibn Rushd on *Book Epsilon* of *Metaphysics*, 89; Ibn Sīnā, demonstration and science, 102–14
inniyya (thatness), 77; Ibn Sīnā, necessary being, 115–116
insurgence, xviii, 5, 12, 15–16, 33, 63, 65, 118–174, 183n15, 196–197n33; collective gathering, 146, 171; Mahmoud Darwish, xxi, 5; indetermined temporal mode, 121; insurgence in form, 137, 170; language 164; matter, 170; non-propertied form of life, 158; non-subjectively determined reading, 65; painting, 158, 166; poetics of things, 118–174; refusal, 148, 171; sonority, 140, 147–148; traditions of insurgence, 66. *See also* anontological form, gathering, poeticality; poetics of things; struggle; refusal
Iraq, xvii, xviii, 121–148, 175n3, 176n7, 181n9, 208n70, 230n3; Etel Adnan, 152, 171, 173; Sinan Antoon, xx; Hanna Batatu, 231–232n9; Sargon Būloṣ, 164; Mahmoud Darwish, 4; genocidal wars and sanctions regime, xvii, 176n7; Khālid al-Maʿālī, 15, 121–148
al-Iṣfahānī, 232n26
Isḥāq ibn Ḥunayn, Syriac translation of *Posterior Analytics*, 88, 221n46; Arabic translation of *Categories*, 94, 221–222n49
Isidore of Seville, 45
iyjāz (concision), 131, 133

Jackson, George, 171
al-Jāḥiẓ, 16, 130–137, 186–187n31, 233n31, 234n35; *balāgha*, eloquence, 131–132; *bayan*, clarity of expression, 131–132; *al-Bayān wa-al-tibyīn*, 131–133; hearing and the poetic, 132–133; inessential linguistic gathering, 134–137; *iyjāz*, concision, 131, 133; *jamāʿa*, collective, 137; *jamāl*, beauty, 132–134; *Kitāb al-ḥayawān*, 134–137; *lafẓ*, utterance, 130–131; *manṭiq al-ṭayr*, language of the birds, 134–137; *tafāhum*, giving one another to understand, 135–137

jamāl (beauty), 132–134
James, C.L.R., 48
jawhar (substance), 75, 80, 92–97, 107–109, 111, 223n60; *Categories*, 94; *Metaphysics*, 105; primary and secondary substance, 93–97, 222–223n52
al-Jawhari, 69, 134
Jenin, xxi
St. Jerome, 39
Jerusalem, 201–202n50, 203n52
Jew, 43–45, 50, 177n12, 185–186n25, 188–189n38, 200–201n49; anti-Jewish violence, 142; Aquinas, 43–45; Las Casas, 209–210n84; Judaeo-Christian, 210–211n85
John of Salisbury, 206–207n65
Johnson, Rebecca C., 191n43, 231n6
Joudah, Fady, xxi, 180n1
jūd (generosity), 112–117
Judy, R.A., 9, 186n26, 186–187n31
al-Jurjānī (ʿAbd al-Qahir), 233n31, 233–234n33

Kanafani, Ghassan (Ghassān Kanafānī), 5, 184n16
Kant, Immanuel, xvii–xviii, 8–9, 10, 64, 126, 172, 186n29; *Ich Denke*, I think, 9; principle of sufficient reason, in Heidegger, *The Principle of Reason*, 9; racialization of form, 9, 11, 177n9, 177n11, 186n26; proper setting of limits, 4, 9, 172; temporality, in Heidegger, *Being and Time*, 187n32; transcendental apperception, xvii–xviii, 9, 157, 186n28. *See also* counterinsurgent pose; settler life
Kantorowicz, Ernst, 45–46, 205n61
Kauanui, J. Kēhaulani, 8, 241n116
Khalili, Laleh, 149
al-Kindī, xviii, 15, 66–83, 120, 215–216n10, 216n13, 221–222n49; *āniyya faqat*, mere being, 76, 82–83; anontological form, 83; Arabic Plotinus, 73–77; Arabic Proclus, 80–83; *fayḍ*, emanation, 83; *Fī al-falsafa al-ūlā*, 77–80; inessential collective, 68; non-capitalist manner of "possession," 69; non-subjectively-determined practice of study, 67–68, 70, 73; philosophical curriculum, 71–73; "Risāla fī kammiyyat kutub Arisṭūṭālīs," 67–73; "Risālat al-Kindī fī ḥudūd al-ashyā' wa rusūmihā, 83; *riwāya*, transmission, 71–72; *riyāḍāt*, propaedeutics, 71; *sabīl*, path, 15, 70; *ṣabr*, patience, 68–73; *tarawwuḍ*, training, 70; *walā'*, devotion, 67, 72

lafẓ (utterance), 124, 130–133, 138. *See also* al-Jāḥiẓ
landscape, 2, 167–168, 169, 239n84, 240n114
Las Casas, Bartolomé de, 48–49, 52, 208n70, 208–209n75; *In Defense of the Indians*, 209–210n84
law, xxi, 5, 16, 17, 21, 38, 41–43, 50, 54, 57, 61–64, 66, 122, 142–143, 173, 181n8, 195–196n28, 205n59, 231n8, 238n76, 239n84; abstraction, 178n13, 214n109; Aquinas, 43–46, 51; Aristotle, *Politics* 1255a5–7, slave by law, *kata nomon*, *secundum legem inter homines positam*, 51; counterinsurgent pose, 59–63, 142; Crusades, 40–41, 42, 63; Samera Esmeir, "On the Coloniality of Modern Law," 142–143; *Entsetzung*, de-posing, of law, xiii, xxi, 5, 173, 182–183n14, 244n136; excess of lingual form over modern legality, xx, 2–3, 5, 18, 66, 117, 121, 123–124, 126, 142, 174; Forensick subject, in Locke, 62; founded in racializing distinctions, 213–214n104; Las Casas, 209–210n84; life, in Paul, Romans 8:6, 39, 45, 48; legal interpretation, in Robert Cover, "Violence and the Word," 63; 1858 Ottoman Land Code, 121, 230n4; pacification, in Paul, Romans 5:1, 52; person, in Locke, 62–63; property and settler colonization, 181n6, 181n8, 241n116; response to non-white, non-Christian forms of social and lingual existence, 43–46, 142; rule of law, 125, 178n13, 181n9; Schmitt, *The Nomos of the Earth*, 39–41, 143, 203n52; subject of interiorizing self-reflection, 7, 18, 122, 142, 177n11, 213–214n104, 214n105, 230n4; Tocqueville, Alexis de, 54, 57; transference of definitions from theology to law, in Ernst Kantorowicz, *The King's Two Bodies*, 45–46, 206–207n65; Vitoria, Francisco de, 46–48, 208n70; Vulgate translation of *nomos* as *lex*, 40, 203–204n55. *See also* abstraction; Aquinas; Benjamin, Walter; counterinsurgent pose; settler life; Locke, John; Hegel, G.W.F.
Lebanon, 16, 121, 150, 152, 237n70, 238n76
Leibniz, 6–10
Lévinas, Emmanuel, 8, 64, 147, 159–164; babbling, 163; child, 163; "Ethics and politics," 163; fraternity, 162–163; "God and Philosophy," 162–163; hostage,

161–162; "Is Ontology Fundamental?," 159–160; *Otherwise Than Being*, 160–162; *Paul Celan: De l'être à l'autre*, 240n106; substitution, 163; Sabra and Shatila massacres, 163; subject-centric pose, 163; pacification of the social, 162; primitive, 163. *See also* genocide; settler life; Zionism
lex (law), 40, 203–204n55
Lezra, Jacques, 37, 199n43
Lienau, Annette Damayanti, 183n15
lisān (language, tongue), xvii, 69, 71, 128, 130–132, 133, 135–137, 232n26, 234–235n37
Lloyd, David, 9, 17, 176n3, 177n9, 186n26, 191n45, 241n115
Locke, John, xvii, xxi, 8, 14, 58–64, 192–193n3, 213–214n104, 214n105, 241n116
Long Soldier, Layli, 1, 6, 11–13, 18, 19, 174
love, xiii, xxi, 6, 11, 13, 14, 18, 38–40, 42, 116, 142, 153, 154, 171, 174, 205n61, 208n70, 245n138
Lowe, Lisa, 35
Lubin, Alex, 183n15
Lucretius, xix, 153, 166, 178n16, 199n43, 238n79
Luxemburg, Rosa, 185n21

al-Maʿālī, Khālid, xviii, 15–16, 21, 120–121; Etel Adnan, 126–127; *Aʿīsh khārij sāʿatī*, 170; American and British-led wars against Iraq, 125; *Anā min Arḍ Kilkāmish*, 137–138; *Aṭyāf Hūldirlīn*, 126–127, 130; *al-ʿAwda ilā al-ṣaḥrāʾ*, 128; genocidal sanctions regime, 125, 176n7; *ghināʾ*, song, 122, 127–128; *Ḥidāʾ*, 124, 128; *ḥidāʾ*, singsong, 128, 130; *al-Hubūt ʿalā al-yābisa*, 123; Ibn Manẓūr, *Lisān al-ʿarab*, 128; indistinction of being and the poetic, 147; inessential performance, 146; *al-Iqāma fī al-ʿarāʾ*, 147–148; al-Jāḥiẓ, 130–140; *jamāl*, beauty, 132–134; *Khayāl min qaṣab*, 138–140; *lafẓ*, utterance, 130–131, 138; materiality in the poetic, 124, 127, 147; poetic gathering, 135–137, 146; poetic subject, 121–124, 129–130; poetics of things, 144–145, 147–148; post-Ottoman juridical state form, 122–124; question's origin, 121–124; *ranīn*, reverberation, 125–126, 147; *siyāsa*, governance, 122, 231n8; sonority, 125–130, 147; *ṣahīl*, neighing, 130; *tartīl*, chanting, 127, 130; translation of Paul Celan's "The Meridian," 140–148; Paul Tsilān, "Khaṭṭ al-ẓahīra," 144–147; *ʿUyūn fakkarat bi-nā*, 121–122. *See also* anontological form; collective; poeticality; poetics of things; refusal
McKittrick, Katherine, 180n4
mabdaʾ (principle), 91, 97, 102, 103, 106, 108–109, 226–227n83
māhiyya (whatness), 93–96, 115, 226n81
Mahomet, 14, 44–45
Makdisi, Saree, 181n9
Makdisi, Ussama, 238n76
manṭiq (logic), 71, 84, 135, 219n38, 219–220n39, 221–222n49. *See also* al-Fārābī; Ibn Sīnā
Marx, Karl, 3, 7, 8, 14, 27–38, 64, 65, 144, 159, 164, 176n5, 194n26, 196n30, 196–197n33; Althusser, 198n39; anontological form, 37; *Capital*, Volume 1, 27, 28, 33, 35, 194–195n26, 197n34; Étienne Balibar, 198–199n41; bees, 196n31; *Bildung*, 35; "capitalist production" standing on its "own feet," 197n34; *1844 Economic and Philosophic Manuscripts*, 14, 28–33; freedom, 31–32; *Grundrisse*, 7, 14, 27, 28, 29, 33–37, 199n45, 200n46; Hegel, *Philosophy of Right*, 32, 195–196n28; interiority, 30–31; language, 38, 199n45; non-selfsame, 37; ontological uncertainty, in Jacques Lezra, *On the Nature of Marx's Things*, 199n43; primitive accumulation, 3, 7, 14, 27–28; private property, 29–30; property-centric orientation, 28, 30, 36–30; *der Sklave*, the slave, 35, 197n34, 200n46; *Stoff*, material, 30–31; temporal determination of capitalist relation of production, in Denise Ferreira da Silva, *Unpayable Debt*, 27; *das Their*, the animal, 32–33; universality, 31–32; *der Wilde*, the savage, 33; *zōon politikon*, 27, 29. *See also* property; Ferreira da Silva, Denise; Robinson, Cedric J.
Massad, Joseph A., 189n38
Mastnak, Tomaž, 39, 41, 63, 177n12, 188–189n38, 200n48, 204–205n56
Masuzawa, Tomoko, 176n5, 210–211n85
mawjūd, mawjūdāt (being, beings), 85, 86, 88, 97, 100, 105, 106, 109, 115
McLaughlin, Kevin, 187–188n36
milites christi, 202–203n51. *See also* Crusades

Mount Tamalpais, 155–157, 165–168, 171
Moten, Fred, 4, 17, 18, 64, 174, 182n12, 245n138
Moumtaz, Nada, 237n70
Muḥammad, 71, 132, 134
muqawama (resistance), 5
al-Musawi, Muhsin, 216n13, 230n3

Nakba, xvii, 176n7, 181–182n10, 242n125. *See also* genocide; Zionism
Negri, Antonio, 199n42
New World, 26, 40, 48–52, 170, 177n12, 212n88; Hortense Spillers, 26; Sylvia Wynter, "1492: A New World View," 48–52
niyya (intention), 133–134
noise, 59, 231n7, 242n125; Locke, *Essay Concerning Human Understanding*, 59; Paul, 1 Corinthians 14:33, 60. *See also* riot
al-Nuwayrī, 234–35n37

Olson, Charles, 172, 243–244n129
ontology, xviii, 4, 6–11, 16–17, 22, 111–112, 117, 120, 123, 159–164, 179n23, 185–186n25, 223–224n64, 225–226n72, 239n84, 239–240n100; settler ontology, 4, 172. *See also* anontolgical form; Aristotle; al-Fārābī; Heidegger, Martin; Ibn Sīnā; al-Kindī; Lévinas, Emmanuel
Ottoman, xvii, xix, 16, 18, 122, 123, 130, 141, 154, 173, 178n13, 178n14, 189–190n41, 218–219n34, 231n8; 1858 Land Code, 121, 230n4, 231–232n9, 237n70; 1856 Treaty of Paris, 143
Ottoman Land Code (1858), 121, 230n4, 231–232n9, 237n70. *See also* Ottoman; property

pacification, 38–48, 52, 53–64, 143, 162, 171, 202–203n51. *See also* counterinsurgent pose; Crusades; law; Paul; property; settler life
Palestine, xv–xvi, 4, 5, 16, 150, 152, 154–155, 173, 176n5, 180n1, 181–182n10, 184n16, 185–186n25, 242n125; Etel Adnan, *The Arab Apocalypse*, 150–153, 154–155; Mahmoud Darwish, "The 'Red Indian's' Penultimate Speech to the White Man," 1–6; Ghassan Kanafani, *The Literature of Resistance in Occupied Palestine*, 5, 184n16; Edward W. Said, *The Question of Palestine*, 152; Zionist colonization, xx–xxi, 4, 152, 181n19. *See also* Adnan, Etel; Darwish, Mahmoud; Gaza; genocide; Kanafani, Ghassan; Joudah, Fady; Makdisi, Saree; *muqāwama*; Sabra; Said, Edward W.; settler life; Shalhoub-Kevorkian, Nadera; Shatila; Tell al-Zaʿatar
Paul, 14, 38–41, 45, 48, 60, 162, 177n11, 201–202n50, 205–206n63, 206–207n65; *akatastasias*, "confusion," 60; 1 Corinthians, 38, 60, 162; flesh, 45, 48; Crusades, 202–203n51; Galatians, 40, 203–204n55; letter of the law, 206–207n65; Locke, 60, 63–64; *pax*, Vulgate, 52; peace, 14, 39, 45–48, 52; rephrasing of *nomos* as modern law, 40–41, 203–204n55; Romans, 39, 45, 48, 52. *See also* Aquinas; Christianity; Crusades; Hegel, G.W.F.; John of Salisbury
philology, xvi–xvii, xviii, xix, 18, 52, 57, 60, 132, 133, 176n5, 183n15, 187–188n36, 192n49, 241–242n118. *See also* Hamacher, Werner; Said, Edward W.
Plato, 75, 189n40, 215–216n10, 184–185n19, 225n68
Plotinus, 15, 73–77, 83, 117, 120, 215–216n10, 229n97; *āniyya faqaṭ*, mere being, 76; *Enneads*, 73–76; "Letter on Divine Science," 74–76, 83; "Theology of Aristotle," 73–77
poeticality, xiii, 5, 12–13, 15–16, 17–18, 26, 66, 120–121, 155, 174; Etel Adnan, 148–173; anaccumulative form, xix, xxi, 5–6, 18, 65, 134, 158, 164; being indistinct from the social, 26, 111–112, 117, 145, 149, 164–165; Paul Celan, 140–148; collective being in the poetic, 5, 18, 133, 136–137, 147, 172, 179n23; Mahmoud Darwish, xxi, 5, 174; indistinction of *praxis* and *poiēsis*, 26, 121, 127, 164; language in excess of subjective form, xviii, 26, 28, 37, 82–83, 101, 120–121, 123, 137, 140, 144, 145, 147, 170–171, 173–174; Khālid al-Maʿālī, 121–148; painting, 156, 157–158, 168; the poetic indistinct from being, xxi, 5, 18, 118, 137, 144–145, 147, 149, 164–165, 170; sociality of things, 13, 18, 28, 65, 165; sonority, xviii, xxi, 3, 8, 18, 19, 124, 126, 128, 130, 140, 148, 153, 161, 174, 231n7, 232–233n28, 233n31; temporal excess in linguistic address, 68, 89, 96–97, 123, 137, 140, 143–146, 174.

See also Adnan, Etel; anontological form; Būloṣ, Sargon; Celan, Paul; collective; Darwish, Mahmoud; insurgence; al-Jāḥiẓ; Kanafani, Ghassan; Long Soldier, Layli; al-Maʿālī, Khālid; Marx, Karl; poetics of things
poetics of things, xxi, 2, 5–6, 15–18, 26, 65, 118, 126–128, 140, 145, 149, 154, 164–165, 166, 171–172, 191n48; Black Study, 17–18; Paul Celan, 141–142, 143–145; Mahmoud Darwish, 1–6; inessential sharing, 140; Layli Long Soldier, 12–13; Lucretius, in Etel Adnan, xix, 153, 166; material doing with and in and as things, 15, 17–18, 37, 120, 126, 128, 141–142, 145, 152, 154, 158; matter, xix, 2, 13, 18, 118, 126, 133, 141–142, 149–150, 153–154, 157, 164–165, 170, 173; non-self-determined lingual practice, xxi–xxii, 5, 15, 65, 66, 123, 134, 137, 139, 144, 146, 148, 171–173; non-propertied poetic mode, 166, 172; sociality of poetic doing, 1, 13, 65, 132–134, 136–137, 140, 144, 145, 152, 164–165; painting, 148–149, 157–159, 166; poetic excess over interiorizing self-understanding, 18, 126, 137, 140, 147, 152, 157–158, 171, 174; poetic life of things, 124–130; the sea, 18, 118, 148–150, 153–154, 164, 166, 170; sonority in utterance, 18, 124–130, 132–133, 147, 153–154, 171–172. *See also* Adnan, Etel; Celan, Paul; Darwish, Mahmoud; Long Soldier, Layli; Lucretius; al-Maʿālī, Khālid; poeticality
poiēsis (making), 26, 28, 121, 164, 186–187n31. *See also* Aristotle; *eū zēn*
Pope Urban II, 39, 42, 48, 201–202n50, 202–203n51, 204–205n56, 206–207n65. *See also* Christianity; Crusades; Jerusalem; Saracen
Porphyry, 95, 187n34, 188n37, 222n51; Abū ʿUthmān Dimashqī, 95; Boethius, 187n34, 188n37, 222n51; *Isagoge*, 95; *On Aristotle Categories*, 223–224n64
post-Latinate, xviii, 14, 15, 16, 25–26, 38, 120, 192–193n3, 194n14
praxis (doing), 26, 121, 164, 215–216n10. *See also* Aristotle; *eū zēn*
primitive accumulation, 3, 7, 14, 27–28, 149, 174, 181n6, 196–197n33, 197n34, 198n39, 198–199n41; in the field of language, 3, 61. *See also* Locke, John; Marx, Karl; Cedric J. Robinson; settler life
Proclus, 15, 80–83; *Elements of Theology*, 80–83; "What Alexander of Aphrodisias Excerpted from Aristotle's Book titled 'Theologia,' which Means 'On Divinity,'" 80–83
proper listening subject, xx, 7–8, 10, 162, 184–185n19, 242–243n126
property, xvii, xvii, xxi, 14, 37–38, 63–64, 120, 121, 142, 154; Brenna Bhandar, *Colonial Lives of Property*, 61, 181n8; proper, in Derrida, 7–8; earth as property, in Marx, 36, 37; *Eigentum*, 7, 28, 144–145; epistemic practice, 10; Cheryl I. Harris, "Whiteness as Property," 8; individual land title, 122, 231–232n9, 241n116; individuated social form, 142; Locke, 61–64, 214n105; mode of social organization, in Robert Nichols, *Theft is Property!*, 241n116; modern grammar of interiority, in Nada Moumtaz, *God's Property*, 237n70; 1858 Ottoman Land Code, 121, 230n4; post-Ottoman frames, 121, 122, 231–232n9, 237n70; private property, in Marx, 28–30; property-centric form, 3, 4, 7–8, 28, 30, 37, 61–62, 145, 146, 174, 185n20, 199n45; property-centric reading, 67, 123; self-consciousness, 61–62; settler colonization, 54–56, 58, 63–64, 181n6, 241n116; social logic of property, 2, 7, 10, 16, 26, 36, 120, 145, 164, 239n84, 241n116; slave, in Aristotle, 26, 48, 51–52; slave, in Marx, 35; Hortense Spillers, "Mama's Baby, Papa's Maybe," 17, 26, 51; subject of property, in Hegel, 195–196n28; *terra nullius*, in Vitoria, Francisco de, 47; transatlantic chattel slavery, xvii, 5, 7, 11, 13, 16–17, 26, 50, 120; transmutation of earth into property, 120, 150, 154, 168. *See also* abstraction; law; Marx, Karl; settler life
Pursley, Sara, 122

al-Qifṭī, 219n38
Qurʾan, 57–58, 135–136, 190n42, 192n49

race, xiii, xvi, xvii, xviii, 5, 8, 9, 11, 16, 17, 25, 27, 43, 48–52, 142, 149, 172, 175n3, 176n5, 176n6, 177n9, 177n11, 179n24, 186n26, 186–187n31, 199n45, 205n61, 208n70, 213–214n104, 239n84. *See also* Robinson, Cedric J.; Ferreira da Silva, Denise; whiteness; Wynter, Sylvia

ranīn (reverberation), 121–130; indistinction of speaking subject, 127; inheritance in language, 128; sonority, 126; temporality, 130. *See also* al-Maʿālī, Khālid; poetics of things
Rastegar, Kamran, 123, 184n16, 191n43, 192n49, 231n6
Redfield, Marc, 141
refusal, xviii–xix, xxi–xxii, 5, 12, 18, 65, 121, 143, 153, 167–168, 170; collective refusal, 149, 172; ethnographic refusal, in Audra Simpson, *Mohawk Interruptus*, 178–179n17; insurgence, 171; manner of reading, 173, 174, 181–182n10, 184n16; marronage, in Cedric J. Robinson, *Black Marxism*, 178n14; non-self-determined form, xxi–xxii, 5, 16, 65, 121, 123, 146, 172; non-subjective linguistic existence, xviii–xix, 16; not critique, xvii; overflow of the form of a subject, 171; post-Ottoman state-juridical formations, xix, 121, 122, 125–126, 143, 148, 178n14, 238n76; refusal of nomo-centric legalities, xxi, 16, 148, 178n13; refusal of the social logic of property, xxi, 16; refusal of settler life, xix, 12, 121, 148, 153, 167–168, 172–173; re-use, xix, 172; sonic gatherings, 171, 174; withdrawal, xix. *See also* collective; insurgence
riot, 4, 11, 25, 63, 172, 244n137. *See also* collective
riyāḍa (training), 71, 189n40, 189–190n41
Robinson, Cedric J., xiii, xvii, 7, 16, 27, 33, 176n6, 178n14, 185n21, 194n14; *Anthropology of Marxism*, 196–197n33; marronage in *Black Marxism*, 178n14. *See also* Black Study; refusal
Rodney, Walter, 185n21
Rodríguez, Dylan, 25, 182n13, 243n126
Rousseau, Jean-Jacques, xx

sabīl (path), 15, 70
ṣabr (patience), 68–73
Sabra, 163
Salaita, Steven, 2
Saracen, 44–45, 48, 52, 188–189n38, 200–201n49; Aquinas, 44–45; Las Casas, 209–210n84; blurring, 204–205n56; catachresis, 48, 52, 187n34, 188–189n38; 209n82; Crusades, 202–203n51, 204–205n56, 205–206n63, 206–207n65; disorder, 204–205n56; Locke, 60; Pauline demand, 45, 48; Pope Urban II, 201–202n50; schismatic, 42–45, 188–189n38; schismatic collectives, 60. *See also* abstraction; collective; Crusades; Jew; Paul; riot
ṣawt (sound, voice), 122, 127, 130–131, 138, 232–233n28. *See also* al-Jāḥiẓ
Schmitt, Carl, xvi, 39–41, 45, 46, 143, 176n3, 203n52
Said, Edward W., 152; *Orientalism*, xvi; *The Question of Palestine*, 238n76; "Zionism from the Standpoint of its Victims," 185n25
See, Sarita Echavez, 3, 176n3, 241n115
Seikaly, Sherene, 231n6, 232n9
Seneca, 215–216n10
Septuagint, 203–204n55
Sepúlveda, Ginés de, 49, 52, 208n70, 208–209n75
settler life, xvii–xviii, xix, 1–65, 120, 121, 148, 166, 168, 173–174, 177n11, 181n9, 192; abstraction, 59–60; accumulative form, xvi, 3, 16, 134, 142, 173; animal, xviii, xx, 8, 11, 20, 21, 25, 27–29, 32–33, 35, 37–38, 40, 175n2, 187n34, 189–190n41, 193–194n11, 195–196n28, 196n30, 199n45, 209–210n84, 222n51; agriculture, 54; atotal, 10; *Bildung*, 3, 7, 10, 35, 195–196n28; catachresis, 38, 48, 52, 60, 187n34, 188–189n38, 209n82; containment, 11–13, 18, 26, 33, 157, 163, 170, 172, 174; Crusades, xvii, 14, 25, 38–39, 41, 202–203n51, 204–205n56; subsistence, 69, 241–242n11, 8, 244n137; division between "life" and "the good life," xix, 14, 21, 24, 48; division between native and settler, 19–20; form, 6; form of life, xviii, 11, 13–14; genocide 5, 171; genocidal formation, 1, 243n126; globality, 52, 152, 171; Indigenous extermination, 3–4, 12–13, 166, 180n4, 192–193n3, 240n114; interiority, xix, 3, 13, 18, 30–31, 66, 150, 237n70; language, xvii, 58–64, 184–185n19, 199n45; law, 5, 42–46, 54–55, 62–64, 181n9, 213–214n104; non-Christian alterities, xv, 14, 39, 43, 45, 48, 52, 142, 188–189n38, 211–212n86, 204–205n56, 209–210n84; non-White, non-European collectives, xv, 4, 39, 142, 194n14, 200–201n49; ontology, 6–11, 16; pacification,

38–48, 64, 162; plantation, xix, 2, 18, 154, 169, 174, 180n4, 212–213n99; Pauline demand, 39, 45; post-Ottoman frames, 16, 18, 121–123, 130, 137, 140–141, 154, 173; primitive accumulation in the field of language, 3, 27–28, 61; properly comported subject of linguistic existence, xx, 3, 19, 21, 37, 38, 58–64, 162; property-centric manner, 4, 7–8, 28, 30, 36–38, 55–56, 61–64, 146, 158; racial capitalism, xvii, 5, 13, 27; reduction of the social to the experience of a subject, 16, 18, 184–185n19; Saracen, 44–45, 48; savage, xviii, 28–29, 33, 35–35–38, 54, 60, 195–196n28, 199n45, 212n88, 213–214n104; self-determined form, xvii, xxi–xxii, 5, 9, 15, 52, 54, 66, 123, 134, 144, 172; self-governed acts, 20; settler ontology, 4, 172; self-consciousness, 9, 14, 17, 33, 49, 52, 61–62, 65, 142; self-exteriorization, 13, 120, 205n61; slave, xviii, 35–38, 48–49, 51–52; social form, 174; social logic of property, 2, 7, 10, 16, 26, 36, 120, 145, 164, 241n116; society, 55–56, 64; subordination of sound to sense, 3, 8, 57–58, 60, 65, 124; subject of self-representation, 3, 9, 13, 154, 177n9; subjects of the political, 154; terminological exertion, 192–193n3; transatlantic chattel slavery, xvi, xvii, 5, 7, 11, 13, 16, 17, 26, 48–52, 120, 178n14, 209n82; translation, 3, 14, 24, 26, 40, 48–52, 57, 58, 60, 154, 162, 168, 187n34, 222n51; twelfth Latin-Christian century, xvii, 14, 16, 24, 26, 39, 41, 47, 52, 60, 120, 125, 176n6, 187n34, 188n37, 188–189n38, 192–193n3, 194n14, 198n39, 200–201n49, 205n61; whiteness, xviii, 177n11, 241–242n118, 243n126; Zionist genocide in Gaza, xi, xiii, xx–xxi, 171, 173. *See also* abstraction; counterinsurgent pose; Crusade; Ferreira da Silva, Denise; Fanon, Frantz; genocide; Hegel, G.W.F.; law; Lévinas, Emmanuel; Locke, John; Kant, Immanuel; Marx, Karl; primitive accumulation, property; riot; Robinson, Cedric J.; Saracen; settler war; Spillers, Hortense; Tocqueville, Alexis de; Vitoria, Francisco de; whiteness; Wynter, Sylvia

savage, xviii, 28–29, 192–193n3, 199n45, 212n88, 213–214n104; Hegel, 195–196n28; Locke, 60; Marx, 33, 35–38; Tocqueville, 54

settler war, xv, xvii, 3–4, 12, 25, 39–41, 41–43, 44, 47, 53–58, 60, 125, 130, 149, 150–152, 154, 171, 175n3, 176n7, 178n13, 181n9, 200n49, 201–202n50, 202–203n51, 204–205n56, 208n70, 209–210n84, 212–213n99. *See also* genocide; law; property; settler life; Zionism

al-Shahrastānī, 92

Shalhoub-Kevorkian, Nadera, xx, 179n24, 185–186n25

Shatila, 163

Sheehi, Stephen, 181–182n10, 191n43, 231n6

shi῾r (poetry), xxi, 2, 71, 126, 132–133, 146. *See also* poeticality; poetics of things

Shohat, Ella, 177n12, 185–186n25

Sibawayh, 133

al-Sijistānī, 221–222n49

Simpson, Audra, xix, 167, 180–181n4, 241n116; ethnographic refusal, 178–179n17

sīra (form of life), 92, 215–216n10, 221n45

siyāsa (governance), 122, 189–190n41, 231n8

Spillers, Hortense, 17, 26, 51, 209n82

struggle, xi, xiii, xvi, 16, 54, 168, 172, 180n4

Tageldin, Shaden, 18, 191n43, 192n49, 231n6, 235n38

tätigkeit (activity), 28, 31–33, 194–195n26

Taylor, Malissa, 230n4, 231n9, 237n70

Tell al-Za῾atar, 150–152, 170

Terada, Rei, 186n29

terra nullius, 47

al-Tha῾ālabī, 235n37

Themistius, 106–108, 109, 110–111, 120

Tocqueville, Alexis de, 14, 53–58, 61, 64; colonization of Algeria, 53–58; agriculture, 54–56; law, 54, 57–58; property, 56–57; Qur᾽ān, 57–58; settler form, 54; society, 55–56; subordination of sound to sense, 57–58; translation, 57; war 56–57

Toufic, Jalal, 172

Traboulsi, Fawwaz, 172

transatlantic chattel slavery, xvi, xvii, 5, 7, 11, 13, 16, 17, 26, 48–52, 120, 178n14, 209n82

Turtle Island, xxi, 167, 243n126

al-Ṭūsī, 101

Vitoria, Francisco de, 14, 40–42, 50, 203n54, 208n70; *Relectio de Indis*, 46–48

wājib al-wujūd (necessary being), 101, 106, 115, 227n85. *See also* Ibn Sīnā
whiteness, xvi, xviii, 8, 120, 142, 174, 177n11, 181n6, 185n25, 189n38, 238n76, 241–242n118; law, 64, 142, 213–214n104; Mahmoud Darwish, "The 'Red Indian's' Penultimate Speech to the White Man," 1–6, 8; white settler subject, 1–4, 51–52, 64, 169, 175n3, 203n54, 240n114, 243n126; white social being, xxi, 63, 152, 167, 180–181n4, 212–213n99. *See also* settler life
William of Moerbeke, 51, 188n37, 208n71
Williams, Eric, 185n21
Wolfe, Patrick, 176n6, 192–193n3
wujūd (being), 77, 89, 93, 101, 106, 109, 111, 112–115, 165, 223n60, 226n81, 226–227n83, 227n85. See also *wājib al-wujūd*
Wynter, Sylvia, 14, 48–52, 177n12; Aristotle, *Politics*, 50–52; Las Casas, 48–52; Judaeo-Christian, 52, 210–211n85, 211–212n86; Latin Christianity, 49–50, 211–212n86; secularization, 212n88; slavery, 48–52

Zionism, xi, xvii, xx–xxi, 4–5, 16, 152, 179n24, 180n1, 181n9, 181–182n10, 185–186n25, 210–211n85; Zionist genocide in Gaza, xi, xvii; *Nakba*, xvii, xx–xxi. *See also* genocide; settler life
zōon politikon (political living being), 21–22, 27, 29, 199n45

JEFFREY SACKS is Professor of Arabic and Comparative Literature at the University of California, Riverside. He is the author of *Iterations of Loss: Mutilation and Aesthetic Form, al-Shidyaq to Darwish* (2015), which was awarded the Harry Levin Prize from the American Comparative Literature Association.

www.ingramcontent.com/pod-product-compliance
Lightning Source LLC
Chambersburg PA
CBHW041227070526
44584CB00006B/321
9781531512330